The Sociocultural Brain

The Sociocultural Brain
A cultural neuroscience approach to human nature

Shihui Han

OXFORD
UNIVERSITY PRESS

OXFORD
UNIVERSITY PRESS

Great Clarendon Street, Oxford, OX2 6DP,
United Kingdom

Oxford University Press is a department of the University of Oxford.
It furthers the University's objective of excellence in research, scholarship,
and education by publishing worldwide. Oxford is a registered trade mark of
Oxford University Press in the UK and in certain other countries

Published in the United States of America by Oxford University Press
198 Madison Avenue, New York, NY 10016, United States of America

British Library Cataloguing in Publication Data

Data available

Library of Congress Control Number: 2017932494

ISBN 978-0-19-874319-4

Printed and bound by
CPI Group (UK) Ltd, Croydon, CR0 4YY

Preface

People from different cultures have evolved distinct patterns of behavior that can be observed widely in daily life. What drives the cultural diversity of human behavior? Anthropologists and sociologists have extensively documented the diversity of human behavior and developed theories to explain their observations from a macroscopic perspective. Neuroscientists have provided a large body of empirical findings that help us to understand micro- (e.g., cellular and genetic) mechanisms of animal behavior. Can we understand the cultural diversity of human behavior from a neuroscientific perspective? During the last decade, a new approach to the examination of cultural diversity of human behavior emerged through the integration of cultural psychology, cognitive neuroscience, and other related research fields. Cultural psychologists investigate behavioral diversity by exploring the underlying psychological traits and cognitive/affective processes. Cognitive neuroscientists employ brain-imaging techniques to investigate neural underpinnings of human cognition and emotion, as well as neural correlates of behavior. The integration of cultural psychology and cognitive neuroscience has taken advantage of elegant behavioral paradigms and theoretical frameworks developed by cultural psychologists, as well as state-of-the-art brain imaging techniques (e.g., functional magnetic resonance imaging and event-related brain potential) from cognitive neuroscience, and this has prompted the emergence of cultural neuroscience.

Cultural neuroscience investigates many interesting and important questions regarding human behavior and the brain from a cultural perspective. For example, to what degree does cultural diversity of behavior reflect distinct functional organization of the brain? Do cultural experiences shape neural mechanisms involved in cognitive tasks that are commonly performed by people in different sociocultural environments? Can brain activity be changed by short-term cultural experiences? Does the brain process culturally familiar and unfamiliar information in the same way? How do cultural experiences interact with genes to influence brain functional organization? Additionally, cultural neuroscience studies raise general questions related to the brain and culture. What is the nature of the human brain? Is it a pure biological or a biosocial organ? What is the nature of culture? Is it a pure social or sociobiological construction?

This book does not aim to answer all these questions; however, given the increasing number of cultural neuroscience studies that have examined the aforementioned issues and reported interesting empirical findings, I believe that now is the right time to provide an overview of the methods and findings of cultural neuroscience research during the last 10 to 15 years, which have substantially enriched our knowledge about the relationship between culture and the functional organization of the human brain. These findings suggest that brain functional organization is shaped by sociocultural experiences to guide our behaviors to fit into a specific sociocultural environment. In particular, recent cultural neuroscience studies have shown evidence that East Asian and Western cultures produce significant influences on neural activities involved in multiple cognitive/affective processes such as perception, attention, mental attribution, self-reflection, and emotion regulation. Genes also interact with a specific cultural trait to modulate the functional organization of the human brain. By summarizing recent cultural neuroscience findings, the book aims to provide a new perspective on human brain functional organization by high-lighting the role of human sociocultural experience and its interaction with genes in shaping the human brain and behavior.

There are 9 chapters in this book. Chapter 1 provides a brief overview of cultural differences in human behavior by comparing and contrasting examples of individuals' behaviors in East Asian and Western societies. It reviews the concept of culture that emphasizes its two key components—shared beliefs and behavioral scripts—and cross-cultural psychological findings that reveals differences in multiple cognitive and affective processes between individuals in East Asian and Western cultures. It also gives an overview of the short history of cultural neuroscience research.

Chapter 2 examines brain activity that is engaged in differential processing of culturally familiar and unfamiliar information by reviewing functional magnetic resonance imaging and event-related potential studies of neural activity involved in the processing of gesture, music, brand, and religious knowledge.

Chapter 3 introduces a theoretical framework for understanding the relationship between sociocultural experiences and cognition, and it provides evidence for differences in brain activity between East Asian and Western cultures involved in cognitive processes related to perception, attention, memory, causality judgment, mathematical operation, semantic relationship, and decision making. Further, it discusses neural bases for a cultural preference for context-independent or context-dependent strategies of cognition.

Chapter 4 examines the difference in self-concept between Western and East Asian cultures and behavioral and brain-imaging findings that have uncovered the neural mechanisms underlying self-face recognition and self-reflection in Western and East Asian cultures.

Chapter 5 presents cross-cultural neuroimaging studies of neural processes underlying social interactions that reveal how East Asian and Western cultural experiences influence specific cognitive and neural strategies in perception of face and expression, empathy for others' emotional states, regulation of emotion, understanding others' beliefs, perception of others' social status, and processing of social feedback.

Chapter 6 examines how temporary shifts of a cultural knowledge system toward independence or interdependence modulates brain activities involved in pain-related sensory processing, visual perception, self-face recognition and self-reflection, monetary reward, empathy, and a resting state. These findings are discussed in terms of a causal relationship between cultural belief/value and functional organization of the human brain.

Chapter 7 reviews empirical findings that allow consideration of biological and environmental influences on human behavior from an evolutionary perspective (e.g., gene-culture coevolution) and from a perspective of individual development (e.g., gene-culture interaction). Moreover, it introduces a cultural neuroscience approach to uncovering genetic influences on the coupling of brain activity and cultural traits by presenting studies that examined how serotonin transporter functional polymorphism and the oxytocin receptor gene moderate the association between interdependence and brain activities involved in self-reflection and empathy.

Chapter 8, based on cultural neuroscience findings, introduces a culture–behavior–brain (CBB)-loop model of human development, which posits that culture shapes the brain by contextualizing behavior, and the brain fits and modifies culture via behavioral influences. Moreover, genes provide a fundamental basis for and interact with the CBB loop at both individual and population levels. This model aims to advance our understanding of the dynamic relationships between culture, behavior, and the brain.

Chapter 9 discusses the implications of cultural neuroscience findings for understanding the biosocial nature of the human brain and the sociobiological nature of culture. It also examines how cultural neuroscience findings help us to rethink strategies of school education, cross-cultural communication, and clinical treatment of neuropsychological mental disorders in different cultures.

This book draws on a number of relevant articles, chapters, and books. I am grateful to the researchers who have contributed to the development of cultural neuroscience by conducting empirical studies and developing theoretical frameworks. It would have been impossible to have this book published without the findings of the cultural neuroscience studies. My special thanks go to Prof. Ying Zhu, who initiated cross-cultural brain-imaging research in China and has been working with me since 2001. My special thanks go also to post doc fellows, graduate, and undergraduate students who worked with me during the last 10 years, including Jie Sui, Lihua Mao, Yina Ma, Yan Mu, Jianqiao Ge, Chenbo Wang, Feng Sheng, Siyang Luo, Zhenhao Shi, Yi Liu, Moritz de Greck, Sook-Lei Liew, Meghan Meyer, Michael Varnum, Kate Woodcock, John Freeman, and others. I am most grateful to Prof. Sik Hung Ng, Yi Rao, Georg Northoff, Shinobu Kitayama, Andreas Roepstorff, Michele Gelfand, Kai Vogeley, and Ernst Poppel for our exciting discussions and productive cooperation. I owe a great deal to Prof. Glyn Humphreys and Jane Riddoch, whom I have been working with since 1996. They hosted me as a visiting professor in 2015 and 2016 at the University of Oxford, where I finished this book. Prof. Jane Riddoch also helped by proofreading all chapters of this book. I thank Weiqiang Wang for providing Figure 1.2. Finally, I am most grateful to my wife Lijuan Liu, who supports my research all the time.

I wish to thank the National Natural Science Foundation of China (Projects 31421003; 31661143039; 31470986) for funding support of my research on the relationship between culture and the brain, and the Leverhulme Trust that supported my visit to the University of Oxford in 2015 and 2016, when I was able to devote myself to the writing of this book.

Oxford, UK

June 2016

Table of Contents

List of Abbreviations

A/A	Adenine/Adenine		L	Left
ACC	anterior cingulate cortex		LG	Lingual gyrus
A/G	Adenine/Guanine		LMF	Left middle frontal cortex
Amyg	amygdala		LPC	Late positive complex
BOLD	Blood-oxygen-level-dependent		LPP	Late positive potential
			MEG	Magnetoencephalography
CBB	Culture-behavior-brain		MEP	Motor-evoked potentials
CC-Behavior	Culturally contextualized behavior		MO	Middle occipital cortex
			MPFC	Medial prefrontal cortex
CV-Behavior	Culturally voluntary behavior		MR	Magnetic resonance
			MZ	Monozygotic twins
DACC	Dorsal anterior cingulate		OXTR	Oxytocin receptor gene
DLPFC	Dorsal lateral prefrontal cortex		PET	Positron emission topography
DMPFC	Dorsal medial prefrontal cortex		PrecCu	Precuneus
DZ	Dizygotic twins		R	Right
EA	East Asian		RMF	Right middle frontal cortex
ECG	Electrocardiography		SNP	Single-nucleotide polymorphisms
EEG	Electroencephalography			
ERN	Error-related negativity		SP	Superior parietal cortex
ERP	Event-related potentials		TMS	Transcranial magnetic stimulation
G/G	Guanine/Guanine		ToM	Theory-of-mind
GWAS	Genome-wide association studies		TP	Temporal pole
			TPJ	Temporoparietal junction
IAT	Implicit association test		VMPFC	Ventral medial prefrontal cortex
Ins/IF	insula/inferior frontal cortex			
			WC	Western Caucasian
IP	inferior parietal cortex		WEIRD	Western, Educated, Industrialized, Rich, and Democratic
IPA	Implicit positive association			
IRI	Interpersonal reactivity index			

Chapter 1

Cultural diversity: From behavior to mind and brain

Diverse human behaviors

In 1996, after I had obtained my PhD in China, I had my first experience of visiting another country. As a visiting research fellow, I was continuing my research on visual perception and attention at the University of Birmingham, United Kingdom. My host professor and his daughter entertained me the first weekend after I had arrived in Birmingham with a trip to Warwick, a small city close to Birmingham. Besides visiting an old and beautiful castle, we visited a shop that specifically sold products for left-handed people such as tools and musical instruments (the professor's daughter was left-handed). The shop came as a great surprise as I had never experienced a similar shop in China. My curiosity was roused again while I was working on this book in 2015. I asked friends and colleagues (even left-handed ones) in Beijing about such shops in China, but they too were unaware of any in China. I performed and Internet search for shops in China that sell left-handed products but had difficulty finding one. However, it was quite easy to find English websites for left-handed products and shops. Why is there such a difference in the availability of left-handed products in the UK and in China? The difference between the two countries may reflect peoples' thoughts and attitudes toward left-handed people, who consist of less than 10% of the population (Van der Elst et al. 2008). It seems that people in a Western society, such as my host professor in the UK, not only tolerate left-handed people but also encourage their tendency to use the left hand as well. In contrast, most Chinese children who attempt to use the left hand to hold chopsticks or intend to hold a pen using the left hand are "corrected" by their parents to change to the right hand. Why does this happen? A possibility is that using a left hand appears discrepant from the majority of the Chinese population (though parents may explain that it would be more convenient to use the right hand than the left hand to hold chopsticks or to write with a pen).

My Birmingham experience was not such a "cultural shock" compared with one of my experiences in California. A couple of years after working at the University of Birmingham, I moved to a laboratory in California, in the United

States, to continue my research on visual perception and attention. I rented a room in a single house owned by a young property owner in a small town. My proprietor, his parents, and two married sisters all lived in the same town and often gathered together at weekends or over holidays. I was once invited by my proprietor to join a birthday dinner at a restaurant for one of his nephews. This pleasant dinner party consisted of a gathering of grandparents, parents, aunts and uncles, and cousins. The family members and I presented gifts and enjoyed the food and the conversation. After the dinner, I was very surprised to notice that the grandparents, parents, and aunts and uncles all paid their own bills (as a guest, I was honored to be "treated" by the grandparents). Why was I surprised? Well, I had never witnessed such a way to pay bills for a family dinner in China! In China, always, one person would pay for such a family dinner, either the father, the grandfather, or someone else. In Chinese society, a family consisting of grandparents, parents, grandchildren, and even other relatives is ONE unit in such social events. It appeared to me that my proprietor's family took split bills as a matter of course while still maintaining good family relationships.

I was to experience more cultural discrepancies in California. For instance, what might occur at a funeral? During a traditional funeral service in Chinese society, relatives, friends, and colleagues usually pay their respects to a deceased person's body quickly, and then console the family members with handshakes and a few words to give comfort and express condolences. There is a sorrowful atmosphere, and most attendees cry with the family members. The core of a traditional Chinese funeral is that attendees show family members their respects to the decedent and, more meaningfully, they comfort the family members in their sadness, and NOBODY is expected to have a smile. What surprised me at a funeral in California was that after getting back from the burial, the family members gathered with other relatives and friends to recall stories about the decedent, praising his traits and excellence. During the event, nobody cried. What shocked me even more was that someone started to tell funny stories about the decedent, causing much laughter! Such behavior would not be tolerated anywhere in Chinese society. It seems to me that the attendees' behavior and stories at the funeral in California focused on the deceased person by recalling his past and praising his virtues. In contrast, attendees at a Chinese funeral emphasize the feelings of the family members, and stories about the decedent are avoided.

The more opportunities one has to travel to different countries, the more chance one has to witness how people behave in distinct ways. A child may sleep in a separate bedroom after birth in one society, as in the United States, whereas a child may share a bedroom with his/her parents until early adulthood in another society, as in China. Whereas an American girl who is unsatisfied with the food she has ordered might expect a response from her mother such as "that's your own choice and you have to take it." In a similar situation, a Chinese mother may tell her daughter, "Mom will take it, and you can order another one." Whereas an American student may choose his/her major for college study based on his/her own interest, Chinese parents are more likely to give strong suggestions or even make decisions about their children's major at college that imply the parents' expectations of their children's future and, to a certain degree, reflect the parents' own life goals. How seat guests during a banquet also varies remarkably between East Asian and Western societies. Conventionally, for a Chinese banquet, people sit around a round table (Figure 1.1A). A modern table even has an upper layer that can rotate so that dishes placed on the upper layer can reach everyone easily. Such a system makes it possible for people to share food and to talk to everyone around the table. In contrast, during a traditional Western banquet, people sit at a long table and everyone has his/her own food (Figure 1.1B). The arrangement only allows one to talk to a couple of his/her neighboring guests. The key discrepancy of these table arrangements is that everyone around a round table is connected with all of the guests through shared foods and conversation during a Chinese dinner, whereas a Western dinner is characterized by communication between two individuals. The arrangement of foods and seats during a Western dinner also gives prominence to each individual guest, whereas an individual is more or less embedded in a social group during a Chinese dinner.

Divergent human behaviors are not limited to individual observations. One social group, collectively, can be extremely different from another one in terms of social behaviors. I would like to give two more examples of distinct social behaviors that exist in the contemporary societies. The first example is about a small ethnic group called "Mosuo," living in the Yunnan and Sichuan provinces in China. Unlike the most common family structure in the world (i.e., a man and a woman get married and live together to raise their children), the Mosuo have very different, unique marriage practices and household configurations. They adopt a matrilineal family system in which large extended families with several generations (grandmothers, mothers, aunts and uncles, grandchildren, etc.) live together within the same house. Everyone lives within communal quarters except women between certain ages, who can have their own private bedrooms. The Mosuo are well known for their walking marriages or "zou hun" in Chinese. A Mosuo woman invites a man she likes to walk to her house after dark and to spend the night with her in her room. However, the man cannot stay there in the next day and has to return to his own home early the next morning. Even after the couple has a child, the man still does not live with the woman. Instead, the woman continues to live with her family and

(A)

(B)

Figure 1.1 Illustration of banquet organization in China (A) and in a Western country (B).

bring up her children with the help from her grandmother, aunts and uncles, etc., whereas the man helps his sisters to take care of his nephews and nieces. Thus in general, Mosuo children are raised by the mother's family, growing up with "aunts" and "uncles" (but not the father), and they even take on the mothers' family name. The walking marriage system produces families that are different from the majority of Chinese families, which are dominated by the father and son, and which lose their female children after daughters get married and live with their husbands' families. The more sons a family has, the bigger a family will be. In contrast, a Mosuo family will become big only if it has many female children.

Both social scientists and development psychologists have long observed fathers' influences on child development. Apart from providing economic and social support to partner and offspring, fathers can affect children development through interaction and education (Paquette et al. 2013). For instance, fathers can play the role of moral teacher by ensuring that their children grow up with an appropriate sense of values. Fathers typically encourage children to choose gender-specific games and toys and play a strong and unique role in the development of children's sex roles (Parker 1996). The quality of father–child relationships has been shown to predict adolescents' greater academic success and prosocial behaviors toward peers (Amato and Gilbreth 1999; Coley 1998). There has been no systematic research on child development in Mosuo families. However, given the findings of the father's important role in child development, one can image how the lack of a father may influence the development of a child in terms of personality, social behavior, and future career success.

The second example is a unique type of architecture that characterizes the rural dwellings distributed in southeastern Fujian province in China, most of which are located in the mountainous regions and surrounded by streams and/or fields (Liu 1984). Local people call these rural dwellings "Tulou" ("earthen house") (Figure 1.2). Each of these residential quarters, made from a rammed earth wall, is a large enclosed grand building, circular or rectangular in configuration and with two or more floors. Each Tulou usually has only one main entrance guarded by a thick wooden door. Within are small interior buildings, all enclosed by the huge peripheral walls of the main building. Rooms on the ground floor are used for storehouses, kitchens, etc. The upper floors provide living areas and, on occasion, the top level of these earth buildings may have apertures for guns for defensive purposes. The most amazing feature of the Tulou is that each grand building actually can house as many as 80 families, which together become one unit once the door at the main entrance is closed. Thus, many facilities inside a Tulou, such as wells, a ceremonial hall, and bathrooms, are shared property. The architecture of the Tulou engenders that people living inside have many things in common and many chances to interact with each other, which allows the building of close connections between them. Public duties such as cleaning common areas and opening/closing the main gate are assigned to different families on a rotational basis. Therefore, a Tulou is different from independent houses in Western societies and modern high-rise buildings in big cities that house families who seldom meet each other. A child growing up in a Tulou has close relationships with many peers and many families. Even adults who live inside one of such rural dwellings must learn how to deal with neighbors appropriately in order to live in harmony with others.

(A)

(B)

Figure 1.2 Illustration of the outside (A) and inside (B) structure of a Tulou in Fujian province, China.

Fujian Tulou were initially built for housing people from the same clan or close clans, with a sound defensive function in specific natural and social environments. What caused the development of such an architectural style? These rural dwellings actually reflect many Chinese traditions and concepts. For example, the circular or rectangular configurations of the grand buildings correspond to the traditional Chinese concept of "round heaven and square earth." The layout of a Fujian Tulou is also consistent with the Chinese dwelling tradition of the "closed outside, open inside" concept. This concept means that people living inside a Tulou share many things and are strongly connected, owing to common family ancestors or tight social relationships, but they keep a social distance from those living outside. Besides representing an architectural style, a Tulou also dictates a lifestyle for the people who live inside. Imagine that child A lives in a Fujian Tulou and child B lives in a single house in a Western society. Everyday child A will meet others who live in the same Tulou. Child A will play with other children and remember their names, their families and the relationships between them, and will take care not to disturb others even within his/her own room because houses are very close to each other inside a Tulou. In contrast, child B meets few others outside his/her family, and therefore does not have to think about relationships with others frequently. Child B does what he/she wants to do by him/herself. These distinct life experiences in different social environments can produce profound influences on a child's development that significantly affect his/her adulthood.

Besides such everyday observations, divergent human behaviors have been widely documented in studies of anthropology and psychology. Anthropologists and psychologists have conducted qualitative and quantitative measures of distinct behaviors in different societies around the world. People always feel excited and interested when observing how people from other societies behave differently from themselves and are curious about the variability of different societies. For anthropologists and psychologists, the comparison of humans from different societies and discoveries of what makes people different from one another and what they share in common are important for understanding the complexity of human thoughts, feelings, and behaviors. However, researchers do not simply attribute the observations of distinct behaviors to "geographical differences" or "skin color differences." They go beyond visible behaviors and try to find mechanisms deeper in the mind and brain in order to interpret various human behaviors. A core concept in this approach to an account of human divergent behaviors is *culture*. But what is culture?

Culture: From observation to concept

The word *culture* is frequently used by the public. In most cases when we notice "unusual behaviors" in people from other societies, the thought that immediately jumps into our mind is "cultural difference" or "cultural diversity." Here "difference" or "diversity" simply reflects our observations that sometimes people from different societies do not behave in the same way. But what does *cultural* mean here? A simple definition of *culture* from the Concise Oxford Dictionary reads "the customs, civilization, and achievements of a particular time or people" (Eighth edition 1990, p. 286). This definition of *culture* is frequently used by the public and it refers to noticeable distinct behaviors and the visible consequences of them. In addition, this definition refers to something that is possessed by a group of people rather than by an individual person.

Apart from the definitions of culture in dictionaries, there have been numerous definitions of *culture* in the academic literature. In an early book, Kroeber and Kluckhohn (1952) collected 161 definitions of *culture* given by researchers from different academic disciplines such as anthropology, sociology, psychology, and philosophy. The meanings of those definitions of *culture* are either broad or specific and they emphasize different aspects of culture. For example, some definitions of *culture* emphasize tradition and heritage: "Culture means the whole complex of traditional behavior which has been developed by the human race and is successively learned by each generation" (Mead 1937, p. 17) or "Culture includes everything that can be communicated from one generation to another. The culture of a people is their social heritage, a "complex whole," which includes knowledge, belief, art, morals, law, techniques of tool fabrication and use, and method of communication" (Sutherland and Woodward 1940, p. 19). Some definitions take culture as ideas and information by claiming, "culture may be briefly defined as a stream of ideas that passes from individual to individual by means of symbolic action, verbal instruction, or imitation" (Ford 1949, p. 38) or "Culture is information capable of affecting individuals' behavior that they acquire from other members of their species through teaching, imitation, and other forms of social transmission" (Richerson and Boyd 2005, p. 5). Some definitions give prominence to the role of culture in guiding behavior, by claiming, "By culture we mean all those historically created designs for living, explicit and implicit, rational, irrational, and nonrational, which exist at any given time as potential guides for the behavior of men" (Kluckbobn and Kelly 1945, p. 97) or "Culture is generally understood to mean learned modes of behavior which are socially transmitted from one generation to anther within particular societies and which may be diffused from one society to another" (Steward 1950, p. 98). Culture is not given by the natural environment. Instead, culture is created by humans. Thus, some definitions lay stress on its nature of artifact by stating that "By culture we mean every object, habit, idea, institution, and mode of thought or action which man produces or creates and then passes on to others, especially to the next generation" (Huntington 1945, pp. 7–8) or "The immense diversity of imagined realities that Sapiens invented, and the resulting diversity of behavior pattern, are the main components of what we call 'culture'" (Harari 2014, p. 37).

Consistent with the aforementioned understanding of culture, social and cultural psychologists often use the concept of culture in three basic senses (Chiu and Hong 2006). *Material culture* refers to all material artifacts produced by human beings such as buildings that host varieties of human social activities, methods by which people make and exchange food and goods, and the ways by which people communicate with each other. *Social culture* refers to social rules and social institutions such as family and marriage that guide and contextualize human behaviors. *Subjective culture* refers to shared ideas, values, beliefs, and behavioral scripts in human mind. These aspects of culture are dynamically related, and together they form a unique social environment for a group of individuals. As pointed out by Kuper (1999, p. 6), "Unlike scientific knowledge, the wisdom of culture is subjective." Thus, subjective culture is relatively more fundamental because material and social culture essentially reflect the outcome of shared beliefs and behavioral scripts.

Examining these definitions of *culture* reveals several key properties. First, subjectivity is an essential feature of culture. Beliefs and values can be conceptualized as mental activity that tells people what is good and what is bad, what we should do and what we should not do. Behavioral scripts are stored in our minds and they instruct us how to communicate and behave during social interactions. The subjective mental activity is dissociated from physical environments and it plays a much more fundamental role in guiding human behavior. Second, beliefs and behavioral scripts can be a part of culture only when they are shared by all or specially designated members of a social group. An individual in a society may create new ideas and behavioral scripts, but these cannot constitute culture unless they are transferred across and accepted by the majority of a social group. Shared beliefs are extremely powerful in connecting a large amount of people for social coordination. Third, culture is "hereditary," but not in a biological sense. Culture can be passed on from one generation to the next via social learning. It can be delivered across generations and it does not die out unless it is destroyed during natural disasters.

Cultural psychologists have realized that culture should not be considered a rigid set of stereotypes about a social group but rather a dynamic knowledge system owned by the collective minds in a social group (Markus and Hamedani 2007). Culture represents a dynamic concept of the social environment that is not part of the innate biological condition of humans. Humans are not born with propensities for any particular culture but with the potential and the capacity to acquire and to create culture (Harris 1999). Thus, an individual may change his/her cultural beliefs and values and absorb new beliefs and values because of experience (e.g., emigrating from one's native country). People from the same social groups or living in the same geographical scope can be quite heterogeneous in terms of the beliefs and values they acquire and behavioral scripts they practice. This is particularly true in contemporary societies where cultural exchange and emigration occur much more often and rapidly than in the past.

The majority of a population in one society shares a cultural knowledge system that is generally discrepant from that owned by people in another society. East Asian and Western societies have been extensively investigated by cultural psychologists and are believed to have different cultural knowledge systems that are often denoted as East Asian culture and Western culture. These two cultures differ in several dimensions, such as how to view the relationship between oneself and others, and how to make causal attributions of physical and social events. However, people in modern societies are not definitely monocultural because they are usually exposed, often deeply, to other cultures' beliefs and practices in multiple sociocultural contexts. Therefore, it is likely that an individual can have multiple cultural systems and, consequently, is often required to switch back and forth between such systems during social interactions (depending on specific contexts of social encounters; Hong et al. 2000). This view of culture allows researchers to build a dynamic model of people's beliefs and behavioral scripts that can be tested in laboratories.

Culture is different from nationality, which is defined by social group membership based on a shared nation state of origin. Whereas culture emphasizes shared beliefs, ideas, values, and behavioral scripts, people of the same nationality do not necessarily share these things or practice the same behavioral scripts. For instance, Southern Americans, relative to Northern Americans, own a stronger belief in the importance of an individual's reputation and greater motivation to defend one's own reputation at all cost (Nisbett and Cohen 1996). Residents of Japan's northern island Hokkaido are similar to European Americans in North America in valuing personal achievement and in showing a dispositional bias in causal attribution, whereas these marker effects of independence are largely absent for non-Hokkaido residents in Japan (Kitayama et al. 2006). In contrast, people from different countries, such as Christian believers in Western and in East Asian societies, may have similar beliefs and behavioral scripts even though they are geographically located in difference places.

Culture is also different from race, which is a way of categorizing human beings based on external attributes, such as the skin tone and facial features that differentiate human populations. In many racial theories, and in lay theories, racial groups also possess different fixed and biologically determined psychological traits and tendencies. Race is viewed as fixed both over the course of the lifespan and across cultural contexts. People from the same racial group are thought to be homogenous in terms of heritage and physical appearance.

However, in reality individuals classified as belonging to the same race do not necessarily share the same cultural values and experiences. For example, Native Chinese and Chinese Americans may be thought to belong to the same racial group, but may have distinct cultural values and beliefs, and experiences.

Researchers such as cultural psychologists use the term *culture* in the sense of a social group whose members share social values, knowledge, and practices. Some studies have recruited participants from two different cultural groups (e.g., Westerners and East Asians) based on cultural psychology findings that suggest that the two groups differ in specific cultural values or specific cognitive processes. In some cases, race and language are concomitants that also differentiate the two cultural groups. Other studies have investigated cultural groups who are from the same nation but are defined by religious or political beliefs (e.g., Han et al. 2008, 2010; Yilmaz and Bahçekapili 2015). In such cases, two groups of participants share the same nationality, race, and language and differ only in a set of shared beliefs/values and practices that are hypothesized to be relevant to a particular pattern of behavioral performance and related brain activity.

To understand the nature of culture, it is necessary to measure and estimate culture quantitatively, and this makes culture shift from something to be described to something to be interpreted. Because culture is a complicated concept with many dimensions, researchers have developed measures that are used to evaluate cultural values or cultural traits in specific dimensions. For example, to estimate to what degree people value close links among individuals who view themselves primarily as parts of a whole (e.g., a social group or a nation) or emphasize the importance of one's own goals/preferences, needs/desires, and rights in thought and behavior, Triandis (1995) developed a questionnaire to measure individualistic and collectivistic cultural values. Singelis (1994) created the Self-Construal Scale to evaluate cultural traits such as whether an individual views the self as an autonomous and bounded entity and emphasizes independence and uniqueness of the self, or views the self as interconnected and overlapping with close others and emphasizes harmony with close others. Tsai et al. (2006) developed a measure of how people want to feel ("ideal affect") and how they actually feel ("actual affect") to examine culturally preferred ideal affective states. These questionnaires have been used widely to quantify differences in cultural orientations between individuals from different societies. In addition, these measures have been used to assess and understand the relationship between cultural values and human behavior by capturing both within and between-group variations in cultural values. Measuring cultural values allows researchers to examine whether group differences in behavior and the underlying mental processes are associated with specific cultural values and whether cultural group differences in behavior are mediated by specific cultural values. Most importantly, these measures provide frameworks for specifying cultural differences in various cognitive and affective processes that are critical for understanding diverse human behaviors.

Behind cultural differences in behavior: Mental processes

Why do people from various societies behave differently? How can we understand diverse human behaviors? Researchers can take very different approaches to address these questions and provide causal explanations from different perspectives. For instance, anthropologists tried to understand the evolution of culture in primates by asking questions about "(a) how socioecological variables affect cultural transmission dynamics, (b) the proximate mechanisms by which social learning is achieved, (c) developmental studies of the role of social influence in acquiring behavioral traits, and (d) the fitness consequences of engaging in social learning" (Perry 2006, p. 171). By describing and analyzing peoples' communication, family structure, social relationship, religious activity, etc., cultural anthropology aims to understand the origin, structure, and adaptive function of cultural systems (Fortun and Fortun 2009). Environment, behavior, and social learning attract much attention from anthropologists, but less interest is paid to the role of mental processes in the evolution of culture, owing to the anthropological approach characterized by behavioral observations.

Because behavior is guided by the mind, researchers spontaneously seek for mental processes that are associated with diverse human behaviors. Cultural psychology is such an approach that investigates "the way cultural traditions and social practices regulate, express, and transform the human psyche, resulting less in psychic unity for humankind than in ethnic divergences in mind, self, and emotion" (Shweder 1991, p. 73). Cultural psychology has its origin in cultural anthropology, but its own research questions, methods, and theories have developed (Kitayama and Cohen 2010). In particular, the scientific effort of cultural psychology focuses on the similarity and dissimilarity of mental processes underlying human behavior. One of the main goals of cultural psychology during the last two decades has been to reveal cultural group differences in the multiple cognitive and affective processes that support human behavior and to attribute diverse human behaviors to distinct underlying mental processes.

The main approach of cultural psychology research, based on the assumption that cultures are comparable, tests two or more subject groups from different cultures with specific cognitive/affective tasks in order to make inferences of culturally universal and distinct mental processes from participants' behavioral performances or from the results of questionnaire surveys. Because cultural psychology research was initiated by psychologists from North America and European countries and was later on joined by researchers from East Asian countries (China, Japan, Korea), the majority of cross-cultural comparisons were conducted between Westerners and East Asians, with relatively fewer comparisons of other cultural groups. To ensure that the research participants from different cultural samples were recruited from comparable populations, most of the cross-cultural studies tested college students because this made it easier to control confounding factors such as age, education, intelligence, and occupation. However, as pointed out by Henrich et al. (2010), current behavioral scientists (including cultural psychologists) routinely test participants from Western, Educated, Industrialized, Rich, and Democratic (WEIRD) societies and assume that these WEIRD subjects are as representative of the species as any other populations. Because there is substantial variability in experimental results across populations and WEIRD subjects are particularly unusual compared with the rest of the species, researchers (including cultural psychologists) must be cautious if they try to generalize about humans based on the results obtained from the members of WEIRD people.

Nonetheless, it is important not to underestimate the increasing findings from cultural psychology that have revealed cultural differences in various mental processes. To date, there has been increasing evidence for cultural group differences in multiple aspects of human psychological constructs. For example, Kitayama and colleagues (2003) developed a framed-line test to assess the ability to incorporate or to ignore contextual information during visual processing, and they compared the performance of people from two cultures. During the famed-line test, participants were first presented with a square frame that includes a vertical line. After the stimulus had been withdrawn, participants were shown another square frame of the same or different size and were asked to draw a line that was identical to the first line in either absolute length (absolute task) or proportion to the height of the surrounding frame (relative task). The authors initially tested two different culture groups in the framed-line test and found that Japanese undergraduate students recruited in Japan were more accurate in the relative task, whereas American undergraduate students recruited in the United States were more accurate in the absolute task. More interestingly, to illustrate cultural influences on performances in the framed-line test, the authors further tested American undergraduate students recruited in Japan and found that they also performed more accurately in the relative than in the absolute tasks. Japanese undergraduate students recruited in the United States, however, showed comparable performances in the two tasks. These results were interpreted in terms of individuals engaging in Asian cultures being more capable of incorporating contextual information and those engaging in North American cultures being more capable of ignoring contextual information during visual perception.

Cultural differences in perception exist not only in the visual modality. Ma-Kellams and colleagues (2012) examined cultural differences in visceral perception by recording heartbeat rates via electrocardiogram (ECG) from Asian and European American participants during a heartbeat discrimination task during which participants were also required to count and report their own heartbeats. The calculated difference scores between actual heart rate and reported heart rate was used to index the accuracy of self-perception of heart rate. Asian participants turned out to display greater difference scores between actual and perceived heartbeats compared with European American participants, suggesting that their visceral perception was less accurate. Kitayama et al.'s (2003) framed-line test was also used to examine whether Asians' greater attention to and reliance on contextual cues cause them to be poorer visceral perceivers. MaKellams et al. computed a contextual dependency score (i.e., the difference between the errors in the absolute and relative tasks) and found that the contextual dependency actually mediated the association between culture and heartbeat detection scores.

Researchers have also reported cultural differences in high-level cognitive processes. To explore cultural influences on memory, Wang (2001) asked American and Chinese college students to report their earliest childhood memory on a memory questionnaire. Participants were told that the memory must be their own memory from earliest childhood, not something they only saw in a picture or heard from someone else. Interestingly, memory reports from the two cultural groups had very different orientations. American participants reported lengthy, specific, self-focused, and emotionally elaborate memories, and their memory descriptions placed emphasis on individual attributes in describing themselves (e.g., "Because, as I was staring at the ceiling, I realized that no one else was around. I remember being taken aback by the ability to amuse myself without any toys."). Contrariwise, Chinese participants reported more collective activities, general routines, and a great number of social roles in their self-descriptions. Thus American and Chinese cultures foster different focuses during retrieval of personal experiences from episodic memory. Such cultural differences in episodic memory were also observed in American and Chinese preschool children (Wang 2004). When asked to recount autobiographical events, American children often provided elaborate and detailed memories focusing on their own roles, preferences, and feelings; they also frequently described themselves in terms of personal attributes, abstract dispositions, and inner traits, all cast in a positive light. In contrast, Chinese children provided relatively skeletal accounts of experiences that centered on social interactions and daily routines, and they often described themselves in terms of social roles, context-specific characteristics, and overt behaviors in a neutral or modest tone.

Another example of cultural differences in high-level cognitive process is how people from different cultures categorize objects. In an early work, Chiu (1972) tested how Chinese and American children from middle- and working-class families classified objects into different categories. Children aged between 9 and 10 years from the two cultures were presented with an item consisting of three pictures representing human, animal, vehicle, furniture, tool, or food categories. The children were asked to select any two out of the three objects in a set, which were alike or went together, and to state the reason for their choices. For example, when an item consisted of a cow, a chicken, and grass, American children tended to put the chicken and the cow together and they justified this categorization by stating, "both are animals." Thus, American children seemed to pay attention to the properties shared by different objects during object categorization. Nevertheless, Chinese children were more likely to put the cow and the grass together and gave a reason for their object sorting by emphasizing that "the cow eats the grass." Chiu's findings suggest that American children tend to classify objects based on inferred characteristics of the stimuli (i.e., an inferential-categorical style), whereas Chinese children prefer to classify objects based on functional or thematic interdependence between the elements in a grouping (i.e., a relational-contextual style). Similar differential tendencies have been observed in college students. Norenzayan et al. (2002) found that East Asian students tended to group objects based on their shared family resemblance, whereas European Americans were more likely to classify objects that can be assigned by a rule into a group. These observations indicate cultural differences in mental processes engaged in object categorization in both children and adults.

The studies aforementioned illustrate cultural group differences in visual/visceral perception, memory, categorization, etc. Apparently, cultural group differences are exhibited in multiple cognitive processes. However, researchers have tried to understand the cultural differences in these cognitive processes in a coherent way by searching for a more fundamental interpretation of cultural disparity in multiple cognitive processes. Drawing upon an early idea that different cultural environments lead to the development of different patterns of ability (Ferguson 1956), it has been proposed that people from different cultures develop various cognitive styles to deal effectively with problems encountered in daily living. These proposals, being against the traditional Western and early psychological thoughts, stress distinct patterns of perceptual/attention and social/political processes across different cultural groups. For instance,

Nisbett and colleagues (2001) proposed that collectivistic East Asian (e.g., Chinese, Japanese) cultures foster a holistic style of thinking that encourages attending to the entire field and the relationships between objects when viewing complicated visual scenes, and the attended information is used for other cognitive processes such as categorization and causal attribution. In contrast, individualistic Western (e.g., Greek or American) cultures cultivate an analytic style of thinking that guides attention primarily to objects and their internal attributes, which in turn lead to characteristics-based object categorization and causal attribution. Nisbett and colleagues further speculate that the distinct thinking styles can be traceable to markedly different philosophical thoughts and social systems developed in these cultures.

Markus and Kitayama (1991) took another perspective on the fundamental basis of cultural differences in mental processes by scrutinizing self-construals (i.e., how people think about the self and relationships between the self and others). They proposed that there are two basic ways to view the self and others. East Asian cultures insist on the fundamental connectedness of individuals to each other (including the connectedness between oneself and others) and encourage attending to others, fitting in, and harmonious interdependence with them. The interdependent self-construal provides a basis of cognition and emotion and deteriorates the role of one's own internal attributes and autonomy in social behavior. Western cultures (North American in particular) inspire individuals to seek and maintain their independence from others by attending to the self and by discovering and expressing their unique inner attributes. The independent self-construal places one's own abilities and opinions at a dominant position when deciding what to do, and how to behave in a social context. There have been empirical findings that reveal how self-construals differ remarkably between Westerners and East Asians and influence other cognitive and affective processes. These will be discussed in Chapters 4 and 7.

Cultural differences can also be assessed from a sociopolitical perspective related to social norms. Gelfand and colleagues (2011) conducted a survey of 33 nations to assess the strength of social norms and tolerance of deviant behavior. By asking individuals from different nations to evaluate items such as "People in this country almost always comply with social norms," they managed to differentiate between cultures that are tight (have many strong norms and a low tolerance of deviant behavior) or loose (have weak social norms and a high tolerance of deviant behavior). Interestingly, the tightness-looseness measures obtained from individuals of a nation are associated with ecological and human-made societal threats during the history of a nation. Tight nations have higher population density, fewer natural resources, more natural disasters, and more territorial threats from their neighbors. People from tight nations also report stronger self-regulation and higher self-monitoring, and these psychological characteristics are attuned to autocratic rules that suppress dissent, strict laws and regulations, and political pressures in tight nations. This tightness-looseness analysis suggests a dimension that distinguishes nations in terms of cultural systems and accounts for how psychological processes and institutional factors are shaped along this dimension to enhance order and social coordination to respond effectively to ecological and historical threats.

The theoretical accounts of cultural differences in cognitive processes are helpful in improving our understanding of diverse human behaviors. As I mentioned earlier, there are novel cultural differences in how parents control sleep behavior in their children. Thus, middle-class European American parents behave differently from most other societies. A survey of 136 societies revealed that infants slept in bed with their mother in two-thirds of the communities and in the same room with their mother in other communities (Whiting 1964). Middle-class European American parents, however, reported that their infants slept separately from them by a few weeks of age, usually in another room (Morelli et al. 1992). Middle-class American infants are encouraged to depend not on people for comfort and company, but on objects such as pacifiers and blankets. Why do middle-class European American parents behave differently from parents from other societies in organizing their infants' sleeping? One account, based on Markus and Kitayama's (1991) theory of independence self-construals in North American culture, is that middle-class European American parents view themselves as independent and autonomous entities and believe that their children should also become independent and autonomous in the future. Indeed, Richman et al. (1988) reported that middle-class European American parents identified independence as the most important long-term goal for their infants. Thus sleeping in a separate room is taken as a training individuality from early childhood. After entering school, children in middle-class European American families are further encouraged to demonstrate self-expression and freedom from others in action and thought. Consequently, the cultural value of independence is transmitted from parents to their children through early education.

Accumulating findings for cultural differences in multiple psychological processes start to challenge the idea that mental processes underlying human behavior are universal across all people at all times. These findings help us to understand diverse human behaviors and meanwhile raise important questions regarding the human brain. Given that mental processes are essentially the function of the human brain, the findings of diverse mental processes across cultures force us to rethink the nature of the human brain. Is the human brain functionally organized in the same way regardless of social environments?

Does the human brain work in the same way regardless of individuals' cultural experiences? These issues have not been addressed by traditional neuroscience studies because neuroscientists usually study animals that are raised in simple environments that are much less colorful and variable than the social environments humans create. In addition, traditional neuroscience research, similar to physics and chemistry research, seeks universal principles of brain function that guide animal and human behavior. An immediate question arising from the findings of cultural psychology is whether and how the human brain mediates distinct mental processes in different cultures. New research techniques such as brain imaging shed new light on these great questions and allow neuroscience to enter the culture arena.

Behind cultural differences in mind: Brain activity

During the last two decades, several historically distinct research disciplines have promoted the emergence of studies of the relationship between culture and brain and inspired neuroscience understanding of variations of behavior and mind across cultures. Brain imaging techniques that can be applied non-invasively to humans to record their brain activities during specific tasks and behavioral performance have developed rapidly since 1990s. Among these imaging techniques, functional magnetic resonance imaging (fMRI) and electroencephalography (EEG) have been widely used to explore neural substrates in the human brain involved in multiple cognitive and affective processes.

fMRI allows researchers to record blood-oxygen-level-dependent (BOLD) signals, which are sensitive to changes in oxygen levels in the circulating blood. Blood flow and glucose consumption far exceed the increases in oxygen consumption (Fox et al. 1988) and this leads to increased amounts of oxygen in the blood that is manifested in the ration of deoxygenated hemoglobin and oxygenated hemoglobin, which can then be detected with fMRI. Although the BOLD signal does not directly measure neuronal activity in the brain, a spatially restricted increase in BOLD signal corresponds with local field potentials (i.e., slow electrical activity reflecting predominantly input to neurons that can be recorded from electrodes over the scalp) (Logothetis 2008). The spatial resolution of BOLD signals is typically approximately 1 to several millimeters depending on the intensity of magnetic field generated by MRI scanners (1.5 to 7 tesla scanners have been used for testing human subjects). A BOLD signal begins to increase after a few seconds and reaches a peak between 4 and 6 seconds after the presentation of a stimulus. It takes 10 to 12 seconds for a BOLD signal to return to a baseline. Thus fMRI allows researchers to assess neuronal activity associated with cognition and behavior with high spatial resolution but low temporal resolution. BOLD signals recorded in the sensory cortex vary systemically with stimulus duration and intensity, whereas BOLD signals recorded from other brain regions such as the frontal lobe show complicated patterns during social cognitive processes.

EEG is a graphic representation of the difference in voltage that can be recorded between metal electrodes mounted over the scalp and a reference electrode and varies across time (Luck 2014). Synaptic activity that contributes to the transmission of information between two cortical neurons is believed to be the most significant source of EEG potentials. EEG activity reflects a combined synchronous electrical activity of a neuron population. EEG activity can be recorded within a millisecond and thus has an advantage of high temporal resolution. EEG activity that is time-locked (phase-locked) to an external event (or stimulus), a motor response, and an internal mental activity can be calculated to produce event-related potentials (ERPs), which have been widely used to explore neurophysiological activity underlying human behavior and cognitive/affective processes. However, as EEG is essentially a two-dimensional projection of neuronal activity in a three-dimensional space, theoretically it is impossible to develop an algorithm to determine the location of the EEG generator, though researchers are developing different algorithms for estimation of sources of EEG activity recorded over the scalp. This is why fMRI and EEG/ERP are often combined by researchers who are interested in both spatial and temporal information of neural activity related to cognition and behavior.

Starting in the 1990s, brain imaging such as fMRI and EEG/ERP began to be used widely among psychologists and neuroscientists who aimed to examine the neural basis of human mental events, and these studies gave birth to *cognitive neuroscience*. The early cognitive neuroscience research focused on the neural mechanisms underlying perception, attention, memory, language, motor skills etc. (Gazzaniga 2004). Cognitive neuroscientists created behavioral paradigms that can be used to disentangle transient neural activities or sustain neural activities in association with specific cognitive functions. By combining fMRI and EEG/ERP, cognitive neuroscientists attempt to account for the neural correlates of cognitive processes by localizing these processes in specific brain regions and clarifying related time courses. Early cognitive neuroscience studies were conducted with the assumption that the human brain mechanisms of cognition are universal across cultural populations and thus seldom considered potential cultural differences.

Social cognitive neuroscience emerged during early 2000s when social psychologists became interested in brain mechanisms that allow people to understand the self and others, to behave appropriately during social interactions, and to navigate complicated social environments efficiently (Ochsner and Lieberman 2001). Early social cognitive neuroscience research focused on the neural substrates underpinning social cognition with the aid of combining brain imaging and social psychological paradigms. Most of these studies aimed to uncover the neural mechanisms of social cognition and behavior without considering potential cultural differences because of the lack of cross-cultural comparisons of brain imaging findings. However, an important feature of social cognition and behavior is their context dependence. People are always situationally embedded in a certain sociocultural environment—the "context"—that substantially influences their perception of others and themselves and others' and their own behavior. This context dependency itself underlies substantial influences exerted by cultural beliefs and values. What social information is processed and how it is processed relies heavily on one's interaction partners (in the case of dyadic interactions), and, more broadly, on the social context in which the interactions occur. As I mentioned early in this chapter, cultural differences in human behaviors are very well documented in anthropology (e.g., Haviland et al. 2008), and human development has been viewed as a process of acquiring and embodying cultural belief/value systems (Rogoff 2003). Researchers who were involved in social cognitive neuroscience studies were well aware of the findings of cultural psychology that have revealed cultural differences in self-construals (Markus and Kitayama 1991 2010), causal attribution of physical and social events (Choi et al. 1999; Morris and Peng 1994), and analytic versus holistic attention (Masuda and Nisbett 2001), among many others. Owing to the considerable evidence for cultural divergence of human subjective experiences and psychological processes, soon after the development of social cognitive research, researchers started to show interest in whether parallel differences in neural mechanisms of cognition and behavior are also present among people who are born and educated in different sociocultural environments.

On the theoretical basis alone, cultural influences on the neural substrates underlying human cognition and behavior would seem highly plausible given that it takes almost 20 years for a large portion of the brain to mature (e.g., the decrease of gray matter density in the cortical surface; Gogtay et al. 2004). From the very beginning of their lives, people engage in complex social environments that are composed of physical entities, social rules, and the folk-beliefs of their respective local communities. Social interactions in such environments may shape people's brains in a way that the functional organization of the brain is attuned closely to the surrounding sociocultural contexts that are characterized by specific cultural beliefs/values and behavioral scripts. Biological research has shown ample evidence for the intrinsic plasticity of the human brain, that is, the brain changes both structurally and functionally in response to environments and experiences (Shaw and McEachern 2001). To give a couple of examples, the occipital cortex, which is commonly involved in visual processing in sighted individuals, can be engaged in auditory processing in blind individuals (Burton et al. 2002; Gougoux et al. 2009). Auditory deprivation results in the recruitment of the primary auditory cortex in the processing of vibrotactile stimuli (Levanen et al., 1998) and sign language (Nishimura et al. 1999) in deaf humans. The medial prefrontal cortex is engaged during self-reflection on visually but not aurally presented trait words in sighted humans, whereas this brain region is recruited during self-reflection on aurally presented trait words in congenitally blind individuals (Ma and Han 2011). These findings exemplify an intrinsic property of the brain, plasticity, which enables the nervous system to respond to environmental pressures, physiological changes, and personal experiences (Pascual-Leone et al. 2005), and to adapt to social contexts during development (Blakemore 2008). Given that human thoughts and behaviors differ substantially across a variety of sociocultural contexts, it is not surprising that the human brain, the carrier of human thoughts and the direct guider of human behaviors, is modulated by sociocultural environments and it develops unique neural mechanisms that help an individual to adapt to culturally specific changes and pressures. Thus, sociocultural-context-dependence can and should be taken as an intrinsic feature of the human brain.

In the beginning of the twenty-first century, researchers started to examine potential cultural differences in human brain mechanisms involved in specific cognitive and affective processes by comparing brain imaging results obtained from different cultural groups. These researchers, similar to cultural psychologists, take the view that human cognitive and affective processes vary as a function of cultural environments that provide unique social contexts, in which mental processes and underlying neural substrates develop and are shaped. They also take the theoretical frameworks, such as individualistic versus collectivistic values (Triandis, 1995), independent versus interdependent self-construals (Markus and Kitayama 1991; 2001), and holistic versus analytic cognitive tendencies (Nisbett et al. 2001), to guide their empirical brain imaging studies that examine cultural discrepancy in the neural correlates of human cognition and behavior. The increasing brain imaging findings of distinct patterns of brain activity involved in cognition and behave in different sociocultural contexts promote the emerging field of cultural neuroscience.

Cultural neuroscience

Cultural neuroscience emerges from the integration of different branches of social sciences and natural sciences. It arises mainly from two disciplines: cultural psychology, which has provided the insight that cognitive, emotional, and motivational tendencies and habits are shaped by culture, and neuroscience, which has demonstrated that the brain is shaped by experience. The term *cultural neuroscience* was initially coined by Chiao and Ambady (2007, p. 238), who defined it as, "a theoretical and empirical approach to investigate and characterize the mechanisms by which [the] hypothesized bidirectional, mutual constitution of culture, brain, and genes occurs." This definition was further refined by Chiao (2010, p.109) who described cultural neuroscience as an "interdisciplinary field bridging cultural psychology, neurosciences and neurogenetics that explains how the neurobiological processes, such as genetic expression and brain function, give rise to cultural values, practices and beliefs as well as how culture shapes neurobiological processes across macro- and micro-time scales." These concepts resonate with the effort to integrate research findings from neuroscience, genetics, developmental psychology, and sociology by highlighting the role of postnatal neuroplasticity in human development (e.g., Li 2003; Wexler 2006). The basic assumption of cultural neuroscience is that culture provides a framework for social behavior, communication, and interaction that generates social values and norms, assigns meaning to social events, interacts with biological variables (e.g., genes), and codetermines the functional organization of the brain.

Taking culture as a shared dynamic environment (e.g., social institutions) and knowledge system (e.g., belief, value, and rule), cultural neuroscience aims to address whether and how cultural contexts and individuals' sociocultural experiences interact with and shape the functional organization of the human brain, and to what degree the observed cultural differences in human behavior can be attributed to distinct neural underpinnings across cultures. Cultural neuroscience research aims to provide a neuroscientific account of cross-cultural variations in human psychological functions and behaviors by discovering socioculturally patterned neural mechanisms and the trajectory of their development. The final goal is to unveil both culturally universal and culturally unique neural processes by which human brains predispose us to perceive self and others, to communicate and interact with conspecifics, and to guide our actions.

Early cultural neuroscience studies examined distinct neural correlates of the processing of culturally familiar/unfamiliar information (see Chapter 2 of this book). Another main endeavor is to investigate whether, and how, two cultural groups differ in neural substrates of specific cognitive and affective processes (see Chapters 3–5 of this book). A typical way to address this issue is to compare fMRI or EEG/ERP results obtained from individuals who were raised in two different sociocultural contexts. One basic assumption of this approach is that, because participants from two cultural groups differ in cultural knowledge, beliefs/values, and/or cognitive and affective processes, the underlying neural activity should illustrate differences between the groups in a specific way. The findings of cultural psychological research have been used to guide hypotheses about neural differences between specific cultural groups. However, selection of participants from two different nations or sociocultural contexts does not necessarily imply that the participants have distinct cultural values (Oyserman et al. 2002). Thus cultural neuroscience studies also assess cultural values/traits from participants, using well-established measures that are developed by social and cultural psychologists, and control for potentially confounding variables such as participants' gender, age, language, and education, as well as socioeconomic status. The measures of cultural values/traits allow researchers to assess whether participants recruited in a cross-culture brain imaging study actually differ in specific cultural beliefs/ values/traits. Measuring cultural values/traits also allows researchers to test the association between cultural values and brain activity across individuals and to explore whether cultural values mediate observed differences in brain activity associated with specific tasks between two cultural groups.

The findings of cross-cultural brain imaging research essentially reveal correlations between culture and brain activity but cannot logically demonstrate a causal relationship between them although the relevant findings are interpreted as cultural influences. To illustrate causal relationships between culture and brain activity, it is necessary to manipulate cultural orientations in the same population and demonstrate variations of brain activity as consequences of the manipulation. It is difficult to conduct such brain imaging experiments outside laboratories. This challenge, however, has been resolved by cultural neuroscientists who adopted an elegant paradigm, cultural priming, from cultural psychology. Based on the assumption that individuals can acquire more than one set of cultural knowledge and can use different sets of cultural knowledge depending on contextual cues (Hong et al. 2000), cultural neuroscience studies investigate whether, and how, priming a specific cultural value gives rise to dynamic changes in brain activity involved in cognitive and affective processes. The findings provide information that allows for causal inference regarding the relationship between cultural values and specific brain activity. This line of research will be discussed in Chapter 6.

A key issue for cultural neuroscience research is how culture interacts with biological factors such as genes to shape the functional organization of the human brain. It is becoming more and more pressing to clarify the consequence of culture-gene interactions on the human brain owing to the recent behavioral findings. For instance, recent research indicates that psychological tendencies and behavioral outcomes associated with specific genotypes are moderated by cultural experiences or even illustrate opposite patterns in individuals from different cultures (Kim and Sasaki 2014). This line of research has provided a strong clue to culture-gene interaction occurring in the underlying brain mechanisms. Recent studies also reported evidence for the association between specific cultural values (e.g., interdependence) and the allelic frequency of a specific gene across different cultural populations. For example, populations dominated by stronger collectivistic values comprise more individuals carrying the short allele of the serotonin transporter functional polymorphism (5-HTTLPR) (Chiao and Blizinsky 2010) and more individuals carrying the A allele of the oxytocin receptor gene (OXTR rs53576) (Luo and Han 2014). These observations encourage researchers to clarify to what degree the findings of cultural differences in brain activity can be attributed to the contribution of genes. Nevertheless, to address such a critical issue requires new paradigms and cooperation of researchers from different cultures who are able to test genotyped individuals using brain imaging. It is thus difficult to conduct empirical research to examine how culture interacts with gene to shape human brain activity. In addition, as there has been substantial brain imaging findings regarding genetic and cultural influences on the brain, mind, and behavior, and gene-cultural interactions on brain and mind; therefore, new theoretical analyses and models are demanded to rethink human development in complicated sociocultural environments. These will be discussed in Chapters 7–8.

Cultural neuroscience is young but developing rapidly. Since the publication of early empirical research, a number of review article have been published in top neuroscience and psychology journals (Ambady and Bharucha 2009; Ames and Fiske 2010; Chiao and Bebko 2011; Chiao et al. 2013; Han and Northoff 2008; Han et al. 2013; Han 2015; Kim and Sasaki 2014; Kitayama and Uskul 2011; Park and Huang 2010; Rule et al. 2013). Several journals have published special issues on cultural neuroscience, including *Progress in Brain Research* (2009), *Social Cognitive and Affective Neuroscience* (2010), *Asian Journal of Social Psychology* (2010), *Psychological Inquiry* (2013), and *Cognitive Neuroscience* (2014). Other contributions to the development of cultural neuroscience include the collective volume titled *Cultural and Neural Frames of Cognition and Communication* (Han and Pöppel 2011) and *The Oxford Handbook of Cultural Neuroscience* (Chiao et al. 2016). A new journal titled *Culture and Brain* was launched in 2013 by the publisher Springer, with a focus on "cultural differences in neural activity" and "the mutual constitution of culture and the brain" (Han 2013).

Despite the rising research interests and accumulating empirical findings, cultural neuroscience is still envisaging omnifarious challenges. These include, for example, the search for new dimensions of cultural orientations along which brain activity is modulated, development of new paradigms that allow the inference of causal relationships between culture and the brain, and the invention of new methods for comparing brain imaging results from two or more cultural groups. Cultural neuroscience also demands new concepts and theoretical frameworks to understand the nature of culture and the brain and the relationships between culture, the brain, and genes. Deep considerations of the social significance of cultural neuroscience findings and their social implications are also on the agenda for future research (see Chapter 9 of this book).

Chapter 2

Neural processes of culturally familiar information

Cultural learning

Human beings are the only species on earth who manage large-scale and long-term systematic education of their offspring. The development of each individual person is essentially a cultural process in a specific social environment (Rogoff 2003). Right from birth, infants receive specific information in their interactions with familiar others, including parents, siblings, kinfolks, and others from the same sociocultural group. Members of the group have similar facial features, own similar cultural values and shared beliefs, and comply with the same behavioral scripts and social rules. As caregivers they may be depended on for social support and deliver culturally specific information through, for example, language, gesture, music, social media, routine ways of doing things, and religious rituals. Individuals in most of the current human societies are educated in well-designed institutions and assimilate systematic cultural knowledge until young adulthood. Therefore, cultural learning is a long process in human development, and of course, it varies greatly across sociocultural environments.

According to Tomasello et al. (1993), there are three types of cultural learning. *Imitative learning* refers to reproducing others' behavioral strategies in an appropriate functional context with an understanding of the intentional state underlying the behavior. *Instructed learning* occurs when learners internalize teachers' instructions and use them to self-regulate their own cognitive functions during subsequent behavior. These two types of learning play a key role in cultural transmission over generations because adults pass to their children cultural knowledge, values, and beliefs by modeling or instruction. A third type of cultural learning is *collaborative learning*, referring to the process during which peers collaborate to construct something new such as novel social values/norms and fancy behavior. Thus, collaborative learning plays a pivotal role in creating new cultural concepts and values. Relative to learning in non-human primates, human learning is unique in that human cultures have some cultural traditions that are learned by almost all group members. In addition, modifications of human cultures can occur during cultural learning and be transmitted over generations. In some cases, an individual failing to assimilate cultural learning would be considered an abnormal member of the social group in human societies.

The brain is sculptured by cultural learning in two different ways. First, parents from different cultures may teach their children to respond during cognitive and social tasks in different fashions, which would lead to the development of distinct cognitive strategies and related functional organization of the brain. For example, during free play, Chinese toddlers, as compared with Canadian toddlers, spend more time in direct physical contact with their mothers and take longer before they approach strangers to play together (Chen et al. 1998). During parent–child interaction, mothers in the United States and other Western cultures are more likely to increase their children's level of arousal or to make them feel excited by playing and chatting, whereas mothers in East Asian cultures are more likely to rock and lull their babies to reduce their levels of arousal or to make them calm down (Minami and McCabe 1995; Morikawa et al. 1998). Cultural differences in behavioral and emotional inhibition in early childhood may lead to the development of distinct patterns of brain activity engaged in self-regulation so that adult brains may be activated differently in response to social interaction and emotion in East Asian and in Western cultures. Second, during early education, children in most societies are exposed to information that is related to their own culture and are less likely to receive information from other cultures. Gesture, music, and brand information, for example, are highly culturally specific, and, in some societies, individuals would have little knowledge of gestures, music, or brands from other cultures until young adulthood. Frequent exposure to culturally familiar information may give rise to unique neural representation of the information. This chapter focuses on differential neural processes of culturally familiar and unfamiliar information.

Culturally familiar information plays a fundamental role in the formation of shared beliefs and behavioral scripts among individuals of the same social group. Relative to individuals from earlier societies, people in current societies have greater opportunities, during adulthood and even early childhood, to encounter people from different cultures who bring beliefs/values/behavioral scripts that may be similar to or different from what an individual has learned during development. Imagine that you are traveling in a country where people live in buildings of different architectural styles, speak different languages, listen to music of different styles, and enjoy food cooked in different ways than those with which you are familiar. In such a new sociocultural environment, suppose you suddenly hear someone singing a familiar song using your own mother tongue. How would you respond and how would you feel about that? Your attention may be attracted immediately by the song that may also remind you of something in your memory and provoke warm or sad feelings in reminisce.

Culturally familiar and unfamiliar information can have a distinct significance for human lives. Culturally familiar information is obtained during early life experiences in a specific sociocultural environment. Cultural familiarity is discrepant from perceptual familiarity. Sensory/perceptual processing of objects or scenes will induce modifications of neural activity in brain regions underlying those sensory/perceptual processes. For instance, research using positron emission topography (PET) showed that viewing new learned, versus unlearned, faces increased the regional blood flow in the right middle occipital gyrus, right posterior fusiform gyrus, and right inferotemporal cortex (Rossion et al. 2001). These brain regions constitute the occipitotemporal (or the ventral) visual pathway in the right hemisphere that underlies perceptual processing of facial features and supports object and face recognition. Participants had not had any form of social interaction with the owners of the new learned (versus unlearned) faces; all they had done was to spend some time viewing some faces but not others in a laboratory. Such a perceptual learning procedure resulted in perceptual experience with learned faces but not with unlearned faces, and it increased familiarity with the perceptual properties of learned faces. Cultural learning in real life is of course different because it not only allows observers to remember perceptual features of others' faces but also to assign deeper values/concepts/beliefs to familiar others via social interactions. It is the case that a cohort can acquire similar values/concepts/beliefs about objects or people through similar cultural experiences, and engender shared values of beliefs about culturally familiar objects or persons. Consequently, the influences of cultural familiarity on human cognition and the underlying neural processes can go beyond the modulations of brain activity in those simply performing sensory/perceptual processing tasks.

Researchers have tried to address the issue of how the human brain processes culturally familiar and unfamiliar information and whether the human brain develops specific neural processes for culturally familiar compared with unfamiliar information. Because the functional organization of the brain is shaped during cultural learning and people have many more experiences with culturally familiar than unfamiliar information, one would expect that the human brain may develop different mechanisms to process such information. There is empirical support for this expectation, cultural neuroscience studies have revealed unique brain mechanisms underlying the processing of culturally familiar and unfamiliar information in several domains. These will be summarized and discussed in this chapter.

Gesture

In addition to languages which are used for verbal communication, humans also develop a form of non-verbal communication, that is, gestures that consist of visible body actions (e.g., of the hand or face). Gestures can be used independently or in conjunction with speech to deliver specific messages during social interactions. In some cases where auditory information is blocked, gestures provide the only way for communication and have been developed into sign languages. People use simple gestures (or emblems) to deliver message (e.g., waving a hand for *goodbye*), as well as using series of gestures to express more complicated instructions, thoughts, and feelings (e.g., the gestures used to guide traffic in a city or to instruct a plane to land at an airport).

Symbolic or intransitive gestures are learned and familiarized through one's cultural experiences (Kendon 1997) and so the meanings of gestures are strongly culturally specific. Early research used video recordings to capture a large sample of international gestures to investigate whether there are universally understood hand gestures and whether the exact same gesture can have different or even opposite meanings in two cultures (Archer 1997). Not surprisingly, the findings indicate cultural differences in meanings of gestures and even more profound differences involving deeply embedded categories of meanings such as make cultures unique. Subsequent studies have further reported evidence for cross-cultural variations of gestures in different dimensions (Kita 2009). For example, some of the conventional gestures are assigned with distinct meanings in different cultures. A typical example is a ring formed by the thumb and the index finger. This gesture means "*OK/good*" in most European cultures such as in Britain, Scandinavia, southern Spain, and Italy. However, the dominant meaning of the same gesture is "zero" in France, and a bodily orifice in Greece and Turkey (Morris et al. 1979). Different gestures can also be used to express the same meaning. The meaning of negation is evinced using a horizontal head-shake in the northern part of Italy, whereas a head toss (i.e., a head jerk upward and backward) in southern Italy indicates "*No*" (Morris et al. 1979). Another dimension of cultural variations of gesture meanings is related to spatial cognition. The speakers of Arrernte in Central Australia use open-hand pointing with the palm vertical to indicate each straight segment of a complex route. "Horn-hand" pointing (with the thumb, the index finger and the pinkie extended) is used to tell the direction of the end of a route (Wilkins 2003). However, these gestures are not used to express similar meanings in other cultures.

What are the neural correlates of performing and perceiving cultural familiar gestures in the human brain? The behavioral observations of cultural differences in gestures and the meanings of gestures have inspired cultural neuroscientists to explore the underlying brain mechanisms. These cultural neuroscience studies have raised questions based on early findings of neural activity related to action perception and imitation. For instance, the accumulating neuroscience studies of both animals and humans have revealed two neural systems, that is the mirror neuron system and the mentalizing system, which perform complementary roles in understanding others' actions. The mirror neuron system consists of motor-related brain regions in the inferior frontal gyrus and inferior parietal lobule (Rizzolatti and Craighero 2004). Animal studies where responses of a single neuron have been recorded revealed that neurons in these brain regions fire both when an animal (e.g., a monkey) performs an action and when the animal observes the same action performed by an experimenter (Fogassi et al. 2005; Gallese et al. 1996). Consistent with the findings of animal studies, fMRI research of human participants has shown that BOLD signals in the brain regions corresponding to the monkey's mirror neuron system (e.g., the pars opercularis of the inferior frontal gyrus and the rostral posterior parietal cortex) increase during action execution, as compared with observation of action, and show the highest activity during imitation that requires both execution and observation (Iacoboni et al. 1999). Given the specific patterns of responses during action perception and execution, the mirror neuron system is proposed to play a key role in mapping observed actions onto one's own motor representations so that one can easily simulate observed actions, and understand and predict others' intentions. The mentalizing system, mainly consisting of the medial prefrontal cortex, posterior cingulate cortex, and the bilateral temporoparietal junctions (Frith and Frith 2003) is activated when individuals infer others' intentions and beliefs while reading stories about others or watching cartoons, images, or movies of others (Gallagher et al. 2000; Han et al. 2005; Saxe and Kanwisher 2003).

Based on the previous neuroscience findings of the functional roles of the mirror neuron system and the mentalizing system, Liew and colleagues (2011) investigated whether observations of culturally familiar and unfamiliar gestures used to express specific meanings similarly recruit the mirror neuron system, the mentalizing system, or both. Because the previous research reported that expert dancers watching their own dance form, versus an unfamiliar dance form, increased the activity in the mirror neuron system (Calvo-Merino et al. 2005; Cross et al. 2006), one may expect that culturally familiar gestures may similarly activate the mirror neuron system, whereas culturally unfamiliar gestures may recruit the mentalizing system to understand the mental states of the performers. An alternative hypothesis is that watching culturally unfamiliar gestures may simply provoke imitation and engage the mirror neuron system, whereas watching culturally familiar gestures may automatically lead to inference of performers' intentions and/or beliefs and activate brain regions in the mentalizing system. Liew et al. (2011) tested these competing hypotheses by scanning Chinese university students using fMRI while they watched 2-second movie clips that depicted an actor performing expressive hand gestures that were either familiar (i.e., thumbs up) or unfamiliar (i.e., "*quail*" in American Sign Language) with his right hand (Figure 2.1). In addition, half of the clips depicted a Caucasian performing these gestures and the other half depicted a Chinese actor making identical gestures. This manipulation allowed the authors to address whether and how neural responses to culturally familiar gestures are modulated by culturally familiar/unfamiliar faces given that Chinese participants may have shared beliefs that a Chinese model is a racial "in-group" member, whereas a Caucasian model is a racial "out-group." To motivate participants to infer actively actors' intentions by attending to their hand movements, the participants were informed that they would be asked to describe the meaning of each gesture immediately after scanning. One of the most interesting observations in this study was that culturally familiar compared with unfamiliar gestures more strongly activated brain regions associated with mentalizing, including the posterior cingulate cortex, dorsal medial prefrontal cortex, and bilateral temporal-parietal junctions. In contrast, culturally unfamiliar compared with familiar gestures more strongly activated regions in the mirror neuron system, including the left inferior parietal lobe and left postcentral gyrus (Figure 2.2). These activations, however, did not differ as to whether the gestures were performed by a Chinese or Caucasian model, indicating independent

Familiar Gesture – Chinese   Unfamiliar Gesture – Caucasian   Control Still – Chinese

Figure 2.1. Illustrations of visual stimuli used in Liew et al. (2011). The stimuli consisted of 2-second videos of familiar gestures (left panel), unfamiliar gestures (middle panel), and control still images (right panel). Each gesture and still image was performed by an actor of the participants' own race (Chinese) and an actor of a different race (European American).

Adapted from Sook-Lei Liew, Shihui Han, and Lisa Aziz-Zadeh, Familiarity modulates mirror neuron and mentalizing regions during intention understanding, *Human Brain Mapping*, 32 (11), pp. 1986–1997, DOI: 10.1002/hbm.21164, Copyright © 2010 Wiley-Liss, Inc.

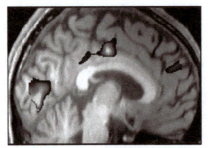 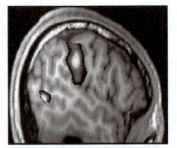

Culturally familiar > unfamiliar gestures   Culturally unfamiliar > familiar gestures

Figure 2.2 Illustrations of brain regions activated by perceiving culturally familiar and unfamiliar gestures. Culturally familiar compared with unfamiliar gestures more strongly activated brain regions associated with mentalizing, including the posterior cingulate cortex, dorsal medial prefrontal cortex, and bilateral temporal-parietal junctions. In contrast, culturally unfamiliar compared with familiar gestures more strongly activated regions in the mirror neuron system, including the left inferior parietal lobe and left postcentral gyrus. (See colour plate.)
Adapted from Sook-Lei Liew, Shihui Han, and Lisa Aziz-Zadeh, Familiarity modulates mirror neuron and mentalizing regions during intention understanding, *Human Brain Mapping*, 32 (11), pp. 1986–1997, DOI: 10.1002/hbm.21164, Copyright © 2010 Wiley-Liss, Inc.

neural processing of culturally familiar gestures and faces. The brain imaging results uncover an interesting interplay between culturally familiarity with gestures and the neural regions underlying both action observation and intention understanding. The brain seems to engage the mirror neuron and mentalizing systems in different degrees to process culturally familiar relative to unfamiliar actions. A motor-based representation of culturally unfamiliar actions is likely to be constructed in the brain to prepare for action imitation, given the lack of understanding of the meaning of these actions. Viewing culturally familiar actions performed by others, however, requires deeper understanding of others' intentions and/or beliefs that are necessary for further complicated social interactions.

Although Liew et al. (2011) failed to find evidence that understanding others' mental states by watching culturally familiar gestures is influenced by culturally familiar/unfamiliar faces of actors, a transcranial magnetic stimulation (TMS) study has shown evidence for complicated interactions between culturally familiar/unfamiliar gesture and actors' faces. TMS is a noninvasive method that has been widely used to stimulate a specific brain region by applying a coil that produces weak electric currents through electromagnetic induction in the region of the brain under the coil. Molnar-Szakacs et al. (2007) gave a single pulse TMS to the right or left primary motor cortex that induced motor-evoked potentials (MEPs) that can be recorded from the electrode placed over the first dorsal interosseous muscle of each hand. The amplitude of TMS-induced MEPs was used as an index of the excitability at the cortical or spinal level or corticospinal excitability, with a larger MEP amplitude being associated with higher corticospinal excitability. Molnar-Szakacs et al. (2007) recorded MEPs from European Americans during observation of American and Nicaraguan gestures performed by both a Euro-American and a Nicaraguan actor. Overall, watching American versus Nicaraguan actors increased the MEPs, and this finding indicates a stronger motor resonance between an observer and culturally familiar others. It was initially predicted that viewing culturally familiar emblems would increase corticospinal excitability than culturally unfamiliar emblems would. Indeed, this was confirmed when participants watched the European American actor who performed American versus Nicaraguan emblems. Nevertheless, watching the Nicaraguan actor who performed American versus Nicaraguan emblems decreased the MEP amplitudes, thus the American emblems performed by the Nicaraguan did not lead to facilitation of corticospinal excitability, but rather to a decrease. These findings were interpreted as reflecting influences of the perceived incongruence in culturally familiarity between the actor and the action they are performing on the motivation for imitation, which resulted in decrease corticospinal excitability during observation of gestures performed by culturally unfamiliar others. Thus, the excitability of the motor system is modulated by whether the perceived emblems are culturally familiar and by who (culturally familiar or unfamiliar others) perform the gestures. From an evolutionary perspective, coding culturally familiar gestures in the brain is particularly important for efficient social interactions that require information exchange among individuals. In particular, automatically catching another's mental states from culturally familiar gestures is critical for productive cooperation among individuals from the same cultural group. The brain imaging findings implicate neural responses at multiple levels that are specific to culturally familiar gestures and facilitate understanding of others' intentions and beliefs.

Music

People in every human culture enjoy music. However, individuals from different cultures have created very different musical traditions and practices (Campbell 1997). People from various societies make distinct musical instruments, and musicians from these societies compose melodies that have unique styles and express unique emotions. Even different generations of musicians from the same society put great effort in composing music of different styles.

Behavioral research has shown that Western adults performed better during detection of randomly located mistuning in a Western major-scale context than in a Javanese pelog-scale context (Lynch and Eilers 1992). More interestingly, even 1-year-old Western infants showed better performance during detection of mistuning in culturally familiar than in unfamiliar scale contexts. How does the brain process culturally familiar and unfamiliar music? One way to clarify the underlying neural mechanisms is to record brain activity from musicians or nonmusicians from different cultures. Universal or culturally specific neural mechanisms involved in music perception can be elucidated by comparing brain responses to culturally familiar and unfamiliar music.

An early work examined brain activity from college students who were trained in both the Western and Javanese systems (experimental group) or were trained in the Western system only (control group) (Renninger et al. 2006). In one condition, participants were presented with tones that fell within the Western C-major diatonic scale (80%, denoted as "standards") and tones that fell outside of the C-major diatonic scale (20%, denoted as "targets"). In another condition, they were presented with tones that are used frequently in Javanese pieces (80%, denoted as "standards") and tones that are rarely used in Javanese pieces (20%, denoted as "targets"). Participants were asked to identify scalar deviations within the Western diatonic scale and within the Javanese pelog scale while electroencephalogram (EEG) was recorded from electrodes over the scalp. This design is a typical oddball paradigm in which targets that appear less frequently elicit a large positive-going waveform (usually denoted as P300) at 300–700 ms after stimulus onset compared with standards that appear more frequently. The P300 is a brain response to the presentation of a rare or surprising stimulus, with the largest amplitude over the parietal region, and is believed to be involved in the updating of an operating context in working memory (Donchin and Coles 1988). Thus, the P300 amplitude in response to targets was used to estimate whether students who had or did not have prior experience with the Javanese musical system were similarly sensitive to scalar deviations within culturally familiar and unfamiliar music tones. It was found that scalar deviations (targets) within both the Western C-major diatonic scale and Javanese pelog scale evoked a large P300 relative to the standards in students who were trained in both the Western and Javanese music systems or trained only in the Western music. However, students with prior experience with the Javanese system showed a larger P300 amplitude in response to scalar deviations within the Javanese pelog scale compared with those without prior experience with the pelog scale. This finding reflects different strategies in adopting contextual information during the processing of culturally familiar and unfamiliar music. Hearing culturally familiar versus unfamiliar music may increase the allocation of attentional resources during the memory updating processes indexed by the modulation of the P300 amplitude.

Distinct neural responses to culturally familiar and unfamiliar music were also observed in studies of other cultural groups. Nan et al. (2006) compared brain activities recorded from German and Chinese musicians while they listened to Western and Chinese music. Traditional Chinese music mainly uses five penta-tonic basic scales and differs from Western music, which uses seven heptatonic scales. By integrating the oddball paradigm and ERPs to the biphrasal melo-dies of which targets (two phrases with the pauses between them were filled by one or several notes) were presented among standards (short melodic excerpts clearly structured into two phrases), Nan et al. found that both German and Chinese musicians performed better in detection of targets among standards by showing higher percentage of correct answers when listening to culturally familiar rather than unfamiliar music. For both cultural groups phrased rather than unphrased melodies induced a positive shift of the brain activity at 450–600 ms after the pause between two phrases, and this effect was more salient for Chinese than for Western music. Neural responses in an earlier time win-dow (100 and 450 ms post phrase-boundary offset) were modulated by both the participants' cultural background and music style. For German musicians, the differential amplitude of phrased versus unphrased melodies was greater when they listened to culturally unfamiliar (Chinese) than to culturally famil-iar (Western) music, whereas this effect was much weaker for Chinese musi-cians (Figure 2.3), possibly because Chinese musicians are also familiar with Western music, though to a less degree than Chinese music. It appears that the early neural processes of culturally familiar and unfamiliar music are driven by both stimulus features (i.e., bottom-up processes in an early time window) and cultural-specific knowledge (i.e., top-down processes at a late time window).

Another study recorded ERPs while American participants listened to melodies based on the Western folk tradition or North Indian classical music (Demorest and Osterhout 2012). Each melody was presented in its original form and a deviation form that contained out-of-key notes. Similar to the previous work, it was hypothesized that, when individuals listen to a piece of music, they would use the content of what they are listening to predict what may come next. However, these predictions or expectancies must depend on individuals' prior cultural experiences with the music. A stronger prediction or expectancy would be applied to culturally familiar relative to unfamiliar music. This hypothesis was tested by asking American participants to make judgments on the congru-ence of Western and North Indian melodies that were presented in the original form or had one target note changed. All participants reported that the Indian melodies were less congruous overall, and they were less sensitive to deviations

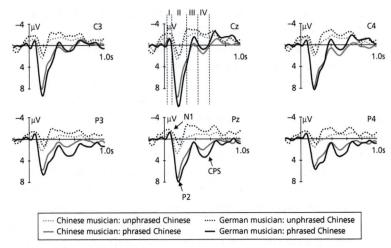

Figure 2.3 Illustration of ERPs to music recorded from Chinese and Germany musicians. The differential amplitude to phrased versus unphrased melodies recorded from the electrodes over the central and parietal regions of the scalp was greater in German than in Chinese musicians when they listened to Chinese music.
Reprinted from *Brain Research*, 1094 (1), Yun Nan, Thomas R. Knösche, and Angela D. Friederici, The perception of musical phrase structure: A cross-cultural ERP study, pp. 179–91, DOI:10.1016/j.brainres.2006.03.115, Copyright © 2006 Elsevier B.V., with permission from Elsevier.

in the Indian melody condition. This is not surprising given that American participants do not have much experience with Indian music. The brain activity to the target note was characterized by a long latency-positive activity over the parietal region, which was denoted as P600 in the study, though it was similar to the P300 observed in the previous research. In addition, the P600 was of larger amplitude when participants listened to Western melodies than to North Indian melodies. This finding is consistent with the idea that, when listening to culturally familiar music, individuals do not passively receive the information. Instead, they generate predictions of what should be heard in the following piece of music. Individuals may remain unable to develop such expectancies when hearing culturally unfamiliar music. The difference in such mental contexts during listening to culturally familiar than unfamiliar music gives arise to distinct sensitivity to changed note in a piece of culturally familiar relative to unfamiliar music.

There is also evidence that cultural familiarity affects the brain regions involved in processing of out-of-key tones. Matsunaga et al. (2012) used magnetoencephalogram (MEG) to measure brain responses to Western and Japanese melodies that contained tonal deviants from Japanese nonmusicians and amateur musicians. MEG is a functional neuroimaging technique that allows the recording of magnetic fields produced by electrical currents in the brain in responses to stimuli during various tasks. Similarly to EEG signals, MEG signals that arise from synchronized neuronal populations can be recorded with excellent time resolution (i.e., milliseconds) and can be used to estimate the origin of neural activity inside the brain. An early MEG study of neural processing of tonal deviations identified increased activities originating in the inferior frontolateral cortex in both hemispheres in response to tonal deviant chords in Western music in Westerners (Maess et al. 2001). Thus Matsunaga et al. further explored whether or not the same brain regions (e.g., the inferior frontolateral cortex) were engaged in the processing of tonal deviations regardless individuals' cultural experiences with the music. Japanese participants, who were born and grew up in Japan, had not received formal music education but had been exposed to both Western and traditional Japanese music. During MEG recording, participants were presented with Western and Japanese melodies that could contain an ending either with a tonally deviant note or not, and they had to respond to this deviant by pressing a button. While participants were able to detect tonal deviations of both Western and Japanese with high accuracy, the MEG data revealed a slight difference in the locations of brain regions activated by tonal deviations of Western and Japanese melodies. Source estimations based on MEG data identified activity around 150 ms following the onset of the final tone in a melody within the right inferior frontal gyrus and the left premotor cortex during listening to both Western and Japanese melodies. However, analyses of coordinates of these brain regions in the standardized Talairach space suggested that, relative to Japanese music, Western music activated the right inferior frontal gyrus more medially and activated the left premotor cortex more superiorly. It is thus likely that the neural activity related to detection of tonal deviations of Western and Japanese music do not completely overlap in the frontal and premotor cortices.

Distinct brain regions engaged to process culturally familiar and unfamiliar music have been examined using fMRI because of its high spatial resolution. To investigate the neural basis of musical-phrase boundary processing during the perception of music from native and non-native cultures, Nan et al. (2008) recorded BOLD responses in German musicians during fMRI scanning while participants categorized phrased Western (native) and Chinese (non-native) musical excerpts, as well as modified versions of these. The impression of phrasing had been reduced by removing the phrase boundary-marking pause (i.e., "unphrased" excerpts). The auditory stimuli were presented binaurally through specially constructed MR compatible headphones, which helped to reduce the influence of scanner noise. Based on prior fMRI findings, Nan et al. made several predictions regarding neural correlates of the processing of musical-phrase boundaries and related effects of cultural familiarity of music. For instance, because the posterior superior temporal cortex showed activations during recognition of musical features such as timbre (Menon et al. 2002), it was predicted that this brain region may be also engaged during the processing of phrase boundaries. In addition, as there has been evidence that the opercular part of the inferior frontal gyrus is associated with the processing of sequential rules in language/music syntax (Friederici 2002; Maess et al. 2001) and motion rhythms (Schubotz and von Cramon 2001), it was further assumed that this brain region ought to be activated during the perception of phrased melodies. Regarding the brain regions that may show effects of cultural familiarity on the processing of phrased melodies, the retrosplenial cortex and neighboring parietal cortex were predicted to differentiate between culturally familiar and unfamiliar music because this brain region is activated by familiar stimuli such as voices and faces (Shah et al. 2001) and familiarity-based judgment (Iidaka et al. 2006). Moreover, because the semantic memory of melodies was associated with activation in the medial and orbital frontal lobe (Platel et al. 2003), culturally familiar music may induce more memory related to the music, compared with unfamiliar music, and thus activate this brain region.

As with the behavior measures that revealed better performance (a higher recognition rate) for the Western than Chinese melodies, culturally familiar and unfamiliar music activated distinct brain regions. First, listening to unphrased compared to phrased melodies activated the posterior superior temporal cortex bilaterally and this effect was present in both Western and Chinese music for the anterior part of the superior temporal cortex but more posteriorly located in the left hemisphere for the Western music, suggesting the distinct involvement of subregions in the superior temporal cortex in response to the increased difficulty of identifying phrase boundaries in unphrased Western and Chinese melodies. Second, a network involving frontal and parietal regions showed increased activations for the phrased compared with unphrased melodies, but these activations did not differ significantly between Western and Chinese music. It was suggested that these results reflect similar attention and working memory processes during listening to culturally familiar and unfamiliar music. Third, the direct comparison between Chinese and Western music listening uncovered activations in the posterior insula, as well as the middle frontal and angular gyri in the right hemisphere, possibly reflecting higher demands on attention systems for the detection of phrase boundaries in unfamiliar music. The contrast of Western versus Chinese music listening was associated with activations in the motor cortex, including the superior frontal gyrus and the posterior precentral gyrus, representing the putative mouth area of the primary motor cortex in the left hemisphere and the precentral gyrus in the classical hand and mouth area in the right hemisphere. The results manifested that familiarity with certain abstract rules and conventions of music of one's own culture may be sufficient to activate the motor cortex to support perception-production integration by internal tapping or swinging when listening to culturally familiar music (e.g., Western music for German musicians).

A recent fMRI study employed an elegant design to disentangle the brain activity underlying encoding and retrieving culturally familiar and unfamiliar music (Demorest et al. 2010). Previous research has verified the role of the left and right lateral frontal cortex in the encoding and retrieving of language and music information, respectively. Brain imaging research has shown consistent evidence for the role of the left inferior frontal lobe in encoding and retrieval of semantic stimuli (Bookheimer 2002). However, brain lesion studies have shown that the left-lateralized anterior frontal trauma disrupted recall of verbal information, whereas the right frontal damage degraded recall of music information (Samson and Zatorre 1992). Thus, encoding and retrieval of language and music appear to be dissociated in the left and right frontal cortices. This allowed one to hypothesize that modulations of culturally familiar and unfamiliar music should occur in the right hemisphere. To test this prediction, Demorest et al. (2010) scanned American and Turkish adults using fMRI, both when participants listened to novel musical examples from their own culture and an unfamiliar culture and when the participants had to identify a series of brief excerpts that had been taken from the examples. The design allowed the authors to isolate neural activities associated with the musical encoding and retrieval of culturally familiar and unfamiliar music. Both American and Turkish participants were significantly more successful in remembering music from their home culture. In addition, participants demonstrated stronger neural activity in response to culturally unfamiliar music during music listening in the right angular gyrus, posterior precuneus, and right middle frontal area extending into the inferior frontal cortex. Similarly, the recall of both culturally unfamiliar and familiar music induced greater activations in the cingulate gyrus and right lingual gyrus. However, activations in these brain regions were greater when participants engaged in recall of culturally unfamiliar music compared with culturally familiar music. These results demonstrate cultural influences on music perception and memory performance at both a behavioral and a neurological level. The increased neural activity in response to culturally unfamiliar music suggests an enhanced cognitive load both when listening and recalling. In addition, the modulations of brain activity by cultural familiarity were most salient over the right hemisphere. These findings are congruent with the fMRI finding of modulation of musical-phrase processing by cultural familiarity (Nan et al. 2008).

By comparing brain responses to culturally familiar and unfamiliar music, researchers have demonstrated that cultural familiarity of music affects music processing at multiple stages of the processing stream, including attention, memory updating, and even motor preparation. Thus, it is not surprising that familiarity with particular music pieces modulates neural activity in a large neural network, covering the frontal, parietal, and temporal cortices. However, these studies showed that cultural familiarity of music could give rise to opposite modulations of brain activity (either increase or decrease) in the neural network.

Brand

There is a long history in many societies that people use names or terms to feature their products or brand their work. For example, Roman glassworkers started to brand their products with significance almost two thousand years ago. In modern societies, brands have become extremely important, not only for the sale of a specific product but also for the survival and persistence of an enterprise. A brand of an enterprise can subsist continuously even if the enterprise hires different employees and makes different products. Thus, a brand is essentially a cultural symbol or identity that distinguishes one enterprise from others and it reflects shared concepts and beliefs in consumers and manufacturers about the enterprise and its products. Products under a specific brand that consumers choose can symbolize a group of consumers and reflect their general values, social status, and their social identity. People tend to be fond of specific brands and choose to buy products of certain brands among almost identical goods. Given the magnificent influences of brand names on human economic decision, much interest has been generated into how familiar and unfamiliar brands are represented in the brain and how a culturally familiar brand may influence human brain activity underlying reward experiences and economic decisions.

A question posed by an early fMRI study was whether cultural information about cars can modulate reward-related brain responses (Erk et al. 2002). Cars are artificial objects invented and designed for the convenience of transportation. However, different types of cars have been assigned with distinct social significance/value, and thus cars can signal people's social rank, power, and wealth. For example, sport cars, as compared with other small cars, are thought in most cultures to be owned by rich people with high social ranking. Such shared beliefs across populations may lead to modulations of the reward system, which consists of the multiple cortical (e.g., the orbital cortex and anterior cingulate cortex) and subcortical (e.g., the ventral tegmental area and striatum) structures (Haber and Knutson 2010; Kringelbach 2005), when viewing cars that are assigned with high versus low social significance. To test this hypothesis, Erk et al. (2002) scanned male adults in Germany while they viewed pictures of sport cars, limousines, and small cars, which they had to rate for attractiveness. Behaviorally, participants rated sport cars more attractive than limousines and small cars. Moreover, brain activations while viewing sports cars versus other categories of cars were verified in the reward circuit consisting of the ventral striatum, orbitofrontal cortex, and anterior cingulate. In addition, the brain activations were positively associated with behavioral preferences of sport cars. Although this study did not directly compare brain activations elicited by sport cars and other reward-related stimuli (e.g., food), the brain regions activated during viewing sport cars are similar to those activated by reward-related stimuli such as food (Volkow et al. 2002), beautiful faces (Aharon et al. 2001), and monetary rewards (O'Doherty et al. 2001). These observations are interesting because sport cars are cultural objects with a short history, unlike natural reward stimuli such as food and sex, which have bonded with the reward system over a long evolutionary process. The findings suggest that culturally familiar objects assigned with high values and significance can activate the "old" reward system, and cultural familiarity with these objects is pivotal for the reward system to respond them. It is unlikely that individuals who have no cultural knowledge about these objects would show activations of the reward system by looking at pictures of apparently meaningless objects.

McClure and colleagues (2004) explored whether and how a brand biases preference decisions for two soft drinks, and whether a brand can modulate brain responses when tasting the drinks. Coca-Cola (Coke) and Pepsi are two types of drinks that are nearly identical in the chemical composition. However, individuals display strong subjective preferences for one or the other, although they are generally familiar with both. Thus Coke and Pepsi provide a good model for testing how a familiar brand affects preference and neural correlates of behavioral preference by controlling the contribution of bottom-up sensory feelings and somatosensory activity. The authors developed an elegant design that required testing four groups of participants. After participants had reported their taste preference between Coke and Pepsi, they performed a forced-choice taste test. In this taste test, the first two groups chose between two unmarked cups, one contained Pepsi and the other contained Coke. The other two groups had to make preference decisions, but in this case, both cups contained the same drink (Pepsi or Coke), and one cup was unlabeled, whereas the other indicated the brand of the drink. Subjects were told that the unlabeled cups contained either Pepsi or Coke. The taste test collected self-reported preferences and was conducted twice, once outside an fMRI scanner and once inside. In the latter condition, a picture of a Pepsi or a Coke can was presented first to give brand information, and soda was occasionally delivered after the visual brand.

McClure et al. found that self-report of preferences did not differ between Pepsi and Coke for Groups 1 and 2, who chose between the two anonymous drinks, even though the participants reported preference for one of the two drinks in daily life. For Groups 3 and 4 who were asked to choose between labeled and unlabeled cups, however, participants showed a strong bias toward the beverage in the labeled cup. This result suggests that brand influences participants' preference for Pepsi or Coke much more strongly than sensory experience does. A linear regression analysis using behavioral preferences as a regressor revealed differences in brain responses evoked by Coke and Pepsi only in the ventromedial prefrontal cortex, that is, a greater preference for Coke was linked to stronger activity in the ventromedial prefrontal cortex in response to soda delivery. This finding suggests that the ventromedial prefrontal cortex provides a neural basis for judgment decisions on preferred drinks based on sensory information. Participants from Group 3 performed the Coke label task in two conditions. In one condition, a picture of a Coke can was presented first, and followed by Coke delivery. In another condition, a light cue was presented and followed by Coke delivery. The critical contrast compared the brain response to a surprising delivery of Coke when it was known to be Coke with the surprising delivery of Coke and when it could have been Coke or Pepsi. This contrast identified significant differential activity in several brain areas including the bilateral hippocampus, parahippocampus, midbrain, dorsolateral prefrontal cortex, thalamus, and left visual cortex. Group 4 performed the same task, as did Group 3, with the only exception that the drinks and brand were changed to Pepsi. Interestingly, a similar analysis of the fMRI data did not find any significant activation in Group 4, indicating that the influence of brand knowledge seemed to be specific to Coke. The previous findings were used to interpret the effects of brand knowledge that were observed in Group 3. First, the dorsolateral prefrontal cortex has been shown to be necessary for employing affective information in biasing behavior (Davidson and Irwin 1999; Watanabe 1996). Second, while the hippocampus is engaged in processing affective information, it has also been shown to play a role in the acquisition and recall of declarative memories (Eichenbaum 2000; Markowitsch et al. 2003). Thus McClure et al. proposed a two-system model in which cultural information biases preference decisions through the dorsolateral region of the prefrontal cortex, with the hippocampus engaged to recall the associated information. This neural model helps us to understand how the appeal or repulsion of culturally familiar brand influences food and drink preferences by modulating brain activity in the two interacting systems.

Neural representations exist for not only images of familiar products but also icons of brands as well. Evidence for this came from Schaefer and colleagues who tested Germany participants when they viewed logos representing familiar car manufacturers in Germany and Europe and logos that were taken from car manufacturers from outside of Europe (Schaefer et al. 2006; Schaefer and Rotte 2007). Participants were instructed that they would see logos of familiar and unfamiliar car manufacturers and that they should imagine using and driving a product of the brand they see. If they saw the logo of a car manufacturer they did not know, they should imagine driving and using a generic car. Questionnaire measures showed that the brands of the group of culturally familiar logos were rated significantly more familiar than the brands of car manufacturers that do not sell their products in the country of the participants (unfamiliar logos) were. There are several interesting observations regarding brain activity in response to icons of brands measured using fMRI. First, the logos of the familiar brands compared with the logos of the unfamiliar brands elicited stronger activation in the dorsal region of the medial prefrontal cortex. Activations were also observed in the right hippocampus, posterior cingulate, and parietal lobe. Schaefer et al. further compared the subgroup of sports and luxury cars with unfamiliar car brands, and this analysis revealed a stronger activation of the medial prefrontal cortex. Apparently, these results are different from the early findings that viewing pictures of sport cars versus other categories of cars activated the reward-related brain regions such as the ventral striatum and orbitofrontal cortex (Erk et al. 2002). Because the medial prefrontal cortex is well known to be associated with self-reflection and self-relevant processing (Johnson et al. 2002; Kelley et al. 2002; Ma and Han 2010; Ma et al. 2014a; Zhu et al. 2007; also see Chapter 4 of this book for more discussion on this topic), Schaefer et al. interpreted the medial prefrontal activation as developing self-relevant thoughts during imagination of driving a familiar car. The observation of activations in the hippocampus is consistent with McClure et al.'s (2004) finding, which is likely to be employed together with the posterior cingulate and the parietal lobe to recall the information associated with culturally familiar brands. The posterior cingulate cortex and precuneus extending into the posterior cingulate have been shown to play a key role in episodic memory retrieval (Wagner et al. 2005). Thus, the influences of icons of culturally familiar brands on human behavior seem to depend on retrieval of relevant information and further evaluation of the information in relation to oneself. These neurocognitive processes may complement the affective reward feelings mediated by the ventral striatum and orbitofrontal cortex in order to make appropriate economic decisions and to enjoy related good feelings.

The mounting brain imaging findings strongly suggests that several key processes are important for perception of brands, in particular, emotion (e.g., feelings of reward related to brands), social relevance (cultural knowledge about brands), and self-relevance. Do these processes contribute equally to perception of brands and related economic decisions? Does one process override the others in inducing individuals' preference for a specific brand and related products? These issues cannot be clarified in the aforementioned studies, where familiarity and values of brands were the main manipulations. Santos and colleagues (2012) addressed these issues by carefully selecting 237 colored brand logos that had been evaluated by an independent group of individuals along four dimensions (i.e., negative, indifferent, positive, and unknown) before scanning a small group of participants using fMRI. During scanning, logos from each category were presented in a random order, and participants had to rate each logo as negative, indifferent, positive, or unknown. Words without emotional content were presented as the baseline condition, and participants were asked to read each word covertly. This design allowed examination of neural correlates of brands related to both familiarity and emotion. Because a small number of unknown logos were used in the study, and few logos were identified as being negative, the fMRI data analysis focused on the comparison between logos judged as being positive and indifferent.

The conjunction analysis of positive logos versus baseline and indifferent logos versus baseline revealed activations in a widely distributed network. This included the orbital frontal cortex, anterior insula, and anterior cingulate gyrus. The hippocampus and parahippocampal gyrus and subcortical structures such as putamen, caudate nucleus, and nucleus accumbens, were also activated by positive and indifferent logos. The network covered brain regions related to reward, memory, affective process, and cognitive control, and overlapped with those observed in the previous research. However, a direct comparison between positive and indifferent logos showed activations in the ventral medial frontal cortex and ventral paracingulate gyrus. The reverse contrast revealed activations in the lateral prefrontal cortex, suggesting greater brain activity in response to the indifferent logos. The ventral medial frontal activity was again interpreted as encoding self-relatedness when viewing positive logos because participants might prefer products of positive logos to those of indifferent logos. Viewing positive logos may produce a stronger reward and induce activations of the ventral medial prefrontal cortex. When watching indifferent logos, however, participants did not show any activation in the reward-related brain regions. This can possibly be attributed to the increased lateral prefrontal activity to indifferent logos that has been demonstrated to play a key role in emotion regulation (Ochsner and Gross 2005). Thus, whether neural processes of emotion, social relevance, and self-relevance are engaged during perception of logos are to some degrees determined by participants' familiarity, affective feelings with the logos, and their motivation to regulate their emotion.

How early during child development do culturally familiar logos induce specific brain responses? It is important to answer this question to understand why children exposed to advertisements of products of specific brands prefer advertised foods at much higher rates than children who were not exposed do, and attempt to influence their parents' purchases (Coon and Tucker 2002). For example, when asking children aged 3–5 years to taste identical foods and beverages labeled in McDonald's™ or unbranded packaging, they indicated a statistically significant preference for the taste of food and drinks labeled with the McDonald's™ brand logos (Robinson et al. 2007). To scrutinize the character of teenagers' brain activity in response to food logos, Bruce et al. (2014) scanned children between 10 and 14 years using fMRI when they were presented with food and non-food logos. The logos were selected based on the evaluation by an independent group of children, allowing food and non-food logos to be matched for cultural familiarity, valence, and intensity. Blurred images of logos matched on color composition and brightness to the experimental logos were used as a baseline condition to control for perceptual processing. During fMRI scanning, children passively viewed images of food/non-food logos and the blurred images that were shown for 2.5 seconds with an interstimulus interval of 0.5 seconds. fMRI data analyses revealed activations in the left orbital frontal cortex, bilateral inferior frontal gyrus, left temporal cortex, and bilateral visual cortex when viewing food logos compared with blurred logo images. The contrast of non-food logos and blurred images showed increased activity in the left medial prefrontal cortex, left inferior frontal gyrus, right thalamus, and bilateral fusiform cortex. Direct comparisons between food and non-food logos identified increased activity in the right occipital cortex and the right paracentral lobule that extended into the posterior cingulate cortex. Food logos also activated the left parietal and left lingual gyrus compared with non-food logos. One interesting finding of the study was that the occipital cortex was also activated by both food and non-food logos, perhaps because these logos attracted more attention relative to the blurred images and were processed with greater attention engagement as a result. This account is supported by the fact that top-down visual attention strongly modulates the neural activity in the visual cortex (Ungerleider 2000) and that the brain region that guides top-down attention (e.g., the left parietal cortex; Han et al. 2004) was more strongly activated by food logos than by non-food logos. Similar to the findings of studies with adults, food logos may trigger evaluation of motivational values and so require cognitive control, which is associated with the orbital frontal cortex and lateral frontal cortex (McClure et al. 2004). However, food logos did not induce significant activations in the subcortical reward regions such as caudate and nucleus accumbens, suggesting that these regions may not be involved in children between 10 and 14 years. These observations support a developmental perspective because one can speculate that culturally familiar logos may modulate the cortical and subcortical affective systems with different developmental trajectories. The brain regions involved in food motivation, reward processing, decision making, and self-control change throughout childhood and adolescence (Bruce et al. 2011). Bruce et al.'s (2014) findings suggest an early link between culturally familiar good logos with the attention and motivation systems in the brain.

The findings of brain imaging studies of brands demonstrate that multiple systems in the brain are responsive to culturally familiar symbols of products, although brand has a limited history during human evolution. Culturally familiar logos can engage enhanced attentional processing, induce memory retrieval, activate the reward system, and bias individuals' preference decisions. The precondition of these processes is the shared beliefs, values, and significance of logos among a social group with the same cultural identity.

Religious knowledge

Religious believers and non-believers differ in terms of shared beliefs and behavioral scripts—the core components of culture. For example, Christians are different from nonreligious people in that Christians believe in God, worship God via rituals, read the Bible, and behave in accordance with the doctrines of Christianity. Christians' cultural experiences make them more familiar with Christian specific documents and personages compared to non-believers and thus may give rise to unique neurocognitive processes of culturally familiar (Christian) information and characters in Christians. This proposal has been tested and supported by brain imaging studies that compare brain activity recorded from Christians with that from non-believers.

An early PET imaging study measured regional blood flow in the brain in German participants who were self-identified as either Christians or nonreligious, while participants read silently or recited different texts from memory (Azari et al. 2001). The texts used in different tasks included the biblical Psalm 23, a well-known German children's nursery rhyme, and instructions on using a phone card from a telephone book. The texts were matched on length and rhyme. The PET images that contrasted reading and reciting the biblical

Psalm compared with nursery rhyme (or phone card instructions) revealed significantly stronger activations in the right dorsolateral prefrontal cortex and dorsomedial frontal cortex in the religious participants, compared with the nonreligious participants. The nonreligious participants, however, showed significant left-amygdala activation when reading and reciting the nursery rhyme compared with the religious participants. The authors argued that reading/reciting familiar religious documents engages specific cognitive processes, such as memory retrieval and conscious monitoring of thought in the medial prefrontal cortex, rather than emotional responses in the limbic system.

The following research unveiled additional neurocognitive processes of religious information that differentiate between believers and non-believers. Ge et al. (2009) tested a neurocognitive model of personality trait judgments on Jesus (the Christian leader) that differentiates between Christians and nonreligious people. Cognitive psychologists have proposed two different models of trait judgments of an individual (Klein et al. 1992; Klein and Loftus 1993; Klein et al. 2002, 2008). According to these models, trait judgment of oneself is achieved by accessing a database of summary traits in semantic memory, which are abstracted from multiple experiences with one's own trait-relevant behaviors. Trait judgments of the self can be made without reference to behavioral evidence stored in episodic memory, although trait-inconsistent episodes may be retrieved to constrain the use of trait summary about the self. Unlike trait judgments of the self, trait judgments of other people require retrieval of behaviors from episodic memory when there are not sufficient experiences to form a trait summary about them. Accordingly, relative to trait judgments of the self, trait judgments of others may require enhanced episodic memory retrieval to provide information for further evaluation. However, trait judgments of a specific other person may be accomplished by accessing trait knowledge in semantic memory, if the amount of experience with that person is sufficient to form a trait summary. On the grounds of these cognitive models of trait judgments, Ge et al. hypothesized that Christian belief and practice help to form a trait summary about the religious leader (Jesus) in believers so that episodic memory retrieval is engaged to a minimum degree when making trait judgments of Jesus in believers, but not in non-believers.

This hypothesis was tested in two experiments. In Experiment 1, Ge et al. recorded behavioral performances in a paradigm that consisted of two successive tasks that required responses to trait adjectives (Klein et al. 1992). The initial task required participants to think of the definition of a trait adjective (the define task) or to recall a specific incident in someone's behaviors to exemplify that person's trait (the recall task). The second task required participants to judge if a trait adjective could describe a specific person (the trait-judgment task). The rationale was that, if trait judgment of a person engages episodic memory retrieval, the initial recall task that activated related episodic memory should facilitate responses to the second trait-judgment task compared with the initial definition task. If Christians have formed a trait summary about Jesus and do not engage episodic memory retrieval during their trait judgment of Jesus, the initial recall task should not promote responses to the second trait-judgment task on Jesus in Christians. In contrast, the initial recall task should facilitate responses to the second Jesus trait-judgment task in nonreligious participants who had not constituted a trait summary of Jesus and thus engaged episodic memory retrieval during Jesus trait judgment. To test these hypotheses, the normalized facilitation effect was defined as the percentage benefit of RTs in the trait-judgment task, i.e., (RTs preceded-by-define-task minus RTs preceded-by-recall-task) divided by RTs preceded-by-define-task. It was found that non-believers showed a greater percentage benefit of RTs to Jesus compared with self-trait judgments, whereas the percentage benefit of RTs did not differ between Jesus and self-trait judgments for Christian participants. These behavioral differences suggest that, for nonreligious subjects, the recall task facilitated behavioral performances in the following trait judgment to a greater degree when they judged Jesus compared with the self. For Christian participants, the recall task also facilitated behavioral performances to the following trait-judgment task, but such facilitation did not differ significantly between Jesus and self-judgments. This finding suggests that Christian participants had a constructed database of summary traits in semantic memory for both the self and Jesus, and this is why the recall task similarly facilitated behavioral performances in the following trait judgment on both the self and Jesus.

This conclusion was further supported by a following fMRI experiment, in which Ge et al. (2009) recorded brain responses from Christians and non-believers using fMRI during trait judgments of the self, a government leader (the former Chinese premier Zhu-Rongji), and Jesus. Because the posterior parietal cortex and precuneus are involved in retrieval of information from episodic memory (Cavanna and Trimble 2006; Wagner et al. 2005) and the enhanced process of episodic memory retrieval during trait judgment is associated with increased functional connectivity between the medial prefrontal cortex and posterior cingulate cortex/precuneus (Lou et al. 2004), Ge et al. tested the hypothesis that, relative to a self-judgment task that engages little retrieval of behavioral evidence from episodic memory, trait judgments of others (both government and religious leaders) would induce enhanced functional connectivity between the medial prefrontal cortex and posterior cingulate cortex/ precuneus in nonreligious participants to support episodic memory retrieval.

However, increased functional connectivity between the medial prefrontal cortex and posterior cingulate cortex precuneus may be observed during trait judgments of the government leader but not during trait judgments of Jesus in Christian participants who had constituted a trait summary about Jesus. Indeed, the analyses of fMRI data revealed that, for nonreligious participants, trait judgments of both government and religious leaders resulted in enhanced functional connectivity between the medial prefrontal cortex and posterior cingulate cortex/precuneus compared with self-judgments. For Christian participants, however, the functional connectivity between the medial prefrontal cortex and posterior cingulate cortex/precuneus differentiated between trait judgments of the government leader and the self but not between trait judgments of Jesus and the self (Figure 2.4). These brain imaging findings further suggest that Christian belief and practice may lead to specific neurocognitive processes (e.g., increased employment of semantic trait summary but decreased memory retrieval of behavioral episodes) in Christian believers when they performed trait judgments of Jesus.

A review of eleven fMRI studies related to religious beliefs revealed common modulations of the neural activity along the midline structure of the brain, including the medial prefrontal cortex and posterior cingulate cortex (Seitz and

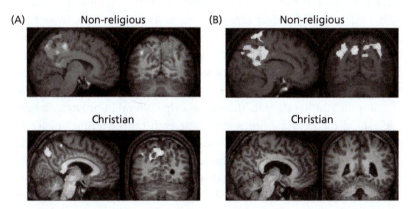

Figure 2.4 Increased functional connectivity between the medial prefrontal cortex and posterior cingulate cortex/precuneus during trait judgments of the government leader (A) and Jesus (B) (versus the self). Christian and non-religious participants were different in the functional connectivity between the medial prefrontal cortex and posterior cingulate cortex/precuneus during trait judgments of Jesus compared with the self. (See colour plate.)

Adapted from Jianqiao Ge, Xiaosi Gu, Meng Ji, and Shihui Han, Neurocognitive processes of the religious leader in Christians, *Human Brain Mapping*, 30 (12), pp. 4012–4024, DOI: 10.1002/hbm.20825, Copyright © 2009 Wiley-Liss, Inc.

Angel 2012). The specific patterns of brain activations in response to familiar religious statements or characters have implications for understanding religious influences on human behavior. For instance, unique neural representations of Psalms and Christian leaders in believers can provide a neural basis of automatic judgments on what is right or wrong and can guide subsequent behaviors during social interactions. Specific neurocognitive processes of familiar religious information and people make it easy for believers to fit into a sociocultural environment in which the religious beliefs, values, and norms dominate human behavior.

In summary, the brain imaging findings indicate that long-term cultural experiences may result in specific neural mechanisms in the human brain that deal with culturally familiar information in multiple dimensions. The unique neural mechanisms underlying culturally familiar stimuli may arise from specific value/beliefs assigned to the stimuli during cultural learning, rather than specific low-level features of stimuli (e.g., the taste of Coke or the tonality of music) and provide a default mode of neural processing of culturally familiar information received in daily life. Neural representations of culturally familiar information are involved in various social behaviors, such as enjoying music and making economic decisions. The unique neural coding of culturally familiar information may allow individuals to comprehend quickly the meaning of social information in one's own cultural context by activating culturally specific cognitive/neural strategies and motivate culturally appropriate behaviors in a specific cultural context. The development of unique neural mechanisms for the processing of culturally familiar information facilitates communication between members of the same cultural group who, via similar underlying neural substrates, have consistent comprehension of culturally familiar stimuli. This would help cultural in-group members to understand each other's minds and share each other's feelings easily. One implication of these cultural neuroscience findings for cross-cultural communication is that people from different cultures first must overcome their distinct mind and feelings mediated by instant automatic brain responses to one set of stimuli that are culturally familiar for one person but culturally unfamiliar for another. To bear in mind that there are distinct neural and cognitive strategies applied to the processing of culturally familiar information and unfamiliar information, one may agree that considering the perspective of a person with different cultural background than the self's is in most cases a good start to cross-cultural communication.

Chapter 3

Cultural differences in non-social neural processes

Neural correlates of cognition: Cultural universality and cultural diversity

How does the brain generate complicated mental activity? This question has always been inspiring and challenging for psychologists and neuroscientists. During the early stage of cognitive neuroscience research, integrating brain imaging techniques such as EEG/ERP and fMRI to investigate the neural mechanisms of various cognitive processes, such as perception, attention, memory, language, and motor control, researchers from North America and Europe reported increasing numbers of findings revealing neural correlates of cognition in Western participants. These studies identified brain activations in specific brain regions and at particular time windows during multiple cognitive processes. Because there were relatively fewer cognitive neuroscience studies of individuals from other cultures, it was unclear at that time, whether or not the brain imaging findings obtained from Western participants could be observed in a similar way in individuals from other cultures. This is a fundamental question regarding whether neural processes involved in human cognition and behavior are culturally universal or divergent.

To survey this issue from an evolutionary perspective provokes distinct speculations about the relationship between the environment and functional brain organization. On the one hand, humans around the globe are confronted with the same challenges for survival, reproduction, and development. They have to detect threats in environments, to fight against antagonists in order to compete for resources, to produce enough food to avoid hunger, and to find appropriate mates to reproduce offspring of their own kind. The similar life goals and requirements across cultures may result in humans evolving similar cognitive repertoires and neurocognitive processes of cognition to mediate varieties of behaviors. On the other hand, both physical and social environments vary tremendously in different societies around the world. Distinct physical and social environments coerce people to develop different social structures, create different methods to reach their goals, and even perceive and understand environments from different perspectives. Accordingly, it is likely that environments, in particular, social contexts, shape cognitive strategies and underlying neural processes and lead to cultural diversity of brain functional organization in humans.

Indeed, cross-cultural comparisons of brain imaging findings have revealed both culturally universal and divergent neural correlates of cognitive processes. Although these studies focus on individuals from East Asian (e.g., Chinese, Japanese, and Korean) and Western (e.g., North American and European) societies owing to the rapid development of brain imaging research in these regions, the cross-cultural comparison of brain activity has covered multiple basic cognitive processes involved in perception, attention, memory, language, and the like. In addition, it appears that various findings of cultural differences in the neural correlates of cognitive processes can best be understood in a specific framework. A relatively recent approach to the understanding of cultural differences in human cognition(Nisbett et al. 2001; Nisbett 2003; Nisbett and Masuda 2003) proposes that Western culture, which originated from ancient Greek thought, encourages an analytic style of cognition that is characterized by focused attention to a salient object and analysis of the properties of that object. Objects are assigned to various categories in order to find abstract/logical rules that governed their behavior. Ancient Chinese and other East Asian cultures, however, advocate a holistic style of cognition that is characterized by distributed attention to the field in which a salient object is located and analysis of relationships among objects and events in the field. Nisbett and colleagues (2001, pp. 291–292) proposed a theoretical framework to account for the relationships between sociocultural environments and cognition:

1 Social organization directs attention to some aspects of the field at the expense of others.

2 What is attended to influences metaphysics, that is, beliefs about the nature of the world and about causality.

3 Metaphysics guides tacit epistemology, that is, beliefs about what it is important to know and how knowledge can be obtained.

4 Epistemology dictates the development and application of some cognitive processes at the expense of others.

5 Social organization and social practices can directly affect the plausibility of metaphysical assumptions, such as whether causality should be regarded as residing in the field versus the object.

6 Social organization and social practices can influence directly the development and use of cognitive processes such as dialectical versus logical ones.

Applying these propositions to the understanding of East Asian/Western differences in cognition, it is purported that social environments and practices make individuals engaging in East Asian (e.g., Chinese, Japanese, and Korean) cultures believe that relationships between objects (or persons) and contextual information are important for explanation and prediction of causal changes of objects (or social events), and such beliefs engender the development of unique cognitive processes that facilitate a holistic cognitive strategy. By contrast, social environments and practices make persons engaging in Western (North American and European) cultures believe that the attributes of a focal object (or a person) are crucial for understanding and predicting causal changes of objects (or persons) and for developing unique cognitive processes that support an analytic cognitive strategy. Multiple distinct processes in perception, attention, memory, and decision making, for example, underlie both holistic and analytic cognitive strategies, and mounting behavioral studies have revealed a cultural diversity of cognitive styles, which raises many questions. What are the common neural underpinnings of cognitive processes in Western and East Asian cultures? Are there specific neural mechanisms underlying cultural differences in holistic/analytic processing styles? The behavioral findings inspire researchers to address these issues by comparing brain imaging results obtained from Western and East Asian cultures. This chapter summarizes cross-cultural brain imaging findings related to multiple cognitive tasks that help to provide a coherent understanding of East Asian/Western cultural differences in neural correlates of basic cognitive processes.

Visual perception and attention

Do people from different cultures perceive the world in exactly the same way? Traditionally, most psychologists have based their research of human perception on the cardinal assumption that the basic processes involved in perception are the same for healthy adults, regardless the ecological and cultural environments in which they are fostered. Nevertheless, since the early time of studies of visual perception on the grounds of certain contemporary philosophical and social scientific concepts, there has been interest in whether human perception is culturally influenced. For example, based on the hypothesis that people have learned different but always ecologically valid visual-inference habits, Segall et al. (1966) tested whether individuals from different cultures are differentially susceptible to geometric illusions by collecting data from the Müller-Lyer illusion task from a large sample in fourteen non-European locations and in the United States. The Müller-Lyer illusion refers to a phenomenon where people routinely perceive straight-line segments of equal length to be longer when they are attached with inward-pointing rather than outward-pointing arrows (Figure 3.1). Interestingly, Segall et al. found that European and American samples made significantly more illusion errors than did the non-Western samples. It was concluded that to a substantial extent, the character of our perceptions is determined by perceptual inference habits, and that various inference habits differ in different societies.

A number of behavioral studies have reported additional evidence for cultural differences in visual perception and attention. For example, in a rod-and-frame task, Ji et al. (2000) had Chinese and American participants look down a long box in which a rod was hung. The orientations of the box and rod could be changed independently. When asked to rotate the rod so that it was aligned to the direction of gravity while ignoring the frame, Chinese participants' performance was more influenced by the position of the box than was the American participants' performance, and the Americans were more confident than the Chinese were when able to position the rod as they had wished. Masuda and Nisbett (2001) tested Japanese and American participants with short video clips of underwater scenes with salient, focal objects (fish), as well as contextual objects (small animals, plants, and rocks). When asked to report what they saw in the clip, American participants tended to first report salient objects more frequently than did Japanese participants. By contrast, Japanese reported contextual information almost twice as frequently as the Americans did. Kitayama and colleagues (2003) developed a framed-line test to examine the ability of incorporating or ignoring contextual information during visual perception. During the framed-line test, participants were first shown a square frame with a vertical line. They were then presented with a new square frame of a different size and were asked to draw a line that was identical to the first line in either absolute length (absolute task) or in proportion to the surrounding frame (relative task). Interestingly, it was found that the Japanese were more accurate in the relative task, whereas the Americans were more accurate in the absolute task. In addition, both Japanese students who were studying in the United States and American students who were studying in Japan tended to show the cognitive characteristics common in the host culture, reflecting influences of their cultural experiences. The behavioral findings are intriguing in that they highlight

Figure 3.1 Illustration of visual stimuli that produce the Müller-Lyer illusion. The lower horizontal line segment appears to be shorter than the upper one, even though the two are actually the same length.

the importance of social environments and personal experiences in shaping perceptual processes in humans. Further, the findings put forward challenging questions such as whether cultural diversity of perception and attention is mediated by distinct neural underpinnings. Tackling this question may help us to comprehend the neural basis of cultural variation of perception and attention, and to provide a broad view of the degree that the functional organization of the human brain is sensitive to sociocultural environments and experiences.

Lewis and colleagues (2008) first used EEG/ERP technique to explore cultural differences in brain activity in response to salient objects and contextual information. They adopted a modified oddball paradigm that employed a typical three-stimulus novelty P3 design. In their design, three types of stimuli were displayed. The frequent nontarget (or standard) stimuli (the number "8" in 76% of trials) were presented with infrequent (i.e., oddball) target stimuli (the number "6" in 12% of trials) and infrequent nontarget stimuli (three-character words, e.g., "DOG"), consonants (e.g., "TCQ"), and numbers (e.g., "305") in 12% of trials). Participants were asked to press a button to respond to the appearance of target oddballs during EEG recording. Infrequent nontarget stimuli were different from standards but, like the standards, did not require behavioral response. Early research has shown that neural responses in this paradigm are characterized by a positive wave peaking around 300–400 ms after stimulus onset over the parietal scalp region, in response to target stimuli, called target P3, and a positive wave in the same time window but with the maximum amplitude over the frontocentral scalp region, in response to infrequent nontarget stimuli, called novelty P3. The amplitude of the target P3 is positively correlated with stimulus probability and task relevance and is thought to reflect attentional resources allocated to processing the target for detecting rare, meaningful events (Johnson, 1988; Herrmann and Knight 2001). The amplitude of the novelty P3, however, is sensitive to deviations from the immediate stimulus context (Debner et al. 2005) and has been used as an index of attention to deviations of stimulus contexts (Ranganath and Rainer 2003).

A direct prediction from Nisbett et al.'s (2001) propositions is that East Asians are more sensitive to contextual information, whereas Westerners are more sensitive to a salient target. Lewis et al. tested this hypothesis by analyzing the amplitude of target P3 and novelty P3 elicited by infrequent targets and infrequent nontargets from East Asian Americans (of Chinese, Korean, and Japanese descent) and European Americans. Comparison of the P3 amplitudes revealed two interesting results. First, infrequent targets elicited a target P3 with the maximum amplitude over the parietal region, indexing attention to target events, and the European Americans displayed relatively greater target P3 amplitudes compared with East Asian Americans. Second, infrequent nontarget events evoked a novelty P3 with the maximum amplitude over the frontocentral region, indexing attention to contextual information, and East Asian Americans, as compared with European Americans displayed relatively larger novelty P3 amplitudes. Because East Asian and European Americans were fostered from families with different cultural backgrounds, these ERP results suggest cultural group differences in the brain activities engaged in the processing of salient targets and contextual information. However, the observed group differences in brain activity did not indicate which cultural values might contribute to the distinct patterns of P3 amplitudes in the two cultural groups. To evaluate this, Lewis et al. measured participants' interdependent self-construal—a cultural trait of viewing the self as interconnected and overlapping with close others, using the Triandis (1995) Individualism and Collectivism Attitude Scale. They conducted a mediation analysis to estimate whether a mediating variable transmits the effect of an independent variable on a dependent variable, and found that the observed group differences in novelty P3 amplitudes were mediated by self-report of interdependence, thus establishing a potential relationship between a specific cultural value and a group difference in brain activity underlying visual perception and attention.

The specific patterns of neural activity associated with established cultural differences in the processing of object and context have been demonstrated in studies using different types of visual stimuli. Lao et al. (2013) examined cultural differences in brain activity underlying the processing of global and local properties of Navon (1977)-type visual stimuli that consist of global shapes (or letters) made up of local shapes (or letters) (Figure 3.2). The previous ERP studies of Chinese participants found modulations of an early positive wave peaking at about 100 ms after stimulus onset over the lateral occipital regions (i.e., P1 component) and the long-latency P3 by attention to the global and local aspects of Navon-type stimuli (e.g., Han et al. 1997; 1999). In addition, relative response speed in identifying global and local targets varied in accordance with the P3 amplitude and peak latency. Lao et al. recorded EEG from Western Caucasians and East Asians while viewing two Navon-type shapes that were

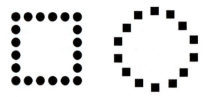

Figure 3.2 Illustration of hierarchical stimuli in which global shapes (square or circle) are composed of local shapes.

successively presented with an interstimulus interval of 150–300 ms. The first (or adaptor) and the second (or target) stimuli could be identical in both global and local shapes, congruent in global or local shapes, or different in both global and local shapes. The EEG data analysis focused on the reduction in neural activity following stimulus repetition or repetition suppression. Thus, ERPs to an adaptor were subtracted from those to its following target to create a neural marker of sensitivity to information at the global or local level of Narvon-type stimuli. Interestingly, East Asians showed greater repetition suppression of the neural activity at 60–110 ms over the lateral occipital regions in response to global relative to local congruent trials. Western Caucasians exhibited greater repetition suppression of the neural activity to global relative to local congruent trials, which, however, occurred at about 270 ms over the centroparietal regions. Caucasians also showed greater repetition suppression of the neural activity to local than to global congruent trials at a later time window (310 ms) over the central scalp region. These ERP results provide electrophysiological evidence that, relative to individuals engaged in the Western culture, people from the East Asian culture develop earlier neural processing of global information over the occipital cortex, whereas Western Caucasians show later neural responses to global/contextual information during visual perception.

The discrepant patterns of ERPs to global/local information and salient targets/contextual information thus provide neural bases of the distinct cognitive strategies that East Asians are more sensitive to situational contexts and attend more to the perceptual field, whereas European Americans tend to be more focused on salient objects and are more context independent during visual perception. The time course and spatial distribution of the ERPs sensitive to cultural effects give a hint that neural activity in both the visual cortex and frontoparietal cortex engaged in visual perception and attention may be shaped by cultural experiences. However, the limited spatial resolution of ERPs does not allow researchers to identify unambiguously the brain regions in which the activity during visual perception differs across two cultural groups. Hedden et al. (2008) thus integrated the framed-line test developed by Kitayama et al. (2003) with fMRI scanning of East Asians in the United States and Americans of Western European ancestry. While being presented with stimuli depicting a vertical line inside a box, participants had to judge whether the box and line combination of each stimulus matched the proportional scaling of the preceding combination (relative task) or whether the current line matched the previous line regardless of the size of the accompanying box (absolute task). There were two conditions in terms of task difficulty; the two rules (relative and absolute match) led to the same matching response (congruent condition) or opposing matching responses (incongruent condition). Brain activity underlying attention to the context or object was examined by contrasting the neural activity in the incongruent and congruent conditions during the relative and absolute tasks, respectively. Given that East Asians and Americans performed better in the relative and absolute task, respectively (Kitayama et al. 2003), the fMRI results can help to address two questions. First, do people engaged in East Asian and Western cultures employ the same or different neural networks during tasks that require taking into account or ignoring contextual information? Second, do people display greater brain activation in culturally nonpreferred tasks than in culturally preferred tasks owing to task difficulty? Hedden et al. found that, for both cultural groups, culturally nonpreferred compared with culturally preferred judgments induced increased activations in the frontal, precentral, and parietal regions. These brain regions constitute a neural network that is in charge of sustained attentional control and top-down modulation of early sensory/perceptual processing in the visual cortex (Nobre et al. 1997; Hopfinger et al. 2000; Han et al. 2004). Thus, the culturally nonpreferred task because of its greater task difficulty, engaged stronger top-down attentional control compared with the culturally preferred task, and this seems culturally universal. However, direct comparison of the absolute and relative tasks in each cultural group revealed opposite patterns of task modulations of the brain activity. Americans displayed greater activations in the frontoparietal network during the relative compared with absolute tasks, whereas East Asians showed the opposite pattern (i.e., greater activations in the frontoparietal network during the absolute tasks than during the relative tasks) (Figure 3.3). Moreover, for both groups, self-report of greater affiliation with the American culture (i.e., viewing the self as autonomous and bounded entity and emphasizing the independence and uniqueness of the self) was correlated with reduced activation in the absolute task. The results suggest an increased need for sustained attentional control during tasks requiring a processing style for which individuals are less culturally prepared. Ideas and practices prevalent in one cultural group can convert a culturally preferred task in a relatively automatic fashion, and thus, fewer neural resources are required for attentional control of the task.

East Asian/Western cultural differences in the activity of the frontoparietal network were replicated in a simple visuospatial judgment task by Goh et al. (2013). In this study, East Asians and Westerners were scanned using fMRI while they performed two different tasks. In the coordinate task, participants were first shown a reference vertical line and had to remember the length of the line. Thereafter, a dot was shown either above or below a horizontal bar, and participants had to judge whether the dot was farther away from the bar than the length of the reference line, by pressing two buttons upon the appearance

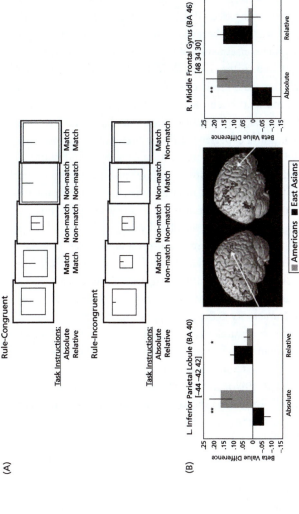

Figure 3.3 (A) Illustration of the stimuli used in the relative and absolute tasks. Participants had to judge whether the length of a vertical line inside a box matched the length of a previously shown line regardless of the size of the box (a context-independent [absolute] judgment task), or whether the box-line combination of each stimulus matched the proportional scaling of the preceding combination (a context-dependent [relative] judgment task). (B) Illustration of fMRI results. Frontoparietal activation associated with judgment tasks in Americans and East Asians. The frontoparietal activity was greater in East Asians (red bars) than in Americans (yellow bars) in the context-independent (absolute) judgment, whereas a reverse pattern was observed in the context-dependent (relative) judgment task. (See colour plate.)

Adapted from Trey Hedden, Sarah Ketay, Arthur Aron, Hazel Rose Markus, and John D.E. Gabrieli, *Psychological Science*, 19 (1), pp. 12–17, DOI:10.1111/j.1467-9280.2008.02038.x, Copyright © 2008, © SAGE Publications. Adapted with permission from SAGE Publications, Inc.

of each stimulus. The control task asked participants to press alternately two buttons upon the appearance of a horizontal bar between two dots to controlling for motor responses. Relative to the control task, the coordination task required more attention to contextual relationship between the dot and line. Goh et al. found that, behaviorally, Westerners responded more slowly than East Asians did in the coordination task. This behavioral index of greater task difficulty was associated with stronger neural engagement in the frontal and parietal cortex in Westerners compared with East Asians. Greater activity in the middle occipital gyrus was also observed in Westerners relative to East Asians, possibly reflecting the consequence of top-down attentional modulation of the activity in the visual cortex. These fMRI findings provide evidence suggesting that, although the same kinds of cognitive processes are invoked across cultures, the frontoparietal attention network is engaged in a culturally nonpreferred task during visual perception, similar to findings of Hedden et al. (2008). In addition, cultural experiences also influence visual perceptual processing in the occipital cortex because of attentional modulation by culturally preferred or non-preferred tasks. Cultural influences on perception and attention are also manifest in individuals from the same cultural environment because activity in the frontoparietal attention network varies depending on the degree to which the individual endorses cultural values.

Distinct patterns of neural responses to salient objects and contexts in individuals engaged in Western and East Asian cultures are further explored in brain imaging studies using pictures of objects against visual scenes. Early brain imaging research has revealed separate neural substrates for the processing of objects and scenes. The activity in the parahippocampal cortex and lateral occipital complex distinguishes natural scenes of different categories (Walther et al. 2009) and shows adaptation to background scene repetition (Goh et al. 2004). The activity in the middle temporal cortex is sensitive to knowledge of object properties (Martin et al. 1996), and activity in the inferior occipital and temporal cortex (e.g., the fusiform area) shows adaptation to object repetition (Goh et al. 2004). These early brain imaging results allow researchers to test whether Western and East Asian cultures increase the sensitivity of activity in object and scene brain regions, respectively. Gutchess and colleagues (2006) had East Asian and American participants watch pictures from three categories: (1) a target object (e.g., an elephant) presented against a white background, (2) a background scene with no discernable target object, and (3) a distinct target object against a meaningful background. Each picture was presented for 4 seconds, followed by a fixation cross of 0–12 seconds. During the 4-second presentation interval, the participants were asked to rate how pleasant they found the picture by a keypress. The fMRI results revealed that Americans relative to East Asians activated more regions implicated in object processing, including the bilateral middle temporal gyrus, left superior parietal/angular gyrus, and right superior temporal/supramarginal gyrus.

Jenkins et al. (2010) further investigated cultural differences in contextual processing by manipulating the congruence of visual scenes using an fMR-adaptation paradigm. They had young Chinese and American participants passively view sets of novel or repeated scenes in which the central object was either congruent with the background (e.g., a deer in the woods) or incongruent with the background (e.g., a television in the desert). Both objects and background varied across trials for sets of novel scenes but remained unchanged across trials for sets of repeated scenes. Because the parahippocampal area and the lateral occipital cortex are respectively engaged in background processing (Epstein and Kanwisher 1998) and object processing (Grill-Spector et al., 2001), Jenkins et al. (2010) expected BOLD signal adaptation for repeated versus novel scenes in these two brain regions. In addition, they predicted that, if Chinese individuals are more sensitive to contextual information than American individuals are, Chinese participants would show greater adaptation to incongruent than to congruent scenes because of their cultural bias to attend to and elaborate upon contextual relationships. Indeed, it was found that BOLD signals in both the parahippocampal area and lateral occipital cortex were significantly lower when viewing repeated scenes, as compared with novel scenes, indicating involvement of these brain regions in the processing of objects and scenes. Moreover, within both the right and left lateral occipital complexes, Chinese participants showed significantly greater adaptation to incongruent scenes than to congruent scenes, relative to American participants. This finding provides evidence that activity in these brain regions was more sensitive to contextual incongruity in Chinese than in American participants.

Do cultural effects on brain activity during visual perception vary across age? Do elderly adults show larger cultural differences in brain activity underlying perception and attention than young adults do? An intuitive prediction would be that elderly East Asians and Westerners would show greater differences in brain activity mediating the processing of objects and contexts compared with their younger counterparts, owing to their prolonged experience within their own cultures. Goh et al. (2007) tested this hypothesis by scanning four groups of subjects, that is, elderly East Asians, elderly Westerners, young East Asians, and young Westerners, during perception of novel and repeated scenes similar to those used in Goh et al. (2004). They found that relative to young adults, elderly adults showed larger group differences in brain activity during perception of scenes. Specifically, elderly East Asians showed significantly reduced adaptation responses in the lateral occipital region (i.e., the object area) than did elderly Westerners. In other words, the lateral occipital activity in East Asians was less sensitive to the repeated presentation of objects than that in Westerners, and the cultural group difference was more salient in elderly than in young adults. Prolonged experience within an object-biased culture may induce stronger modulations of brain activity underlying object processing in elderly than in young adults.

How do cultural group differences in brain activity during perception come about? This question cannot be clarified simply by the findings of distinct patterns of brain activity in East Asians and Westerners. If cultural experiences play a key role in producing group differences in brain activity, one should predict that individuals from East Asian and Western societies should exhibit similar group differences to those mentioned above, regardless of their ethnicity (e.g., Asians vs. Caucasians). Unfortunately, there has been no brain imaging research on people of the same ethnicity from East Asian and Western societies during perception. However, Kitayama et al. (2003) reported that, during the framed-line test, while Americans in the United States were more accurate in the absolute task than in the relative task, Americans who had stayed in Japan for up to 4 months showed similar performances to Japanese living in Japan, being more accurate in the relative task than in the absolute task. Apparently, cultural experiences can assign participants in a foreign culture with cognitive biases that resembles the pattern typical in the host culture. Lewis et al.'s (2008) finding that cultural group difference in brain activity (i.e., novelty P3 amplitude) was mediated by a cultural trait (i.e., interdependence) further supported the idea that various cultural values from different societies contribute to the cultural group differences in the neural underpinnings of perception.

Do physical environments contribute to the observed cultural difference in brain activity underlying perception? To analyze the perceptual environments from different cultures, Miyamoto et al. (2006) examined randomly sampled pictures of scenes from small, medium, and large cities in Japan and the United States. They then asked individuals to estimate the following: How ambiguous is the boundary of each object? How many different objects do there seem to be? To what degree do there seem to be parts of the scene that are invisible? To what degree is the scene either chaotic or organized? They also used a computer program to count the number of objects in an image by scanning across the image and outlining the boundaries of objects. Both subjective and objective measures indicated that Japanese scenes were more ambiguous and contained more elements than American scenes did. Miyamoto et al. also found that priming Japanese and American participants with Japanese scenes shifted their attention more toward contextual information than priming with American scenes.

Therefore, it is likely that culturally specific patterns of attention are afforded at least partially by the perceptual environment of each culture. Physical environments, cultural value, and personal experience together give rise to the cultural group differences in brain activity underlying perception and attention. An interesting question for future research is whether cultural belief/value or physical environments dominate the development of culturally specific cognitive styles in perception and attention.

Memory

Memory is a series of processes in which information is encoded, stored, and retrieved. Information from the outside world has to be processed or registered first. The encoded information then needs to be consolidated to be recollected in the future in case the information is required for making decisions for actions. Grön et al. (2003) were the first to investigate cultural group differences in brain activity during spatial memory encoding. They scanned Chinese and German Caucasian participants while they viewed a pattern of green rectangles appearing within a 3×3 black matrix with white grid lines. Participants had to remember the locations of green rectangles during the learning block, which was immediately followed by a recall task. During the recall task, participants saw an empty 3×3 black matrix with white grid lines and were asked to fill the matrix by pressing the corresponding buttons of a keyboard to reproduce the pattern of rectangles seen during learning. Relative to a control task (watching a red circle), encoding the spatial information of green rectangles gave rise to different patterns of brain activations in the two cultural groups in the five learning blocks, although behavioral performance in the recall task was alike in the Chinese and the German participants. Specifically, in the first two learning blocks, Chinese relative to German participants showed stronger activations in the frontal and parietal cortex that consist of the dorsal stream (or the "where" system) serving for the analysis of spatial features (Ungerleider and Haxby 1994). The comparison of German versus Chinese, however, identified increased activations in the inferior occipital/lingual/fusiform gyrus, and hippocampus, which constitute the ventral stream (or the "what" system) serving the analysis of object features. The distinct engagement of the dorsal and ventral systems in the two cultural groups showed a reversed pattern in the two subsequent learning blocks. Chinese participants showed more engagement of the inferior occipital/lingual/fusirorm gyrus, whereas German participants were more likely to recruit the frontal and parietal cortex. These findings illustrate culturally specific dynamic changes in the "what" and "where" neural systems during information encoding. It seems that Chinese participants adopted a strategy of initial coding of spatial information, which was followed by focusing visual properties of stimuli during the learning procedure, whereas German participants showed a reverse temporal order of processing spatial information and object features. Interestingly, the findings indicate that the outcome of different culturally imprinted neural processing routines can lead to similar behavioral performances during memory retrieval. This raises a more general question regarding the relationship between behavioral performance and related brain activity in complicated cognitive tasks. Cultural experience allows the human brain to develop different neural strategies in coping with the same cognitive task.

Causal judgments

Finding causal relationships between objects, events, and human behaviors plays a fundamental role in the production of human knowledge. Humans from different cultures are similarly motivated to understand the physical laws that govern object interactions. Hence, observation of physical events that are governed by universal laws may lead to similar cognitive processes of causal attribution. However, making causal judgments of physical events and human behaviors is strongly modulated by cultural experiences. Social psychology research has shown evidence that, when making causality judgments on social behaviors, East Asians are more sensitive to contextual constraints compared with European Americans who are more prone to individuals' internal dispositions (Choi et al. 1999; Morris and Peng 1994). Similarly, causal attribution of physical events also varies across cultures by emphasizing the disposition of objects or the contextual nature of object interactions. When interpreting the causes of physical events (e.g., the changes of motion of objects), Americans are more likely to attribute the causes of physical events to dispositional factors (e.g., weight or shape), whereas Chinese participants are more likely to account for the same events in terms of contextual factors (e.g., gravity and friction) (Peng and Knowles 2003). The cultural differences in the style of causal attribution are consistent with the posit that Western cultures encourage an analytic style of cognitive processes, whereas East Asian cultures foster a holistic fashion of cognition (Nisbett et al. 2001) and inspire the exploration of culturally universal and culturally specific neural substrates of causal attribution in the human brain.

To do this, Han and colleagues (2011) compared the neural correlates of causal judgments of physical events that had been recorded from several different cultural groups. In Experiment 1 the brain regions involved in causal attribution of physical events were identified by scanning Chinese participants using fMRI while they viewed video clips depicting physical events. Each video clip began with a 2-second display showing five stationary balls. Four balls with different colors (gray, red, green, and tan) were grouped together while a blue ball was separated from the others (Figure 3.4). A sentence presented at the center of the screen indicated a possible cause for the forthcoming change of the blue ball's motion direction or speed. For example, a physical event began with the blue ball staying at the center of display for 2 seconds or it moved horizontally from left to right (or from right to left) at a constant speed for 2 seconds while the grouped balls moved toward the blue one. The blue ball would then collide with the gray ball when its leading edge was positioned at the center of the screen. Immediately after the blue ball made contact with the gray one, the blue ball moved horizontally, either in the same direction with a speed change or in the opposite direction for 2 seconds, and the blue and the grouped balls then stopped moving. Participants were asked to judge (1) the causes for the blue ball's movement change or (2) the blue ball's motion direction at the end of a video clip. During the causality judgment task, participants judged if each statement of the possible cause of target object's movement change was appropriate. The causes given emphasized either dispositional factors (e.g., "the blue ball is heavy" or "the blue ball moves quickly") or the contextual factors (e.g., "the gray ball is heavy" or "the air resistance is large"). During the motion judgment task, subjects judged whether a statement of the blue ball's final motion direction ("the blue ball moved rightward at the end of the clip" or "the blue ball moved leftward at the end of the clip") was correct. Participants made a "yes" or "no" response after each video clip by pressing one of the two buttons using the right index or middle finger.

By contrasting dispositional or contextual causality judgments with motion direction judgments, Han et al. found that, relative to motion direction judgments, both contextual and dispositional causality judgments activated a neural circuit consisting of the medial prefrontal cortex, bilateral frontal cortices, left parietal cortex, left middle temporal cortex, and right cerebellum (Figure 3.5). It was further verified that the medial prefrontal activity was similarly activated during causality judgments, regardless of the complexity of contextual information (i.e., whether only a gray ball and a blue ball were presented or with this gray ball was grouped with other colored balls), whereas the left parietal activity during contextual causality judgments decreased significantly when the gray ball was presented on its own versus when it was grouped with other colored balls. These results show a dissociation in the functional role of the medial prefrontal and left parietal cortices by showing that the former plays a key role in inferring causes of physical events, whereas the latter encodes contextual information during causality judgments.

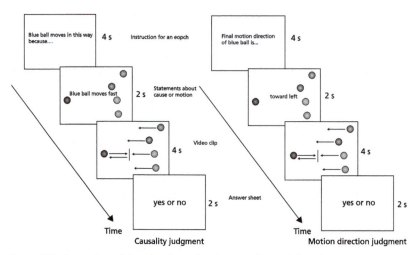

Figure 3.4 Illustration of the stimuli used in the causality and direction judgment tasks. (See colour plate.)

Adapted from *Neuropsychologia*, 49 (1), Shihui Han, Lihua Mao, Jungang Qin, Angela D. Friederici, and Jianqiao Ge, Functional roles and cultural modulations of the medial prefrontal and parietal activity associated with causal attribution, pp. 83–91, DOI:10.1016/j.neuropsychologia.2010.11.003, Copyright © 2010 Elsevier Ltd., with permission from Elsevier.

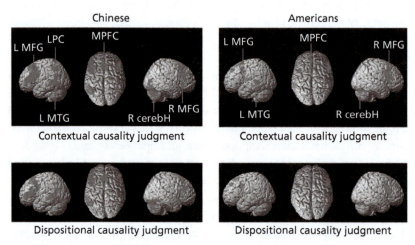

Figure 3.5 Brain activations during the causality and direction judgment tasks in Chinese and American participants. (See colour plate.)

Adapted from *Neuropsychologia*, 49 (1), Shihui Han, Lihua Mao, Jungang Qin, Angela D. Friederici, and Jianqiao Ge, Functional roles and cultural modulations of the medial prefrontal and parietal activity associated with causal attribution, pp. 83–91, DOI:10.1016/j.neuropsychologia.2010.11.003, Copyright © 2010 Elsevier Ltd., with permission from Elsevier.

To clarify cultural differences in neural correlates of causal attribution, in a second experiment, Han and colleagues scanned two independent groups of Chinese and European American participants and focused on the medial prefrontal and left parietal activity associated with causal attribution of physical events. If the inferential process of causality is a unique human trait linked to causal attribution (Penn and Povinelli 2007), the medial prefrontal activity related to inference of causes of physical events should be necessary and should be comparable for both Americans and Chinese participants. However, because the Chinese tend to attribute physical events more to contextual factors than Americans do (Peng and Knowles 2003), the left parietal activity that is sensitive to contextual information during causal judgments should be stronger in Chinese than in American participants. It was further hypothesized that, relative to American participants, Chinese participants would show greater neural activity related to contextual processing, particularly when they conduct dispositional causal judgments because considering contextual information during dispositional causal attribution may be specific to East Asian cultures. Indeed, it was found that while the medial prefrontal activity involved in causality judgments was comparable in the two cultural groups, the left parietal activity associated with causality judgments was stronger in Chinese than in American participants, regardless of whether the contextual information was attended (Figure 3.5). Thus, the findings identified culturally universal causal inference in the medial prefrontal cortex but culturally sensitive activity in the left parietal cortex, which appears to be specifically engaged in the processing contextual information during causality perception.

The cultural differences in the left parietal activity are interesting in that the left parietal cortex was activated in Chinese participants, regardless of whether the causal judgments asked them to pay attention to the contextual information (i.e., in both the dispositional and contextual causal judgments), whereas this brain region failed to show activation in American participants in either type of causal judgments. It seems that Chinese and American participants in this study manifested two extremes of neural strategies when involved in contextual processing during causal attribution. The differential engagement of the left parietal cortex in the causal attribution of physical events in the two cultural groups provides a neuroscience account of the finding that the Chinese compared with the Americans are more likely to attribute causes of the same events to contextual factors (Peng and Knowles 2003). Might it be possible that individuals from other cultures could exhibit flexible neural strategies in the left parietal cortex so that this brain region is activated when causal attribution focuses on contextual possibilities but not on the disposition of target objects? Cross-cultural behavioral research that has compared North America, Western Europe, and East Asia persons has positioned the Germans between Americans and East Asians when comparing psychological and behavioral traits (e.g., attentional bias toward contextual information and self-concept, Kitayama et al. 2009). In this case, one may expect that German participants may adopt a flexible neural strategy to recruit the left parietal cortex during contextual but not dispositional causal judgments. To test this hypothesis, Han et al. (2015) scanned a group of German participants during causal judgments and motion direction judgments using the same experimental stimuli and design as that described by Han et al. (2011). Indeed, they found that German participants showed increased activity in the left parietal cortex during contextual causal judgments compared with motion direction judgments. However, no activation in the same brain region was observed when German participants performed dispositional causal judgment on physical events. Thus, the left parietal activity underlying the processing of contextual information during causality judgments seems to be highly sensitive to individuals' cultural experiences. Taken together, these brain imaging findings have uncovered cultural-universal and cultural-sensitive neural activity involved in causal attribution and provided a neuroscientific account of East Asian/Western cultural bias in causal attributes. In addition, these findings raise interesting questions regarding cultural effects on brain activity underlying causal attribution of social events. One may expect similar cultural differences in the neural underpinnings of causal judgments on social events; however, this should be tested in future research.

Math

Mathematical skill is one of the most fundamental cognitive abilities humans possess and it plays a key role in daily life in every human society. Thus, one may expect involvement of similar neural processes during mathematical operations in different cultures. Indeed, brain imaging studies that have examined neural activity related to mathematical operations have shown that the intraparietal sulcus is activated during simple mathematical tasks (e.g., subtraction) in Americans (Prado et al. 2011) and in Chinese (Zhou et al. 2007) and it is therefore supposed to be associated with the representation of quantity. The precuneus, a medial area of the superior parietal cortex, is also activated during multiplication and subtraction in Americans (Prado et al. 2011) and Koreans (Lee 2000). These findings, however, cannot help to explain differential performance when solving mathematical problems across cultures. For example, a study comparing Flemish-speaking Belgians, English-speaking

Canadians, and Chinese speaking Canadians showed that Chinese Canadians were faster than the other two groups when solving complex additions (Imbo and LeFevre 2009).

There are multiple reasons for cultural group differences in the performance mathematical operations. Language, reading experience, and education (e.g., where different strategies may have been taught) all may produce differential effects on the achievement of mathematical operations. It is also possible that people from different cultures activate distinct neural strategies during mathematical operation. This idea has been tested by recording BOLD signals from Chinese and English speakers from the United States, the UK, Canada, and Australia (Tang et al., 2006). Participants were asked to perform judgments of the spatial orientation of numerical stimuli (number task), judgments of whether the third digit was equal to the sum of the first two in a triplet of Arabic numbers, judgments of whether the third digit was larger than the larger one of two Arabic numbers, and judgments of the spatial orientation of nonnumerical stimuli (as a control task). In both cultural groups, the number task activated a neural circuit consisting of the bilateral occipital and parietal cortex. However, the comparison between Chinese and English speakers revealed distinct patterns of brain activity in several brain regions during these tasks in the two cultural groups. During the three tasks relating to operations on numbers, English compared with Chinese speakers showed greater activity in the perisylvian language region including both Broca's area and Wernicke's areas, which have been demonstrated to be respectively engaged in language production and understanding. Chinese relative to English speakers, however, showed increased activity in the left premotor association area. A further functional connection analysis suggested strong connections between the visual cortex and supplementary motor area during the comparison task in Chinese but not English speakers, and there was a strong correlation between the visual cortex and intraparietal cortex during the comparison task in English but not Chinese speakers. These results suggest that native English speakers may largely employ a language process in the left perisylvian cortices for mental calculation, whereas native Chinese speakers may largely depend on a visuo-premotor association network for the same task. A similar process may underlie the two apparently different strategies. The parietal cortex, which supports numerical quantity comparison, was activated during mathematical operations in both cultural groups.

Typically, Chinese and English speakers are taught with different strategies for simple mathematical operations. For example, adults in North America are educated to employ both retrieval and calculation strategies when solving single-digit multiplication problems (e.g., 9 × 8) (Lefevre et al. 1996).

Adults educated in China, however, are taught to remember all the answers of single-digit multiplication problems in elementary school and rely exclusively on memory retrieval when solving single-digit multiplication (Campbell and Xue 2001). The differences in strategies used in mental calculation tasks can lead to great variations of patterns of performance. For instance, although single-digit multiplication problems involving relatively large numbers (e.g., 9 × 8) take longer to solve (and are more error prone) than problems involving smaller numbers (e.g.,2 × 3), this problem-size effect is much more salient in North American than in Chinese participants (Campbell and Xue 2001). Prado et al. (2013) examined the neural mechanisms underlying the cultural differences in the problem-size effect on single-digit multiplication in adults who had been educated in China or in the United States. Participants were scanned using fMRI when performing multiplication tasks with different levels of difficulty. The two operands were smaller than or equal to 5 (e.g., 3 × 4) in the small multiplication problems but were larger than 5 in the large multiplication problems (e.g., 6 × 7). Each problem was presented twice, once with the correct answer and once with an incorrect answer. Participants were asked to make "right" or "wrong" judgments for each problem. Both groups responded more slowly during the large relative to the small multiplication problems. However, Chinese participants compared with American participants responded faster overall and showed a smaller problem-size effect. Brain activations that distinguished the cultural groups in the problem-size effect were observed in parallel with the group differences in behavioral performance. Across both Chinese and American participants, the contrast of large versus small multiplication problems showed increased activity in the left intraparietal sulcus, bilateral inferior frontal gyrus, left middle frontal gyrus, and anterior cingulate. However, there was a greater neural problem-size effect for Chinese relative to American participants in the bilateral superior temporal gyrus, as well as in the left precentral/postcentral gyri and precuneus. A greater neural problem-size effect for American relative to Chinese participants was identified in the right intraparietal sulcus and anterior cingulate. In addition, the neural problem-size effect in the right intraparietal sulcus and anterior cingulate positively predicted the behavioral problem-size effect in reaction times.

The distinct patterns of neural and behavioral problem-size effects were interpreted in the light of the previous brain imaging findings. The mid-superior temporal cortex has been associated with the impaired retrieval of multiplication facts (Lampl et al. 1994) and the storage of the semantic association between a multiplication problem and its answer (Prado et al. 2011). The left superior temporal cortex is engaged in phonological coding (Friederici 2012), and both the left and right superior temporal cortices play an important role in letter to speech sound mapping (Hickok and Poeppel 2007). These facts allow us to speculate that the multiplication problem-size effect might be a verbal retrieval effect in Chinese participants, who may memorize multiplication facts as rhyming formulas during early school education. Unlike the Chinese, Americans may use calculation procedures to a greater degree during large relative to small multiplication problems. The problem-size effect observed during mathematical operation can therefore be linked to various neural strategies employed during simple calculation tasks. The fact that the Chinese choose to memorize the answers of single-digit multiplication problems does not necessarily link to their language. Rote verbal teaching methods and multiplication tables are employed in both China and the United States to improve mathematical skill, but these methods are used earlier and more extensively in China than in the United States, possibility owing to the long history of using multiplication tables in Chinese education (Zhang and Zhou 2003). The fact that Chinese children spend more time practicing multiplication facts than American children do also reflects the difference in cultural values such that the Chinese culture emphasizes improvement of students' skill using the same procedures across operations, whereas American culture encourages learning via an individual's exploration. Individuals from any other cultures can adopt the same strategy during math education and the practice of rote verbal teaching methods and multiplication tables may induce the engagement of the temporal cortex during single-digit multiplication.

Semantic relationship

Both behavioral and brain imaging studies have shown East Asian/Western cultural differences in perception/attention that were accompanied with distinct underlying neural substrates. It appears that individuals in Western cultures engage enhanced cognitive and neural processing of focal and target objects, whereas individuals from East Asian cultures are more likely to facilitate cognitive and neural processing of contextual information and the relationships between objects. Does the unique processing style in East Asian and Western culture go beyond perceptual/attention processing? Would East Asian/Western cultural differences in cognitive styles be present during the processing of more abstract information, such as semantic meaning and relationship, independently of whether the information is delivered via perceptual stimuli or language? Two brain imaging studies addressed these issues using quite different stimuli and paradigms.

Goto and colleagues (2010) recorded EEG from Asian Americans and European Americans while viewing pictures of an object presented against a background. They manipulated the semantic relationship between the foreground object and background scenes. For instance, one picture might show a crab on beach, whereas another might show a crab on a parking lot. The object and background scene are semantically congruent in the former condition but are semantically incongruent in the latter condition. If Asian Americans are oriented toward the context and the relationship between the foreground and the background, and European Americans are more oriented to the target object, Asian Americans should be more sensitive to the semantic incongruity between the object and background compared with European Americans. Goto et al. measured a specific ERP component, termed N400, to estimate brain sensitivity to the semantic incongruity between the object and background. The N400 is a negative potential that was initially observed in response to a word in a sentence that was semantically incongruent with the preceding words in the same sentence (Kutas and Hillyard 1980). When reading sentences like "I like my coffee with cream and socks," the last word evoked the N400 compared with reading the last word in the sentence "I like my coffee with cream and sugar." The N400 peaks between 300 and 600 ms after stimulus onset with the maximum amplitude over the parietal region. The N400 amplitude is sensitive to semantic incongruity between stimuli regardless of whether the semantic items are delivered through visual or auditory modalities. The N400 is believed to serve as an index of semantic expectancy because its magnitude is inversely related to semantic relatedness (Kutas and Hillyard 1980). An MEG study revealed that the N400 reflects dynamic activity from the posterior to anterior temporal cortex and frontal cortex in response to semantically anomalous sentence endings (Lau et al. 2008).

Goto et al. (2010) predicted that, if Asian Americans disperse their attention across the field and process relationships among events in their environment to a greater degree than do European Americans, semantically incongruent objects and backgrounds should elicit a larger N400 in Asian Americans than in European Americans. This indeed was what they found: Asian Americans showed a greater negativity to stimuli in which the object and background were incongruent than congruent in semantic meanings, and the differential activity to incongruent versus congruent stimuli showed the largest amplitude over the central/parietal region at about 400 ms. Surprisingly, European Americans failed to show difference in amplitude in response to semantically incongruent and congruent stimuli, suggesting ignorance of the background information. To estimate the relationship between the N400 amplitude difference and cultural value, Goto et al. measured participants' cultural traits using the Singelis (1994) independent and interdependent self-construal scales. This measure showed that European Americans were more independent than Asian

Americans were. In addition, it was found that smaller magnitude N400 incongruity effects were positively correlated with higher independent self-construal scores. The results are in agreement with the hypothesis that East Asians cultures show greater holistic processing. Asian Americans processed the semantic relationship between foreground and background objects to a greater degree than European Americans did. At the individual level, the N400 incongruity effect was correlated with participants' cultural trait (i.e., independence). This provides further support for the connection between cultural experience and the neural marker of semantic relationships.

Cultural influences on the neural processing of semantic relationships were further tested using a triad categorization task (Gutchess et al. 2010). East Asians and American participants underwent fMRI scanning while alternating between categorical or thematic strategies when sorting triads of words (e.g., panda, monkey, and banana). When the three words were presented simultaneously on each trial, participants had to select the two words that were categorically related (e.g. panda and monkey in the category-match task) or selected the two words that shared a functional relationship (e.g. banana and monkey in the relationship-match task). During a control task, participants selected the two words that were identical (e.g., flower, paper, and paper). As mentioned in Chapter 1, Chiu (1972) found that Chinese children tended to categorize the objects based on functional relationships, whereas American children tended to group objects based on taxonomic categories. Such distinct tendencies of using particular semantic strategies cannot be explained by language difference because bilingual participants (i.e., Chinese from Hong Kong and Singapore who learned English early in life and use both English and Chinese frequently in daily communication) showed similar tendency of categorizing objects in terms of their relationship, regardless of whether the objects were named in Chinese or in English (Ji et al. 2004). To test whether the frontal-parietal network associated with attentional control is more engaged when participants performed culturally nonpreferred categorization, Gutchess et al. (2010) first identified the neural circuit involved in the triad categorization task by pooling the category-match and relationship-match tasks together to contrast with the control task. This revealed increased activations in the inferior frontal, superior parietal and inferior temporal cortices, insula, and cerebellum. When directly comparing the two cultural groups in the category-match task, the frontal-parietal network, including the middle/superior frontal cortex, inferior parietal cortex, and angular gyrus were more strongly activated in East Asian than in American participants. Unexpectedly, the same frontal-parietal network also showed stronger activations during the relationship-match task when comparing East Asian with American participants. Interestingly, the cultural differences in these brain activations were more salient over the right than the left hemispheres, possibly owing to the use of semantic stimuli in this study. American relative to East Asian participants exhibited greater activity in the cingulate cortex and lateralized middle frontal cortex during the category-match task and only in the right insula during the relationship-match task. Because the frontal-parietal network plays a key role in attentional control and is increased during culturally nonpreferred perceptual tasks (Hedden et al. 2008), and the middle frontal gyrus has been associated with tasks requiring more extensive search of lexical or categorical knowledge during semantic tasks (Kotz et al. 2002), Gutchess et al. speculated that East Asians had to engage controlled executive processes in both category- and relationship-match tasks, whereas the Americans responded strongly to conflict in the semantic content of information. For both cultural groups, the right insular activity was activated during culturally nonpreferred categorization tasks (i.e., East Asians during the category-match task and Americans during the relationship-match task), possibly reflecting increased affective processing when confronted with culturally nonpreferred tasks.

Decision making

Making decisions is an important part of everyday life and it determines how we behave. For instance, when a new product becomes available in the market, some people may buy it immediately regardless of cost, whereas others would rather wait for some time to buy it (when the price may happen to drop to a certain degree). Similarly, some people may like to take an immediate small reward, whereas others would prefer to wait sometime for a large one. How do cultural experiences influence decision making and the underlying neural mechanisms? The preference for taking an immediate current reward implicates lack of taking future possibilities into consideration, whereas the decision of giving up a current reward but taking a remote reward must rely on considering the current and future as a whole. If this proposal were correct, one would expect that East Asians with a holistic cognitive style would tend to favor a large but remote reward and Westerners with an analytic cognitive style would prefer a small but immediate reward.

To test potential cultural difference in decision making where it relates to selection between a more proximate outcome and another with an extended delay, Kim et al. (2012) scanned American and Korean participants during a decision-making task. The task required participants to make a series of choices between smaller, more immediate rewards ($r1$ available at delay $t1$), and later, larger rewards ($r2$ available at delay $t2$). After the choice was displayed on a screen, participants indicated their preference by pressing one of two buttons. After a choice was selected, feedback was given to indicate that the response was recorded successfully. The behavioral data were believed to fit a discounted value function such as V(r,t)=r/(1+kt), where r is the reward amount available at delay t and V is the subjective value of the offer. V depends on time through a discount rate k, such that higher k indicates a stronger preference for immediate outcomes. Two possible neural mechanisms could influence the participants' decision. A greater activity in the brain reward system in response to the current offer may lead to an immediate reward, whereas a greater activity in the brain control system may allow individuals to take a long-term perspective that emphasize the future and thus choose a large but remote reward. Behavioral measures demonstrated a dramatic difference in behavior with Americans being more prone to accept an immediate reward compared with Koreans. By contrasting choices involving an immediate reward (today) versus other choices, Kim et al. identified brain activations in response to sensitivity to delays in the ventral striatum and ventral medial prefrontal cortex. Moreover, greater activity in these brain regions predicted larger delay discounting (or greater preference for the small but immediate reward). However, the posterior parietal cortex and the lateral prefrontal cortex were equally activated in all intertemporal choices. Most interestingly, cross-cultural comparison confirmed stronger activity in the ventral striatum in responses to the delay of reward in Americans compared with Koreans (Figure 3.6), whereas the activity in the lateral prefrontal

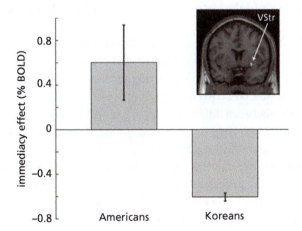

Figure 3.6 Brain activity in the VStr associated with reward processing was greater in Americans than in Korean participants when choices involved an immediate reward compared with choices involving only delayed rewards. (See colour plate.)
Adapted from Bokyung Kim, Young Shin Sung, and Samuel M. McClure, *Philosophical Transactions of the Royal Society B: Biological Sciences*, 367 (1589), pp. 650–656, Figures 3b and 4, DOI:10.1098/rstb.2011.0292, Copyright © 2012 The Royal Society.

cortex related to executive control did not show significant cultural group difference. The cultural difference in behavioral and brain imaging results suggest that the Koreans compared with the Americans are less sensitive to immediate reward because of decreased activity in the reward-related neural structure rather than enhanced activity underlying executive control. These findings provide a potential neural mechanism underlying the difference in financial preferences involving time between Eastern and Western populations.

Culture and neurocognitive style

The increasing numbers of studies have shown evidence for cultural group differences in neural substrates of a number of basic cognitive processes by comparing brain activity of individuals from East Asian and Western cultures. The findings demonstrate cultural variations of neural processes underlying perception, attention, memory, causal attribution, math operation, semantic relationship, and decision making. The influence of cultural experiences is evident over multiple brain structures, including the frontal, parietal, temporal, insula, and cerebellum. Can these findings be reconciled to fit into the notion of East Asian/Western difference in holistic and analytic processing styles (Nisbett et al. 2001)? Do East Asian/Western cultural influences on neurocognitive processes undergo a fundamental principle independently of the domains of information processing or tasks with distinct cognitive requirements?

Inspecting the results of these studies allows one to integrate the findings in a coherent account in terms of Nesbett et al.'s proposition. If the East Asian culture promotes a cognitive style of paying attention to contextual information such as the connection between foreground objects and background scenes or the relationship between different targets for processing, such a cognitive style can be consistently applied to different cognitive tasks and can be associated with specific neural substrates involved in the tasks. These together generate a neurocognitive style that is specific to the East Asian culture and is applied to various culturally preferred mental processes and behaviors. These include enhanced neural sensitivity to the variation of background scenes during perception (Jenkins et al., 2010), decreased activity in the frontal-parietal cortex during integration of object and contextual information (Hedden et al. 2008), greater activity in the dorsal visual pathway in responses to encoding of spatial relationships between objects during memory (Grön et al. 2003), and stronger activity in the parietal cortex during causal attribution of physical events (Han et al. 2011). Both the activity in the visual cortex sensitive to the repetition of global shapes (Lao et al. 2013) and the activity in the temporal cortex in response to the problem-size effect during single-digit multiplication (Prado et al. 2011) reflect a Chinese preference for integrating multiple elements into a unified unit during perception and math operation. By contrast, the favoring of an analytic cognitive style in individuals from Western culture results in a different neurocognitive style such as increased brain activity to salient foreground targets (Lewis et al., 2008), decreased activity in the frontal-parietal cortex in response to an object dissected from contexts (Hedden et al. 2008), greater activity in the ventral visual pathway in responses to object features during memory (Grön et al. 2003), decreased parietal activity during causal attribution (Han et al. 2011), and greater intraparietal and anterior cingulate activity in response to the problem-size effect during math operation (Prado et al. 2011). The human mind can be characterized by either "a context-independent processing style—aggregating and integrating across situations, ignoring situational variance in one's thoughts, feelings, and responses" or "a context-dependent processing style—paying attention to specific social contexts" (Kühnen and Oyserman 2002, p. 492). While psychologists provide behavioral evidence for Western/East Asian cultural difference in holistic/analytic cognitive styles, the cultural neuroscience findings revealed neural bases for a cultural preference of context-independent or a context-dependent strategy of cognition in multiple neural systems that are involved in different tasks and behaviors. The diversity of cognitive and neural processing styles challenges the classic psychological and philosophical view that the basic processes of human cognition are culturally universal.

In general, people who are brought up in the same society live in the same environmental landscape, speak the same language, share similar beliefs about the world, behave in accordance with the same social rules, and are governed by the same social system. These common sociocultural experiences contribute to development of similar mental processes (or cognitive style) and related neural substrates for individuals in that society, whereas different sociocultural experiences lead to distinct cognitive styles as is the case in different societies. Similarity in cognitive styles and, in particular, the underlying neural substrates, in a population make it easy for members of a social group to understand each other quickly, reach agreement easily, and come to a decision efficiently. These in turn engender the psychological and neural bases for social cooperation and interaction. Nevertheless, individuals from the same society may also vary in selection of different cultural values and in the degree of acculturation, leading to heterogeneity of neurocognitive styles in individuals from the same society. What factors lead to variations of individuals' acculturation in the same society? Chapter 7 will discuss potential contribution of the interaction between culture and gene to individual differences in neurocognitive styles in a cultural population.

Chapter 4

Cultural differences in neurocognitive processing of the self

Culture and self-concept

Starting from the early stage of development, a child learns to recognize his/her own face in a mirror and to perform self-oriented behavior guided by the image in the mirror (such as doing up one's hair). Later on, the individual learns social roles from interactions with family and school companions and begins to reflect on his or her own personality traits, behavior, and life goals. Such experiences give rise to a self-concept—an idea or abstraction of "who I am," and help to develop specific cognitive and neural processes related to oneself, which consist of key components of social cognition and play a fundamental framework for coordinating social interactions with others. Since William James (1950), psychologists have started to ponder and investigate the nature and constituents of self-concept and have tried to break it down into different dimensions such as physical attributes, mental traits, and social roles of an individual. Carl Rogers and others have also proposed that people not only formulate a concept of the "actual self" (i.e., beliefs of what attributes a person actually possesses) but also create a concept of the "ideal self"—a schema of oneself that a person strives to reach in the future (Higgins 1987; Rogers 1961). Self-concept is highly related to an individual's mental health because distorted or negative schemas of the self can make individuals susceptible to mental disorders such as depression (Beck 1976).

The essentiality of self-concept has been long accredited by philosophers from different societies. However, self-concept is marked with salient cultural imprints and assigned with different meanings. Ancient philosophers in the Western cultures took the existence of the self for granted and acknowledged its essential importance. Aristotle (384–322 BC) claimed that the whole self, soul and body alike, is something given and not questioned, and knowing the self is the beginning of all wisdom of human beings. Other Western philosophers have tended to pursue invariants of the self or self-identity that are consistent across time and social environments. For instance, Locke (1731) viewed the self as a continuity of consciousness or memory that provides a basis for an individual's identity across time and space. Baars (1997) asserted that self-concept or self-identity provides a framework that remains largely stable across many different life situations. Western thoughts also emphasize mental activity such as self-consciousness or self-awareness as one of the essential features of the self. In the modern European Western tradition, the self is considered as a thinking substance, as explicitly denoted in the declaration "I think therefore I am.... But what I am? A thing which thinks" (Descartes, 1912, p. 89). Contemporary scholars from Western societies also stress a notion of self-concept that gives prominence to the uniqueness of oneself and makes one distinguishable from others. Seigel (2005, p.3), in his book, *The Idea of the Self*, gave the following definition "By 'self' we commonly mean the particular being any person is, whatever it is about each of us that distinguishes you or me from others." This idea of self-concept emphasizes an individual's independence in social life such that the self is an agent who is capable of acting freely and taking responsibility for his/her own actions (Searle 2004). Obviously, self-concept as developed in the Western culture puts a lot of stress on the individuality of a person, as noted by Solomon (1990, p. 178) that "it is a matter for serious reflection that in our self-absorbed, individualistic society, so much is written and said on self-realization and individual self-identity, while somewhat less has been written, at least on the same level of self-conscious philosophical profundity, on the nature of our relations with one another."

Ancient philosophers in East Asian cultures also believed in the existence of the self, but they took a different perspective in terms of the nature of self-concept. A Chinese philosopher named Zengzi (曾子) (505–435 BC) asked his students to examine the self on three counts every day (here "three" is taken to mean "many") to stress the importance of knowing the self. However, rather than asking his students to consider exactly in which aspects the self is different from others, Zengzi requested them to reflect on their loyalty to their peers and their reputation among friends. Zengzi's teaching highlights self-reflection in relation to close others. Proverbially, Chinese philosophers focus on men much more often than on a man (or the self) in order to understand human nature in general, and, even when explicitly addressing the concept of the self, they tend to stress the relationship between the self and others. As pointed out by a modern Chinese scholar Shih Hu (1929/2006, p. 107), Chinese tradition reckons that "a person cannot exist alone; all action must be in the form of interaction between person and person." Some Chinese philosophers even believe that to realize no distinction between oneself and others and no distinction between the individual and the universe is an ideal mental state for human beings (Fung 1948/2007, p. 124). Indeed, Chinese Buddhism takes an extreme view of the self by attributing human non-enlightenment to the existence of self-concept in our minds, and asks people to learn their original identification with the Universal Mind (or Pure Consciousness) in order to get rid of the eternal Wheel of Birth and Death (Fung 1948/2007, pp. 400–402). More recently, a modern Chinese philosopher has been trying to formalize self-concept as a knot of the universal connection with the ability to think consciously of the self and to be capable of transcending itself (Zhang 2005). In such a model of the self, the existence of the self completely depends on its connections with others, and the "self" makes sense only when it interacting with others. According to this "relational self" concept, people are able to see others in the self and vice versa.

The cultural differences in self-concept that have unfolded in the philosophical literature can be summarized by stating that the self in Western cultures is experienced as single and subjective given whereas the self in East Asian cultures is experienced as a socially connected entity that depends on social context and social relationships. How are the philosophical thoughts on self-concept manifested in human cognition related to the self and the relationship between the self and others? Are there self-specific cognitive processes that are universal across sociocultural environments? Another interesting question is how cultural differences in self-concept affect human cognition/emotion and behavior, given that self-concept promotes differential sampling and processing of information from the environment (Triandis 1989); plays an integral part in human motivation, cognition, affect, and social identity (Sedikides and Spencer 2007); and provides an "integrative glue" that functions to integrate parts into perceptual wholes, binds memory to source, and links attention to decision making (Sui and Humphreys 2015).

Contemporary psychologists have proposed several theoretical frameworks to capture the essential difference in self-concept across cultures. For instance, Triandis and colleagues (Triands et al. 1988; Triands 1989) proposed that individualistic (e.g., Western) cultures give priority to personal goals over the goals of collectives, whereas collective (e.g., East Asian) cultures make no distinctions between personal and collective goals or even subordinate personal goals to the collective goals. Nisbett (2003) purported that the self as a bounded, impermeable free agent in Western cultures can move from group to group and setting to setting without significant alteration. The self in East Asian cultures, however, is connected, fluid, and conditional, and can be understood only in relation to others.

One of the most influential theoretical frameworks of cultural differences in self-concept was put forward by Markus and Kitayama (1991). The basic idea behind their framework is that Western cultures that emphasize self-identity lead to an independent view of the self and individuals with independent self-construals are inclined to be self-focused and to attend to the self more than to others (including intimate others). In contrast, the emphasis of fundamental social connection in East Asian cultures favors an interdependent view of the self (interdependent self-construal) that is generally sensitive to information about significant others and attends to intimate others as much as to the self. The cognitive schemas of the self in Western and East Asian cultures proposed by Markus and Kitayama are illustrated in Figure 4.1. An early version of the self-schemas only includes the part in the big circle (Markus and Kitayama 1991). The Western, independent view of the self, illustrated as the central circle in Figure 4.1, is characterized by inner attributes (the Xs), such as desire, preference, attribute, or ability, that can only belong to the self. Such representations of the inner self are the most elaborated in memory and the most accessible when thinking of the self, and are most significant in regulating behavior. The central circle and the surrounding circles can intersect, suggesting a representation of the self in relation to others. However, there is a clear and solid boundary between the self and others (even close others). With an independent self, the interaction with others produces a sense of self as separate, distinct, or independent from others, and an individual's behavior is driven by one's own trait, motivation, and goal. For the East Asian, interdependent self, the significant self-representations (the Xs) are those in relationship to and shared with close and significant others, as illustrated by the overlap of the central and surrounding circles made of dotted lines. The model of interdependent self-construals also implicates potential changes of self-concept structure with the nature of a particular social context. What drives the behavior of those with interdependent self-construals is not invariant personal attributes but the knowledge of the

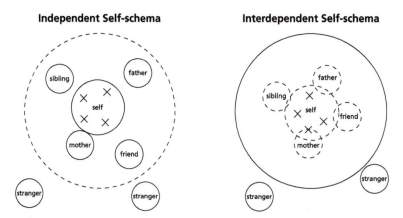

Figure 4.1 Illustration of the schema of self-concept in East Asian and Western cultures.

self in relation to specific others in a particular context. With an interdependent self, interaction with others produces a sense of self as connected to, related to, or interdependent on others. In a later version of the self-schema, Markus and Kitayama (2010) further discussed the implication of independent/interdependent self-construals for building social relationships between in-group and out-group members. It was postulated that the clear and solid boundary between the self and close others for the independent self makes it hard to formulate a sense of in-group identity and, consequently, people with independent self-construals can move between in-group and out-group relatively easily. On the other hand, the close relationship between the self and close others produces a strong sense of in-group identity (consisting of the self and close others) and a significant in-group versus out-group distinction. This then results in difficulty in moving across the solid boundary between in-group and out-group for those with interdependent self-construals.

The theoretical frameworks of cultural differences in self-concept predict variations in other psychological processes related to self-concept during perception, memory, and self-reflection across cultures. One may further predict that the neural mechanisms underlying self-related psychological processes can vary across sociocultural environments. In addition, it is likely that variations of self-construals may also modify the neural underpinnings of other cognitive and affective processes. These issues have been investigated in cultural neuroscience research extensively. This chapter will focus on cultural differences in neurocognitive processes related to self-face recognition and self-reflection: two domains of self-related processing that play key roles in shaping self-identity, and have been investigated relatively extensively in cultural neuroscience research. Chapter 6 will present additional brain imaging findings of how temporary shift of self-construals modulates neurocognitive processes involved in cognition and emotion, and it discusses these findings in the context of causal relationship between cultural beliefs and functional organization of the human brain.

Cultural differences in neurocognitive processing of self-face

Self-face recognition

The ability to look at and recognize oneself in a mirror is not exclusively owned by humans. Gallup (1970) was the first to test the ability of self-recognition in non-human primates. A group of chimpanzees was exposed to a mirror for ten days and then was anesthetized to receive a mark of odorless dye above the eyebrow that could not be seen by the animal unless the animal viewed itself in a mirror. Gallup found that chimpanzees in the training group, but not those without previous mirror exposure, directed touches toward the mark on their foreheads when the mirror was reintroduced. Subsequent studies found that other animals such as Asian elephants (Plotnik et al. 2006), dolphins (Reiss and Marino 2001), and rhesus monkeys (Chang et al. 2015) were also able to pass this "mirror test" by showing self-directed action after being exposed to a mirror for a period of time. The ability to recognize one's own face in a mirror appears during the second year of life in human infants (Amsterdam 1972; Asendorpf et al. 1996), and mirror self-recognition in children is associated with the emergence of social emotion such as embarrassment and shame (Lewis 2011). It is generally accepted that passing the mirror test indicates awareness about one's physical appearance (Suddendorf and Butler 2013) and it has been suggested as an index of self-awareness (Keenan et al. 2000).

Psychologists have tried to elucidate the processes that are unique for self-face recognition using various paradigms. For example, using a visual search task, Tong and Nakayama (1999) revealed faster behavioral responses when American college students searched for their own face compared with a stranger's face among distractor faces. The self-face advantage in search time was observed regardless whether upright or inverted faces were used in the visual search task. The self-face advantage in behavioral responses was also evident over familiar faces during judgments on face identity in American participants (Keenan et al. 1999). Similarly, individuals from East Asian cultures showed self-face advantage in behavior performances. When Chinese college students were presented with images of their own face or a friend's face and were asked to discriminate orientations of those faces but to ignore face identity, they responded faster to self-face than to familiar faces (Ma and Han 2009, 2010; Sui et al. 2006). These findings indicate that the self-advantage in face recognition is robust, independent of tasks performed on the face, and evident across different cultures.

Multiple perceptual and cognitive mechanisms have been proposed to interpret the self-face advantage in behavioral performance. Tong and Nakayama (1999) suggested that the observed shorter searching time to self-face than to a stranger's face may reflect the effect of robust representations of highly over-learned familiar faces. However, an account of the self-face advantage merely based on perceptual familiarity is in contradiction with the fact that people spend much more time seeing their friends' and colleagues' faces than seeing their own faces in a mirror. Moreover, perceptual familiarity cannot explain faster responses to self-face compared with familiar faces in tasks that required identification of inverted faces (Keenan et al. 1999) or identification of facial features unrelated to identity (e.g., orientations of faces; Sui et al. 2006). Ma and Han (2010) have proposed an implicit positive association (IPA) theory of self-face recognition in order to explain the self-face advantage in behavioral responses. They hypothesized that viewing one's own face activates positive attribute in self-concept, which in turn facilitates behavioral responses to self-face. The IPA theory of self-face recognition was put forward based on two lines of research. First, human beings have a basic desire to feel good about themselves (James 1950), and most human adults possess a positive view of the self (Greenwald 1980). Second, human adults responded faster to stimuli with positive than negative valence, such as positively versus negatively toned words (Stenberg et al. 1998) and the names of "good" versus "bad" people (Cunningham et al. 2003). To test their hypothesis, Ma and Han (2010) first had participants undergo a self-concept threat priming procedure in which participants were asked to make judgments on whether a number of negative trait adjectives could be used to describe themselves. Participants then had to respond to pictures of their own faces or their friends' faces by making judgments on orientations of these faces. The rationale was that, if the implicit positive association with self plays a key role in self-face advantage, the self-face advantage should be reduced once the implicit positive association with self is broken or weakened by the self-concept threat priming. It was first shown that, in the typical implicit association test (IAT; Greenwald et al. 1998), participants responded faster to a self-face paired with positive words than with negative words, and the IAT effect was significantly reduced by self-concept threat priming. In addition, self-concept threat priming, which was supposed to reduce the implicit positive association with the self, significantly slowed responses to self-face and led to faster responses to familiar faces than self-face. The findings support the engagement of a social cognitive mechanism (i.e., implicit positive attitude toward the self) in advantages of behavioral responses to the self-face.

The neural mechanisms of self-face recognition have been investigated by recording ERPs to self-face and familiar/unfamiliar faces from healthy adults. It is well known that face stimuli usually elicited a negative activity peaking around 170 ms after stimulus onset over the lateral occipitotemporal brain regions (N170; Bentin et al. 1996), which is believed to be engaged in coding facial structure (Eimer 2000) and facial identity (Heisz et al. 2006). Sui et al. (2006) first recorded ERPs from Chinese adults while they were presented images of a self-face, one familiar other face, and one unfamiliar other face matched for sex and age, all with neutral expressions. In five images of each face, the head was oriented to the left (from 45–90°) and to the right in five other images of the same face. In separate blocks of trials, participants were asked to identify the head orientations of self-faces, familiar faces, or unfamiliar faces by a button press while ignoring other faces. Sui et al. did not find evidence for modulations of early face-specific ERP component (e.g., N170) by face identity regardless whether face stimuli were attended (i.e., required to be responded to) or unattended (i.e., required no responses). However, the self-face compared with familiar faces elicited an increased positive activity over the frontal/central brain areas over a large time window (220–700 ms) after stimulus onset. This long-latency positive shift of the ERP amplitude in response to self-face relative to familiar faces was replicated in other studies that required responses to orientations of faces (Guan et al. 2014), changes of fixation (Geng et al. 2012), and simple detection of the appearance of each face (Kotlewska and Nowicka 2015). These studies failed to find evidence for modulations of the early face-specific ERP component by self-face, possibly because the task demands in these studies had nothing to do with face identity. Keyes and colleagues (2010) presented participants with a series of face stimuli of oneself, a friend, and a stranger with brief exposures. Participants were instructed to monitor a sequence of images for infrequently occurring repeated images and to press the keyboard spacebar when they noticed a repeat. This task required the processing of face identify rather than a global feature of face (e.g., orientation). Keyes et al. found that self-face compared with friend/stranger faces increased the N170 amplitude over the posterior brain regions. Self-face relative to friend/stranger faces also enlarged the amplitude of a vertex positive potential (VPP)—a positive ERP component peaking around 170 ms after stimulus delivery with the maximum amplitude over the frontal/central brain regions. The differences in brain activity between friend and strangers' faces did not emerge until 280 ms and beyond, with positive shift of ERP amplitude to friend faces. The ERP findings suggest that self-face recognition is characterized by enhanced neural activity during both the early stage of facial structure encoding and the late improved cognitive evaluation.

The precise brain regions involved in self-face specific processes have been identified in a number of fMRI studies. A typical design of early fMRI research that aimed to localize the processing of self-face was to compare BOLD signals in response to self-face versus a control face. For example, viewing self-face versus strangers' faces significantly activated the right frontal cortex, right occipitotemporoparietal junction, and left fusiform gyrus (Sugiura et al. 2005). Perceiving self-face versus a familiar famous face (Platek et al. 2004) or perceiving self-face versus personally familiar faces (Platek et al. 2006; Scheepers et al. 2013; Sugiura et al. 2005) also activated the right frontal and parietal lobe and the left middle temporal gyrus. Uddin et al. (2005) created morphed images using different proportions of pixels from self-face and a personally familiar face and found that viewing morphed images containing more self with those containing more personally familiar others also activated the right frontal and parietal cortex. For each individual, the self-face has specific perceptual features and viewing the self-face evokes personal self-identity. To contrast self-face with another's face does not allow researchers to disentangle the different cognitive processes engaged in self-face recognition. To further clarify the functional roles of the brain areas involved in the processing of perceptual features of self-face and self-identity independent of facial perceptual features, Ma and Han (2012) recorded BOLD responses to rapidly presented faces drawn from morph continua between self-face (Morph 100%) and a gender-matched friend's face (Morph 0%) in a face recognition task. They compared BOLD responses to Morph 100% versus Morph 60% that differed in self-face physical properties but were both recognized as the self. This contrast uncovered neural activity sensitive to self-face physical properties in the left fusiform face area—a brain region in the temporal lobe on the lateral side of the fusiform gyrus that has been identified in facial recognition (Kanwisher et al. 1997). On the other hand, contrasting Morph 50% that were recognized as the self versus a friend in different trials revealed neural modulations associated with self-face identity in the right fusiform face area. The contrast of Morph 50% recognized as the self versus a friend also revealed activations in the medial prefrontal cortex and posterior cingulate. Importantly, these activations were not observed when comparing brain activity in response to faces of oneself versus the friend of each participant. The results revealed self-face specific modulations of activity in the fusiform face area and medial prefrontal cortex, and highlight the distinct functional roles of the left and right fusiform face areas in the processing of perceptual features and personal identity of self-face. The left fusiform face area was engaged in coding physical features of self-face independently of face identity, whereas the right fusiform face area and the medial prefrontal cortex was involved in coding face identity of self-face independently of the physical attributes of self-face. Personal self-identity independent of perceptual feature processing also engaged the medial prefrontal cortex that also mediates self-reflection on personality traits (see the following section of this chapter). Thus, perceptual feature and face identity of self-face are encoded in distinct neural subsystems.

Cultural differences in self-face recognition

As mentioned earlier in this chapter, both philosophy and psychology literatures suggest that self-concept is a cultural phenomenon. East Asian cultures tend to promote the interdependent self-construals, whereas Western cultures tend to encourage the independent self-construals (Markus and Kitayama 1991; 2010). If self-concept, which consists of differential dimensions such as physical appearance, personality trait, and social role, varies across Western and East Asian cultures, one would expect that the neurocognitive processes involved in self-face recognition, a key component of the physical dimension of self-concept, would differ in individuals from Western and East Asian cultures. Two predictions arise from Markus and Kitayama's cognitive model of cultural difference in self-concept. On the one hand, given that Western cultures encourage people to be self-focused and to attend to the self more than to others, one would anticipate that the advantage of self-face recognition over the recognition of others' faces should be more salient in Western than East Asian cultures. On the other hand, because self-concept in East Asian cultures is sensitive to information about significant others, one would expect that the advantage of self-face recognition should be more vulnerable to social context such as the presence of significant others in East Asian than Western cultures.

Interestingly, while researchers from the Western cultures focused on the unique neurocognitive processes of self-face recognition, researchers from East Asian cultures embarked on research by investigating the relationship between self-face recognition and its sensitivity to the influences of social contexts and cultural experiences. To test the first prediction that the advantage of self-face recognition is more salient in Western than East Asian cultures, Sui et al. (2009) compared the behavior performance associated with self-face recognition between British college students in Hull, UK, and Chinese college students in Beijing, China. They found that both cultural groups responded faster during judgments of orientations of self-face compared with a familiar face. However, the self-face advantage in response time was much more salient in British than in Chinese participants (Figure 4.2). A possible account of the cultural difference in behavioral responses to self-face and familiar faces is that, according to the IPA theory of self-face advantage, participants assign values that are more positive to the self than to a friend, and this implicit positive association is stronger in British than in Chinese participants. The greater implicit positive association with the self in British compared with Chinese individuals results in faster response to a perceptual symbol of the self (e.g., images of self-face).

The second prediction that the advantage of self-face recognition is more easily affected by social contexts in East Asian than in Western cultures was tested by Han and colleagues using two paradigms (Liew et al. 2011; Ma and Han 2009, 2010). In one study Ma and Han (2010) asked both American and Chinese students to respond to pictures of their own faces or their friends' faces by making orientation judgments on these faces after they had undergone the self-concept threat priming (i.e., a 3-minute procedure that required participants to judge whether a number of negative trait adjectives were able to describe the self) and a control priming procedure. They found that individuals

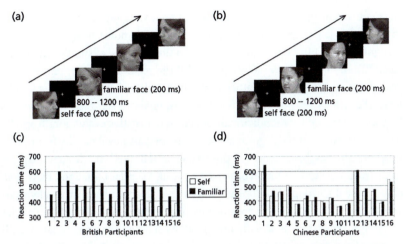

Figure 4.2 (a) and (b) illustrate the stimuli and procedure for the British and Chinese subjects. All participants were asked to decide whether self-face or a familiar face was shown in a left or right profile. The decision was made by a button press to target faces (own face or the familiar face) using the left or right index finger and ignoring the other faces. (c) and (d) show the results of reaction times to self-face and familiar faces for each individual participant in the British and Chinese sample.
Adapted from Jie Sui, Chang Hong Liu, and Shihui Han, *Social Neuroscience*, 4 (5), pp. 402–411, DOI: org/10.1080/17470910802674825, Copyright © 2009 Routledge http://www.informaworld.com.

from both cultural groups responded faster to self-face than to friends' faces, and the self-face advantage was reduced by the self-concept threat priming for both American and Chinese participants. However, the effect of self-concept threat priming on behavioral responses to self-face versus a friend's face was greater in Chinese than in American participants, indicating that self-face recognition in Chinese is more sensitive to social influences manipulated in a laboratory.

Cultural differences in contextual sensitivity of self-face recognition were further verified using relatively more authentic social stimuli in a number of other studies (Liew et al. 2011; Ma and Han 2009). Ma and Han (2009) asked a group of Chinese graduate students to judge orientations (toward left or right) of self-face, their advisor's face, and another faculty member's face. They found that, while participants responded faster to self-face compared with another faculty member's face, the response time was significantly slower to self-face than to the advisor's face. The presence of one's advisor's face relative to another faculty members' face significantly slowed responses to self-face to a greater degree. This effect cannot be explained simply by the sensitivity to people higher in a social hierarchy because the advisor and another faculty member were equivalent in the social hierarchy and both were higher in the hierarchy than the graduate students were. These findings demonstrated that self-face recognition in Chinese is highly sensitive to the presence of significant others. In addition, Ma and Han (2009) quantified the relation between participant's concern of advisor's negative attitude about the self and response times to self-face. The results showed that differential responses to self-face and advisor's face were correlated with individual's concerns of negative evaluations from the advisor. Thus for Chinese graduate students, negative evaluations from advisors constitute higher threats to a positive view of the self and disrupt the positive perceptual representation of self-face. Using a similar paradigm, Liew et al. (2011) tested a group of European American college students. It was hypothesized that the effect of the presence of significant others should be smaller in American participants with independent self-construals compared with Chinese participants with interdependent self-construals. Indeed, it was found that American graduate students maintained the self-face advantage even in the presence of their advisor's face, indicating that self-face recognition was much less influenced by significant others. Interestingly, the self-face advantage decreased in participants who assigned higher social status to their advisors. It appears that, unlike that in Chinese culture, self-face recognition in a culture emphasizing independence (i.e., American culture) is much less influenced by others' attitude toward the self, but it may be associated with perceived social dominance of others. Together these findings indicate that self-face recognition and positive views of the self are more sensitive to social feedback and significant others in Chinese than in American cultures.

The neural correlates of cultural differences in self-face recognition were examined by recording ERPs to self-face and familiar faces from British and Chinese participants (Sui et al. 2009). Several ERP components have been identified to be associated with specific processes during face recognition. For example, a negative activity over the fronto-central electrodes peaking at 200–350 ms after stimulus onset (anterior N2) is sensitive to perceptual salience of stimuli (Folstein and Van Petten 2008) and it differentiates between neutral and emotional facial expressions (Kubota and Ito 2007; Sheng and Han 2012). Sui et al. (2009) predicted that, if Western independent self-construals compared with East Asian interdependent self-construals assign greater social salience to one's own face than to others' faces, there would be enhanced neural coding of self-face in individuals from Western cultures. Thus, they recorded ERPs elicited by self-face and a friend's face from two culture groups.

Chinese university students in Beijing, China, and British university students in Hull, UK, were tested in a task that required orientation judgments of self-face and a friend's face. It was found that a negative activity peaking between

280 and 340 ms over the frontal-central area, denoted as the anterior N2, was sensitive to face identity and showed distinct patterns in British and in Chinese participants. Specifically, British participants showed larger N2 amplitude to self-face relative to the familiar face. In contrast, Chinese participants exhibited smaller anterior N2 amplitude to self-face compared with the familiar face (Figure 4.3). Across all participants, the differential N2 amplitudes to self-face and familiar faces predicted the self-advantage in behavioral responses. The amplitude of a long-latency positive ERP component (i.e., the P300) was enlarged by self-face relative to familiar faces when these stimuli required behavioral responses. This effect, however, did not differ significantly between the two cultural groups. Thus both behavioral and ERP results suggest cultural differences in neurocognitive processes at a specific time window involved in self-face recognition. Individuals from Western cultures that encourage independent self-construals assign greater social salience or positive value to self-face over faces of familiar others and result in enhanced neural coding of

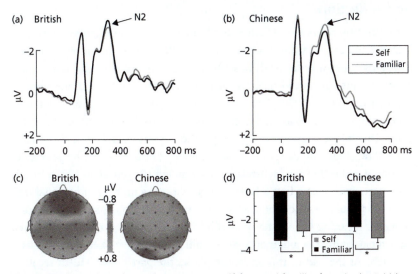

Figure 4.3 Illustration of neural responses to self-face and familiar faces in the British and Chinese sample. The N2 was enlarged to self-face relative to familiar face in British subjects (a) but was of smaller amplitudes to own face than familiar faces for the Chinese (b). Top views of voltage topographies of N2 difference between self-faces and familiar faces from the British and Chinese are shown separately in (c). Difference waves between self-faces and familiar faces were computed at all electrode positions. The mean amplitude of N2 from the British and Chinese at Fz is shown in (d). (See colour plate.)

Adapted from Jie Sui, Chang Hong Liu, and Shihui Han, *Social Neuroscience*, 4 (5), pp. 402–411, DOI: org/10.1080/17470910802674825, Copyright © 2009 Routledge http://www.informaworld.com.

self-face. In contrast, individuals from East Asian cultures that inspire interdependent self-construals may develop neurocognitive processes that assign the faces of familiar others with greater social salience over self-face.

It must be acknowledged that the observation of cultural group differences in behavioral and brain responses to self-face suggests a possible relationship between self-construal and self-face recognition but it does not demonstrate a causal relationship between self-construals and self-face recognition. In Chapter 6, I'll discuss a self-construal priming paradigm that allows the researcher to test variations of behavioral and neural responses to self-face because of temporary shift of independent/interdependent self-construals in a laboratory. This paradigm provides evidence for causal relationships between self-construals and self-face recognition.

Cultural differences in neurocognitive processing during self-reflection

Self-reflection

Self-reflection refers to the ability that human mind can think over the entity that constitutes that mind. The entity, or the self, consists of multiple attributes. A healthy adult can effortlessly describe his/her own physical appearance, personality traits, and social relationships with others—the three dimensions of self-concept (James 1950). Self-related information is encoded and stored in memory systems, and can be retrieved to guide behavior during social interactions. The unique cognitive processing of the self was initially investigated in a behavioral study that developed a self-referential task to assess the priority of encoding and retrieval of self-related information (Rogers et al. 1977). In this task, participants were first asked to judge whether a number of personal trait adjectives could describe themselves. Judgments of phonemic properties and semantic meaning were initially used by Rogers et al. as control tasks, which were replaced by trait judgments for a familiar person (e.g., a celebrity) in later research. At the end of this encoding phase, the participant had to recall as many of the words as they could. A number of studies reported similar results, where healthy adults showed better memory of the adjectives used to describe the self than those used to describe others (Klein et al. 1989). This phenomenon has been described as a self-reference effect that is believed to be associated with more extensive and elaborated processing of self-related information relative to that related to others.

The neural correlates of self-reflection have been explored by combining fMRI and the self-referential task by Kelley et al. (2002). As in the behavioral studies, during fMRI scanning, participants were asked to perform judgments on whether a number of trait adjectives could be used to describe the self or another person (e.g., a celebrity). The contrast of self-judgments versus other judgments was calculated to reveal brain activity that was believed to be specific to the encoding of self-related information. A robust finding that has been replicated by many fMRI studies is that BOLD signals in the ventral medial prefrontal cortex (mPFC) increase significantly while making judgments of the self compared with a celebrity in individuals from both Western (e.g., D'Argembeau et al. 2007; Kelley et al. 2002; Mitchell et al. 2005) and East Asian cultures (e.g., Ma and Han 2011; Wang et al. 2012; Zhu et al. 2007) (Figure 4.4). The increased activity in the ventral mPFC cannot be attributed to differential perceptual/semantic processing or motor responses because these were matched for self-judgments and other judgments. Macrae and colleagues (2004) tested the functional role of the ventral mPFC activation during trait judgments by asking American participants to perform a memory test after they had been scanned during the self-referential task. They found that trait adjectives that were remembered compared with those that were forgotten during the memory test induced greater activations in the ventral mPFC during the trait-judgment tasks. Ma and Han (2011) also found that the greater ventral mPFC activity elicited by trait adjectives during the self-referential task predicted higher recognition scores of these words in the later memory test. The findings support

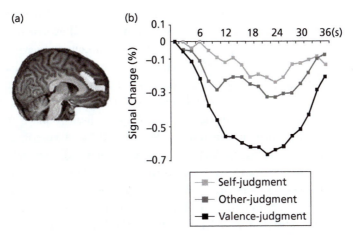

Figure 4.4 Illustration of brain activation in association with self-reflection. (a) The contrast of self- vs. celebrity-judgments on personality traits activated the medial prefrontal cortex. (b) BOLD signals during different judgment tasks. (See colour plate.)

Adapted from Yina Ma and Shihui Han, Neural representation of self-concept in sighted and congenitally blind adults, *Brain*, 134 (1), pp. 235–46, Figure 2b and 2c, DOI: http://dx.doi.org/10.1093/brain/awq299, Copyright ©2011, © The Author (2010). Published by Oxford University Press on behalf of the Guarantors of Brain. All rights reserved.

a hypothesis that the ventral mPFC activity is engaged in elaborated encoding of self-related information or self-relevance of stimuli (Han and Northoff 2009; Northoff et al. 2006).

EEG/ERP studies have also discovered neural activity involved in the self-referential task with high time resolution. For instance, Mu and Han (2010, 2013) obtained EEG recordings from Chinese adults during trait judgments of the self and a celebrity, which were followed by a memory test that demanded recognition of trait adjectives used for the trait judgments during EEG recording. While participants recognized better trait adjectives used to describe the self than the celebrity, the EEG activity related to self-referential processing that was both time- and phase-locked to stimulus onset was characterized by enhanced positivity in a long time window (200–1000ms) over the right frontal area, elicited by self-relative compared with other judgments. In addition, relative to other-referential traits, self-referential traits induced event-related synchronization of theta-band activity over the frontal area at 700–800 ms and of alpha-band activity over the central area at 400–600 ms. The EEG/ERP results are consistent with the fMRI results and further revealed that the self-referential processing during encoding of personality traits occurs quite early in the processing stream.

Cultural differences in self-reflection

According to Markus and Kitayama (1991), the processing of self-related information varies as a consequence of an individual's cultural experiences, such that self-focused processing encouraged by Western cultures may produce enhanced encoding and retrieval of information related to the self than that related to others, while East Asian cultures inspire attention to information about intimate others as much as that to the self. How is the cognitive model of culturally specific self-construals mediated in the human brain? A common expectation is that individuals from Western and East Asian cultures may recruit, to a certain degree, distinct neural substrates underlying self-reflection. Specifically, one may ask whether, in accordance with Markus and Kitayama's cognitive model, there are shared neural substrates involved in reflection of the self and a close other in East Asian but not Western cultures. Do East Asians engage neural substrates underlying inference of others' opinion during self-reflection if they strongly care about other's thoughts of the self? Would self-focused attention engage greater neural activity in individuals from Western than East Asian cultures?

Zhu and colleagues (2007) conducted the first cross-cultural fMRI study to assess cultural differences in neural correlates of encoding personality traits related to the self and a close other. An early behavioral study using the self-referential task found that healthy Chinese adults remembered the trait adjectives associated with the self and close others (such as one's mother) equally well (Zhu and Zhang 2002). The behavioral finding suggests that, for Chinese adults, there would be overlapping neural representations of the self and a close other (e.g., mother) in the ventral mPFC during judgments of personality traits. This, however, might not be true for Westerners. To test this hypothesis, Zhu et al. (2007) scanned two cultural groups—Chinese and English-speaking Westerners—during the self-referential task. Participants were presented trait adjectives and had to make judgments on whether a trait adjective could describe the self or a celebrity. Thus, the contrast of self-judgments versus other judgments allowed to the identification of brain activations that were specifically engaged in self-reflection. Additionally, participants were asked to judge whether a trait adjective was able to describe one's own mother. Brain activity engaged in mother judgments allowed the researchers to assess whether trait judgments of both the self and a close other would induce overlapping activation in the ventral mPFC in Chinese, but not in Westerners. Behavioral measures showed that both Chinese persons and Westerners remembered the adjectives used during self-judgments better than those used during celebrity judgments. The fMRI data revealed several interesting findings. First, relative to trait judgments of a celebrity (i.e., Zhu Rongji, the former Chinese premier, for Chinese, or Bill Clinton, the former American president, for Westerners), judgments on one's own personality traits significantly activated the ventral mPFC in both cultural groups. Thus, the ventral mPFC was engaged in coding self-relevance of stimuli regardless of participants' cultural experiences. Moreover, relative to trait judgments of a celebrity, judgments on personality traits of one's mother also activated the ventral mPFC, and this effect was significant in Chinese but not in Westerners (Figure 4.5). This finding indicated that the ventral mPFC was engaged during both self-reflection and reflection on a close other in Chinese, but only during self-reflection in Westerners. More importantly, when comparing self-judgments versus mother judgments, Westerners demonstrated stronger activation in the ventral mPFC, whereas the Chinese failed to show any activation. This result further supports the proposition that there is overlapping neural representation of the self and mother in the ventral mPFC in Chinese persons but not in Westerns.

The overlapping neural representations in the mPFC are not limited to the self and mother. A recent fMRI study of Chinese couples has shown that trait judgments of one's spouse and one's child also activated the mPFC that overlapped with that observed in trait judgments of oneself (Han et al. 2016). However, the degree of the mPFC involvement in neural representations of close others may depend on one's experiences of social interactions with close others. Wang et al.

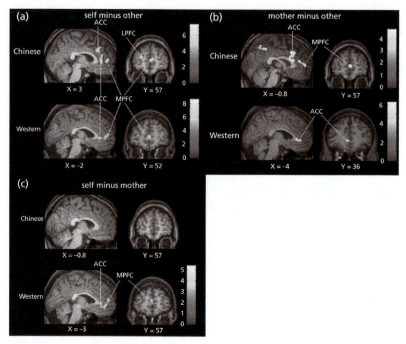

Figure 4.5 Cultural differences in MPFC activations during trait judgments of one's mother. (a) Judgments of the self relative to a celebrity activated the MPFC in both Chinese and Westerners. (b) Judgments of one's mother relative to a celebrity activated the MPFC only Chinese participants. (c) Judgments of the self relative to mother activated the MPFC in Westerners but not in Chinese. (See colour plate.)

Reprinted from *NeuroImage*, 34 (3), Ying Zhu, Li Zhang, Jin Fan, and Shihui Han, Neural basis of cultural influence on self-representation, pp. 1310–16, DOI:10.1016/j.neuroimage.2006.08.047, Copyright © 2006 Elsevier Inc., with permission from Elsevier.

(2012) tested whether the mPFC activity is engaged in the neural representations of different close others in a similar vein in Chinese participants. They scanned Chinese participants when performing trait judgments of the self, one's mother, father, and a best friend. Trait judgments of a celebrity were also included as a baseline. The mPFC activity engaged in self-judgments was first localized by contrasting self-judgments versus celebrity judgments. BOLD signals in the brain region were then extracted in the conditions of mother, father, and best friend judgments and were compared with each other. It was found that the mPFC activity during mother judgments was greater than those during father and best friend judgments, whereas the mPFC activity did not differ significantly between farther judgments and best friend judgments. The findings underscore the functional role of the ventral mPFC activity in encoding social relevance of others related to the self. A more recent fMRI study of bicultural

Asian Americans reported that, during trait judgments on the self and the mother, the dorsal region of the mPFC was even more engaged for the task requiring mother judgments than self-judgments (Huff et al. 2013). The greater mPFC activity linked to the mother than the father/best friend in relation to the self is consistent with stronger behavioral connections during development between the self and the mother (Geary 2000) and may provide a neural basis for the particular bond with one's mother relative to other close relatives and friends (Hodges et al. 1999).

To assess whether Western/East Asian cultures modulate the mPFC activity underlying self-reflection, Ma et al. (2014a) performed fMRI scanning of 30 Chinese and 30 Danish university students. The two cultural groups are respectively dominated by interdependence and independence (Li et al. 2006; Thomsen et al. 2007). To examine the cultural differences in the mPFC activity related to reflection on different dimensions of the self-concept, Ma et al. asked participants to make judgments of their social roles (e.g., student or customer), personality traits (e.g., smart or greedy), and physical features (e.g., black hair and tall) of the self and a celebrity during fMRI scanning. They tested two hypotheses. First, the stronger sense of the self as separate or independent from others in Danes will be mediated by stronger mPFC activity during self-reflection. Second, if individuals from East Asian societies to a larger degree construct self-identity with reference to social relations and emphasize others' expectations and thoughts, self-reflection may engage brain regions involved in the processing of others' thoughts and beliefs. A region of interest for testing the second hypothesis was the temporoparietal junction (TPJ) that is located at the border of the posterior parts of the temporal lobe and the inferior parts of the parietal lobe. The TPJ has been shown to be activated during the processing of what may be in another's mind such as beliefs (Saxe and Kanwisher 2003). Therefore, it was predicted that the Chinese participants would recruit stronger TPJ activity during self-reflection compared with the Danish, particularly during reflection on social attributes. Behavioral measures confirmed a reliable difference in cultural orientations between the two cultural groups. Chinese compared with Danes endorsed more strongly interdependence measured using the Singelis (1994) self-construal scale. Brain imaging results revealed distinct patterns of the mPFC and TPJ activity in the two cultural groups. First, while self-judgments relative to other-judgments activated the mPFC activity along all of the three dimensions, mental, physical, or social attributes, in both cultural groups, the mPFC activity underlying self-judgments was significantly stronger in Danes than in Chinese, and the cultural group difference in the mPFC activity was evident regardless of whether participants performed judgments on social roles, personality traits, or physical appearance (Figure 4.6).

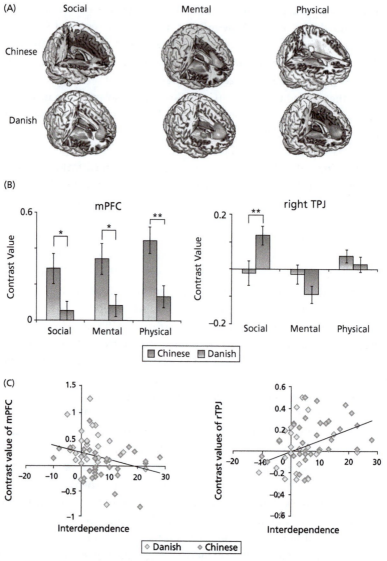

Figure 4.6 (A) Whole-brain analyses revealed greater activity in the MPFC in Danes than in Chinese during self-reflection, whereas Chinese participants showed stronger activity in the TPJ during reflection of one's social roles. (B) The contrast values from the MPFC and TPJ in the cultural groups. (C) The correlation between interdependence and MPFC/TPJ activity associated with self-reflection. (See colour plate.)

Adapted from Yina Ma, Dan Bang, Chenbo Wang, Micah Allen, Chris Frith, Andreas Roepstorff, and Shihui Han, Sociocultural patterning of neural activity during self-reflection, *Social Cognitive and Affective Neuroscience*, 9 (1), pp. 73–80, Figures 2a and b, 1a and b, and 4b and c, DOI: 10.1093/scan/nss103, Copyright © 2014, Oxford University Press.

Second, the analysis of TPJ activity uncovered an opposite pattern—the Chinese showed stronger TPJ activity in both hemispheres than the Danes did during self-judgments of social attributes. Moreover, the functional connectivity between the mPFC and bilateral TPJ associated with self-judgments on social attributes was significantly stronger in the Chinese than in the Danes. Third, a regression analysis of all participants confirmed a significant negative correlation between the right TPJ and mPFC activities associated with self-judgments of social attributes. Finally, Ma et al. examined whether the cultural differences in mPFC and TPJ activities were mediated by the interdependent cultural values. A hierarchical regression analysis confirmed that individuals' interdependence scores were negatively correlated with mPFC activity, but positively correlated with bilateral TPJ activity associated with self-judgments of social attributes. Moreover, the model with cultural affiliation (i.e., Chinese vs. Danes), and interdependence scores regressed on TPJ activity revealed that the measure of interdependence significantly mediated the relationship between the cultural affiliation and the TPJ activity involved in self-reflection on one's social role.

These brain imaging findings have several important implications. First, the interdependent self-construals in Chinese population may lead to overlapping neural representations of the self and close others. In contrast, in accordance with the independent self-construals in Western cultures, there are dissociated neural representations of the self and others (even close others such as one's mother) in the mPFC. Second, cultural group differences in brain activity underlying self-reflection (i.e., the TPJ activity) can be mediated by a specific cultural value (e.g., interdependence), suggesting that the group-level differences in brain activity underlying self-reflection can be partially explained by individual differences in interdependence. Third, East Asian/Western cultures lead to distinct patterns of brain activity in the mPFC and TPJ that support discrepant strategies employed during self-reflection. The relative impacts of the mPFC and TPJ in the social brain network can be shifted via the interconnection between these brain regions during self-reflection owing the degree to which an individual takes others' perspective when reflecting on the self. Fourth, the fact that the TPJ was not activated during self-reflection on mental and physical attributes suggests that the degree to which perspective taking is involved in self-reflection depends on both the dimension of the self-construal and the cultural experiences. Personality traits and physical attributes are thought to be more immutable than are social roles (cf. Hong et al., 2001), and are thus relatively more constant across social contexts and independent of others' thoughts. Finally, while these brain imaging results indicate cultural group differences in the brain activity underlying self-reflection, there were obvious variations of the brain activity underlying self-reflection along the degree of endorsement of a cultural value (e.g., interdependence) even among members within a cultural group. This reflects the fact that, besides the effect of common experiences of a cultural group, each individual's personal experience also plays an important role in shaping the neural substrates of self-representation, which in turn sways peoples' behavior during social interactions. Taken together, the cultural neuroscience findings, in particular the distinct patterns of the mPFC and TPJ activity in coding personal attributes of the self and others, provide potential neural underpinnings of Markus and Kitayama's (1991; 2010) model of Western/East Asian cultural differences in self-construals.

Religious belief and neural correlates of self-reflection

The difference in self-concept exists not only between East Asian and Western cultures, but there are also notable differences in self-concept between subpopulations of the same society. For example, people with different religious beliefs— a subjective culture that influences individuals' behavior significantly (Chiu and Hong 2013)—differ dramatically in how to think about the self. Christianity advocates denial of self or self-transcendence in order to highlight human contingency and dependence on God (Burns, 2003; Lin, 2005). The mandate that "every one of us shall give account of himself to God" (Romans 14:12) emphasizes judgment of oneself from God's perspective rather than from one's own or other individuals' perspectives. One of the extreme claims of Buddhism is that the self does not exist (Albahari, 2006; Ishigami-Iagolnitzer, 1997). According to the teaching of Buddha, the idea of self is an imaginary false belief that has no corresponding reality (Ching, 1984), and Buddha's followers should practice to get rid of any mindset of sense of "me" or "mine." Long-term life experiences under such religious teachings may profoundly influence the neurocognitive processes of the self. For instance, the emphasis of God's judgment of the self can lead to the inference of God's mind about the self when individuals are asked to think about the self. For Buddhists who follow the doctrine of "no-self," a task that requires thinking about the self would not make sense, and the ventral mPFC that is engaged in self-reflection in nonreligious individuals would not be activated. In addition, the task of self-reflection itself may produce conflict with the belief of no-self in Buddhists, and performing such a task may demand conflict monitoring and activate the related brain regions.

Han and colleagues (2008, 2010) tested these hypotheses in two fMRI studies. The first study scanned two groups, self-identified nonreligious participants and Christian participants, during judgments of personality traits of oneself and a celebrity (Han et al. 2008). To obtain independent psychological measurements that could account for differential involvement of the self in trait judgments between the two groups, each participant, after the scanning procedure, was asked to rate how the following factors influenced his/her judgments about the personality of the self or of others: one's behavior; friends' evaluation; one's relationship with others; and Jesus' evaluation. A 7-point scale was used ranging from 0 (no influence) to 6 (very strong influence). This measure revealed that nonreligious participants identified their own behavior as the most important factor that influenced their judgments, whereas Christian participants reported that Jesus' evaluation was the most important factor that determined their judgments. The fMRI data analysis focused on whether Christian beliefs and practices would weaken the process of coding self-relatedness in the ventral mPFC during trait judgments of the self but engage brain regions underlying inference of others' opinions. Because the dorsal region of the mPFC has been shown to be involved in inference and evaluation of others' mental states such as belief or intention (Gallagher et al. 2000; Han et al. 2005), it was predicted that, relative to nonreligious participants, Christian participants would recruit the dorsal mPFC more, but the ventral mPFC less during self-reflection. Indeed, the fMRI data confirmed that, unlike nonreligious participants who showed increased activity in the ventral mPFC during reflection of personality traits of oneself relative to a celebrity, Christian participants showed increased activity in the dorsal region of the mPFC, but decreased activity in the ventral mPFC during self-reflection.

Han et al. (2010) further scanned a group of Chinese Buddhists during self-reflection on personality traits to examine whether self-reflection activated the neural substrates of conflict monitoring (e.g., the anterior cingulate cortex; Botvinick et al. 2004) in Buddhists. Similarly, participants were asked to perform trait judgments of oneself and a celebrity during fMRI scanning. Interestingly, comparing self-judgments versus celebrity judgments failed to generate increased activation in the ventral mPFC in Buddhist participants. Instead, self-judgments significantly activated the dorsal region of the mPFC, rostral anterior cingulate cortex, and midcingulate and the inferior frontal/insular cortex. There has been substantial evidence that the anterior cingulate and midcingulate cortex, as well as the inferior frontal/insular cortex are involved in conflict monitoring and negative emotions such as physical pain and empathy for others' suffering (Fan et al. 2011; Shackman et al. 2011). The fMRI results from Buddhist participants can thus be interpreted as reflecting decreased encoding of self-relevance of stimuli in the ventral mPFC owing to the doctrine of "no-self" but enhanced conflict monitoring and negative affect as the task demand was contradiction with participants' beliefs. The brain imaging findings suggest that religious beliefs and practices can significantly modulate neural substrates underlying self-reflection in human adults so that the default neural underpinnings can afford specific thoughts and behaviors consistent with specific religious doctrines.

Neural roots of culturally specific self-concept and behavior

The models of cultural differences in self-concept proposed based on the findings of cross-cultural behavioral studies are mainly built on explicit self-reports, which are likely to have undergone strong influences of social desirability and social norms. The cultural neuroscience findings summarized in this chapter provide evidence that cultural differences in self-concept have a deep neurophysiological root in the human brain. The brain imaging findings enrich our understanding of cultural influences on the neurocognitive strategies involved in self-reflection in individuals with different cultural experiences and religious beliefs/practices. Western/East Asian cultures modulate the degree to which the mPFC is engaged in self-reflection to code self-relevance of stimuli, whereas Christian and Buddhist beliefs and practices are likely to eliminate or weaken the differential processing of the self and others in the ventral mPFC. Western/East Asian cultures influence whether an individual takes the perspective of other individuals by differentially modulating the TPJ activity engaged in self-reflection of social attributes, whereas Christian beliefs and practices specify the essentiality of inferring mental states of an individual (e.g., Jesus) by recruiting the dorsal region of the mPFC, and Buddhists seem to employ the cingulate cortex to monitor the conflict between the doctrine of "no-self" and the task demand of self-reflection.

If the neural substrates of self-reflection support a chronic mode of cognition of the self, cultural variations of neural underpinnings of self-related processing can help us to comprehend and account for differences in people's behavior across societies. For instance, the enhancement of the mPFC activity underlying presentations of the self over others (even family members such as the mother) can provide a default mode of self-concept that draws stress on the primacy of self-interest and one's own life goals in the Western individualistic culture. Meanwhile, the distinct neural representations of the self and others also support the autonomous self-concept that encourages an individual to make his/her own choices, and meanwhile acknowledges one's own responsibility for behavioral outcomes. The shared neural representation of the self and family members in the mPFC provides a neural basis for an East Asian perspective that regards the self and family members as a unit. The overlapping neural coding of self and family members may give prominence to a family's goal, draw attention to an individual's obligation and responsibility for the family, and improve family members' coordination to reach their common goals. The automatic engagement of the TPJ during self-reflection is another chronic mode of culturally specific brain activity that may contribute to overestimation of others' mental states and increased sensitivity to contextual social information in East Asian cultures (e.g., Ma and Han 2009; Wu and Keysar 2007). These culturally specific default models of brain activity provide a potential neural basis for the emergence of East Asian philosophical thoughts that advocate *harmony* between the self and others and between one and another social group.

Another implication of the distinct and shared neural representations of the self and others is that the motivation to secure the interest of the personal self, which has been considered a fundamental human motive in the Western culture, can vary significantly in individuals from Western and East Asian cultures. The independent self, underpinned by distinct neural coding of the self and others, may be more strongly motivated by the interest of the self than that of other others, whereas this may not be true for the interdependent self. Kitayama and Park (2014) tested this idea by recording the error-related negativity (ERN)—an ERP component contingent on incorrect responses (Falkenstein et al. 1991; Gehring et al. 1990). A typical paradigm to induce the ERN is to ask participants to respond as quickly as possible to targets in a series of rapidly presented stimuli with high task difficulty to trigger incorrect responses. The ERN is usually observed within 100 ms after an erroneous response in speeded reaction time tasks owing to continuous stimulus processing after the actual response is executed and awareness of mismatch of the actual response and the correct response. Both dipole modeling of EEG results and fMRI research have localized the ERN to the anterior cingulate cortex (Carter et al. 1988; Gehring et al. 2000). Kitayama and Park (2014) asked European American and Asian (Chinese and Korean) to identify a center letter among a set of five letters that were flashed at the center of the screen for 100 ms (e.g., HHHHH, HHSHH). Participants were told that their response would be monitored, and correct responses that were faster than their median response time would be converted into points, and the points obtained in separate blocks of trials would be used to trade a gift for oneself and for a close, same-sex friend, respectively. Thus, participants were motivated to earn as many reward points as possible to receive gifts for both the self and the friend. The ERN to incorrect responses were used as a neural index of motivation and self-centric motivation was expected to be associated with a greater ERN amplitude in the condition of responding to earn points for oneself relative to the friend. It was found that, for European Americans, the ERN was significantly greater in the self-condition than in the friend condition, indicating a stronger motivation to bring in benefits for the self than for the friend. For Asians, however, the ERN did not differ between the self and friend conditions, suggesting similar motivations for earning points for the self and the friend. While self-report revealed higher scores of interdependent self-construals in Asians than for European Americans, the interdependent self-construal score was negatively correlated with the ERN index of self-centric motivation (i.e., ERPs to incorrect responses minus those to correct responses) across all participants. It was further shown that the cultural group difference in ERP amplitude was mediated by the interdependent self-construal score, suggesting a possible role of overlapping self-other representations or interdependence in generating cultural group differences in motivations to earn benefits for oneself relative to a friend.

The findings of distinct neural substrates of self-concept and self-centric motivation advance our understanding of the neural roots of independent and interdependent self-construals and cultural variations of social behavior. Independent and interdependent self-construals can also influence behavior via its effects on other cognitive and affective processes. As will be discussed in Chapter 6, a temporary shift of independent/interdependent self-construals via self-construal priming can produce significant influences on neurocognitive processes during perception, attention, emotion, and related behavior. Thus, independent/interdependent self-construals can provide a cultural framework that constrains both behavior and brain activity underlying multiple cognitive and affective processes (Han and Humphreys 2016). Finally, current cultural neuroscience research focuses on the influences of East Asian/Western cultures on the neurocognitive processes of the self. We have known little about neural substrates of self-concept in other cultures. If self-concept and the neural underpinnings play a key role in guiding human behavior, it is of course important to explore these in other cultures such as Arab and African. It is also critical to develop new frameworks for comprehension of the neural substrates of self-concept in these cultures based on new empirical findings.

Chapter 5

Cultural differences in neurocognitive processing of others

Social interactions in cultural contexts

Central to human life are social interactions during which individuals communicate and coordinate with each other and take meaningful actions to reach specific social goals. An infant starts to react to others immediately after birth and interacting with others is extremely important for development of cognitive abilities and underlying neural substrates. Social interactions occur between two or more individuals in a particular sociocultural environment and constitute the foundation of social relationships. The consequences of social interactions can be either good or bad. Social interactions can bring mutual benefits to agents who take part in successful cooperation. Disagreeable consequences may arise from social interactions that produce conflicts between individuals or social groups. Of particular importance, efficient social interactions require information or knowledge of the participants' social identity in terms of their gender, ethnicity, socioeconomic status, etc. Some information can be perceived from a participant's face such as an individual's identity and whether the participant is, for example, a friend or stranger, partner or antagonist. Perceiving others' social and individual identity is vital for determining whether and how to interact with them. Likewise, efficient social interactions depend on understanding of others' mental states. We need to have a sense of what others believe and what they intend to do, which helps us to figure out why others behave in a specific way and to predict their future actions. Further, we need to comprehend others' feelings and, in certain situations, to share their emotional states and possibly take actions resulting from the shared emotional states. By taking advantage of such social information, we are capable of assessing and predicting the outcome of social interactions and are helped in making judgments on the appropriateness of our own behavior. Others' affective states can be easily ascertained from facial expressions, whereas their intentions/beliefs, if not expressed explicitly, have to be inferred from their action and behavior.

The human brain has evolved different neurocognitive systems in correspondence with the requirement of social information processing. For instance, a complicated neural circuit consisting of multiple brain regions has been proposed to extract information from faces (Haxby et al. 2000). There is a brain area in the posterior part of the ventral temporal lobe that can be more strongly activated when viewing faces than viewing objects or scenes, which has been named the fusiform face area (Sergent et al. 1992; Kanwisher et al. 1997). Damage to the fusiform gyrus can lead to a syndrome called "prosopagnosia," where a patient's ability to recognize facial identity of someone known to the patient (e.g., stranger versus friend) is impaired even though other visual abilities (e.g., object recognition) can remain intact. Other neural structures such as the amygdala—a subcortical structure located medially within the temporal lobes of the brain—plays a key role in recognition of facial expression. Patients with amygdala damage have difficulty in recognizing facial expressions such as fear, anger, and happiness, which can be easily discriminated by healthy controls (Adolphs et al. 1994). As mentioned in Chapter 2, the mirror neuron system in the frontal and parietal cortices contributes greatly to the understanding of others' intentions during action perception. Inference of others' mental states also recruits the dorsal medial prefrontal cortex, temporoparietal junction (a brain region at the corner of the parietal and temporal cortex), and temporal pole (the most anterior part of the temporal lobe; Frith and Frith 2003). Humans have also developed specific neural substrates in brain regions, such as the anterior cingulate and anterior insula, for understanding and sharing (or empathize) others' emotional states (Fan et al. 2011). These areas are believed to be associated with prosocial behavior. The multiple neural systems involved in the processing of information (e.g., identity, intention, and affective state) about our conspecifics provide a neural basis for our ability to handle complex social interactions in daily life.

Social interactions occur ubiquitously in human societies but are characterized with novel cultural imprints, such as the examples I mentioned in Chapter 1. State-of-art techniques for communication have increased the number of large-scale, rapid social interactions among people from diverse geographical and cultural regions and backgrounds. As a result, cultural differences in social interactions have been brought into prominence, particularly when individuals from differential cultures start to conduct interactional cooperative ventures or business dealings. What and how social information is processed relies heavily on with whom an individual interacts and in which cultural context such interactions occur. For example, the way people think of and interact with those who sit high or low in a social hierarchy may vary greatly across Western and East Asian societies (Triandis and Gelfand 1998). Cultural contexts also shape the use of communication technology. For example, when using Internet social networks, Korean college students put more weight on obtaining social support from existing social relationships, whereas American students place relatively greater emphasis on seeking entertainment (Kim et al. 2011).

From an evolutionary perspective, the brain evolves to cope with the complexity of social interactions, such that the relative neocortex volume increases as a function of the mean social-group size (Dunbar and Shultz 2007), suggesting that more complex and larger-scale social interactions require more neural resources in the primate brain. Humans have evolved specific patterns of brain activity to mediate social cognition—the processing (e.g., perceiving, encoding, storage, and retrieval) of complicated information relating to the self and others. Recent brain imaging studies have accumulated ample data revealing the functions of different neural systems underlying social cognition (Lieberman 2007). Neural plasticity allows for the development of neural mechanisms during adolescence, which are adapted to the context-dependent nature of social cognition (Blakemore 2008). Culture provides a framework for social interactions by building social values and norms and by assigning meanings to social events. Given the diversity of sociocultural contexts across the world, the human brain has developed neural mechanisms to mediate social interactions with specific cultural imprints. This chapter summarizes and analyzes cross-cultural brain imaging findings related to the processing of information about multiple aspects of others—the main target of social interactions.

Face

A face provides a great deal of information about a person. Face recognition is an ability that enables us to identify a mate (partner), a friend, or a stranger, to differentiate kin from non-kin members of one's social group, and to distinguish between fellows or opponents during group conflict. The ability to recognize faces is obviously critical for survival and reproductive processes. Multiple techniques have been applied to address how a face is processed in the human brain. In particular, brain imaging studies have revealed a distributed neural network that consists of multiple brain regions dedicated to the processing of different facial features (Haxby and Gobbini 2011). This neural network includes the occipital face area, fusiform face area, and posterior superior temporal sulcus, which respond more strongly to images of faces than to images of objects and houses. Relative to neutral expressions, emotional facial expressions (e.g., fear or sadness) evoke stronger responses in the latter two brain regions. Responses in these brain regions also decrease to repeated presentations of faces with the same identity, suggesting that both the fusiform face area and posterior superior temporal sulcus contribute to coding of facial expressions and face identity. The intraparietal sulcus shows responses specifically to eye gaze, which delivers useful information during social interactions. Perception of personal familiar faces also engages modulations of brain activity in the temporoparietal junction, posterior cingulate, and medial prefrontal cortex.

Cultural differences in the processing of face and facial expression are manifested in both the neurocognitive strategy of face perception and distinct neurocognitive processes of culturally familiar and unfamiliar faces/expressions. One technique that has allowed researchers to infer the neurocognitive processes of faces is to track eye movements during face perception. By recording sequences of eye fixations (e.g., trajectory and duration), which describe the way in which overt visual attention is directed and which aspects of the face are focused on, one can examine whether people with different cultural experiences employ the same neurocognitive strategy during face perception. In a series of studies, Caldara and colleagues compared the patterns of eye movements during face perception between Westerners and East Asians. In one study, Blais et al. (2008) presented Western Caucasian and East Asian participants with images of 56 Caucasian and 56 Asian neutral faces of the size of a real face and asked them to learn, recognize, and categorize these faces by race. Each face was randomly presented at one of four locations of a computer screen for 5 seconds during learning and stayed on the screen until participants responded during recognition. The movements of the dominant eye were monitored using an eye-tracking system with a resolution of 1 arc minute during the learning and recognition stages of the face-recognition task and the subsequent face categorization by race task. Previous studies have shown that Westerners exhibited a triangular "scanpath" of eye movements by landing their fixations primarily on the eyes and mouth during face learning and recognition. This finding led to the presumption that the triangular scanpath represented a culturally universal efficient strategy of eye movements during face perception (Groner et al. 1984; Henderson et al. 2005). Blais et al. (2008), however, found a striking cultural difference in eye-movement trajectory during face learning and recognition tasks. Western Caucasian observers consistently fixated the eye region, and partially the mouth, whereas East Asian observers fixated more on the central region of the face (i.e., the nose) (Figure 5.1). The pattern of cultural-group differences in fixation trajectory was evident regardless of whether participants viewed same-race or other-race faces, suggesting the existence of culturally specific strategies of face processing independent of social identify of perceived faces. Blais et al. (2008) also tested how participants recognized learned faces and found that both Western and East Asian participants reported better recognition of same-race compared with other-race faces, replicating the well-known phenomenon

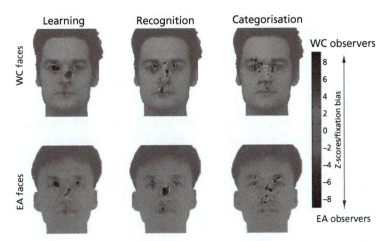

Figure 5.1 Fixation biases for Western Caucasian and East Asian observers. Cultural group differences in fixation biases are highlighted by subtracting Western Caucasian and East Asian Z-scored fixation distribution maps during face learning, recognition, and categorization by race. (See colour plate.)

Reproduced from Caroline Blais, Rachael E. Jack, Christoph Scheepers, Daniel Fiset, and Roberto Caldara, Culture Shapes How We Look at Faces, *PLoS ONE*, 3 (8), e3022, DOI:10.1371/journal. pone.0003022, © 2008 Blais et al.

termed "the other-race effect" during face recognition (Malpass and Kravitz 1969). Blais et al.'s (2008) findings are intriguing in that they suggest that people from different cultures may employ distinct perceptual strategies as reflected in the scanpath, by either focusing on the eye or nose, during face perception, and this seems not to influence the advantage in recognizing same-race faces.

Further research revealed that the cultural difference in eye trajectory during face perception was evident in children aged 7–12 years of age (Kelly et al. 2011). During a training session, participants were shown four examples of real-size faces to familiarize themselves with the stimuli. They were then monitored in a learning session that required the children to learn a series of face images that would be subsequently tested during the recognition phase. Each face was presented for 5 seconds during the learning phase but was presented until the participant made a key press response in the recognition phase. As with the adults, the pattern of eye movements was characterized with a triangular scanpath that covered the eyes and mouth in Western children but with a focus on the region around the nose in East Asian children, suggesting that cultural forces may indeed be responsible for shaping eye movements from early childhood. These findings, however, do not necessarily imply that there is no culturally universal pattern of eye movements during face perception. A study that focused on the first gaze location for face identification found that the first fixation for both East Asian and Western Caucasian adults landed at a featureless point between the eyes and the nose during perception of either Caucasian and Asian faces (Or et al. 2015). The initial fixation is fundamental in the acquisition of most of the information for face identification and thus is less influenced by cultural experiences.

As mentioned in Chapter 3, East Asian and Western cultures respectively foster a holistic cognitive strategy that facilitates the processing of global and contextual information and an analytic cognitive strategy that expedites the processing of local information and salient objects. Do the different patterns of eye-movement trajectory observed in East Asians and Westerners influence the processing of global and local information of faces? Miellet et al. (2013) examined this issue by developing a gaze-contingent technique called the Expanding Spotlight. East Asian and Western Caucasian adults were presented with faces during a learning phase to learn face identity. After a 30 second pause, a series of faces (half new and half old) were presented, and participants had to judge whether each face had been presented in the learning phase. At this stage, each face was masked with a Gaussian aperture centered on the participant's fixation location so that the facial information corresponding to face identity was available only inside the Gaussian aperture. The Gaussian aperture was limited to 2° for each new fixation and dynamically expanded with time (1° every 25 ms). It was assumed that, if the Expanding Spotlight hypothesis were correct, observers would maintain a fixation to a given location until they had obtained sufficient foveal and extrafoveal information from that location to solve the task. The fixation maps replicated the previous observations by showing the central bias for East Asians and eye-mouth bias for Westerners. More interestingly, Miellet et al. reconstructed the visual information of facial stimuli in the frequency domain (e.g., in the high- vs. low-frequency band) in each cultural group. These data showed that Western participants used local high-spatial-frequency information sampling, covering all of the features critical for effective face recognition (the eyes and the mouth) whereas East Asian participants achieved a similar result by using global low-spatial-frequency information from those same facial features. Both behavioral and brain imaging studies have suggested that global or contextual information is mediated via the low-spatial-frequency channel and local or detailed information is delivered via the high-spatial-frequency channel during visual perception (Han et al. 2003; Hughes et al. 1996; Jiang and Han 2005; Shulman et al. 1986). Thus Miellet et al.'s findings indicate that, during face perception, preference for holistic or analytic processing also differentiates the neurocognitive strategies in East Asians and Westerners who utilize local and global information for face recognition, respectively.

Facial expression

Humans deliver nonverbal social information during social interactions by facial expressions, which result from changing the positions of the muscles beneath the skin of the face. Facial expressions are used to express one's feelings, positive or negative, which can be quickly apparent so that others can make decisions on whether to approach or withdraw during social interactions. It is believed that similar muscle movements are engaged across cultures to show basic expressions such as happiness, sadness, anger, fear, surprise, and disgust (e.g., Ekman et al. 1987). However, this does not necessarily mean that people from different cultures perceive and understand these facial expressions in the same way. A meta-analysis of published studies indicates that the percentage of observers who selected the predicted labels of facial expressions varied greatly across cultures (Nelson and Russell 2013). Quantitative analyses of facial expressions also revealed that Westerners represent each of the six basic emotions with a distinct set of facial movements common to the group, whereas Easterners do not (Jack et al. 2012). Further, Easterners represent emotional intensity with distinctive dynamic eye activity. These findings raise two major questions regarding cultural differences in neural processes of facial expressions, that is, are there culturally specific strategies for decoding facial expressions and are there distinct neural mechanisms underlying the processing of expression of culturally familiar and unfamiliar faces?

To address the first question, Jack et al. (2009) recorded the scanpath from Western Caucasian and East Asian observers when they viewed same-race or other-race faces and had to classify these faces into different facial expression categories (i.e., happiness, surprise, fear, disgust, anger, sadness, or neutral). East Asian observers made greater numbers of errors when categorizing the expression of "disgust" compared with Western observers who performed with high accuracy for all the facial expressions. The two cultural groups also exhibited different patterns of eye movements during the expression categorization task. East Asian participants persistently fixated the eye region of facial stimuli, whereas Western participants distributed their fixations evenly across the face. It appears that the strategy adopted by Eastern observers made them focus more narrowly and made it difficult to distinguish between the negative emotions (e.g., disgust, fear, and surprise).

Eye-movement patterns also suggest that Chinese compared with Americans are more easily influenced by contextual facial expressions. Stanley et al. (2013) recorded fixation trajectories during emotion judgments of a target face surrounded by four faces with expressions that were the same or different from the expression of the target face. According to the proposition of dominant holistic or analytic cognitive styles in East Asian and Western cultures, one would expect Americans relative to Chinese participants to be less influenced by contextual information. Indeed, the behavioral performances indicated that Americans were more accurate than Chinese participants were in recognizing emotions embedded in the context of other emotional expressions. Eye-tracking data showed that, relative to the Chinese, Americans attended more to the target faces and made more gaze transitions to the target face, suggesting that they were more likely to treat the target face as independent from the contextual faces in the display during categorization of facial expressions. The neural mechanisms mediating cultural differences in contextual influences on the processing of facial expressions were examined by recording ERPs to a central target face that was surrounded by other faces (Russell et al. 2015). The target and surrounding faces showed the same emotion (e.g., all were happy or sad) or different emotions (e.g., a happy target surrounded by sad faces). Japanese and European Canadian participants were asked to rate the intensity of emotions of the central target face while ignoring the surrounding faces. The data analyses focused on two ERP components, that is, the N400 and the late positive complex (LPC). The N400 can be elicited when a perceived object is shown on a semantically incongruent compared with a congruent background (Goto et al. 2010), and it is believed to be sensitive to contextual information. The LPC is a positive activity over the parietal cortex that usually begins around 500 ms after sensory stimulation, and its amplitude is larger in response to affective incongruent stimuli than to congruent stimuli. If, relative to European Canadians, Japanese participants are more sensitive to facial expressions of the surrounding faces, they should show larger N400 and LPC when the facial expressions of the target and surrounding faces were incongruent than when they were congruent. Indeed, Russell et al. (2015) found that this was the case. Japanese participants exhibited larger amplitudes of the N400 (at 350–500 ms) and LPC (at 500–700 ms) in the incongruent than in the congruent conditions, whereas European Canadian participants did not show differences in the N400 and LPC amplitudes between the two conditions. These findings suggest potential neural mechanisms underlying enhanced processing of facial expressions that serve as a social context during social interactions in Japanese persons.

Distinct neural strategies in the processing of facial expressions in East Asian and Western cultures were further examined in an fMRI study that focused on neural responses during evaluations of facial expressions in terms of arousal (Park et al. 2015). As mentioned earlier in Chapter 1, how people want to feel ("ideal affect") varies significantly across cultures, as European Americans value high-arousal positive affect (e.g., excitement) whereas Chinese prefer low-arousal positive affect (e.g., calm) (Tsai et al. 2006). In addition, European

Americans report valuing high- and low-arousal positive states similarly, whereas the Chinese report valuing low-arousal positive states more than high-arousal positive states. It is thus proposed that European Americans might find excited facial expressions more rewarding than calm facial expressions, whereas the Chinese might show a reverse effect. This proposition was verified by examining cultural differences in neural responses to high- and low-arousal facial expressions (Park et al. 2015). The reward-related neural circuit identified in both humans and animals consists of both cortical (e.g., the orbitofrontal cortex and ventral medial prefrontal cortex) and subcortical (e.g., the ventral striatum, caudate, amygdala) structures that show increased responses to various kinds of rewards (O'Doherty 2004). The cortical and subcortical parts of the reward network play different roles in mediating the reward value. The orbitofrontal and medial prefrontal cortices are engaged in coding the reward value of perceived stimuli, which, together with the amygdala and ventral striatum, also respond to predictors of reward. Park and colleagues (2015) scanned European American and Chinese female adults using fMRI when they viewed and rated faces that varied by expression (excited, calm), ethnicity (White, Asian), and gender (male, female). This design allowed comparison of neural responses of different cultural groups to expressions with high and low arousal. It was found that the European Americans showed greater activity in the bilateral ventral striatum and left caudate while viewing excited (vs. calm) expressions relative to the Chinese. Within cultures, the Chinese showed greater activity in the medial prefrontal cortex in response to Asian calm (vs. excited) expressions, whereas European Americans showed comparable medial prefrontal activity and greater superior frontal activity in response to excited (vs. calm) expressions. Across cultural groups, greater ventral striatal activity while viewing faces predicted greater preference for excited versus calm expressions months later. These findings help to clarify the neural strategy that mediates cultural preference for high- versus low-arousal positive affect. It seems that viewing culturally preferred expressions in European Americans (i.e., exited) activated the subcortical reward system (e.g., ventral striatum), which may coordinate with the cortical system (e.g., superior frontal activity) to generate predictions of an upcoming reward following the stimuli. The Chinese, however, might intend to code the value of culturally preferred expressions (i.e., calm) during perception. Thus, culturally preferred expressions in Chinese and European Americans are mediated by distinct neural underpinnings.

The neural mechanisms underlying the processing of expression of culturally familiar and unfamiliar faces have been tackled by examining neural responses to expressions of same-race and other-race faces. Race is a dynamic set of historically derived and institutionalized ideas, shared by most human societies, which sorts people into ethnic groups according to perceived physical and behavioral human characteristics (Moya and Markus 2011). Although studies using genetic cluster analysis have found correlations between self-reported racial group membership and the genetic cluster of racial groups (Paschou et al. 2010), race is essentially a sociocultural construction that emerges when groups are perceived to pose a threat (political, economic, or cultural) to each other's world view or way of life. A common and fundamental belief in most human societies is that same-race and other-race individuals are perceived as being socially in-group and out-group members, respectively. This cultural world-view has particular sociopolitical implications for understanding facial expressions for same-race and other-race faces.

For example, relative to other-race fear expressions, same-race fear expressions can signal risk or threat when confronted by an in-group member and thus can warn an observer of a dangerous situation. This may lead to greater sensitivity to same-race compared with other-race fear expressions. Chiao et al. (2008) had Japanese in Japan and Caucasians in the United States view Asian and Caucasian faces with neural, happy, fearful, and angry expressions. Participants underwent fMRI scanning while they categorized the perceived faces into the four categories in the light of facial expressions. The fMRI results replicated the early brain imaging finding that fearful compared with neutral expressions activated the amygdala (Whalen et al. 1998), indicating that the amygdala plays a key role in an adaptive function as an early warning mechanism. However, the amygdala activity was strongly modulated by the relationship in race between the observers and perceived faces. For both Japanese and Caucasian participants, the amygdala activity was stronger in response to fearful expressions of same-race relative to other-race faces. The effect was not observed for neutral, happy, and angry expressions. It was suggested that individuals' experiences with and exposure to particular sets of facial expressions of fear during development causes the amygdala to optimally respond to facial configurations of fear specific to one's own cultural group by adulthood.

Similarly, pain expressions of same-race faces, which are perceived as in-group members, can signal the demand of social support and thus induce stronger brain responses compared with those of other-race faces. In a series of studies, Han and colleagues showed evidence for distinct brain responses to pain expressions of same-race and other-race faces (Sheng and Han 2012; Sheng et al. 2014; Sheng et al. 2016). Sheng and Han (2012) recorded ERPs to pain and neutral expressions of Asian and Caucasian models from Chinese adults who were asked to make judgments on ethnicity (Asian vs. Caucasian) of each model. This judgment task drew observers' attention to the feature of perceived faces that stressed the in-group/out-group relationship between the observers and perceived faces. Both Asian and Caucasian faces evoked a positive neural response at 128–188 ms after stimulus onset over the frontal/central brain regions (i.e., P2 component). Source estimation using low-resolution brain electromagnetic tomography (Pascual-Marqui et al. 2002), a linear method of computing statistical maps from EEG data that reveal the locations of the underlying source processes, suggested that the P2 might arise from the anterior cingulate cortex. There were two interesting findings regarding modulations of the P2 amplitude by pain versus neutral expressions. First, the P2 amplitude over the frontal lobe was enlarged in response to pain compared with neutral expressions. Second, the increased P2 amplitude to pain versus neutral expressions was found when Chinese participants viewed Asian faces but not Caucasian faces (Figure 5.2). This indicated greater neural responses in the anterior cingulate cortex to the pain expression of culturally familiar faces. Third, the increased P2 amplitude to pain versus neutral expressions positively predicted self-reported unpleasantness induced by pain expressions, suggesting the frontal activity in the P2 time window as a neural underpinning of the affective link (e.g., sharing) between the observer and same-race faces. The ERP findings were further confirmed in a following fMRI study that employed the same stimuli and procedure (Sheng et al. 2014). It was found that pain compared with neutral expressions induced stronger activations in the anterior cingulate cortex in Chinese adults when viewing Asian rather than Caucasian faces. The ERP and fMRI findings consistently suggest modulations of neural responses to pain expressions of culturally familiar and unfamiliar faces.

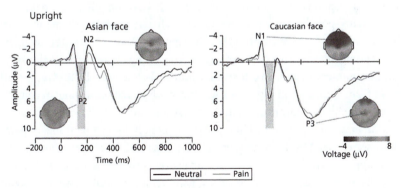

Figure 5.2 ERPs in response to Asian and Caucasian faces with pain and neutral expressions recorded from Chinese participants. (See colour plate.)

Reprinted from *NeuroImage*, 61 (4), Feng Sheng and Shihui Han, Manipulations of cognitive strategies and intergroup relationships reduce the racial bias in empathic neural responses, pp. 786–97, DOI:10.1016/j.neuroimage.2012.04.028, Copyright © 2012 Elsevier Inc., with permission from Elsevier.

The increased neural responses to same-race pain expressions show how racial in-group members' feelings of suffering can facilitate social support. However, perceiving other-race individuals as out-group members can weaken brain responses to their pain expressions.

From a development perspective, infants usually start to recognize the pain expressions of caregivers such as parents who are, in most cases, of the same race, and do not have opportunities to perceive pain expressions of other-race individuals until a late stage of development. Because the function of neurons is strongly modulated by personal experiences, the different time course of exposure to same-race and other-race facial expressions allows one to speculate on the possibility that there are distinct neuronal populations that respectively respond to facial expressions of culturally familiar and unfamiliar faces. This hypothesis was tested in an ERP study that examined the suppression of neural activity in response to pain expressions during repetitive presentations of same-race faces (Sheng et al. 2016). Repetition suppression refers to the relative attenuation of neural responses to repeated occurrence of a stimulus (Henson et al. 2004). It is commonly acknowledged that the repetition suppression of neural activity elicited by two successive stimuli indicates the engagement of an overlapping neuronal population in the processing of both stimuli (Grill-Spector et al. 2006). There are two competitive hypotheses regarding neuronal populations engaged in responses to pain expression of same-race and other-race faces. The distinct-population hypothesis suggests that different neuronal populations are recruited to code painful emotional states of own-race and other-race individuals, respectively, and the neuronal population coding own-race pain responds more strongly relative to that coding other-race pain. The overlapping-population hypothesis predicts shared modules for the processing of both own-race and other-race pain expressions, which therefore suggests overlapping neuronal populations engaged in coding own-race and other-race painful emotional states. To clarify these proposals, Sheng et al. (2016) recorded ERPs from Chinese and European/American white adults viewing an adaptor face (with either a painful or neutral expression) and a target face (with only a painful expression) presented in rapid succession. If distinct neuronal populations are engaged in the coding of pain expressions of different races, repetition suppression of neural activity to pain expressions, that is, decreased neural responses to target faces preceded by pain versus neutral adaptors, should occur when an adaptor and a target are of the same race but not when they are of different races. Sheng et al. (2016) first replicated their previous findings that the P2 amplitude over the frontocentral region was enhanced by pain compared with neutral expressions and this effect was more salient for same-race than other-race faces. In addition, they found that the P2 amplitude in response

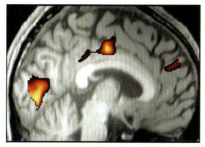 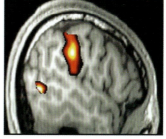

Culturally familiar > unfamiliar gestures   Culturally unfamiliar > familiar gestures

Figure 2.2 Illustrations of brain regions activated by perceiving culturally familiar and unfamiliar gestures. Culturally familiar compared with unfamiliar gestures more strongly activated brain regions associated with mentalizing, including the posterior cingulate cortex, dorsal medial prefrontal cortex, and bilateral temporal-parietal junctions. In contrast, culturally unfamiliar compared with familiar gestures more strongly activated regions in the mirror neuron system, including the left inferior parietal lobe and left postcentral gyrus.

Adapted from Sook-Lei Liew, Shihui Han, and Lisa Aziz-Zadeh, Familiarity modulates mirror neuron and mentalizing regions during intention understanding, *Human Brain Mapping*, 32 (11), pp. 1986–1997, DOI: 10.1002/hbm.21164 Copyright © 2010 Wiley-Liss, Inc.

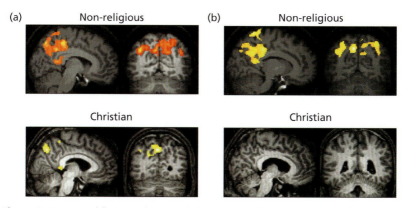

(a) Non-religious   (b) Non-religious

Christian   Christian

Figure 2.4 Increased functional connectivity between the medial prefrontal cortex and posterior cingulate cortex/precuneus during trait judgments of the government leader (A) and Jesus (B) (versus the self). Christian and non-religious participants were different in the functional connectivity between the medial prefrontal cortex and posterior cingulate cortex/precuneus during trait judgments of Jesus compared with the self.

Adapted from Jianqiao Ge, Xiaosi Gu, Meng Ji, and Shihui Han, Neurocognitive processes of the religious leader in Christians, *Human Brain Mapping*, 30 (12), pp. 4012–4024, DOI: 10.1002/hbm.20825 Copyright © 2009 Wiley-Liss, Inc.

(a)

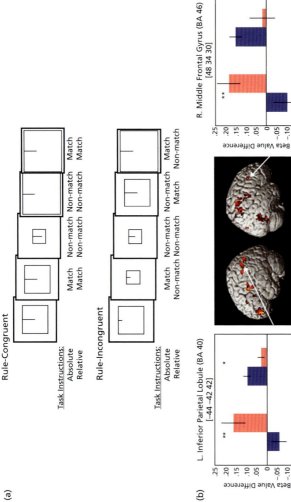

Rule-Congruent

Task Instructions:
Absolute   Match   Non-match   Non-match   Match
Relative   Match   Non-match   Non-match   Match

Rule-Incongruent

Task Instructions:
Absolute   Match   Non-match   Non-match   Match
Relative   Non-match   Non-match   Match   Non-match

(b)

L. Inferior Parietal Lobule (BA 40)
[−44 −42 42]

R. Middle Frontal Gyrus (BA 46)
[48 34 30]

Americans   East Asians

Figure 3.3 (A) Illustration of the stimuli used in the relative and absolute tasks. Participants had to judge whether the length of a vertical line inside a box matched the length of a previously shown line regardless of the size of the box (a context-independent [absolute] judgment task), or whether the box–line combination of each stimulus matched the proportional scaling of the preceding combination (a context-dependent [relative] judgment task). (B) Illustration of fMRI results. Frontoparietal activation associated with judgment tasks in Americans and East Asians. The frontoparietal activity was greater in East Asians (red bars) than in Americans (yellow bars) in the context-independent (absolute) judgment, whereas a reverse pattern was observed in the context-dependent (relative) judgment task.

Adapted from Trey Hedden, Sarah Ketay, Arthur Aron, Hazel Rose Markus, and John D.E. Gabrieli, *Psychological Science*, 19 (1), pp. 12–17, DOI:10.1111/j.1467-9280.2008.02038.x Copyright © 2008, © SAGE Publications. Adapted with permission from SAGE Publications, Inc.

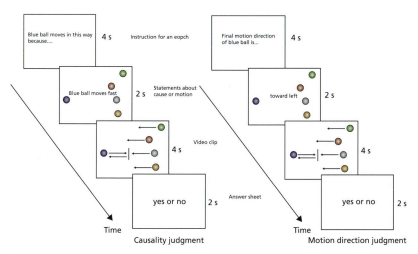

Figure 3.4 Illustration of the stimuli used in the causality and direction judgment tasks.

Adapted from *Neuropsychologia*, 49 (1), Shihui Han, Lihua Mao, Jungang Qin, Angela D. Friederici, and Jianqiao Ge, Functional roles and cultural modulations of the medial prefrontal and parietal activity associated with causal attribution, pp. 83–91, DOI:10.1016/j.neuropsychologia.2010.11.003 Copyright © 2010 Elsevier Ltd., with permission from Elsevier.

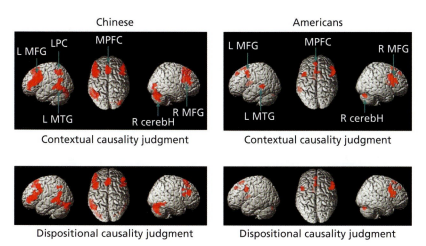

Figure 3.5 Brain activations during the causality and direction judgment tasks in Chinese and American participants.

Adapted from *Neuropsychologia*, 49 (1), Shihui Han, Lihua Mao, Jungang Qin, Angela D. Friederici, and Jianqiao Ge, Functional roles and cultural modulations of the medial prefrontal and parietal activity associated with causal attribution, pp. 83–91, DOI:10.1016/j.neuropsychologia.2010.11.003 Copyright © 2010 Elsevier Ltd., with permission from Elsevier.

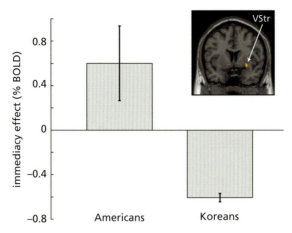

Figure 3.6 Brain activity in the VStr associated with reward processing was greater in Americans than in Korean participants when choices involved an immediate reward compared with choices involving only delayed rewards.

Adapted from Bokyung Kim, Young Shin Sung, and Samuel M. McClure, *Philosophical Transactions of the Royal Society B: Biological Sciences*, 367 (1589), pp. 650–656, Figures 3b and 4, DOI:10.1098/rstb.2011.0292 Copyright © 2012 The Royal Society.

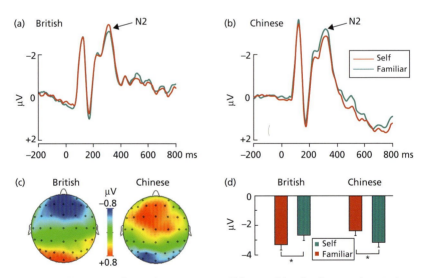

Figure 4.3 Illustration of neural responses to self-face and familiar faces in the British and Chinese sample. The N2 was enlarged to self-face relative to familiar face in British subjects (a) but was of smaller amplitudes to own face than familiar faces for the Chinese (b). Top views of voltage topographies of N2 difference between self-faces and familiar faces from the British and Chinese are shown separately in (c). Difference waves between self-faces and familiar faces were computed at all electrode positions. The mean amplitude of N2 from the British and Chinese at Fz is shown in (d).

Adapted from Jie Sui, ChangHong Liu, and Shihui Han, *Social Neuroscience*, 4 (5), pp. 402–411, DOI: org/10.1080/17470910802674825, Copyright © 2009 Routledge http://www.informaworld.com.

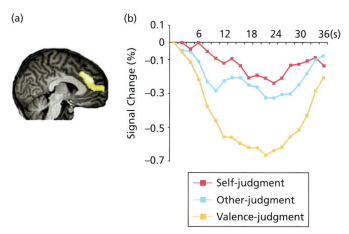

Figure 4.4 Illustration of brain activation in association with self-reflection. (a) The contrast of self- vs. celebrity-judgments on personality traits activated the medial prefrontal cortex. (b) BOLD signals during different judgment tasks.

Adapted from Yina Ma and Shihui Han, Neural representation of self-concept in sighted and congenitally blind adults, *Brain*, 134 (1), pp. 235–46, Figure 2b and 2c, DOI: http://dx.doi.org/10.1093/brain/awq299, Copyright ©2011, © The Author (2010). Published by Oxford University Press on behalf of the Guarantors of Brain. All rights reserved.

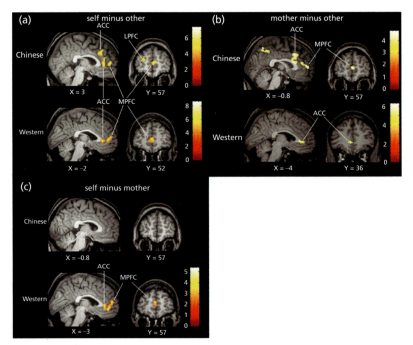

Figure 4.5 Cultural differences in MPFC activations during trait judgments of one's mother. (a) Judgments of the self relative to a celebrity activated the MPFC in both Chinese and Westerners. (b) Judgments of one's mother relative to a celebrity activated the MPFC only Chinese participants. (c) Judgments of the self relative to mother activated the MPFC in Westerners but not in Chinese.

Reprinted from *NeuroImage*, 34 (3), Ying Zhu, Li Zhang, Jin Fan, and Shihui Han, Neural basis of cultural influence on self-representation, pp. 1310–16, DOI:10.1016/j. neuroimage.2006.08.047, Copyright © 2006 Elsevier Inc., with permission from Elsevier.

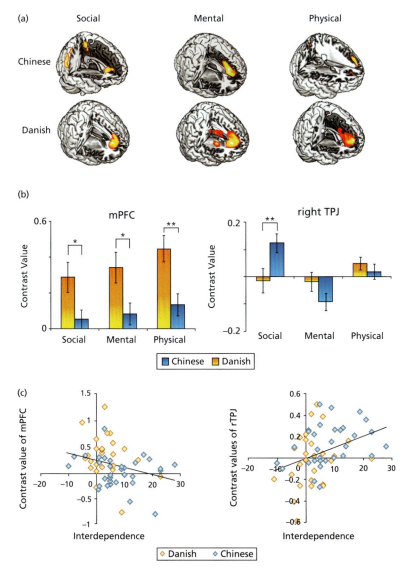

Figure 4.6 (A) Whole-brain analyses revealed greater activity in the MPFC in Danes than in Chinese during self-reflection, whereas Chinese participants showed stronger activity in the TPJ during reflection of one's social roles. (B) The contrast values from the MPFC and TPJ in the cultural groups. (C) The correlation between interdependence and MPFC/TPJ activity associated with self-reflection.

Adapted from Yina Ma, Dan Bang, Chenbo Wang, Micah Allen, Chris Frith, Andreas Roepstorff, and Shihui Han, Sociocultural patterning of neural activity during self-reflection, *Social Cognitive and Affective Neuroscience*, 9 (1), pp. 73–80, Figures 2a and b, 1a and b, and 4b and c, DOI: 10.1093/scan/nss103, Copyright © 2014, Oxford University Press.

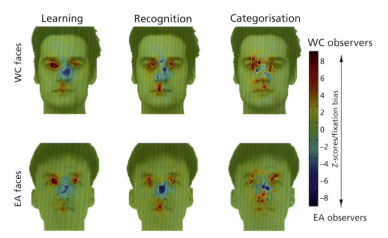

Figure 5.1 Fixation biases for Western Caucasian and East Asian observers. Cultural group differences in fixation biases are highlighted by subtracting Western Caucasian and East Asian Z-scored fixation distribution maps during face learning, recognition, and categorization by race.

Reproduced from Caroline Blais, Rachael E. Jack, Christoph Scheepers, Daniel Fiset, and Roberto Caldara, Culture Shapes How We Look at Faces, *PLoS ONE*, 3 (8), e3022, DOI:10.1371/journal.pone.0003022, © 2008 Blais et al.

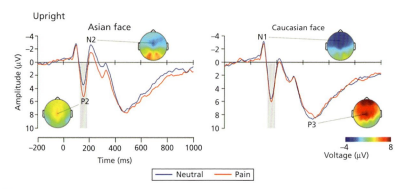

Figure 5.2 ERPs in response to Asian and Caucasian faces with pain and neutral expressions recorded from Chinese participants.

Reprinted from *NeuroImage*, 61 (4), Feng Sheng and Shihui Han, Manipulations of cognitive strategies and intergroup relationships reduce the racial bias in empathic neural responses, pp. 786–97, DOI:10.1016/j.neuroimage.2012.04.028, Copyright © 2012 Elsevier Inc., with permission from Elsevier.

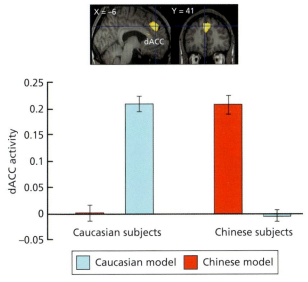

Figure 5.3 Increased brain response to perceived pain in culturally in-group (same-race) and out-group (other-race) individuals. The upper panel illustrates the dACC where BOLD signals were extracted. The lower panel shows the amplitude of BOLD signals in response to perceived painful stimuli applied to same-race and other-race models.

Adapted from Xiaojing Xu, Xiangyu Zuo, Xiaoying Wang, and Shihui Han, Do You Feel My Pain? Racial Group Membership Modulates Empathic Neural Responses, *The Journal of Neuroscience*, 29 (26), pp. 8525–8529, Figure 1c, d, and f, DOI: 10.1523/JNEUROSCI.2418-09.2009 © 2009, The Society for Neuroscience.

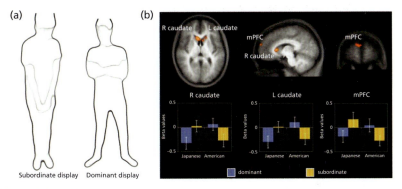

Figure 5.4 (A) Illustration of cartoons showing gestures of either dominance or subordination. (B) Cultural group differences in brain activities in response to cartoons of dominant and subordinate gestures.

Reprinted from *NeuroImage*, 47 (1), Jonathan B. Freeman, Nicholas O. Rule, Reginald B. Adams Jr., and Nalini Ambady, Culture shapes a mesolimbic response to signals of dominance and subordination that associates with behavior, pp. 353–9, DOI:10.1016/j.neuroimage.2009.04.038, Copyright © 2009 Elsevier Inc., with permission from Elsevier.

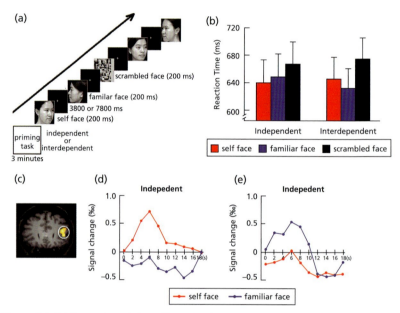

Figure 6.1 (A) Illustration of the self-construal priming procedure and the face-recognition task. After the self-construal priming task, participants were scanned while being presented with their own face, a familiar face, and scrambled faces, and had to indicate the head orientation of the intact faces and the location of the gray bar next to the scrambled faces by pressing a button with the right index or middle finger. (B) Mean reaction times to self-face, familiar faces, and scrambled faces. (C) Illustration of the right frontal activation in association with self-face. (D) The time courses of the BOLD signals in the right middle frontal cortex after the independent self-construal priming. (E) BOLD signal in the right middle frontal cortex after the interdependent self-construal priming.

Adapted from Jie Sui and Shihui Han, Self-Construal Priming Modulates Neural Substrates of Self-Awareness, *Psychological Science*, 18 (10), pp. 861–866, DOI:10.1111/j.1467-9280.2007.01992.x, Copyright © 2007, © SAGE Publications. Adapted with permission from SAGE Publications, Inc.

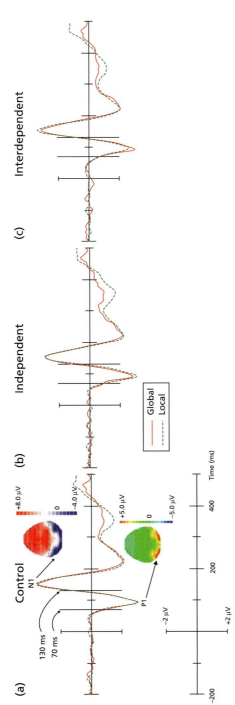

Figure 6.2 Illustration of the variation of P1 amplitude in response to global and local targets of compound visual stimuli after independent and interdependent self-construal priming.

Adapted from *Biological Psychology*, 77 (1), Zhicheng Lin, Yan Lin, and Shihui Han, Self-construal priming modulates visual activity underlying global/local perception, pp. 93–7, DOI:10.1016/j.biopsycho.2007.08.002, Copyright © 2007 Elsevier B.V., with permission from Elsevier.

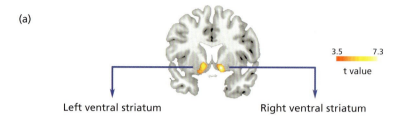

(a)

3.5   7.3
t value

Left ventral striatum   Right ventral striatum

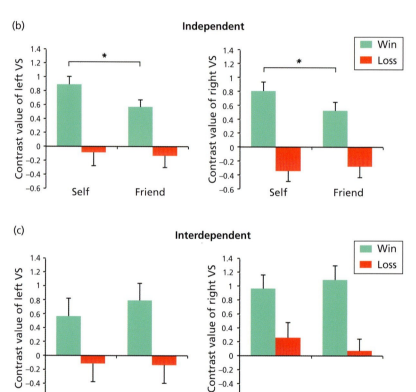

(b)   **Independent**

(c)   **Interdependent**

Figure 6.4 Modulation of reward activity in the ventral striatum in response to winning money by self-construal priming. The upper panel illustrates the reward activity in the ventral striatum. The middle and lower panels show BOLD responses to one's own and a friend's reward. The reward activity to one's own reward was stronger than that to a friend's reward after independent self-construal priming, whereas interdependent self-construal priming tended to produce an opposite pattern. Adapted from *NeuroImage*, 87 (1), Michael E.W. Varnum, Zhenhao Shi, Antao Chen, Jiang Qiu, and Shihui Han, When "Your" reward is the same as "My" reward: Self-construal priming shifts neural responses to own vs. friends' rewards, pp. 164–9, DOI:10.1016/j.neuroimage.2013.10.042, Copyright © 2013 Elsevier Inc., with permission from Elsevier.

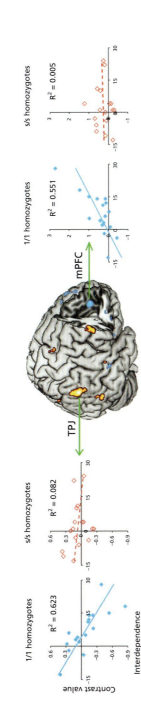

Figure 7.1 Illustration of the interaction between interdependence and 5-HTTLPR on brain activity involved in reflection of one's own personality traits. The middle panel illustrates the TPJ and mPFC in which the neural activity showed significant gene-interdependence interactions in the hierarchical regression analyses. Long/long but not short/short allele carriers showed significant associations between brain activity and interdependence.

Adapted from Yina Ma, Dan Bang, Chenbo Wang, Micah Allen, Chris Frith, Andreas Roepstorff, and Shihui Han, Sociocultural patterning of neural activity during self-reflection, *Social Cognitive and Affective Neuroscience*, 9 (1), pp. 73–80, DOI: 10.1093/scan/nss103, Copyright © 2014, Oxford University Press.

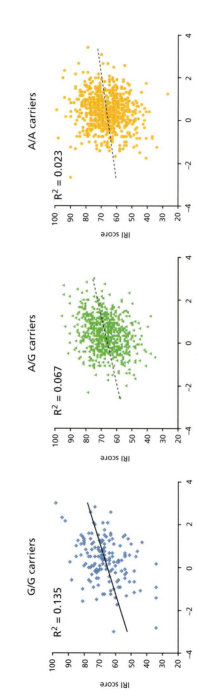

Figure 7.2 Illustration of the interaction between interdependence and OXTR rs53576 on empathy ability in a cohort of Chinese adults. There was stronger coupling between interdependence and empathy ability indexed by the IRI scores in G/G than in A carriers.

Adapted from Siyang Luo, Yina Ma, Yi Liu, Bingfeng Li, Chenbo Wang, Zhenhao Shi, Xiaoyang Li, Wenxia Zhang, Yi Rao, and Shihui Han, Interaction between oxytocin receptor polymorphism and interdependent culture values on human empathy, *Social Cognitive and Affective Neuroscience*, 10 (9), pp. 1273–1281, Figure 1a, DOI: 10.1093/scan/nsv019, Copyright © 2015, Oxford University Press.

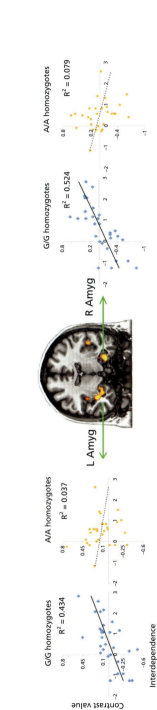

Figure 7.3 Illustration of the interaction between interdependence and OXTR rs53576 on amygdala responses to perceived pain in others in a cohort of Chinese adults. The scatter plots illustrate positive and negative associations between interdependence and amygdala activities in response to perceived pain in others in the two variants of OXTR rs53576.

Adapted from Siyang Luo, Yina Ma, Yi Liu, Bingfeng Li, Chenbo Wang, Zhenhao Shi, Xiaoyang Li, Wenxia Zhang, Yi Rao, and Shihui Han, Interaction between oxytocin receptor polymorphism and interdependent culture values on human empathy, *Social Cognitive and Affective Neuroscience*, 10 (9), pp. 1273–1281, Figure 2, DOI: 10.1093/scan/nsv019, Copyright © 2015, Oxford University Press.

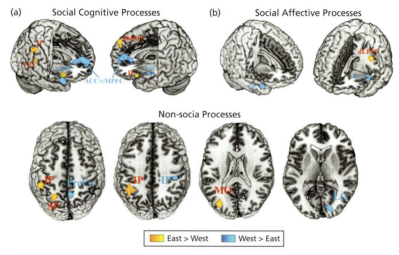

Figure 8.1 Illustration of East Asian vs. Western cultural differences in brain activity. Yellow-to-orange color shows brain regions that indicate stronger activity in East Asians compared to Westerners. Light-to-dark blue color shows brain regions that indicate stronger activity in the reverse comparison. (A) Cultural differences in brain activity involved in social cognitive processes during self-reflection, mentalizing, and moral judgment; (B) cultural differences in brain activity involved in social affective processes during empathy, emotion recognition, and reward; (C) cultural differences in brain activity involved in non-social processes during visual spatial or object processing, visual attention, arithmetic, and causal judgments on physical events. Adapted from *NeuroImage*, 99 (1), Shihui Han and Yina Ma, Cultural differences in human brain activity: A quantitative meta-analysis, pp. 293–300, DOI:10.1016/ j.neuroimage.2014.05.062, Copyright © 2014 Elsevier Inc. Published by Elsevier Inc., with permission from Elsevier.

to a target face with a painful expression was decreased when the target face was preceded by a painful versus neutral face, indicating repetition suppression of brain activity in response to the painful expressions. Most importantly, the repetition suppression of brain activity was evident when an adaptor and a target were of the same race but not when their racial identities differed. This effect was observed in both Chinese and Caucasian participants. These findings support the idea that, at least as a certain stage of neural processing of painful expressions, the human brain recruits distinct neuronal assemblies to code the painful expression of culturally familiar and unfamiliar faces.

Unlike neural responses to fear and pain expressions, human brain activity may be more sensitive to the anger expressions of other-race than same-race faces because a racial out-group member may implicate group conflict/aggression and possible harm toward an observer. This suggestion was tested by Krämer et al. (2014), with German participants who underwent fMRI scanning while watching short video sequences showing faces that displayed either a direct or averted gaze, expressed either anger or happiness, and represented either a cultural in-group (European faces) or a cultural out-group member (Asian faces). Krämer et al. found that when anger was expressed with averted gaze, participants showed more increased activity in the amygdala in response to cultural in-group compared with out-group members, replicating Chiao et al.'s (2008) findings. However, when anger was expressed with direct gaze, more activation was found in the dorsomedial and dorsolateral prefrontal cortices in response to cultural out-group compared with in-group members. Gaze direction also interacted with group relationship to modulate neural responses to happy expressions, but in a different fashion, that is, enhanced neural activation in the medial and lateral prefrontal cortical areas was associated with the processing of cultural in-group compared with out-group members expressing happiness with direct gaze. These findings can be reconciled by considering the distinct significance of gaze direction and expression of cultural in-group and out-group members. To be stared at by an angry face can make one uncomfortable or even scared because it signals a threat. Such a signal is more threatening if coming from an out-group than in-group member owing to its implication of group conflict that could bring more serious consequences relative to conflict between two individuals from the same social group. By contrast, a happy face with direct gaze delivers a friendly message that is more reliable when coming from an in-group than from an out-group member. Therefore, facing both an angry out-group member and a happy in-group member has novel social significance (risky or safe) and require an individual to further process the target's mental states, such as intention and desire, by recruiting the dorsomedial prefrontal cortex. Under both conditions, one may have to regulate his/her own emotional responses with the aid of the dorsolateral prefrontal cortex. Both systems, the dorsal medial and lateral prefrontal cortices, work together to guide a correct decision for one's own actions during social interactions with culturally familiar versus unfamiliar others.

Empathy

Empathy refers to the ability to understand and share the emotional states of conspecific others, and it has been proposed to play a fundamental role in appropriate social interactions. For instance, empathy for the suffering of another person can provide a proximate psychological mechanism mediating altruistic behavior (de Waal 2008; Batson 2009). To understand and to share another's painful emotion drives an individual to assist those who are in need of social support. However, people show different patterns of empathy for cultural in-group and out-group members. In a study to examine how defendant race and empathetic induction affect a subsequent juror decision-making task, Johnson et al. (2002) asked white university students to read a passage involving a black or a white defendant in a criminal case. Participants were then induced to feel empathy for the defendant and to make punishment judgments. It was found that participants reported greater empathy for and assigned more lenient punishments for the white than for the black defendant. Drwecki et al. (2011) also found that pro-white empathy biases to patients' pain expressions in white medical students and nursing professionals predicted their pro-white pain-treatment biases.

To explore the neural basis for the discrepant empathy for cultural in-group and out-group members' pain, Xu et al. (2009) scanned Chinese and European/American white participants using fMRI while they watched video clips showing Asian or white models who received painful (needle penetration) versus non-painful (cotton swab touch) stimulation. Participants had to make judgments as to whether or not the perceived model felt painful after receiving the needle penetration or a cotton swab touch. After fMRI scanning, participants were asked to rate how much pain a model in a video clip was feeling and how unpleasant participants were feeling when watching the video clips. Participants explicitly reported greater pain intensity and unpleasantness when watching a needle compared with a cotton swab applied to a model, and the self-report of the others' pain and one's own unpleasantness did not differ for same-race and other-face models in both cultural groups. The analysis of fMRI data indicated that watching painful (vs. non-painful) stimulations applied to culturally in-group faces significantly activated the anterior cingulate and the inferior frontal/insular cortex in both cultural groups. Nevertheless, the empathic neural response in the anterior cingulate decreased significantly when participants viewed faces of culturally out-group vs. in-group members (Figure 5. 3), and the decreased empathic neural responses in the anterior cingulate to the culturally out-group members was observed in both cultural groups. Similarly, Mathur et al. (2010) found that both European and African Americans showed increased activity in the medial prefrontal cortex in response to pain expressed by cultural in-group members. Moreover, the increased medial prefrontal activity predicted how an observer would like to help cultural in-group members to reduce their suffering. It is not surprising that explicit self-reports of subjective feelings were not enhanced for in-groups possibly because the dominant cultures in current societies discourage racial in-group bias in attitude and behavior. The brain imaging findings, however, revealed implicit distinctions in neural processes during the understanding and sharing of others' emotions, which may further influence social behavior during intergroup interactions.

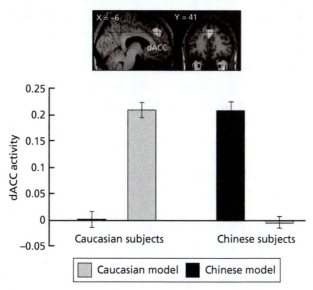

Figure 5.3 Decreased brain response to perceived pain in culturally out-group (other-race) and in-group (same-race) individuals. The upper panel illustrates the dACC where BOLD signals were extracted. The lower panel shows the amplitude of BOLD signals in response to perceived painful stimuli applied to same-race and other-race models. (See colour plate.)

Adapted from Xiaojing Xu, Xiangyu Zuo, Xiaoying Wang, and Shihui Han, Do You Feel My Pain? Racial Group Membership Modulates Empathic Neural Responses, *The Journal of Neuroscience*, 29 (26), pp. 8525–8529, Figure 1c, d, and f, DOI: 10.1523/JNEUROSCI.2418-09.2009, © 2009 The Society for Neuroscience.

Is the in-group bias in empathic neural responses inevitable? Can real-life cultural experiences change brain responses to same-race and other-race individuals' suffering to reduce the in-group bias? Zuo and Han (2013) tested the possibility that real-life cultural experiences with other-race individuals reduce culturally in-group biases in empathic neural responses by scanning 20 Chinese adults who were brought up in Western countries (the United States, the United Kingdom, and Canada) where the majority of the population is white. Participants viewed video clips in which either Asian or Western white models received painful (needle penetration) and non-painful (cotton swab touch) stimulations. It was expected that long-term sociocultural experiences with out-group members would weaken the in-group bias by increasing empathic neural responses to perceived pain in other-race individuals. Indeed, it was found that the neural activity in the pain matrix including the anterior cingulate cortex, anterior insula, inferior frontal cortex, and somatosensory cortex activation was significantly greater in response to painful compared with non-painful stimuli when applied to both Asian and Western white models. Moreover, these empathic neural responses to Asian and Western white models were equally strong and positively correlated with each other. Such results shed a new light on how sociocultural experiences can reduce culturally in-group favoritism in empathic neural responses by enhancing brain activity to out-group members' suffering.

Distinct neural strategies during empathy were also observed in other cultural groups. Cheon et al. (2011; 2013) required Korean and American participants inside an fMRI scanner to observe scenes depicting either Korean or white Americans in an emotionally painful (e.g., in the midst of a natural disaster) or neutral (e.g., attending an outdoor picnic) situation. Relative to white American participants, Korean participants reported experiencing greater empathy and elicited stronger activity in the left temporoparietal junction (a brain region associated with mental-state inference and perspective taking) for in-group compared with out-group members. Moreover, the value of focus on others (calculated on questionnaire measures) was associated with heightened neural responses within the anterior cingulate cortex and insula more so for the Korean participants than for the white American participants (Cheon et al. 2013). Such results suggest that collectivistic East Asian cultures induce a stronger tendency to take others' perspective when viewing others in pain and this tendency may in turn enhance one's emotional sharing with perceived suffering in cultural in-group members.

The influence of cultural experiences is not limited to empathy for pain. de Grez and colleagues (2012) reported brain imaging evidence for differences in empathic neural responses to anger between individualistic and collectivistic cultures. They found that Chinese compared with German adults, who were matched for age, gender, and education, described themselves as significantly more interdependent with significant others. During an intentional empathy task, participants were presented with the angry and neutral faces of culturally in-group (i.e., same-race) members and were asked to empathize intentionally the emotional state of each face. fMRI scanning revealed that the left dorsolateral prefrontal cortex had stronger hemodynamic responses in Chinese subjects during intentional empathy for angry faces. Germans, in contrast, showed stronger hemodynamic responses in the right temporoparietal junction, right inferior and superior temporal gyrus, and left middle insula during intentional empathy for angry faces. These brain imaging results are consistent with the idea that collectivistic cultures value harmony more than individualistic cultures do and thus encourage people such as the Chinese to regulate emotional responses when viewing others in anger. This function may be mediated by the dorsolateral prefrontal cortex that has been demonstrated in numerous brain imaging studies to be engaged in emotion regulation (Ochsner and Gross 2005). In contrast, empathy for anger in individualistic cultures may stress perceptual analyses of facial expressions in the right inferior and superior temporal gyrus and induce similar emotional responses in oneself mediated by the insula. Taken together, these brain imaging results demonstrate that the cultural beliefs of in-group/out-group social relationships influence how the brain responds during empathy for pain expressions. Cultural experiences also shape the neural strategy of perspective taking and emotion regulation in response to different types of facial expressions.

Emotion regulation

Because emotions are critical for guiding social interactions that may result in serious social consequences, how people regulate their own emotions in response to others has an important significance. Interestingly, strategies of emotion regulation vary greatly across cultures because of cultural differences in goals of social activity and interaction. For example, in a collectivistic society (e.g., China) that stresses the importance of positive mood and social peace within a group to achieve social harmony, anger is not encouraged, because this emotion obviously leads to social discord or conflict. Thus, the collectivistic culture makes strong demands of emotion regulation so that people do not express angry emotion easily and frequently. In a society that fosters individualistic culture and stresses the importance of an individual's uniqueness, such as the United States, the control of emotional expression is often considered undesirable and unhealthy, and thus, people are encouraged to disclose rather than control their feelings. Cultural preferences for low-arousal emotions (such as calmness and serenity) in collectivistic cultures also require frequent regulation of emotional responses, and the desirability of high-arousal emotions in individualistic cultures encourages the explicit expression of emotions (Tsai et al. 2006) and thus calls for less emotion regulation in daily life.

Numerous fMRI studies have shown that emotion regulation recruits specific brain regions that constitute a specific network in the frontal and parietal lobes (Etkin et al. 2015). Specifically, the left lateral prefrontal cortex and medial prefrontal cortex are activated during emotion regulation regardless of whether the goal is to increase or decrease emotion (Ochsner and Gross 2005). The right lateral prefrontal cortex and the orbital frontal cortex are engaged during emotion regulation particularly when the goal is to decrease negative emotion. The specific functional roles of these brain regions allow one to speculate that individuals from East Asian and Western cultures may employ the lateral prefrontal cortex to different degrees if the demands of emotion regulation vary in these cultures. A meta-analysis of the cultural differences in brain activity involved in social affective processes (e.g., empathy, emotion recognition, reward) showed stronger activity in the right dorsal lateral frontal cortex in East Asians but greater activity in the left insula and right temporal pole in Westerners (Han and Ma 2014). The cultural difference in the lateral frontal activity provides a possible neural mechanism that satisfies the demands of emotion regulation in East Asian cultural environments.

Murata et al. (2013) directly tested cultural differences in brain activity involved in emotion regulation by recording ERPs from Asian and European American participants. To assess the hypothesis that Asians are culturally trained to down-regulate emotional processing, whereas European Americans are unlikely to down-regulate emotional processing when required to suppress emotional expressions, the researchers focused on the parietal late positive potential (LPP), an ERP component of which the magnitude of the parietal LPP is correlated with subjective feelings of arousal of stimuli (Cuthbert et al. 2000) and self-reported intensity of emotions (Hajcak and Nieuwenhuis 2006). Murata et al. (2013) presented both Asian and European Americans with unpleasant pictures of mutilation and threat (human and animal) and neutral pictures (household items and neutral faces) for 4 seconds each. Participants were instructed to pay attention to the emotional responses that were naturally elicited by the picture, or to minimize and hide the emotional responses that were naturally elicited by the picture. If Asian Americans had been trained to down-regulate their negative emotions, the LPP amplitudes that were elicited by unpleasant pictures and indexed emotional responses should be reduced when participants tried to suppress their emotions. However, European Americans were not expected to show similar LPP amplitude changes because they had not been trained to regulate emotional processing in the same way. Indeed, while both cultural groups exhibited a parietal LPP at about 600 ms post-stimulus, Asian American participants subsequently showed a significant decrease of the LPP amplitude during emotion suppression than they did when paying attention to the emotional responses that were naturally elicited by the picture. As expected, European Americans did not show evidence for modulation of the LPP amplitude by suppression versus attention demands. The different patterns of LPP modulations by task demands may reflect the differences in emotion regulation in the two cultural groups. Cultural experiences of emotion regulation make it easier for Asian Americans to adopt a strategy to down-regulate the arousal induced by emotional stimuli relative European Americans who have less experiences of emotion regulation. However, this study left an open question whether the lateral prefrontal activity that is more directly related to emotion regulation varies across the two cultural groups that could be clarified in future cross-cultural fMRI research.

Mental attribution

A fundamental assumption about the human mind is that our behaviors are driven by internal thoughts such as intention, desire, belief, and emotion. Humans, as well as other primates, attribute mental states to their conspecifics in order to interpret and predict their behaviors (Premack and Woodruff 1978). The process of mental attribution, also referred to as mentalizing, mindreading, or "theory-of-mind" (ToM), can occur automatically and rapidly. Mental attribution has two basic components, that is, the perceptual processing of nonverbal social cues (such as gaze direction) and the social–cognitive processing of invisible mental states. Psychologists have developed various paradigms to induce inference of others' mental states to test the ability of mental attribution. For example, a false-belief task has been used to examine the ability to differentiate between a fact and an individual's belief. After reading the following story, "John told Emily that he had a Porsche. Actually, his car is a Ford. Emily doesn't know anything about cars though, so she believed John," a participant is asked, "When Emily sees John's car, does she thinks it is a Porsche or Ford" (Saxe and Kanwisher 2003). To answer the question accurately, one has to know the truth, and what Emily believes to be the truth. The neural basis of mental attribution has been scrutinized by numerous neuroimaging studies, and there is substantial evidence to indicate that mindreading recruits a neural circuit consisting of the dorsal medial prefrontal cortex, temporal pole, and temporoparietal junction (Frith and Frith 2003).

Are the neural substrates of mental attribution influenced by cultural experiences? To explore this issue, Kobayashi and colleagues (2006) scanned American-English-speaking monolingual adults and Japanese-English late bilingual adults during a ToM task consisting of false-belief stories in the form of "x thinks that y thinks that …." Participants also performed judgments on event outcomes based on an understanding of physical-causal reasoning. Relative to this control task, Kobayashi showed that judgments about others' mental states resulted in increased activation in the right dorsal medial prefrontal cortex, right anterior cingulate cortex, right middle frontal gyrus and dorsal lateral prefrontal cortex in both cultural groups. However, a direct comparison of the two cultural groups revealed that judgments of the mental states in monolingual American participants produced greater activations in the right insula, bilateral temporoparietal junction, and right dorsal medial prefrontal cortex, relative to bilingual Japanese participants who, however, showed greater brain activity in the right orbital frontal gyrus. These brain areas have been shown to subserve distinct functions. For example, the insular cortex has been implicated in the mediation of the connections between the limbic system and frontal regions of the brain (Allman et al. 2005) and to be involved in the processing of emotionally laden face stimuli (Gorno-Tempini et al. 2001). The temporoparietal junction area is thought to have a role in integrating sensory modalities and limbic inputs (Moran et al. 1987), whereas the orbitofrontal gyrus has been shown to be involved in emotional mentalizing tasks (Moll et al. 2002). Thus it appears that, for people who grew up in the American culture, attributing mental states to other people may require the integration of sensory modalities and limbic inputs more than for people who grew up in Japanese culture, whereas growing up in Japanese culture might result in a particular mental-attribution style that involves "feeling" others' emotions.

The same research group also compared cultural and linguistic effects on the neural bases of mental attribution in American English-speaking monolingual children and Japanese bilingual children aged between 8 and 11 (Kobayashi et al. 2007). Both cultural groups were presented with false-belief stories depicted in either languages or cartoons. Both cartoon-based and word-based ToM tasks activated a number of brain regions, including the dorsal medial prefrontal cortex and precuneus in both cultural groups. However, the word-based ToM task generated greater activity in the left superior temporal sulcus in the American children than in Japanese children, whereas enhanced activity was identified in the left inferior temporal gyrus in the Japanese children. In addition, stronger activation in the right temporoparietal junction in the cartoon-based ToM task was observed in the American children than in the Japanese children. This could be interpreted as evidence for a weakened self-other distinction in Japanese culture, as the ability to distinguish self from others engages the right temporoparietal junction (Decety and Lamm 2007), and East Asian cultures encourage the use of collectivistic group-thinking more than individualistic self-thinking to account for human social behaviors. In the cartoon-based ToM task, Japanese children showed higher activation in the left anterior superior temporal sulcus and temporal pole than the American children did. The temporal pole has been suggested to integrate sensory information and limbic inputs (Moran et al. 1987), so it could be agreed that the Japanese children might have had to integrate sensory and limbic inputs more so than the American children did in the cartoon-based ToM task.

Adams et al. (2010) employed a relatively simple task, called the "Reading the Mind in the Eyes" test (Baron-Cohen et al. 2001), to explore the neural correlates of an intracultural advantage in mental attribution. The information derived from the eyes is rich and important for social communication. These facts form the basis of the "Reading the Mind in the Eyes" test, during which a participant is presented with a series of photographs of the eye-region of faces of different actors and actresses, and is asked to choose which of two words best describes what the person in the photograph is thinking or feeling. Performance during the test has been used to estimate how well participants can put themselves into the mind of the other person. The test is assumed to involve the first stage of attribution of ToM (i.e., identifying attribution of the relevant mental state) but it does not include the second stage (i.e., inferring the content of that mental state), and it has been shown to differentiate non-clinical samples from clinical samples with impaired social perception, such as those with autism spectrum disorders (e.g., Baron-Cohen et al. 1999). Given that people usually have more experience with culturally in-group than out-group members and tend to ascribe more complex mental states to members of their own versus other social groups (Paladino et al. 2002), Adams et al. (2010) predicted an intracultural advantage in the ability to infer mental states from the eyes. They presented European American and Japanese adults with photographs depicting just the eye region of Western and Asian individuals. There was a word in each corner of the photograph describing a possible mental state (e.g., friendly, sarcastic, irritated, or worried). During fMRI scanning, participants made judgments on each photograph about the mental state or gender of the perceived eye. Both cultural groups showed a greater proportion of correct responses to culturally in-group eyes than to out-group eyes during mental-state reasoning, suggesting a behavioral intracultural advantage in reading others' mind from the eye. This intracultural advantage in mindreading was shown to be associated with greater activity bilaterally in the posterior superior temporal sulci during same- versus other-culture mental-state decoding in both cultural groups. In addition, the activation in the posterior superior temporal sulci when viewing eyes of culturally out-group individuals was negatively correlated with the behavioral intracultural advantage in the mindreading task.

The findings indicate that the differential recruitment of the posterior superior temporal sulci based on cultural-group membership is associated with both improved mindreading of culturally familiar eyes and dampened mindreading of culturally unfamiliar eyes. Such brain imaging findings suggest that cultural experiences can shape the neurological architecture subserving high-level mental-state reasoning in both adults and children.

Social status

Individuals in many social species are organized into social groups on the ground of their status in a social hierarchy. Among these, humans have constructed the most complicated social hierarchy that frames our behavior, mind, and brain. How to sit or stand in front of another person and how to talk to him/her are strongly influenced by the social status of those involved in social interactions. An individual needs to be aware of the social status of those they are interacting with in order to make correct decisions and behave appropriately. Variations of behavior toward others at different levels of a social hierarchy are influenced by people's attitudes toward others, which, interestingly, show major differences between East Asian and Western cultures. For example, the American culture encourages competitiveness, and most people in the United States are prompted to become dominant in a social hierarchy (Triandis and Gelfand 1998). By contrast, in East Asian culture, subordination and sociability are reinforced, and dominance is not favored. Chinese and Japanese cultures teach individuals from the early stage of development to be agreeable rather than dominant. Another example of cultural variations of behavior toward others is how older adults are treated. Older adults have a higher social status in East Asian traditions, which emphasizes the significance of the family more, compared with Western cultures that encourage independence and self-elevating. When viewing point-light displays depicting the gaits of individuals of different ages, Americans rated older walkers as being less socially dominant, whereas Koreans' rating of social dominance did not distinguish between young and older walkers (Montepare and Zebrowitz 1993). Given that East Asian and Western cultures manifest different attitudes toward people at different levels of a social hierarchy, the positive valence accessed to individuals is likely to vary across the cultures. A neuroscience prediction of such cultural differences in attitudes and feelings about others would be cultural modulations of the neural activity in the reward system, in response to signals to people at different levels of social hierarchy.

Freeman and colleagues (2009) examined whether Americans would show stronger reward-related mesolimbic activity to dominant members of a social hierarchy and Japanese individuals would show stronger reward-related mesolimbic activity to subordinate members. They presented cartoons of human bodies with gestures of either dominance or subordination to Americans and Japanese individuals during fMRI scanning (Figure 5. 4). After fMRI scanning, participants completed a questionnaire to measure their behavioral tendencies toward dominant versus subordinate members of a social hierarchy. Passive viewing of these cartoons activated brain regions in the reward system, including the bilateral caudate nucleus and the medial prefrontal cortex, but with distinct patterns of modulations by perceived dominance and subordination. Specifically, American participants showed greater activity in the caudate and medial prefrontal cortex in response to dominant stimuli than with subordinate stimuli, whereas Japanese participants showed a reverse effect: stronger activity in these brain regions in response to subordinate than to dominant stimuli (Figure 5.4). Consistent with the distinct patterns of brain activations, Americans self-reported a tendency toward more dominant behavior, whereas Japanese self-reported a tendency toward more subordinate behavior. In addition, activations in the caudate and medial prefrontal cortex were able to predict individuals' behavioral tendencies. Stronger responses in the caudate and medial prefrontal cortex to dominant stimuli predicted increased dominant behavioral tendency, and stronger activity in these brain areas to subordinate stimuli predicted more subordinate behavioral tendency. Thus, American and Japanese cultural

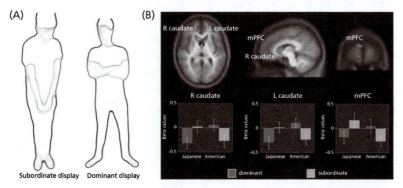

Figure 5.4 (A) Illustration of cartoons showing gestures of either dominance or subordination. (B) Cultural group differences in brain activities in response to cartoons of dominant and subordinate gestures. (See colour plate.)

Reprinted from *NeuroImage*, 47 (1), Jonathan B. Freeman, Nicholas O. Rule, Reginald B. Adams Jr., and Nalini Ambady, Culture shapes a mesolimbic response to signals of dominance and subordination that associates with behavior, pp. 353–9, DOI:10.1016/j.neuroimage.2009.04.038, Copyright © 2009 Elsevier Inc., with permission from Elsevier.

experiences lead to specific patterns of brain responses to people at different positions in a social hierarchy, which can mediate distinct default behavior toward dominant and subordinate others in these cultures.

Brain imaging research has also revealed cultural influences on neural activity in the reward system in response to evaluation of older adults. Krendl (2016) scanned Chinese and white American participants using fMRI while participants viewed images of older and young adults and had to indicate via button-press whether they liked or disliked the person pictured. Participants' attitudes toward older adults were also assessed using the Attitudes toward Old People Scale (Kogan 1961) after scanning. Positive results were higher for images of young models in both cultural groups. Compared with white American participants, the Chinese tended to report higher proportion of liking images of older adults, but this difference was not statistically significant. However, the estimation of attitude after scanning did reveal a moderately higher negative affect toward older adults in white American participants compared with Chinese participants. To examine whether Chinese and white American participants engaged disparate neural mechanisms when evaluating older adults, a contrast between images of older versus young adults was performed. This contrast was then submitted to cultural comparison that showed higher activations in the bilateral ventral striatum and right parahippocampal gyrus in Chinese relative to white American participants. Moreover, self-reported attitudes toward older adults and ventral striatal activity were correlated with the extent to which participants reported being affiliated with their respective cultural traditions. Together, these findings suggest that there is a cultural influence in attitude and brain activity to others of different social hierarchy, though, relative to self-reports of attitudes, brain activity may be more sensitive to social information about others' social hierarchy. Viewing images of culturally favored others induces enhanced neural activity in key regions of the reward system, which may underlie the parallel good feelings in oneself. These brain imaging findings suggest a possible way by which culture promotes individuals' attitude and behavior, that is, to connect culturally favored values with the reward neural system. Nevertheless, values that are attached to the reward system are strongly culturally selective.

Social comparison

Psychologists have long realized that humans have a basic drive to evaluate their opinions and abilities by comparison with other people (Festinger 1954). In addition, social comparison can produce notable affective (either positive or negative) consequences. Given that cultural views of the relationship between the self and others vary across societies (e.g., Markus and Kitayama

1991, 2010), one may expect cultural differences in the motivation to conduct social comparison. Indeed, it has been shown that, relative to European Canadians, Asian Canadians sought more social comparisons as indexed by their greater willingness to check others' scores after an intellectual test (White and Lehman 2005). There was also a positive correlation between self-reported collectivism and the degree of social comparison across student participants from the United States and China (Chung and Mallery 1999). These observations suggest that individuals educated in interdependent cultures that stress relationships with others are more likely to seek social comparison than are individuals in independent cultures that emphasize one's internal attributes, feelings, and thoughts.

One possible account for cultural differences in the tendency for social comparison seeking is that brain activity in individuals from interdependent and independent cultures are differentially sensitive to social comparison. For example, when making economic decisions, East Asians' brain activity may be more sensitive to their income relative to that of others, whereas Westerners' brain activity may be more sensitive to their absolute income. To test this hypothesis, Kang et al. (2013) scanned Korean and American adults performing a financial gambling task simultaneously and independently with a partner. During the task, a participant was presented with three unrevealed cards on each trial and had to choose one of them. Two to four seconds later, the chosen card was turned over to show the monetary outcome for the participant. A second card was turned 4 seconds later so that monetary outcomes for both the participant and the partner were displayed. Another 4 seconds later, the participant had to choose whether to save the results or to repeat the trial later. An interesting finding of this study was that the neural activity in two reward-related brain region, that is, the ventral striatum and ventromedial prefrontal cortex, was differentially sensitive to one's absolute income and relative income in the two cultural groups. Upon seeing their own income, American participants showed stronger activity in these brain areas than Koreans did. By contrast, viewing the partner's income elicited greater activity in the ventral striatum and ventromedial prefrontal cortex in Korean participants than in Americans. In addition, the strength of functional connectivity between the ventral striatum and the ventromedial prefrontal cortex predicted individual variability in the degree to which participants' decisions were affected by relative incomes. Thus, the activity in the reward system seems to be more sensitive to social comparison in Korean participants than in Americans, and it influences individuals' economic decisions.

Korn and colleagues (2014) further revealed cultural differences in behavior and brain responses to feedback from social peers. They first asked groups of five participants of either German or Chinese origin to play a tabletop version of a popular game that is highly engaging and allows players to show a variety of cooperative and competitive behaviors. Before the game participants were told that their personality traits would be rated by the other players in their group and their own ratings would be shown to the other players as well (in an anonymous fashion). After the game, each participant rated three of the four other participants on 80 trait adjectives, on a Likert scale from 1 (this trait does not apply the person at all) to 8 (this trait applies to the person very much). In the second session of the study, participants underwent fMRI scanning while being presented with trait adjectives and then rated to what degree these adjectives can describe themselves or another participant whom they had not rated during the first session. Participants were then shown a score that they believed to be the mean rating of themselves given by three other participants from the first session of the study. After this social feedback, participants were asked to rate themselves and a peer again. This design allowed the researchers to measure how much participants changed or updated their self- and other-ratings after having received social feedback. Behavioral measures revealed that, for both cultural groups, participants updated their ratings more toward desirable than toward undesirable feedback, and were positively biased by social feedback. However, Chinese relative to German participants updated their trait ratings more after receiving the social feedback from others. Analyses of fMRI data identified increased activity in the medial prefrontal cortex when participants received feedback about themselves compared with another participant. The medial prefrontal activity was positively correlated with positive social feedback (e.g., ratings of positive traits from others), suggesting a functional role of coding reward arising from social feedback in this brain region. In addition, it was found that, relative to Chinese participants, German participants showed stronger activity in the self-related medial prefrontal cortex activity during feedback processing, suggesting a neural substrate underlying cultural-group difference in responses to social feedback.

The brain imaging findings in the aforementioned studies support the conclusion that individuals from East Asian and Western cultures get rewards from different psychological sources during social interactions. In an interdependent cultural environment, individuals care more about how others think about themselves, and positive feedback from others lead to stronger reward activity in the brain, whereas individuals from an independent cultural environment may get greater reward from positive social feedback to the self. The other-related and self-related reward activity may in turn facilitate individuals' attention and behavior toward the other or the self.

Moral judgment

In daily life, people often make decisions on whether to take actions by evaluating whether or not the actions are right or wrong, proper or improper. Moral judgments like these are extremely important in guiding human behavior by assigning positive or negative values to the outcome of behaviors. It is believed that moral judgments can be reached by taking into consideration of social rules, contextual information, one's own emotion responses, and outcome of reasoning processes, for instance. Psychological research has suggested distinct cognitive and affective processes involved in moral judgments. For example, Kohlberg (1969) has proposed that the moral reasoning that drives moral judgments engages cognitive processes such as looking at a problem from multiple perspectives. The social intuitionist model, however, emphasizes interpersonal processes during moral judgments that rapidly and intuitively tell people that something is wrong (Haidt 2001). Another approach to the nature of moral judgments suggests that, while moral judgments may make use of social cognitive processes such as the representation of others' mental states, emotions also contribute to moral judgment under some circumstances (Greene and Haidt 2002). Cultural psychology research has reported evidence for cultural differences in moral judgments. Gold et al. (2014) asked British and Chinese participants to solve a trolley problem. Participants were told a story about a runaway trolley that threatens to kill five persons on the track ahead. A bystander can save the five by switching a lever to divert the trolley on to a sidetrack; the consequences of this action are that one person will be killed. Participants were asked to make judgments regarding whether it would be permissible and impermissible to kill one person to save five others' lives. Gold et al. (2014) found that fewer Chinese participants, relative to British participants, were willing to take action and sacrifice one to save five, and this cultural difference was more pronounced when the consequences were less severe than death. Gold et al. speculated that the cultural-group differences in morality-related behavioral tendencies were due to Chinese shared beliefs in fate, a force beyond human control that is chiefly responsible for determining people's destinies, or to Chinese interdependent self-construals that make them more worried about being negatively perceived by others if they caused harm to someone.

Potential neural substrates underlying cultural differences in moral judgments have been examined in an fMRI study of Korean and American adults (Han et al. 2014). Participants underwent fMRI scanning while they read short essays describing moral-personal dilemmas in which a violation causes serious bodily harm that falls a particular person or set of persons. They were then asked to evaluate whether the solution presented at the end of each dilemma is "appropriate" or "inappropriate." It was found that, relative to non-moral judgments on the appropriateness of behaviors that do not cause bodily harm, moral judgments induced greater activity in the right putamen and right superior frontal gyrus associated with cognitive control processes in Korean compared with Americans participants. American participants showed a significantly higher degree of activity in the bilateral anterior cingulate cortex under the moral-personal condition than Korean participants did. Because the activity in the putamen has been associated with intuition (Wan et al. 2011) and the anterior cingulate activity with conflict monitoring (Botvinick et al. 2004), Han et al.'s (2014) findings of stronger activation in the putamen can be understood by assuming that Koreans recruit intuitive processes for making moral judgments to a greater degree compared with Americans. This finding provides a neural basis for the argument that people educated in East Asian cultures usually seek intuitive instantaneous understanding through direct perception of external situations (Nisbett et al. 2001). In contrast, American participants seem to utilize the conflict monitoring system during moral judgments to a greater degree than Korean participants do. This may be due to increased exposure of conflict in a multiple cultural society, as is the case in the United States (Constantine and Sue 2006). Alternatively, individuals living in a collectivistic society (e.g., Koreans) prefer to accommodate conflicting situations (Oyserman et al. 2002) and avoid possible social conflicts (Leung et al. 2002) to maintain social harmony.

Another perspective on the cultural differences in brain activity related to moral judgments is derived from a different dimension of psychological processes. Gelfand et al. (2011) suggested that individuals in societies that have experienced a high degree of ecological and historical threat (e.g., Chinese) may develop stronger norms and punishment of norm violators to coordinate social action relative to those who grow up in societies confronted with a low degree of ecological and historical threat (e.g., American). This theory forecasts that individuals from the Chinese culture (compared with those from the American culture) would be more sensitive in mind and brain activity to social norm violation. This prediction was tested by recording EEG from Chinese and American adults while they were reading sentences that described situations with or without social norm violation (Mu et al. 2015). The first sentence depicted a situation (e.g., "Amanda is at the art museum.") and was presented for 1500 ms. It was then replaced by the second sentence that depicted a specific behavior that is appropriate in the situation (e.g., "She is reading.") or violates a social norm in the situation (e.g., "She is dancing."). This study found that both cultural groups showed consistent negative deflection of event-related potential around 400 ms (the N400) over the central and parietal regions in response to the detection of norm violations. Over the frontal regions, however, only Chinese exhibited the N400 in responses to social norm violations, and the frontal N400 amplitudes predicted a variety of behavioral and attitudinal measurements related to the strength of social norms such as ethnocentrism and self-control. Putting the fMRI and EEG imaging together, it can be concluded that, relative to American culture, East Asian cultures (e.g., Chinese and Korean culture) foster neural mechanisms that facilitate fast and intuitive processes during moral judgments, corresponding to the cognitive style in East Asian cultures that is characterized by higher sensitivity to social contexts and significant others during social interactions. Moral judgments in the American culture may require the processing of conflict between perceived social situations and social rules to be internalized in one's brain.

Chapter 6

Cultural priming on cognition and underlying brain activity

Dynamic behavior, culture, and brain

The saying "When in Rome, do as Rome does" exists in different versions in many societies, all pinpoint a similar phenomenon: people change their social behaviors to fit local cultures. For example, an American graduate student who calls his/her supervisors by their first names when working in the United States will start to call his/her Chinese supervisor "Teacher Han" after working for a short period of time in a Chinese university. There are many similar observations like this. One possible account of the cultural dynamics of human social behavior is that people may simply change and modify their behaviors in response to a new social environment by imitating the behavior of others, even though, in some cases, to do so does not conform to one's own cultural beliefs and values. Alternatively, it is likely that once an individual has lived in a cultural environment for a while, incorporates the local cultural beliefs/values within his/her original cultural system, and embeds new cultural beliefs/values into the brain, he/she may voluntarily and facilely take culturally appropriate actions in a local society. Such self-driven behaviors are essentially different from imitation of others' behavior in terms of motivation.

These analyses raise an important question regarding the nature of cultural systems in the human brain. *Culture* refers to shared beliefs and behavioral scripts shared by a group of individuals, which, together with social institutions, constitute a social environment in which individuals of a social group develop and evolve. Each individual is fostered in a specific sociocultural environment and is engrafted with specific cultural beliefs, values, norms, etc. For instance, as I have discussed in early chapters, individualism and independence are encouraged in Western societies, whereas collectivism and interdependence dominate the main streams of thought in East Asian societies (Hofstede 1980, 2001; Markus and Kitayama 1991, 2010; Zhu and Han 2008). North Americans believe more strongly in individual agency and autonomy, whereas East Asians believe more strongly in group agency and obligations toward the group (Hong et al. 2001). However, there have been increasing numbers of immigrants worldwide who reside outside the country where they were born and educated. These days, even in the same society, people are able to encounter various cultural beliefs and values (Oyserman et al. 2014). Does an adult, who already has learned and obtained a cultural system in the brain, absorb new cultural beliefs/ values? Is it possible that an individual's brain can host more than one cultural system? If so, is it possible that an individual can switch between two cultural systems quickly because of different patterns of brain activity underlying cognition and behavior?

These questions have been addressed by cultural psychologists who view culture as a dynamic knowledge system rather than static monolithic entities deeply rooted with the social groups belonging to those cultures, or a rigid set of stereotypes about a social group (Markus and Hamedani 2007). It is believed that humans are not born with propensities for any particular culture but with the potential and capacity to acquire and to create culture (Harris 1999). Thus, an individual may change his/her cultural values and beliefs as a result of experience (e.g., emigrating from one's native country). People from the same cultural group can also be quite heterogeneous in terms of the values and beliefs they acquire. There are different perspectives on the relationship between cultural dynamics and human cognition. According to Hong and her colleagues (Hong et al. 2007; Hong 2009), the increased frequency and intensity of intercultural interactions expose people frequently to two or more cultural traditions and knowledge. Through cultural learning, people are able to acquire a cultural knowledge that is different from their native knowledge. After integrating the knowledge from different cultural sources to foster a creative synthesis, an individual can switch between his/her native cultural knowledge and the new cultural knowledge so as to increase flexibility in cognition and behavior when meeting more than one cultural tradition or interacting with people from different cultures. Thus, culture provides a dynamic framework within which cognition and behavior occur. Upon meeting two cultural groups, a particular set of cultural systems can be activated by contextual cues or the recent use of specific cultural beliefs/values to guide subsequent cognitive/affective processes involved in social behavior. Oyserman and colleagues (2007, 2009, 2011) take culture as situated cognition or processes. They believe that culture can be understood as a set of associative processes that determines which information is accessible and how information is processed and interpreted. Everyday situations can have downstream consequences on thinking, feeling, and doing. A cultural mindset, for instance, either an individualistic or a collectivistic mindset, can be activated in a specific situation. Thus, culture as situated cognition is dynamic and often it varies across different social situations. Both dynamic views of culture do not take cultural beliefs as rigid and exclusive systems. Instead, cultural systems or mindsets in each individual are flexible, inclusive, and modifiable from moment to moment and across one's life span.

A cultural neuroscience perspective assigns culture with even greater flexibility, given the intrinsic plastic nature of the brain that mediates human cultural knowledge and enables humans to adapt to sociocultural environments (Chiao and Ambady 2007; Han and Northoff 2008; Han et al. 2013; Kim and Sasaki 2014). Cultural neuroscientists regard human neurocognitive processes as being flexible and being continuously shaped by sociocultural experiences and environments. An individual's brain is not doomed by biology to work in a specific way, but rather the brain is strongly shaped by both long-term and short-term cultural experiences. Because cultural neuroscientists believe that there is a causal relationship between cultural experiences and brain functional organization, they not only examine cultural group differences in the neural correlates of multiple cognitive and affective processes to reveal the effects of long-term cultural experiences on the brain, but also investigate whether and how the brain activity engaged in specific cognitive and affective processes varies as a consequence of short-term cultural experiences. This chapter introduces behavioral and brain imaging studies that investigate whether and how human cognition and the underlying brain activity can vary within a short temporal scale owing to recent use or activation of specific cultural knowledge. Cultural psychologists and cultural neuroscientists have developed cultural priming paradigms that encourage or reinforce specific cultural beliefs and values and have examined the subsequent variations in cognition/affective processes and related brain activity. This approach, unlike the paradigms of cultural group comparisons that were mentioned in Chapters 3–5, excludes the effects of individuals' long-term social experience and practices, geographical location, religious values, and language on cognition and brain activity. Cross-cultural differences in cognition and brain activity are arguably only correlational, not causal in nature, and thus require further examination to clarify which facets or dimensions of culture cause the observed cross-cultural differences. Cultural priming paradigms allow researchers to examine causal relationships between a specific cultural belief/value and dynamic brain activity involved in multiple cognitive and affective processes.

Cultural priming and human cognition

Both views that take culture as a dynamic framework or dynamic processes predict that temporary activation of a specific cultural system will causally influence subsequent cognition and behavior. This idea has been tested using cultural priming—an experimental procedure that temporarily shifts individuals' mindsets toward one or another set of cultural beliefs/values. Cultural psychologists have developed several types of cultural priming and found evidence for consistent effects of cultural priming on multiple cognitive processes and behavior. For instance, language has been used as a priming method with the assumption that English carries Western/American values/beliefs, such as individualism/independence, and Chinese or other non-Western language carries the knowledge of a home culture such as collectivisms/interdependence. Trafimow et al. (1997) asked Chinese in Hong Kong, who are supposed to be bicultural because Hong Kong was a British colony before 1997 and students were educated with Western culture at school but fostered with Chinese culture at home, to perform an open-ended task called the Twenty Statements Test (Kuhn and McPartland 1954), which required participants to write twenty sentences all beginning with "I am." It was found that, when the questionnaire was presented in English, participants exhibited frequent use of trait adjectives in their self-descriptions, which emphasized an individual's uniqueness and cross-situational consistency of the self. When the questionnaire was presented in Chinese, participants were more likely to describe themselves with varying social roles. Similarly, Kemmelmeier and Cheng (2004) asked Chinese participants in Hong Kong to complete Singelis's independent and interdependent self-construal scales (Singelis, 1994). These scales have been frequently used to estimate individuals' self-construals. They found that participants scored independent self-construals higher when the questionnaire was in English than when it was in Chinese, though this effect was evident only in female participants. These results suggest that, at least for bicultural individuals who can used two languages (e.g., Chinese and English), language as a tool can trigger or endorse a specific cultural trait (e.g., independence or interdependence) and influence language-based tasks.

Other researchers use pictures of cultural symbols as toolkits that can facilitate the switch between cultural beliefs/values or cultural frames and thus influence the subsequent cognition and behavior. Wong and Hong (2005) used slides of Chinese cultural icons (e.g., a Chinese dragon and a person performing kung fu) or American cultural icons (e.g., the American flag and a scene showing an American football game), or neutral primes (geometric figures) to examine how cultural priming affected subsequent cooperative behavior. During the priming procedure, participants were shown slices of cultural icons and were required to name the objects shown in the pictures and to think about the ideas represented by the cultural icons. After being primed with Chinese or American cultural icons, Chinese college students in Hong Kong played a Prisoner's Dilemma game, which assesses the payoffs of cooperating or defecting, with friends or strangers. During this game, participants have to decide to cooperate or defect, and the outcomes will depend on the strategies that both players have cho-sen. Defecting always brings a better individual outcome for the participant, regardless of whether the partner chooses cooperation or defection. However, participants will get a higher joint outcome if both partners choose to cooper-ate. Participants were told that they would be awarded an amount of money equivalent to the points they scored in the game. Wong and Hong (2005) found that participants were likely to be more cooperative with friends after Chinese rather than American cultural knowledge was primed. However, with stran-gers, low levels of cooperation were shown after both Chinese and American culture priming.

Ng and Lai (2009) assessed whether the self-concept of bicultural Chinese would become more socially connected after Chinese versus Western cultures were primed. They examined the self-reference effect on memory in Chinese college students in Hong Kong after they had been primed with exposure to typ-ical Chinese pictures (e.g., the Great Wall and Chinese food) or Western (e.g., the British parliament and English cake and tea) cultural icons. They found that, with Western cultural priming, participants would recall more information (two-word phrases) that had been used to describe the self than the information related to others (including a nonidentified person and a participant's mother). However, priming with Chinese cultural icons made participants remember the information related to the self and others (both the nonidentified person and the mother) equally well. Sui and colleagues (2007) also reported similar effects with Chinese/American cultural priming in Chinese college students in Beijing, China, using the Twenty Statements Test and the self-referential task. Cultural priming may also modulate how individuals make causal judg-ments about observed events. Benet-Martínez et al. (2002) primed Chinese Americans, who had been born in China or Singapore, and had lived for at least five years in the United States, with American and Chinese cultural icons (e.g., pictures of Mickey Mouse, the US Capitol building, and a cowboy, or pictures of a Chinese dragon, the Summer Palace in Beijing, and a rice farmer) to activate the American or Chinese cultural meaning systems. After priming, participants were shown a computer-generated animation display of a single fish swimming in front of a group of fish, a paradigm adopted from Morris and Peng (1994). After watching the display, participants were asked to explain why the single fish and the group of fish were swimming apart by reporting their agreement with internal causes ("the one fish is influenced by some internal trait (such as independence, personal objective, or leadership)") or external causes (e.g., "the one fish is being influenced by the group (e.g., being chased, teased, or pres-sured by the others)". It was found that participants made more external attribu-tions (a characteristic Asian behavior) after being exposed to Chinese cultural primes, and more internal attributions (a characteristic Western behavior) after being exposed to American cultural primes. Taken together, these results suggest that priming with Chinese compared with Western cultural icons results in the facilitation of processing of social information related to close others, an increased cooperative tendency with close others, and a tendency of contextual interpretation of observed events. However, because Chinese and Western cultures consists of many different dimensions (e.g., individualism vs. collectivism, independence vs. interdependence, analytic vs. holistic thinking, and internal vs. external causal attribution), priming Chinese or Western cultures using pictures or language does not clarify which dimension of culture gives rise to the effects observed on cognition and behavior.

Self-construal priming is a procedure developed by Gardner and colleagues (Brewer and Gardner 1996; Gardner et al. 1999) that allows individuals to shift a specific cultural trait, that is, a self-construal, to either an interdependent or an independent style. The procedure of self-construal priming is simple. Participants were presented with two versions of short essays that describe a trip or a story, and the two versions differ only with respect to whether the pronouns in the essays are independent (e.g., I, mine, and my) or interdependent (e.g., we, ours, and us). Participants were asked to read the essays and circle all the pronouns in the essays. Essays used for the control priming were similar except that no independent or interdependent pronouns appear in them. Thus, different versions of priming materials could lead participants to focus their attention on the self as an individual or as a member of a social group. Self-construal priming has been used in a number of behavioral studies revealing that priming independence or interdependence affects multiple cognitive processes.

Research using self-construal priming on visual perceptual and memory processes assumes that priming interdependent self-construals drives individuals to focus on contextual information or the relationship between perceptual objects, whereas priming independent self-construal biases their attention to focal objects. Several studies have tested these hypotheses using a number of different paradigms. For example, Kühnen and Oyserman (2002) presented participants with compound stimuli (i.e., large letters consisting of small letters). Identification of global large letters depends on the relations between small letters (global task), whereas identification of local small letters requires attention to a focal object (local task). Using Gardner et al.'s self-construal priming procedure, one group of participants was primed with independence and another group with interdependence. Both groups performed the global and local tasks after the priming procedure. An interesting finding was that participants primed with independence were slower to identify global relative to local letters. By contrast, participants primed with interdependence tended to show the opposite effect: slower responses to local than to global letters, though this effect was not statistically significant. Most participants in this study were white, but some self-identified as black, Asian, and Hispanic, in terms of ethnicity. Moreover, the between-subjects design in Kühnen and Oyserman's work (2002) could not reveal whether self-construal priming could produce bidirectional effects on cognitive processes in an individual participant, which would lead to the facilitation of context-dependent processes by the interdependent self-construal priming and facilitation of context-independent processes by the independent self-construal priming. Lin and Han (2009) clarified this issue by including a control-priming condition in their study. They measured reaction times to the global and local properties of the compound letters from a group of Chinese participants after they had been primed for independent and interdependent self-construals. In the control-priming condition, participants read essays that did not include either independent or interdependent pronouns. The visual angle of compound letters was manipulated by Lin and Han so that participants responded equally fast to global and local targets in the control-priming condition. It was then found that, relative to the control-priming condition, interdependent self-construal priming resulted in faster responses to the global than to the local targets, whereas the reverse effect on reaction times was evident for independent self-construal priming (i.e., faster responses to the local than to the global targets in compound letters). Lin and Han (2009) also tested the effect of self-construal priming on performance during a Stroop task that required identification of a central target letter (H vs. E). The target letter was flanked by two peripheral letters that were identical to or different from the target letter. Relative to independent self-construal and control priming, interdependent self-construal priming slowed response speed and decreased response accuracy when the target and peripheral letters were different, suggesting that the contextual information was made more salient by interdependent self-construal priming, causing enhanced interference of the processing of the central target. Similarly, Krishna et al. (2008) found that individuals primed with independent (vs. interdependent) self-construals were more prone to spatial judgment biases in tasks in which the context needed to be included in processing, but were less prone to spatial judgment biases in tasks in which the context needed to be excluded from processing. These behavioral findings together indicate that priming independent or interdependent self-construals can modify visual perception by enhancing attention to a focal object or contextual information.

Self-construal priming has been further shown to modulate social emotion and social behavior. *Social emotion* refers to the affective states that can be induced during social interactions such as embarrassment, shame, envy, and pride. Furukawa et al. (2012) assessed cultural group differences in social emotion by asking children age 8 to 11 years to complete the Test of Self-Conscious Affect for Children (Tangney et al. 1990) to estimate their propensity to experience shame, guilt, and pride. They found substantial differences across cultures in the mean levels of shame, guilt, and pride, with Japanese children scoring highest on shame, Korean children scoring highest on guilt, and US children scoring highest on pride. Could the observed cultural differences in social emotion be related to self-construals? Neumann et al. (2009) tested the hypothesis that individuals with a predominantly interdependent self-construal would experience more pride than individuals with a predominantly independent self-construal would if others are successful. They examined how Chinese and German college students responded to scenarios in which others were successful by asking them to imagine that a person from their own country had received the Nobel Prize for Literature; a person they knew from their childhood had published a world-famous bestseller; or a team at their university had won an international soccer championship. They found that Chinese students felt relatively more pride in these situations than German students did. In a second study, they asked German students to think about the achievements of others or their own achievements after having been primed with either interdependent or independent self-construals. It was found that thinking about the achievements of others resulted in more pride after priming of the interdependent rather than the independent self-construal, whereas thinking about their achievements resulted in more pride after priming of independent rather than interdependent self-construals. These findings indicate a causal relationship between self-construals and one's feelings of pride about others' achievements.

The effects of self-construal priming are not only manifested in social cognition/emotion but are also evident in various social behaviors as well. Colzato and colleagues (2012) tested the hypothesis that people co-represent the actions of a co-actor to a greater degree when primed with interdependent than independent self-construals using a social Simon task. In the experiment, two participants sit next to each other and respond to the color (green or blue) of a dot that might appear to the left or right of a central fixation of circles. One participant responded by pressing one of two keys, while the other key was operated by the other participant. Participants were asked to ignore the location of the stimulus and to base their responses exclusively on its color. The classical Simon effect shows that left and right actions performed by one person are carried out faster if the responding hand spatially corresponds to the stimulus signaling them (Simon 1969). The social Simon effect refers to a similar phenomenon when the two actions are carried out by different people. When two participants sitting side by side are respectively asked to respond to the color of dots that might appear to the left or right of a central fixation, they responded faster when the sitting position and the target required to be responded to are spatially correspondent (e.g., the participant sitting on the right is asked to respond to the target that appears to the right of the fixation) than when incongruent (e.g., the participant sitting on the right is asked to respond to the target that appears to the left of the fixation). It was assumed that, if drawing people's attention to personal interdependence or independence affects the degree to which people integrate others into their own self-concept, one would expect a more pronounced social Simon effect with the former than with the latter. Indeed, Colzato et al. found that, relative to individuals who were primed with independence, those who were primed with interdependence showed a larger social Simon effect in reaction times, suggesting that priming interdependence enhanced self-other integration in a simple color-discrimination task.

There is also evidence that self-construal priming influences social behavior in a real social context. Holland et al. (2004) examined the effects of self-construal activation on behavior conducive to interpersonal proximity. In an initial study, participants were led into a room by the experimenter and seated in front of a computer. After typing in their first name, the participants performed a lexical decision task in which neutral words together with non-words were presented. On half of the trials, a word was subliminally presented for 16 ms. This word could be the first name of the participant (which would activate the independent personal self-construal) or a neutral word *apple* as a control condition. In a second study, participants were asked to write about the similarities between themselves and their friends/family to prime interdependent self-construal or about the differences between themselves and their friends/family to prime independent self-construals. In both studies, after the priming procedure, participants were asked to take a seat in a waiting area, ostensibly to give the experimenter some time to prepare the second part of the experiment. Four chairs were lined up in the waiting area, with a jacket hanging over the chair on the extreme left. The distance between the chair with the jacket on it and the chair that the participant chose to sit on was measured to examine the effect of self-construal priming. Interestingly, relative to control participants, participants who were primed with independence sat further away from where they anticipated another person would sit in a waiting room, whereas participants primed with interdependence sat closer to the anticipated other person. Utz (2004) further showed that priming interdependence versus independence facilitated cooperation when economic decisions had to be made. Participants were asked to reorganize scrambled sentences that contained words such as *individual, self-contained*, or '*independent* to activate the concept of independence, or words such as *group, friendships*, or *together* to activate the concept of interdependence. They were then asked to play a four-coin give-some dilemma game, ostensibly with another participant. At the beginning of each round, each player had four coins, worth 1 Euro to him/herself but 2 Euros to the other person, and had to decide how many (0, 1, 2, 3, or 4) of his/her four coins he/she wanted to give to the other person. Similarly, the other person was supposed to decide how many of his/her four coins he/she wanted to give to the participant. The number of coins given in every round was measured to estimate participants' cooperation in the dilemma game. It was found that participants primed with independence exhibited lower levels of cooperation than did participants primed with interdependence.

The behavioral studies described earlier in this chapter show evidence that cultural priming, using either pictures of cultural icons or semantic single/plural pronouns, generate changes of multiple cognitive and affective processes involved in perception, memory, social emotion, and economic decisions, for example. These behavioral findings lend support to the idea that an individual can have two sets of cultural knowledge systems that under certain circumstances can be dynamically switched in response to sociocultural environments and experiences to adjust social behavior. The findings indicate a causal relationship between culture and cognition/behavior. Culture provides a framework for cognition and behavior and it biases how people think and behave.

Cultural priming and brain activity

Given that cognition and behavior are controlled by the brain, the findings of cultural priming effects on cognition and behavior raise the question of whether and how cultural priming modulates human brain activity related to cognitive and affective processes. To address this question it is important to clarify how flexible the brain needs to be in order to respond to changes in cultural values/norms and how the recent use of cultural knowledge frames neurocognitive processes related to behavior. Most of the current cultural neuroscience studies integrate self-construal priming and fMRI or ERP to examine cultural priming effects on brain activity. These studies have a basic hypothesis that priming independence will facilitate self-focusing and thus will enhance the brain activity related to the processing of self-relevant information. By contrast, priming interdependence promotes the cognitive link between the self and others and thus decreases the brain activity that supports the differentiation between the self and the other.

An early fMRI study assessed whether self-construal priming modulated brain activity related to self-awareness induced during face perception. As mentioned in Chapter 4, the ability to recognize one's own face develops early in children at about two years (Asendorpf et al. 1996). Human adults respond faster to their own faces than to the faces of others in various tasks (Keenan et al. 2000; Ma and Han 2009, 2010). Neural correlates of self-face recognition in adults have been identified in the frontal lobe (including the right frontal cortex and medial prefrontal cortex) in the previous fMRI studies by contrasting perception of one's own face versus a familiar face (Platek et al. 2004, 2006; Uddin et al. 2005) or by contrasting identifications of a morphed face recognized as oneself versus a friend (Ma and Han 2012). To investigate whether and how neural correlates of self-face recognition are modulated by self-construal priming, Sui and Han (2007) took pictures of a participant's face and the face of one of the participant's friends, which either faced left or right. During fMRI scanning, the participants were first asked to read essays containing independent or interdependent pronouns (e.g., I or we). After each type of priming, participants were asked to make judgments of orientations of their own and familiar faces. It was predicted that priming independence versus interdependence would promote a mindset of self-focus that would facilitate self-face recognition by enhancing the underlying brain activity. This prediction was supported by both behavioral performance and BOLD responses related to self-face. Participants responded faster to self-face than to the familiar face after independent self-construal priming but faster to the familiar face than to self-face after interdependent self-construal priming. Brain imaging results revealed that the neural activity in the right middle frontal cortex was specifically modulated by perception of faces and self-construal priming. The right middle frontal activity in response to one's own face was increased after independent self-construal priming but decreased after interdependent self-construal priming relative to that in response to the familiar face. The behavioral and brain imaging results consistently suggest that the neural correlates of self-awareness associated with recognition of one's own face are modulated by short-term self-construal priming in human adults (Figure 6.1), indicating a causal relationship between self-construals and brain responses during self-face recognition. The brain imaging results were particularly surprising because the self-construal priming procedure in this study lasted for only three minutes. The findings demonstrate that the brain activity underlying self-face recognition is very sensitive to temporary shifts of cultural traits in a short period.

Other types of cultural priming also modulate the differential neural processing of the self and others. Ng and colleagues (2010) primed Chinese college students in Hong Kong with typical Chinese (e.g., the Great Wall) or Western (e.g., the British parliament) cultural icons before participants underwent fMRI scanning, during which they performed personality-traits judgments on the self, their mother, and a person whom the participants would not identify

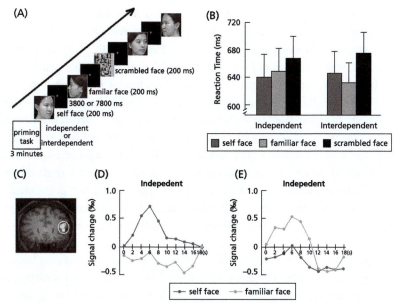

Figure 6.1 (A) Illustration of the self-construal priming procedure and the face-recognition task. After the self-construal priming task, participants were scanned while being presented with their own face, a familiar face, and scrambled faces, and had to indicate the head orientation of the intact faces and the location of the gray bar next to the scrambled faces by pressing a button with the right index or middle finger. (B) Mean reaction times to self-face, familiar faces, and scrambled faces. (C) Illustration of the right frontal activation in association with self-face. (D) The time courses of the BOLD signals in the right middle frontal cortex after the independent self-construal priming. (E) BOLD signal in the right middle frontal cortex after the interdependent self-construal priming. (See colour plate.)

Adapted from Jie Sui and Shihui Han, Self-Construal Priming Modulates Neural Substrates of Self-Awareness, *Psychological Science*, 18 (10), pp. 861–866, DOI:10.1111/j.1467-9280.2007.01992.x, Copyright © 2007, © SAGE Publications. Adapted with permission from SAGE Publications, Inc.

with (i.e., a nonidentified person). The inclusion of a nonidentified target for trait judgments would allow researchers to test whether Chinese culture priming would induce self-inclusiveness, while Western culture priming would induce self-other differentiation regardless of whether the "other" was a close and significant one, and whether cultural priming effects on overlapping neural representations are limited to the self and close others. Given the previous cross-cultural brain imaging findings of overlapping neural representations of the self and mother in Chinese but not Western participants (Zhu et al. 2007), it was predicted that, in Westernized bicultural Chinese adults, priming with Western cultural icons would increase the neural differentiation of the self and others, whereas priming with Chinese cultural icons would enhance the neural overlapping of the self and others. To control for potential influences of language (students in Hong Kong speak both Chinese and English), trait adjectives were presented in both Chinese and English during scanning to minimize any language-related confounds. The critical finding of this study was that, after Western culture priming, self-judgment induced increased activity in the ventral medial prefrontal cortex relative to both the nonidentified person and the mother, whereas after Chinese culture priming, the fMRI results failed to show any brain activation in the contrast of self versus mother and self versus nonidentified person. These effects arose from both increased activity during self-judgments and decreased activity during judgments of others in the medial prefrontal cortex after Western cultural priming. Thus Western versus Chinese cultural priming modulated neural activity related to both the self and others to enhance self-other differentiation in the medial prefrontal cortex.

Chiao and colleagues (2010) further explored whether temporarily heightening awareness of individualism or collectivism facilitates the processing of culturally congruent self-representations within the cortical midline regions of the brain. They tried two different types of cultural priming on bicultural individuals (i.e., Asian Americans), that is, the Sumerian Warrior Story task and the Similarities and Differences with Family and Friends task (Trafimow et al. 1991). The Sumerian Warrior Story describes a dilemma where Sostoras, a military general, has to decide which warrior to send to a king. One version of the story, in which Sostoras chooses the warrior who is the best qualified for the job, is believed to prime individualism, and another version, in which Sostoras chooses the warrior who is a member of his own family, is supposed to prime collectivism. After reading the story, participants made a judgment about whether or not they admire the general. The Similarities and Differences with Family and Friends task asks participants to think for two minutes about what makes them different from their family and friends to prime values of individualism or what they have in common with their family and friends to prime values of collectivism. After the priming procedure, participants were asked to write a short essay about their family and friends. Culturally congruent or incongruent self-representations were tested using a general context-independent self-task (e.g., participants were asked to make judgments on "in general, does this sentence describe you?") and a context-dependent self-task (e.g., to make judgments on "does this sentence describe you when you are talking to your mother?"). Chiao et al. found that activity in both the medial prefrontal cortex and the posterior cingulate cortex was modulated by cultural priming and types of self-description. Participants primed with individualism showed a greater neural response in these brain regions for general self-descriptions relative to contextual self-descriptions, whereas those primed with collectivism showed a greater neural response for contextual relative to general self-descriptions. The findings provide further evidence for the dynamic influence of temporal shifts of cultural frame on neural representations underlying self-reflection. It should be noted that, in the aforementioned three studies, the priming procedures were very different. Reading single/plural first-person pronouns, viewing pictures of cultural symbols, and thinking self-other similarity or differences recruit language, visual perceptual, and memory processes, respectively. However, the priming effects on the neural underpinnings of self-related processing were consistent in these studies, regardless of the different cognitive processes involved in the priming procedure. The findings demonstrate that the cultural beliefs/values/norms of individualism and collectivism are fundamentally and causally important for modulations of brain activity underlying self-related processes.

The findings that self-construal priming modulated self-related brain activity may not be surprising because both the priming and the following tasks were associated with cultural schemas of self-concept. If self-construals play a role of a fundamental cognitive frame, priming independent or interdependent self-construals should alter multiple levels of neural processing in the brain. Indeed, both ERP and fMRI studies have shown increasing evidence that self-construal priming modulates the neural correlates of sensory, perceptual, and high-order cognitive/affective processes. For example, Wang et al. (2014) investigated whether and how temporary shifts in self-construals modulated sensory and perceptual processing during physical pain by recording ERPs to painful and non-painful electrical stimulations from Chinese adults. It is well known that a cortical circuit consisting of the primary (SI) and secondary (SII) somatosensory cortex, anterior cingulate, insula, and supplementary motor area is engaged in physical pain (Peyron et al. 2000). ERP studies have identified human electrophysiological responses over the scalp to painful stimulation, including two early consecutive negative activities (i.e., the N60 at 20–90ms and N130 at 100–160 ms) that arise from the contralateral SI/SII and are related to early somatosensory processing of physical pain, and a long-latency activity that arises from the ACC and is related to the cognitive evaluation of and affective responses to physical pain (Bromm and Chen 1995; Christmann et al. 2007; Tarkka and Treede 1993; Zaslansky et al. 1996). Because priming independent, compared with interdependent self-construals, may facilitate self-focused attention, it was expected that independent versus interdependent self-construal priming may enhance the neural activity to painful stimulations. Wang et al. found that electrical stimulation to the left hand elicited two negative components (N60 and N130) over the frontal/central regions, and two positive components (P90 and P300) over the central/parietal regions with larger amplitudes at electrodes over the right rather than left hemisphere. Painful compared with non-painful stimulation enlarged P90, N130, and P300 amplitudes. More interestingly, it was found that priming independent versus interdependent self-construals induced larger N130 amplitudes to painful stimulation but did not produce significant effects on the amplitude of late neural responses (e.g., P300) to painful stimulation. The N130 was of larger amplitude over the right central electrodes that were contralateral to the stimulated hand and originated from the right somatosensory cortex. This result suggests that self-construal priming modulates the early sensory processing of physical pain. However, although self-construal priming failed to show reliable effects on the P300 amplitude in response to physical pain, there was a significant positive correlation between the differential P300 amplitudes to painful versus non-painful stimulation and the self-report of interdependent self-construals. Separate analyses further clarified that the independent relative to interdependent self-construal priming increased the P300 amplitude in those with high interdependence but decreased the P300 amplitude in those with low interdependence. Thus, the effect of self-construal priming on the late cognitive evaluation of physical pain varies across individuals with different dominant self-construals formed during long-term life experience.

Neural responses during visual perception are also modulated by self-construal priming. Lin et al. (2008) investigated whether the neural activity in the extrastriate cortex underlying the global/local perception of compound stimuli could be modulated by self-construal priming in Chinese participants. EEG recordings were undertaken in Chinese adults who were asked to discriminate the global/local letters in a compound stimulus. The visual angle of the compound stimuli was adjusted so that, under a control-priming condition, the amplitudes of the typical ERP components recorded from occipital electrodes (i.e., the P1 component) did not differentiate between the global and local task. The results showed that the independent self-construal priming resulted in enlarged P1 amplitude to local relative to global targets, while interdependent self-construal priming led to larger P1 amplitude to global than local targets (Figure 6.2). The P1 component originates from the extrastriate cortex and underlies early visual perception (e.g., Martinez et al. 1999). Thus Lin et al.'s findings provide electrophysiological evidence that self-construal priming modulates visual perceptual processing in the extrastriate cortex and suggest a neural underpinning of the finding that independent and interdependent self-construal priming speeded behavioral responses to local and global targets in compound stimuli, respectively (Lin and Han 2009).

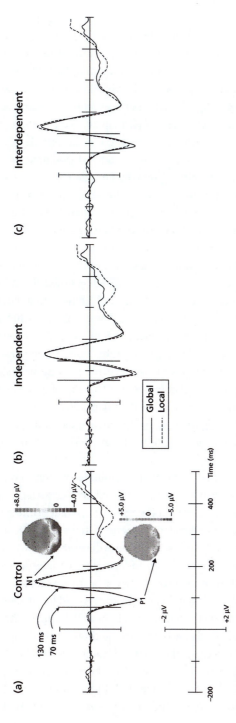

Figure 6.2 Illustration of the variation of P1 amplitude in response to global and local targets of compound visual stimuli after independent and interdependent self-construal priming. (See colour plate.)

Adapted from *Biological Psychology*, 77 (1), Zhicheng Lin, Yan Lin, and Shihui Han, Self-construal priming modulates visual activity underlying global/local perception, pp. 93–7, DOI:10.1016/j.biopsycho.2007.08.002, Copyright © 2007 Elsevier B.V., with permission from Elsevier.

The modulation of contextual information processing by self-construal priming has been further consolidated by Fong et al. (2014), who examine how priming of individualistic and collectivistic culture modulated the neural activity underlying attention to social-emotional contexts in Asian Americans. After being primed with individualistic and collectivistic cultural values using the Sumerian Warrior Story task and the Similarities and Differences with Family and Friends task (Trafimow et al. 1991), participants were presented with visual stimuli consisting of focal figures presented in the middle of a group of background figures (Figure 6.3). Both the target and the surrounding figures had either a happy or a sad facial expression, and the expressions were either congruent (i.e., all figures were expressing the same emotion) or incongruent (the target and surrounding figures showed different facial expressions). Fong et al. sought to determine how priming individualistic and collectivistic cultural values shaped cognitive processing of socioaffective context by analyzing a long-latency negative ERP component, that is, the N400, which was associated with the processing of semantic relatedness of social stimuli in the previous work (e.g., Goto et al. 2013). Fong et al. showed that, after priming with interdependent values, participants displayed a larger N400 amplitude in response to incongruent than congruent affective stimuli. In contrast, after priming with independent values, participants showed comparable neural responses in the N400 time window to incongruent and congruent stimuli. The ERP results support the notion that temporarily heightening the awareness of an interdependence cultural schema led to enhanced attention to contextual information whereas highlighting an independence cultural schema guided participants to focus on the focal figure and to ignore the surrounding socioaffective information.

The effects of self-construal priming are not limited to sensory, perceptual, and attentional processing but can be extended to the social and affective domains. Varnum and colleagues (2014) demonstrated that priming independence or interdependence modulated neural activity in the subcortical structures involved in vicarious reward: a sense of pleasure derived from watching others gain rewards. After being primed with independent or interdependent self-construals, Chinese adults were asked to play a card-guessing game in which they had to guess whether the number on the card would be smaller or greater than 5, indicated by pressing the left or right button. Participants had a chance to win extra monetary rewards for themselves and their friends in addition to their basic payment. After each trial, feedback indicated whether the participant had won or lost for either himself/herself or the friend. It was hypothesized that priming interdependence compared with independence should increase reward activity in response to a friend's benefit owing to increased similarity

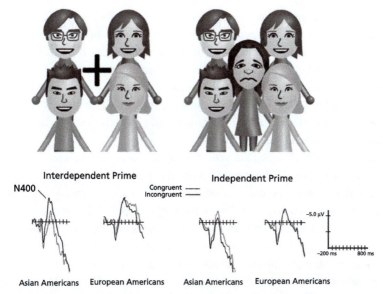

Figure 6.3 The upper panel illustrates visual stimuli of which the surrounding figures are presented first, and a figure expressing a different facial expression as the surrounding figures is shown superimposed with the images of the surrounding figures. The lower panel illustrates the N400 amplitude to stimuli in which the focal and surrounding facial expressions are incongruent and congruent after independent and interdependent self-construal priming. The effect of self-construal priming was evident in Asian Americans but not in European Americans.

Adapted from *Culture and Brain*, 2 (1), Michelle C. Fong, Sharon G. Goto, Colleen Moore, Tracy Zhao, Zachary Schudson, and Richard S. Lewis, Switching between Mii and Wii: The effects of cultural priming on the social affective N400, pp. 52–71, DOI:10.1007/s40167-014-0015-7, Copyright © 2014, Springer-Verlag Berlin Heidelberg. With permission of Springer.

and closeness to the other. Participants reported similar feelings of happiness when winning monetary reward for himself/herself or a friend but were less happy when they lost monetary reward for themselves relative to the friend, even though self-reported feelings were not influenced by self-construal priming. However, fMRI scanning revealed that neural responses to reward were significantly modulated by self-construal priming. Winning compared with losing monetary reward activated the bilateral ventral striatum—the key nodes of the reward network. Losing compared with winning monetary reward enhanced the activity in the bilateral insula and superior frontal gyrus. In addition, after an independent self-construal priming, the bilateral ventral striatum responded more strongly to winning money for the self than for a friend. Priming an interdependent self-construal, however, resulted in comparable activations in these regions in response to winning money for the self and for a friend. Interestingly, independence versus interdependence priming failed to alter neural activity in response to losing monetary to either the self or a friend (Figure 6.4). These findings suggest a neural mechanism by which a notion of self that includes close others causes similar rewards for the self and a friend. The modulations of the subcortical reward activity may provide a neural basis of the motivation for altruistic behavior toward close others when the cultural values of interdependence are activated.

According to Markus and Kitayama (2010), independent and interdependent self-construals have different implications for strength of in-group/out-group relationships. Thus, one may ask whether self-construal priming can change emotional responses to others by modulating the social relationship between an observer and those being observed. As mentioned in Chapter 5, in-group favoritism in empathic neural responses (i.e., greater activity during empathy for in-group than out-group members' pain) was more salient in those coming from collectivistic cultures (e.g., African Americans and Koreans) compared with those coming from individualistic cultures (e.g., Caucasian-Americans, Mathur et al. 2010; Cheon et al. 2011). According to Markus and Kitayama (2010), an independent schema of the self can organize behavior primarily with reference to an individual's own thoughts and feelings and it results in a weakened sense of in-group/out-group relationship so that people can move between in-group and out-groups relatively easily. In contrast, an interdependent schema of self organizes behavior immediately in reference to the thoughts and feelings of others with whom a person is in relationship, and leads to a significant distinction between in-group and out-group. Thus, it can be hypothesized that interdependent self-construals may augment an in-group bias in empathy, which, however, can be reduced when independent self-construals are promoted. This hypothesis was verified by Wang et al. (2015), who examined how a racial in-group bias in empathic neural responses varied following self-construal priming. During fMRI scanning, Chinese adults were first primed with independent or interdependent self-construals and then presented with video clips that depicted painful or non-painful stimulations applied to the faces of Asian and white models. It was predicted that a racial in-group bias in neural responses to perceived pain in others would occur when interdependent self-construals were promoted, whereas a racial in-group bias in the neural responses to perceived pain in others would be decreased when independent self-construals were encouraged. The activity in several brain regions indicated such patterns of modulation. There were stronger neural activities in the mid-cingulate, left insula, and supplementary motor areas in response to racial in-group compared with the out-group members' pain after participants had been

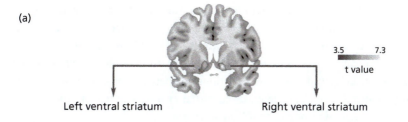

(a)

3.5   7.3

t value

Left ventral striatum   Right ventral striatum

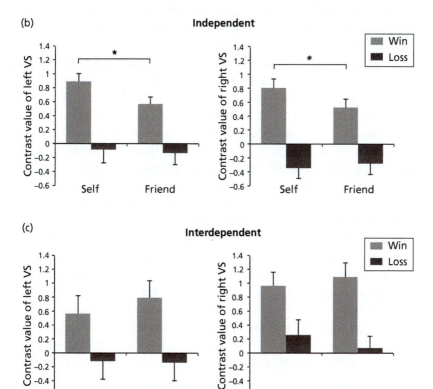

Figure 6.4 Modulation of reward activity in the ventral striatum in response to winning money by self-construal priming. The upper panel illustrates the reward activity in the ventral striatum. The middle and lower panels show BOLD responses to one's own and a friend's reward. The reward activity to one's own reward was stronger than that to a friend's reward after independent self-construal priming, whereas interdependent self-construal priming tended to produce an opposite pattern. (See colour plate.)

Adapted from *NeuroImage*, 87 (1), Michael E.W. Varnum, Zhenhao Shi, Antao Chen, Jiang Qiu, and Shihui Han, When "Your" reward is the same as "My" reward: Self-construal priming shifts neural responses to own vs. friends' rewards, pp. 164–9, DOI:10.1016/j.neuroimage.2013.10.042, Copyright © 2013 Elsevier Inc., with permission from Elsevier.

primed with interdependent self-construals. However, the racial in-group bias in neural responses to others' pain in the left supplementary motor area, mid-cingulate cortex, and insula was significantly reduced by priming independent self-construals. The results suggest that shifting an individual's self-construal modulates perceived intergroup relationships between observers and targets (e.g., reduced by independent self-construal priming), and such interactions determine neural responses to others' suffering.

If interdependent self-construals promote attention to others and social context to a greater degree than independent self-construals do, the effect of self-construal priming may be extended to motivation to execute actions and thus to modulate activity in the motor cortex. This issue was addressed by Obhi et al. (2011), who recorded the motor-evoked potentials elicited with transcranial magnetic stimulation (TMS) during an action observation task. TMS is a non-invasive method that can be used to stimulate small regions of the brain. A head coil generates a transient magnetic field over the cortex that produces small electric currents in the region of the brain under the coil via electromagnetic induction. Obhi et al. used TMS to activate participants' left motor cortex and recorded motor-evoked potentials when participants viewed videos depicting a right hand squeezing a rubber ball between the thumb and index finger such that the rubber ball was substantially deformed. Self-construal primes were administered by superimposing interdependent words (e.g., *Together* and *Integrate*) or independent words (e.g., *Individuality* and *Unique*) on each video clip. The results of motor-evoked potentials indicated that, compared with a no-priming baseline condition, priming interdependent self-construal increased motor cortical output, whereas priming independent self-construal did not. Such changes in the motor system by interdependent self-construal priming are in line with the effects of self-construal priming on other cognitive and affective processing to mediate behavioral changes in response to others' demands of help.

All the above studies tested self-construal priming effects on task-related brain activity. However, the neural correlates of self-construal priming itself remain unknown. In addition, it is unclear whether and how self-construal priming changes the baseline brain activity before task-related brain activity occurs. To clarify these issues would help to construct a general neural model of how self-construal priming modulates task-related brain activity. Wang and colleagues (2013) scanned Chinese adults when they underwent independent and interdependent self-construal priming and when they were in a resting state (i.e., not performing any explicit task) after the priming procedure. The resting-state activity is characterized by spontaneous fluctuations in BOLD signals and, particularly, enhanced activity along the cortical midline structure is associated with self-related processing (Deco et al. 2011). Want et al. found that, relative to a calculation task, reading short essays with plural pronouns (*we, our,* or *us*) or singular pronouns (*I, me,* or *mine*) activated the ventral medial prefrontal cortex and the posterior cingulate cortex. Thus, self-construal priming appears to engage the brain regions that have been demonstrated to be involved in self-reflection. Relative to independent self-construal priming, interdependent self-construal priming induced greater activity in the dorsal medial prefrontal cortex, a key node of the default mode network that is activated during person perception (Han et al. 2005; Mitchell et al. 2002) and interference of others' mental states (Amodio and Frith 2006). The analysis of regional homogeneity of resting-state activity, an index of the similarity of dynamic fluctuations of voxels within a given cluster (Zang et al. 2004), revealed increased local synchronization of spontaneous activity in the dorsal medial prefrontal cortex but decreased local synchronization of spontaneous activity in the posterior cingulate cortex after interdependent versus independent self-construal priming. Thus, the modulations of brain activity both during and after self-construal priming were salient in the default mode network. The brain activity during the resting state, which is shaped by self-construal priming, may render a precondition on which the subsequent task-related brain activity takes place.

Interaction of temporary and chronic self-construals on brain activity

All the brain imaging studies of cultural priming mentioned in the previous section tested bicultural or monocultural individuals from one society. This leaves an open issue of how temporary shifts of cultural values manipulated in a laboratory may interact with individuals' chronic cultural traits to modulate brain activity underlying cognitive/affective processes. For instance, since Westerners and East Asians in general value independent and interdependent self-construals, respectively, would they respond differently when primed with interdependent or independent self-construals? Would a match versus a mismatch between primed cultural values and "chronic" cultural traits give rise to different response patterns of brain activity? Such interactions, if they exist, may occur both when temporary activation of a cultural value is congruent with or incongruent with an individual's chronic cultural trait. The consequence of such interactions can provide a cognitive frame under which the brain carries out various cognitive and affective functions. A limited number of brain imaging studies have examined the two issues regarding the interactions of temporary shifts of cultural values and the chronic cultural traits on brain activity. First, whose brain activity, those educated in Western or East Asian cultures, is more prone to being influenced by cultural priming? Second, which types of cultural priming, congruent or incongruent with individuals' chronic cultural traits, produce greater effects on brain activity? These questions have been addressed by recording brain activity from Western or East Asian participants after self-construal priming.

To investigate whether an individual's culturally specific pattern of neural activity to faces is modulated by temporary access to independent/interdependent self-construals, Sui et al. (2013) recorded ERPs from British and Chinese adults during judgments of the orientation of one's own and a friend's face after the participants had been primed with independent or interdependent self-construals by reading short essays carrying semantic single or plural pronouns. They tested the hypothesis that priming independence or interdependence opposite to (versus similar to) one's chronic cultural traits would produce stronger effects on brain activity in response to one's own face and a friend's face. For example, as the British on average prefer independence, priming interdependent versus independent self-construals should produce larger changes of neural responses to self-face and friend's faces relative to a baseline condition without self-construal priming. Conversely, as the Chinese on average favor interdependence, priming independent versus interdependent self-construals should change their brain activity to their own face and friend's faces to a larger degree relative to the baseline condition. Sui et al. found that both British and Chinese participants responded faster to their own face compared with a friend's face during judgments of orientations of faces by responding with a button press. British participants showed faster responses to their own faces than to their friends' faces in the no-priming and independent-priming conditions but not in the interdependent-priming condition. Chinese participants also responded faster to their own faces but their response speeds were not influenced by self-construal priming. Thus, the effects of self-construal priming on British participants' performance were consistent with the hypothesis. The hypothesis was further supported by the modulations of ERPs to faces by self-construal priming. ERP recordings revealed that an early frontal negative activity at 220–340 ms (the anterior N2) was sensitive to both face identity and self-construal priming. For British participants, the anterior N2 was of a larger amplitude to one's own face compared with a friend's face in the baseline condition, and priming an interdependent self-construal reduced the anterior N2 amplitude to their own faces. For Chinese participants, the friend's face elicited a larger anterior N2 compared with their own faces, and priming an independent self-construal decreased the anterior N2 amplitude to their friend's faces. Both behavioral and brain responses to the self and a friend in this work at least partially support the posit that individuals from a Western society are more sensitive to interdependent self-construal priming, whereas individuals from an East Asian society are more sensitive to independent self-construal priming.

The conclusion of the interaction between temporary shift of self-construal and chronic cultural traits, however, does not apply to empathic neural responses to unknown others. Jiang et al. (2014) recorded ERPs to stimuli depicting the hands of unknown others experiencing painful or non-painful events from Chinese and Western participants after they had been primed in independent/interdependent self-construal priming. The ERP results first replicated the previous findings by showing that viewing stimuli depicting painful versus non-painful stimuli applied to others elicited a positive shift of the fronto-central activity at 230–330 ms and of the central-parietal activity at 440–740 ms. There was also evidence for priming effects on empathic neural responses. Relative to the control-priming condition, empathic neural responses at 230–330 ms were decreased by interdependent self-construal priming among Chinese participants but by independent self-construal priming among Western participants. Apparently, empathic neural responses to unknown others were more sensitive to interdependent self-construal priming in Chinese but more sensitive to independent self-construal priming in Westerners. According to Markus and Kitayama (2010), the independent self-construal dominates Western cultures and defines a solid boundary between the self and any others. The interdependent self-construal dominates East Asian cultures and induces a solid boundary between in-group (including the self and close others) and out-group (non-close others such as strangers). Jiang et al.'s findings can best be understood in terms of that activating an independent mindset causes all others to be excluded from the self in Western culture and thus reduces empathic responses to out-group members (i.e., unknown others). In contrast, activating an interdependent mindset may enhance the boundary between an in-group (i.e., self and close others) and out-group (i.e., unknown others) in East Asian culture, which in turn weakens empathic neural responses to perceived pain in unknown others.

Sui et al.'s (2013) and Jiang et al.'s (2014) findings allow one to conclude that a temporary shift of the self-construal does not always produce greater effects on brain activity when temporarily activated cultural values are inconsistent versus consistent with an individual's chronic dominated cultural traits. The interacting pattern between a temporary shift of self-construal and chronic cultural traits on brain activity seems to depend upon the social information required to be processed (e.g., self, familiar others, or strangers). Brain activity can be modulated by priming of cultural values that are in line with or contrary to individuals' chronic cultural traits.

Cultural frames for brain function

The cultural priming studies of brain activity summarized in this chapter complement cross-cultural brain imaging findings by showing that both a temporary switch of cultural knowledge systems manipulated in laboratories and chronic cultural value systems formed during long-term sociocultural experiences can influence human brain activity engaged in a number of sensory, perceptual, cognitive, and affective processes. The findings strengthen our understanding of a causal relationship between culture and functional organization of the human brain. Individuals start to learn specific cultural beliefs/values/norms and practice culturally specific behavioral scripts from early childhood. Cultural learning and experience help to formulate belief/value systems and routine ways of doing things, and shape styles of cognitive and affective processing. However, even during adulthood, one's cultural knowledge system can be temporarily changed, and the short-term shift of cultural values/norms similarly modulates cognition and behavior. In this sense, culture can provide both a sustained and a transient frame for structuring both behavior and mental processes.

Cultural neuroscience findings provide evidence that cultural influences go beyond behavioral and psychological effects and extend the function of culture to shape the neural basis of behavior and mental processes. The findings indicate that performing the same task involving the same stimuli can engage distinct patterns of brain activity in individuals from different cultures, and the cultural group differences in brain activity can be mediated by a specific cultural value (e.g., interdependence). More importantly, cultural (e.g., self-construal) priming induces transient shifts in the default style of processing toward interdependent or independent ways of thinking, and this in turn gives rise to changes of related brain activity. The findings show evidence that brain responses to stimuli during a task are to a certain degree, constrained by both sustained (owing to long-term cultural experiences) and transient cultural frameworks (owing to short-term exposure to cultural values). The sustained cultural frames built during long-term social experiences are relatively stable and they offer a default mindset under which the brain functions to guide behaviors during daily life. Most of the findings of cross-cultural brain imaging studies indicate the effects of long-term cultural experiences on the functional organization of the brain so it is shaped to fit a specific sociocultural environment. The pattern of brain functional organization arising from long-term cultural experiences provides default neural underpinnings of culturally specific cognitive styles. However, the sustained cultural frame can change over time under certain conditions (e.g., emigration across the globe), which can generate new long-term cultural experiences.

Unlike sustained cultural frames, the transient cultural frames adjust neural correlates of multiple cognitive and affective processes in a short period, and such modifications are not expected to last long if cultural priming is not repeated in a long-term fashion. Multicultural environments provide the precondition of building transient cultural frames during the switch between cultural schemas according to the immediate sociocultural context (Hong et al. 2000). The capacity of changing patterns of brain activity in response to rapidly formulated cultural schemas is critical for the brain to respond to various social tasks in dynamic changing sociocultural environments. Both sustained and transient cultural frames influence multiple levels of neural substrates of sensation, perception, attention, emotion, self-reflection, empathy, and mental state inference. These cultural neuroscience findings demonstrate that the effect of cultural learning on brain activity differs from the effect of domain specific (e.g., perceptual and motor) learning, which selectively alters neural activity in the visual cortex, motor cortex, etc. The interaction between sustained and transient cultural frames constrains neural strategies and biases the brain to respond in a specific way to guide our behaviors (Han and Humphreys 2016).

Chapter 7

Gene-culture interaction on human behavior and the brain

Nature versus Nurture: A cultural perspective

The importance of heredity relative to environment in shaping our biological functions, mental processes, and social behaviors during human development and evolution has long been debated. The phrase *nature versus nurture* has been coined to characterize the pivotal issue of the relative contributions of hereditary and of environmental differences in accounting for individual variations in any particular behavioral tendency and psychological trait and the biological basis. While early research was aimed at determining the influences of heredity and environment, it is now commonly accepted that nature and nurture are not alternatives, and there are complicated heredity-environment interacting effects. If we consider that genes are affected by their environments, and learning requires the expression of genes, it would be misleading to exaggerate the nature-nurture distinction when studying human nature. By asking questions such as how genes are expressed in response to environments, researchers have been able to move toward in the investigation of whether and how heredity and environment interact to modify multiple aspects of the trajectory of human development, and how the effects of one can be constrained, multiplied, or even reversed by the effects of the other.

Empirical research on the effects of nature versus nurture on human development has covered an astonishing range of topics in different fields. One approach of the empirical studies has been to compare measures from identical (or monozygotic, MZ) twins, who share nearly 100% of their genes, and nonidentical (or dizygotic, DZ) twins, who share only about 50% of their genes, to explore the genetic contributions to physiological and psychological variables. For example, ophthalmologists have investigated whether monozygotic and dizygotic twins tend to resemble each other in refractive error and the ocular component values of their eyes, to estimate to what degree the variance of myopia can be explained by heredity and whether myopia is associated with the amount of time spent in reading activities and level of education (Mutti et al. 1996; Saw et al. 2000). Psychologists have studied to what extent intelligence and psychological traits vary across monozygotic and dizygotic twins and have assessed how specific cognitive abilities such as memory are subject to influences of both heredity and life experience (Turkheimer 2000; Kan et al. 2013). There is also an interest in the contributions of heredity and environment to complex human social behaviors such as cooperation and aggression (Moffitt, 2005; Cesarini et al. 2008) and political/economic decision making (Hatemi et al. 2015). Neurobiologists have examined the degree to which the structural and functional organization of the human brain is tied with specific genes (Wright et al. 2002; Toga and Thompson 2005; Chen et al. 2012; Richiardi et al. 2015) and to what extent brain functional organization varies as a consequence of an individual's life experiences (Sadato et al. 1996; Ptito et al. 2005; Lupien et al. 2009). Psychiatrists have pursued causal relationships between the heredity-environment interaction and mental disorders such as anxiety and depression (Caspi et al. 2003; Caspi and Moffitt 2006; Wilkinson et al. 2013).

In the Nature-versus-Nurture discussion of human development, the concept of *heredity* has an unambiguous biological basis—deoxyribonucleic acid (DNA)—a molecule with an identified structure. DNA molecules consist of two biopolymer strands in the form of a double helix with four types of nucleobase—cytosine (C), guanine (G), adenine (A), and thymine (T). DNA stores biological information, part of which contributes to variations of phenotypes, by serving as patterns for producing proteins. Early behavioral genetic research took advantage of the different DNA patterns in monozygotic and dizygotic twins to examine to what degree behavior traits are inheritable. The rationale is that, because monozygotic twins' genetic similarity is twice that of dizygotic twins, monozygotic twins' behavior ought to be at least twice as similar as that of dizygotic twins if nothing but genes has an influence on their behavior. If this is not the case, one can infer that environments must interact with genes to contribute to patterns of behavior. Recent genome-wide association studies (GWAS) have taken further steps to identify the genetic variants in specific single-nucleotide polymorphisms (SNP) that are associated with biological and behavioral traits such as stature and educational attainment (e.g., Yang et al. 2010; Rietveld et al. 2013; Evangelou and Ioannidis 2013). The findings of behavioral genetics have helped to account for individual differences in biological and behavioral traits coming from people experiencing the same culture from the perspective of heredity. However, it remains a big challenge for behavioral genetics research to unravel the biological pathways through which genes influence human traits and behavior.

The concept of *environment* used in the Nature-versus-Nurture discussion of human development, however, is much more complicated than the concept of heredity. People can have very different life experiences owing to social contexts, family structures, the language one speaks, schools one attends, the occupation one carriers on, the religion one practices, cultural beliefs/values one endorses, etc. Which among these factors is the most homogenous in a cohort of people, and thus plays the most critical and stable influence on their behaviors? Considering human development from early childhood to adolescence, children from different families have distinct experiences with parents who provide reward and render punishment as a part of education at home. Although children from the same family tend to share similar experiences with their parents, research has shown that the environmental factors shared by family members have not been found to make their members similar in almost all the human behavioral traits studied (Rowe 1994). Studies of psychological characteristics (such as personality and cognitive ability) in adopted children reared in the same family have revealed that correlations for adoptive siblings in most psychological characteristics hover near zero, which implies that environmental differences outside family between children from the same family represent the major source of environmental influence (Plomin and Daniels 1987). More interestingly, it has been shown that shared environmental effects that can make siblings growing up in the same family similar in terms of general intelligence are important in childhood but are negligible after adolescence (McGue 1993). Such findings raise a fundamental issue of what is shared by individuals during and after adolescence that is able to produce crucial effects on the development of behavioral traits and the underlying brain mechanisms.

Both brain structure and cultural beliefs undergo rapid change during adolescence. For example, in a study that examined the dynamic anatomical sequence of human cortical gray matter development between the ages of 4–21 years, Gogtay et al. (2004) found that human cortical development is characterized by a decrease of gray matter density, and the process of cortical maturation starts from lower-order somatosensory and visual cortices and occurs in the higher-order association cortices including the frontal lobe—the key node of the social brain network underlying social cognition and behavior—during adolescence. A study of acculturation of Hong Kong immigrants in Canada found that a longer duration of life experience in Canada was found to be associated with greater identification with Canadian culture only in immigrants younger than 15 years, whereas such an association was not observed at later ages of immigration (Cheung et al. 2011). These neuroscientific and behavioral findings suggest that adolescence may be a sensitive period for digesting new cultural beliefs/values and that shared beliefs/values—the core component of culture—are relatively more consistent across individuals than the individuals' life experiences. Therefore, it is likely that the homogeneity of cultural beliefs/ values in a social group plays a key role in shaping behavioral traits and underlying brain mechanisms. Indeed, it has been suggested that the processes of socialization through which the skills and values needed to thrive in a given culture are acquired take place in the peer group rather than the family (Harris 2000). Children care about and are eager to learn what is valued and shared in their peer groups, and this eventually teaches them how to compete for status and mates, rather than to surrender to their parents' teaching. Thus, a cultural perspective on the relationship between nature and nurture puts stress on the functional role of shared beliefs/values and learned behavioral scripts and their interactions with human biological processes in forming an individual's psychological traits and behavioral tendencies. Particularly in current societies, most individuals develop in artificial environments that are full of cultural imprints. Such individuals acquire cultural beliefs/values through social learning at schools and from social media. It is inevitable for each individual to be strongly influenced by the cultural experiences that are, to a certain degree, common to the majority of a population in a society.

Gene-culture coevolution

Geneticists and biological anthropologists take a broad view of culture as information that is acquired from other individuals through teaching, imitation, and other forms of social learning and is capable of affecting an individual's behavior (Richerson and Boyd 2005). This view of culture has led to the notion of inheriting two kinds of information, that is, biological and social information that is respectively encoded by genes and culture, and so has created analogies between cultural change and biological evolution. Culture can be transmitted from one generation to the next, in a way similar to genetic inheritance. However, cultural transmission also takes place obliquely (e.g., learning from teachers) and horizontally (e.g., among peers of the same generation), which are different from the transmission of genetic information. Cultural selection occurs through the specific cultural beliefs and values that are promoted in a population owing to adoption of these beliefs/values by individuals (Cavalli-Sforza and Feldman 1981). Cultural selection also takes place when individuals learn culturally specific behavioral scripts and modify their behaviors because of their personal experiences (Richerson and Boyd 2005). The transmission and selection processes suggest that culture develops in human history in a way similar to that of genetic evolution and that genetic and cultural processes interact over evolutionary time. The gene-culture coevolutionary theory proposes that genetic propensities can influence what cultural organisms learn, and culturally transmitted information and culturally constructed environments can modify the selection pressures that influence genetic transmission in populations (Richerson and Boyd 2005; Laland et al. 2010; Richerson et al. 2010).

Early research related to gene-cultural coevolution considered how a learned behavior coevolves with the allele frequency of specific genes that in turn may affect acquisition of the behavior. For example, milk consumption requires the enzyme lactase: it has been shown that there is a high correlation between the incidence of the gene for lactose absorption and a history of dairy farming in populations (Durham 1991), suggesting coevolution of a specific gene and culturally preferred foods. Recent research has tried to break down culture into specific traits to investigate further covariation of allele frequencies of specific genes and cultural values across nations. Chiao and Blizinsky (2010) assessed the association between cultural values of individualism and collectivism and the allelic frequency of the serotonin transporter functional polymorphism (5-HTTLPR). The 5-HTTLPR has two variants, that is, the short (s) and the long (l) alleles (Canli and Lesch 2007), and it has been suggested to interact with an individual's life experiences to influence their traits and behaviors. For example, depression symptoms (Caspi et al. 2003; Taylor et al. 2006) and neuroticism (Pluess et al. 2010) are more closely associated with stressful life events in the short allele carriers than in the homozygous long allele (l/l) carriers of 5-HTTLPR. One interesting finding reported by Chiao and Blizinsky (2010) was that collectivistic cultural values are significantly more likely to be apparent in individuals carrying the short allele of the 5-HTTLPR across 29 nations. There is a higher proportion of short allele carriers in East Asian countries dominated by collectivistic cultural values than in Western European countries dominated by individualistic cultural values. In addition, it was found that the collectivistic cultural values and the frequency of short allele carriers negatively predict a global prevalence of anxiety and mood disorders, and the increased frequency of short allele carriers predicts decreased anxiety and mood disorder prevalence owing to increased collectivistic cultural values. Mrazek et al. (2013) further reported that the short allele frequency in the 5-HTTLPR is correlated with another cultural value, tightness and looseness, which indexes the strength of norms and tolerance for deviance from norms (Triandis 1989; Gelfand et al. 2011). Similarly, Way and Lieberman (2010) found that variations within the genes of central neurotransmitter systems such as the 5-HTTLPR and opioid (OPRM1 A118G) are associated with individual differences in social sensitivity. In addition, the relative proportion of these alleles is correlated with lifetime prevalence of major depression across nations, and this relationship is partially mediated by individualism and collectivism cultural values.

Luo and Han (2014) have further revealed that the association between collectivistic cultural values and the allelic frequency of the 5-HTTLPR is mediated by the allelic frequency of the oxytocin receptor gene that is localized to human chromosome 3 (Gimpl and Fahrenholz 2001). One variant of the oxytocin receptor gene, called OXTR rs53576, is a SNP (G or A) located in intron 3 of the coding region, which has been associated with variations of emotion-related behaviors. Luo and Han (2014) examined whether OXTR rs53576 can explain the relations between pathogen prevalence, collectivistic cultural values, and prevalence of major depression disorders. Interestingly, they found that, across twelve nations, the A allelic frequency of OXTR rs53576 correlates with collectivistic cultural values endorsed by these nations. Moreover, the A allelic frequency of OXTR rs53576 mediates the relationship between pathogen prevalence, allelic frequency of the 5-HTTLPR and collectivistic cultural values. Finally, the A allele frequency of OXTR rs53576 is predictive of a major depression disorder prevalence across nations and that is mediated by collectivistic cultural values. Taken together, these findings suggest that covariations of cultural values (rather than a specific behavior) and specific genes may not be a contingency in human societies, and that, at the population level, there may exist direct interactions between allele frequencies and cultural values/beliefs. Thus, cultural heritage and genetic heritage are woven together during human development and evolution to shape our behavior and influence global variations in pathogen prevalence and the epidemiology of affective disorders.

Gene-culture interaction on psychological trait and behavioral tendency

While the aforementioned empirical research of gene-culture coevolution focuses on the distribution of specific genes within different cultural groups, another line of research investigates gene-culture interaction by examining culturally moderated associations between specific genes and behavioral/psychological tendencies (Sasaki 2013; Kim and Sasaki 2014). This approach tries to explain whether and how genetic and sociocultural factors interact to shape psychological traits and behavioral tendencies at an individual level. A fundamental hypothesis underlying this approach is that variants of a gene can be differentially susceptible to sociocultural environmental input, and thus, how an individual engages culture-specific behaviors is modulated by his/her genetic makeup. The variant that is more sensitive to cultural influences then should embody to a greater degree culturally preferred patterns of psychological and behavioral tendencies in a specific society. A number of studies have shown evidence supporting this proposal.

For example, Kim and colleagues (2010) examined individuals' sensitivity to cultural norms regarding emotional-support seeking as a type of social environment in two cultural groups. Korean and American participants were genotyped for OXTR rs53576 and completed questionnaire assessments of psychological distress and emotional-support seeking. Kim et al. predicted a three-way interaction of culture, distress, and OXTR genotype on emotional-support seeking because OXTR has been shown to be related to socioemotional sensitivity. Interestingly, it was found that, among distressed American participants, those with the G/G (and A/G) genotypes reported seeking more emotional social support, compared with those with the A/A genotype. By contrast, seeking emotional support did not significantly differ between G/G (and A/G) and A/A genotypes in Korean participants. Moreover, for those with low distress, OXTR groups did not differ significantly in either cultural group. These findings provide the first evidence that variants of OXTR rs53576, particularly those with high distress, are differentially sensitive to input from the social environment (e.g., specific cultural norms regarding emotional social support seeking). Moreover, psychological distress and culture appear to be important moderators that can shape behavioral outcomes associated with OXTR genotypes.

The following studies have revealed further evidence for an interaction between OXTR and culture on other psychological traits and behavioral tendencies. Since emotional suppression is normative in East Asian cultures but not in the American culture, Kim and colleagues (2011) tested an interaction of culture and OXTR rs53576 in emotional suppression by asking genotyped Korean and American participants to complete assessments of emotion regulation. They found that, among American participants, those with the G/G genotype reported using emotional suppression to a lesser degree than those with the AA genotype did, whereas Koreans showed the opposite pattern, indicating that the variants of OXTR rs53576 are differentially sensitive to input from cultural norms regarding emotion regulation. Another study tested how the association between religiosity and psychological well-being may depend on the interplay between cultural context and OXTR rs53576 (Sasaki et al. 2011). Because religion in East Asian cultures tends to emphasize social affiliation more than in a North American cultural context, it was predicted that culture (European American vs. Korean) and a specific gene polymorphism (OXTR rs53576) may interact to affect the association between religiosity and psychological well-being (as assessed by questionnaire measures of psychological distress). It was found that among individuals with the G/G genotype who were genetically predisposed toward social sensitivity, Korean participants reported greater psychological well-being if they were more religious. On the contrary, European Americans with the G/G genotype had lower psychological well-being if they were more religious. The opposite patterns of genetic differences in psychological well-being between the two cultures suggest that religion as a cultural system may benefit well-being for those who are genetically predisposed to be socially sensitive but only to the extent that the cultural context provides adequate opportunities for social affiliation.

Increasing evidence has revealed cultural interactions with other genes to influence behavioral tendencies and psychological traits. For example, Kitayama and colleagues (2014) investigated whether and how cultural acquisition of interdependence versus independence was moderated by polymorphisms of the dopamine D4 receptor gene (DRD4), which regulates the efficiency of the central dopaminergic pathways. The exon 3 variable-number tandem repeat polymorphism of DRD4 has three types of variants, with the most common alleles of 2, 4, and 7 repeats (i.e., 2R, 4R, and 7R alleles). Among these the 7R allele shows less in vitro dopamine functioning and is characterized by diminished dopamine feedback inhibition (Seeger et al. 2001; Wang et al. 2004). Interestingly, relative to Caucasian populations, the 7R allele is less frequent in Asian populations, such as Koreans (Reist et al. 2007), and has been suggested to be a plasticity allele that is sensitive to environmental influences (Belsky and Pluess 2009). Such findings motivated Kitayama and colleagues to test the hypothesis that the 7R compared with other variants of DRD4 is associated with greater adoption of cultural norms in a specific cultural context. They measured independence and interdependence, using Singelis's (1994) Self-Construal Scale, from European American and Asian American students and genotyped these participants for DRD4. Questionnaire measures first identified that European American students were more independent, whereas Asian American students were more interdependent. Further analyses revealed that the cultural difference in interdependence/interdependence in the predicted direction was significant in the 7R/2R carriers but was negligible for the 7R/2R non-carriers. Because the 2R allele is derived from the 7R allele (Wang et al. 2004) and these two alleles share some biochemical properties and functions (Reist et al. 2007), it is not surprising that 7R/2R carriers exhibited high sensitivity in absorbing cultural values/beliefs. This finding suggests that the social orientation (interdependence) measured with explicit belief-based questionnaires is modulated by variants of the DRD4 carried by individuals.

If the 7R/2R variants compared with other variants are more susceptible to sociocultural experiences, these variants should illustrate a stronger effect of cultural priming in laboratories. Taking religion as a cultural system, Sasaki et al. (2013) examined whether individuals carrying the 7R/2R alleles would show greater prosocial behavior when primed with religion relative to 7R/2R non-carriers. They adopted a priming procedure from Shariff and Norenzayan

(2007), which gave each participant a set of ten five-word strings. Participants were asked to unscramble the words to make a four-word phrase or a sentence by dropping the irrelevant word. The religion-related prime consisted of words relevant to religion (e.g., *God* and *divine*) and the control prime contained non-religion words (e.g., *shoes* and *sky*). To estimate whether prosocial tendencies in 7R/2R carriers and non-carriers were differentially susceptible to religion priming, Sasaki et al. measured participants' willingness to donate for prosocial causes supporting the environment. It was found that individuals implicitly primed with religion-related words reported a greater willingness to volunteer than those receiving the control priming did. Importantly, this main effect was qualified by a significant interaction of DRD4 variant and religion prime, which showed that the religion prime enhanced prosocial behavioral tendency in the 7R/2R carriers but failed to influence willingness to volunteer for 7R/2R non-carriers. By showing that prosocial tendency in one variant of DRD4 was more sensitive to religion priming than in other variants of DRD4, Sasaki et al. provide an elegant laboratory illustration of dynamic interactions of cultural priming and individuals' genetic makeup on behavioral tendency.

Ishii et al. (2014) also reported evidence for an interaction between the 5-HTTLPR and culture on the processing of social emotion. It has been shown that short/short compared with long/long allele carriers of 5-HTTLPR showed elevated depressive symptoms or risk in high-stress environments but reduced depressive symptom levels or risk in low-stress environments (Caspi et al. 2003). This led to the suggestion that the short compared with the long allele carriers of 5-HTTLPR would be more susceptible to both good and bad environmental inputs (Belsky et al. 2009). Thus it is likely that short/short carriers of 5-HTTLPR would be likely to respond more strongly to culture-specific norms and practices relative to the long allele carriers. To verify this prediction, Ishii et al. (2014) tested genotyped Japanese and American participants on the 5-HTTLPR while participants viewed movie clips showing models whose facial expressions changed from happy to neutral. Their task was to judge the point at which the emotional expressions disappeared. The idea was to assess individuals' sensitivity to the gradual disappearance of a smile: a dynamic cue manifesting violation of others' expectations. It has been shown previously that, compared with European Americans, Japanese participants judged the disappearance of smiles faster (Ishii et al. 2011), possibly because of being more sensitive to signs of social disagreement. Ishii et al. (2014) found that Japanese participants with the short/short genotype detected the disappearance of smiles with greater perceptual efficiency than did those with short/long and long/long genotypes, whereas such a tendency was not observed in Americans. This finding implies that short/short carriers are more sensitive to facial expression changes that function as social feedback only when the change is culturally important such as in Japan but not in America.

Each of the aforementioned studies has shown evidence of an interaction between culture and a specific gene. In addition, for each gene, one variant compared with another appeared to be more sensitive to cultural environments and experiences. These findings raise an interesting question of whether consideration of multiple genes rather than a single gene would yield more reliable results overall as an explanation of cultural influences on behavioral traits. A recent work tested this by genotyping American and Korean participants on four genes including OXTR, DRD4, 5-HTTLPR, and 5HTR1A polymorphisms (LeClair et al. 2014). The serotonin receptor type-1A (5HTR1A) gene encodes for the serotonin HT1A receptor, and the G allele of the 5HTR1A rs6295 polymorphism prevents binding of repressor proteins, resulting in reduced serotonin levels, and it has been linked to depression (Lemonde et al. 2003). LeClair et al. defined a genetic susceptibility index based on polymorphisms from the four genes to build an integrative measure of genetic susceptibility. They calculated susceptibility scores by assigning a value of 2 to the most susceptible homozygote of 5-HTTLPR (short/short), 5HTR1A (G/G), and OXTR (G/G). The least susceptible homozygotes of 5-HTTLPR (long/long), 5HTR1A (C/C) and OXTR (A/A) were assigned with a value of 0, and heterozygotes were assigned a value of 1. For DRD4, individuals having the 7R or two 2R alleles were assigned with a value of 2; those with at least one 2R allele were assigned with a value of 1; and no 2R or 7R allele carriers with a value of 0. Thus the overall genetic susceptibility index, ranging from 2 to 0, was believed to reflect an individual's susceptibility by considering multiple genes. Behavioral tendencies of self-expression were estimated by integrating questionnaire measures of values of self-expression, emotion suppression, and emotional-support seeking. LeClair et al. performed a moderated hierarchical regression analysis that confirmed a gene-culture interaction on individuals' behavioral tendencies. There was a negative relationship between genetic susceptibility and the index of self-expressive tendencies in Korean participants: those with less genetic susceptibility exhibited a greater tendency to assign high values to expression, showing less emotion suppression and more emotional-support seeking. In contrast, American participants showed a positive relationship between genetic susceptibility and self-expressive tendencies. This study created a model for examining the effects of multiple genes simultaneously, and the findings suggest that the genetic susceptibility index predicts a wider range of self-expression outcomes than is predicted by individual polymorphisms.

Taken together, these studies open a gene-culture interaction approach to understanding the causes of human psychological trait and behavioral tendencies. The findings that the same genotype can be associated with different patterns of phenotypes in different cultural groups cast doubts on the concept of a simple relationship between genotype and phenotype in humans, and have important implications for understanding genetic effects on human behavioral tendencies. Importantly, the findings can be interrelated by assuming that the degree of cultural acquisition is influenced by polymorphic variants of genes (Kitayama et al. 2016). One variant relative to another variant of the same gene is more susceptible to cultural influences so as to more easily adopt a local cultural value (e.g., the 7R allele carriers of DRD4 prefer independence in European Americans but prefer interdependence in Asian Americans, Kitayama et al. 2014) or a behavioral tendency that is encouraged by a local cultural context (e.g., the G/G compared with A/A genotype showing less emotional suppression in Americans but more emotional suppression in Koreans; Kim et al. 2011). The greater susceptibility of one compared with another variant of the same gene is manifested when considering both chronic cultural influences (e.g., comparing measures from two cultural groups) and temporary cultural effect (e.g., cultural-value priming). The distinct patterns of phenotypes related to a gene in different cultures are caused by specific challenges/goals and specific behavioral scripts through which individuals approach these goals in different cultural environments.

Genetic influences on the brain

It is commonly believed that, as a biological organ, both anatomical and functional organizations of the brain develop along the trajectory that, to a certain degree, is predetermined by an individual's genetic makeup, although this view does not exclude influences of environments and experiences on brain development. Thus before moving forward to studies of the gene-culture interaction in the human brain, I believe that it would be helpful to give a short overview of the brain imaging research of genetic effects on the structural and functional organization of the human brain. Imaging genetics is a field that has emerged recently to integrate brain imaging and genetics in order to examine the genetic associations of brain morphology and function in healthy individuals and abnormal structural and functional organization of the brain in patients with mental disorders. Brain morphology and function are used as endophenotypes, which are closer to genes relative to psychological traits and behavior tendencies, to assess genetic variability. Three main approaches in this field are twin studies that explore heritability of brain structure and function, candidate gene association studies that assess the association between a specific gene and brain structure and function, and GWAS that search for a SNP associated with the variation of brain structure and functions.

Twin studies compare imaging results from MZ twins and DZ twins of different ages. The rationale of this line of research is that increased similarity in structural or functional imaging results in MZ than DZ twins would suggest genetic contributions to brain morphology and function. By contrast, increased similarity between DZ twins would be more likely to implicate the effects of shared environments. To examine the relative contributions of genetics and non-genetic factors to the variation of brain morphology or function, researchers in the field define heritability and consider heritability estimates below 20% as low, 20%–50% at moderate, and above 50% and high (Strike et al. 2015). To date, there have been increasing numbers of findings that indicate genetic contributions to brain morphology. For instance, by scanning elderly male twins aged between 68 and 78 years, Sullivan et al. (2001) calculated the volume of brain structures related to memory such as the hippocampus, temporal horn, and corpus callosum. It was found that 40% of the hippocampal variance was attributable to genetic influences, whereas about 60% of the temporal horn variance and 80% of the callosal variance were attributable to genetic influences. The moderated heritability of the hippocampal structure allowed the potential of environmental modification of this structure during dynamic memory processes. Recent twin studies of cortical structure even make it possible to develop a brain atlas of human cortical surface area based on genetic correlations. Chen and colleagues (2012) scanned 406 twins aged between 51 and 59 years and compared MZ and DZ brain structures to estimate genetic correlations between different areas on the cortical surface to assess shared genetic influences on relative areal expansion between cortical regions. The brain was segmented into the frontal, parietal, temporal, and occipital subdivisions to evaluate genetic correlations. It was found that genetic correlations were higher between clusters within the same lobe than between clusters in different lobes. The most distinct genetic partitions were observed in the anteroposterior division between motor and sensory cortices, suggesting distinct genetic contributions to the morphology of these two brain regions. Heritability of brain network properties has also been estimated by collecting imaging data from twins. Bohlken et al. (2014) examined structural network topology using diffusion tensor imaging on 156 adult twins between the ages of 18 and 67 years. Network properties such as path length and the clustering coefficient were calculated to characterize the binary connections between 82 structurally defined brain regions per subject. Both properties were estimated to be under substantial genetic influence with 68% heritability of the clustering coefficient and 57% heritability for path length. Thus, there is evidence for genetic influences on the size of a brain structure, segmentation of brain regions, and connections between brain regions.

Heritability of the functional organization of the brain has been investigated by recording neural activity during various cognitive tasks, using both fMRI and EEG/ERP. For instance, Koten et al. (2009) tested MZ twins and non-twin brothers from ten families during a digit memory tasks in which participants had to verify (recognition phase) whether a single digit was contained in a previously memorized digit set (encoding phase). Participants were asked to perform a simple arithmetic task (either addition or subtraction) or an object categorization task (fruits and tools) between the encoding and recognition phases as a distractor. The heritability of neural activities that were activated in these tasks was high (>80%), but genetic influences were evident in different brain regions depending upon which task was performed, such that the temporal cortex exhibited genetic effects during the encoding phase, the occipital and intraparietal cortex showed genetic influences during the recognition phase, and the inferior frontal gyrus illustrated genetic effects during the distractor phase. The heritability of brain activity engaged in working memory was further confirmed in a large sample of 319 twins aged between 20 and 28 years (Blokland et al. 2011). Participants underwent fMRI scanning while performing the 0-back or 2-back versions of a spatial working memory task, which asked for a simple button press in response to a number displayed at one of four locations (0-back) or the number presented two trials before the current one (2-back) and thus required online monitoring, updating, and manipulation of remembered information. The contrast of the 2-back compared with the 0-back condition across all participants revealed working memory related activations in a neural circuit consisting of the frontal, parietal, temporal cortices, and cerebellum. The analysis of twin correlations for task-related brain activation revealed that the overall MZ twin correlations of brain activity activated by the working memory task were more than twice the size of the DZ correlations with the heritability estimates varying from 40% to 65%. This is consistent with heritability estimates of 57% for response accuracy in individuals' performance during the 2-back condition. Therefore, individual variations in both functional activity and behavioral performance related to the working memory task were possibly influenced by genetic factors.

Additionally, many EEG/ERP findings exemplify genetic associations with task-related and resting-state brain activity. To give two examples, Wright et al. (2001) examined whether the variation of P3 amplitude and latency—a sensitive electrophysiological index of the attentional and working memory demands of a task— could be attributed to genetic factors. They recorded ERPs during a delayed response working memory task in which a target stimulus was briefly presented and participants had to remember the target location for a short time and then responded to indicate the target location. Targets in this paradigm elicited a P3 component peaking around 300 ms after the onset of a target stimulus over the frontal, central, and parietal regions. It was found that 48% to 61% of the variance in P3 amplitude and 44% to 50% of the variance in P3 latency could be accounted for by additive genetic factors, and approximately one-third of the genetic variation at frontal sites was mediated by a common genetic factor that also influenced the genetic variation at parietal and central sites. It thus appears the P3 component that is phase-locked to stimulus onset is a promising endophenotype that may mediate genetic influences on attention/memory processing. Genetic influences may be even stronger on non-phase-locked EEG activity. The analysis of resting-state EEG activity with eyes closed recorded from MZ and DZ twins found that twin correlations pointed toward high genetic influences for spectral powers of multiple band EEG activity over wide scalp locations (Van Beijsterveldt et al. 1996). The averaged heritability for the delta, theta, alpha, and beta activities during resting was as high as 76%, 89%, 89%, and 86%, respectively. Genetic contributions to individual differences in a variety of electrophysiological measures was further verified by a meta-analysis of a number of EEG studies by confirming that the heritability estimate of the P300 amplitude was as high as 60% and the heritability estimate of alpha band neural oscillations was as high as 81% (Van Beijsterveldt and Van Baal 2002). A recent magnetoencephalography (MEG) study of twin pairs similarly showed evidence that gamma band (45–80 Hz) activity elicited by the perception of moving sine wave gratings illustrated a heritability of 91% (van Pelt et al. 2012). Taken together, these EEG and MEG findings lend support to the idea that brain functioning, as indexed by rhythmic neural activity during a resting state or during a task, is one of the most heritable characteristics of the human brain. However, it should be noted that, while the findings of brain imaging studies of twins inform us of how much of the variability in brain structure and function is due to genetic differences between people, calculations of heritability do not provide information about the underlying genes that contribute to brain structure and function. However, the magnitude of the heritability estimate can inform researchers of the statistical power for searching for a causal gene (Bochud et al. 2012).

The candidate gene approach to the understanding of genetic influences on the brain has investigated the effect of a specific gene on brain structure and function. Research along this line has usually been driven by a hypothesis based on psychiatric illness and behavioral findings, which have indicated that a specific gene is associated with behavioral tendency, psychological trait, or a mental/behavioral problem. An excellent example of a candidate gene study is the effect of 5-HTTLPR on the brain. 5-HTTLPR is the promoter region of a single gene, SLC6A4, which encodes the 5-HTT protein that removes serotonin released into the synaptic cleft. The short 5-HTTLPR variant produces less 5-HTT mRNA and protein than the long variant does, resulting in higher concentrations of 5-HT in the synaptic cleft. An early study of 505 individuals compared self-report of neuroticism (a personality trait that is principally composed of anxiety and depression-related subfactors) from short and long allele carriers of 5-HTTLPR (Lesch et al. 1996). Individuals with one or two copies of the short form of the 5-HTTLPR reported higher neuroticism scores than did individuals homozygous for the long variant. Another work recruited 1037 individuals between 3 and 26 years to examine interactions between 5-HTTLPR and environment on depression (Caspi et al. 2003). It was found that the effect of life events on self-reports of depression symptoms was significantly stronger among individuals carrying a short allele than among long/long homozygotes. In addition, more depression symptoms in short compared with long/long carriers were evident only in those who had experienced stressful life events. Similarly, the probability of suicide attempts was higher in short relative to long/long carriers, but this difference was only evident in those who had experienced stressful life events. Following these early studies, there have been increasing reports of association between 5-HTTLPR polymorphism and risk behavior showing the presence of at least one short allele to be associated with significant increases in alcohol-use problems and sexual risk behaviors (Rubens et al. 2016). These findings have suggested the possibility that a specific gene may exacerbate or buffer the effect of stressful life events on depression and suggest that brain imaging research should be performed to clarify the neural structures that may undergo 5-HTTLPR influences.

Hariri and colleagues (2002) published the first fMRI study to test the hypothesis that short allele carriers of 5-HTTLPR, who presumably have relatively lower 5-HTT function and expression and relatively higher levels of synaptic 5-HT, would exhibit a greater amygdala response than would long/long allele carriers, who presumably have lower levels of synaptic 5-HT and have been reported to be less anxious and fearful (Lesch et al. 1996). This study employed a simple paradigm that required subjects to match the affect (angry or afraid) apparent in one of two faces to that of a simultaneously presented target face. fMRI data were collected from participants in America. The contrast of this emotion task with a control condition (while participants viewed a trio of simple geometric shapes [vertical and horizontal ellipses] and selected one of two shapes identical to the target shape) significantly activated the amygdala and other brain regions related to face processing (e.g., the fusiform gyri and inferior parietal cortex). Moreover, the response of the right amygdala was significantly greater in short carriers than in long/long carriers of 5-HTTLPR. Short carriers also exhibited greater activity in the right posterior fusiform gyrus, which was attributed to possible excitatory feedback from the amygdala. 5-HTTLPR effects on neural activity in response to emotional stimuli in the amygdala and insula have been reported in other ethnic groups such as Chinese (Ma et al. 2015) and have been confirmed by a meta-analysis (Munafò et al. 2008). Moreover, 5-HTTLPR influences the volume of the amygdala and its functional connection with other emotion-related regions. Pezawas et al. (2005) scanned a large sample of genotyped individuals during a perception task similar to that used in Hariri et al. (2002). They examined 5-HTTLPR effects on both brain morphology and functional connectivity: a measure of correlated activity in brain regions that reflects functional integration of the brain regions during a specific task. It was found that, compared with long/long allele carriers of 5-HTTLPR, short allele carriers showed a reduced volume of the amygdala and perigenual anterior cingulate cortex. In addition, s allele carriers showed a significant reduction of the functional connectivity between the amygdala and perigenual anterior cingulate cortex. These findings shed new light on the neural mechanisms in emotion-related regions through which 5-HTTLPR influences human traits and behavior.

Another example of candidate gene approach to the understanding of genetic influences on the brain tested the association between OXTR rs53576 and the brain activity involved in cognitive and affective processes. Behavioral studies have suggested associations between OXTR rs53576 and psychological traits/behavioral tendencies such that carriers of the G relative to the A allele of OXTR rs53576 show enhanced empathic parenting (Bakermans-Kranenburg et al. 2014 and higher empathic accuracy (Rodrigues et al. 2009). Individuals homozygous for the G allele also show higher trust, empathic concern, and prosocial behavior than do A allele carriers (Tost et al. 2010; Kogan et al. 2011; Smith et al. 2014). These behavioral findings have inspired examination of the association between OXTR rs53576 and brain activity related to relevant psychological traits and behavioral tendency. For instance, by scanning a large sample of genotyped young adults (all white of European ancestry), Tost and colleagues (2010) investigated how structural and functional organization of the brain regions related to emotional processing vary across variants of OXTR rs53576. Examination of gray matter volume revealed a significant allele-load-dependent decrease in hypothalamus gray matter volume, with A/A allele carriers showing the smallest gray matter volume of the hypothalamus, G/G allele carriers with the largest, and G/A allele carriers with the middle. Functional activations were observed in the amygdala in an emotional face-processing task used in Hariri et al. (2002). A/A allele carriers of OXTR rs53576 showed the lowest task-related amygdala activations, and G/G homozygotes showed the highest response to fearful faces. Moreover, there was increased coupling of hypothalamus and amygdala in A/A compared with other variants of OXTR rs53576. The effect of OXTR rs53576 on amygdala responses to emotional faces has been replicated in another cohort of individuals (Dannlowski et al. 2015) and is consistent with an observation of smaller amygdala volumes in the AA compared with the G/G genotype (Wang et al. 2014). The variation of structure and function of subcortical regions related to emotion processing provides a possible neural basis for variations of psychological trait behavioral tendencies in allele carriers of OXTR rs53576.

Cortical structures related to emotional processing, parenting behavior, and altruistic attitude also exhibit variations of functional responses across the variants of OXTR rs53576. Michalska et al. (2014) invited women whose children were 4–6 years old to participate in a mother-child interaction task in which the mothers played freely with their children in a room with scattered clothes, papers, and empty containers. Mothers and their children were videotaped to code the mothers' positive parenting behavior (e.g., praising and giving positive affective and physical support to their children to clean the room). Later on, the mothers were scanned using fMRI while they viewed photos of their own versus an unrelated child. Watching their own versus an unrelated child significantly increased neural responses in regions subserving motivation, reward, and emotion processing, such the midbrain, dorsal putamen, thalamus, anterior cingulate, and prefrontal cortices. OXTR rs53576 effects were also observed in parenting behavior and brain activity. Michalska et al. first observed positive correlations between positive parenting behavior and neural activity in the orbital frontal cortex and anterior cingulate in response to a parent's own child's photos. In addition, they found evidence for significant associations between rs53576 alleles and positive parenting and between rs53576 alleles and activity in the orbital frontal cortex and anterior cingulate with A/A allele carriers, showing more positive parenting behavior and greater activity in the orbital frontal cortex and anterior cingulate compared with G allele carriers. Luo et al. (2015b) examined the association of OXTR rs53576 with empathic neural responses in a context of the presence of social in-group and out-group members. By scanning A/A and G/G allele carriers during the perception of painful and neutral stimulations applied to same-race or other-race individuals, Luo et al. found that G/G compared with A/A individuals showed stronger activity in the anterior cingulate and supplementary motor area in response to racial in-group members' pain, whereas A/A relative to G/G individuals exhibited greater activity in the nucleus accumbens in response to racial out-group members' pain. Moreover, the in-group bias of activity in the anterior cingulate and supplementary motor area positively predicted participants' implicit attitudes toward in-group/out-group members, and the nucleus accumbens activity to racial out-group individuals' pain negatively predicted participants' motivations to help racial out-group members. These findings provide evidence that the two variants of OXTR rs53576 are associated with in-group bias in neural responses to others' pain that are linked to implicit attitude and altruistic motivation, respectively.

The candidate gene approach has also revealed a number of other genes that contribute to the development of brain morphology and function. These hypothesis driven studies cast new light on influences of a potential gene on brain development but are unable to disclose new genes or SNPs that contribute to the brain development by affecting brain structure and function. The GWAS approach developed in the past decade has made it possible to identify SNPs that influence brain morphology and functions by examining many common genetic variants in a large sample. The GWAS approach requires a sample of DNA from each individual participant and the extraction of a phenotype that can be a disease, a trait, a behavior tendency, a feature of brain structure, or a brain activity related to cognitive and affective processes. Millions of genetic variants are read from the DNA sample using SNP arrays to examine whether one type of the variant (one allele) from the entire genome is more frequent in individuals or is associated with a specific phenotype. Because hundreds of thousands to millions of SNPs are tested in GWA studies, the conventional threshold is usually set very high (p-value is 5×10^{-8}), and a discovery cohort is tested first, which is followed by a test of an independent validation cohort to validate the most significant SNPs identified in the first cohort. Because a large sample is required for GWA studies, data are usually collected from multiple sites, and a meta-analysis is then performed on these data sets.

For example, because twin studies suggest that the hippocampal, total brain, and intracranial volumes are highly heritable in humans (Peper et al. 2007), a GWAS aimed to search for common genetic polymorphisms influencing hippocampal, total brain, and intracranial volumes by testing seventeen cohorts of European ancestry that comprised a full sample ($N = 7,795$) and a healthy subsample ($N = 5,775$) using directly genotyped SNPs (Stein et al. 2012). Phenotypes were computed from anatomical MRI from each individual by focusing on the hippocampal, total brain, and intracranial volumes. Two SNPs in the same linkage disequilibrium block showed strong associations with hippocampal volume after controlling for intracranial volume (rs7294919 and rs7315280). The association between rs7294919 and hippocampal volume was also evident in cohorts consisting of elderly subjects and in a meta-analysis. The intracranial volume was associated with an intronic SNP (rs10784502) near a positional candidate gene underlying an observed quantitative trait locus in this work. Another example of GWAS identified SNPs associated with structures in subcortical regions by collecting the MRIs of 30,717 individuals from 50 cohorts (Hibar et al. 2015). A meta-analysis of imaging data from different sites revealed associations of different SNPs with the volumes of subcortical structures such as the putamen (rs945270, rs62097986, and rs6087771) and caudate nucleus (rs1318862). While identification of these genetic variants in GWAS provides insight into the causes of variability in volumes of brain structures that are critical for both normal brain function and neuropsychiatric dysfunction, it remains unclear whether and how specific genetic variations linked to volumetric brain differences are associated with brain function and other cognitive traits. In addition, there is still a big gap between SNPs and brain phenotypes. Big challenges for future research are to identify molecular and neural substrates that mediate genetic influences on the brain, and, in particular, how the intermediate molecular and neural mechanisms are moderated by environments and experiences.

Gene-culture interaction on the brain

The aforementioned studies provided behavioral evidence for gene-culture interaction on psychological trait and behavioral tendency. These studies examined gene-culture interaction by comparing questionnaire or behavioral measures from two genotyped cohorts of individuals from Western and East Asian cultures. Different patterns of phenotypes in two variants of the same gene across cultures are taken as the index of gene-culture interaction. The findings can be interpreted as cultural influences on genetic effects on human trait/ behavior or genetic constraints on cultural effects on human trait/behavior. The behavioral research on gene-culture interactions raises novel questions for cultural neuroscientists such as whether gene-culture interaction can also be observed on the brain underlying cognition and behavior. A challenge for parallel brain imaging research on gene-culture interaction is to collect brain imaging data from genotyped individuals from at least two cultures. This requires two research groups who have shared research interests on the same gene and psychological process, and researchers must be able to genotype participants at two sites and collect brain imaging data using MRI scanners or EEG systems produced by the same manufacturer. Owing to the requirements, there has been little cross-cultural brain imaging research of genotyped individuals.

However, researchers have opened an alternative approach to investigate gene-culture interaction with brain activity by examining the association between cultural values and brain activity in a population from the same culture. Identifying individuals from one society who exhibit heterogeneity of cultural values/traits such as independence/interdependence would allow assessment of the correlation between brain activities in response to cognitive/affective tasks and self-reports of cultural values/traits. A possible way of gene-culture interaction on the brain is that genes moderate the association between cultural values and brain activity across individuals in the same society. Given that the candidate gene research has suggested that one or another variant of the same gene is more vulnerable to environmental influences (Belsky et al. 2009), it is likely that the coupling of brain activity and cultural values/traits may be stronger in the vulnerable variant than in the other variant of the same gene. Such genetic moderation effects on brain culture coupling may be particularly salient in the brain regions engaged in social/affective processing that are sensitive to cultural influences.

To date there have been two fMRI studies published following this line of research. Ma and colleagues (2014b) investigated the interaction between 5-HTTLPR and interdependence on brain activity underlying reflection of oneself and one's mother in Chinese university students. As mentioned in Chapters 4 and 5, neural processes of the self and others engage a social brain network including brain regions such as the ventral and dorsal medial prefrontal cortex, precuneus/posterior cingulate, and temporoparietal junction (Kelley et al. 2002; Ma and Han 2011; Jenkins and Mitchell 2011; Gallagher et al. 2000; Saxe and Kanwisher 2003). In addition, activity of the social brain network showed distinct patterns in response to the self and others in individuals from East Asian and Western cultures (e.g., Zhu et al. 2007; Ma et al. 2014a). Activity in some regions of the social brain network was also correlated with self-reports of cultural values such as interdependence across individuals. However, activity in the social brain network related to the processing of the self and others not only undergoes influences of cultural experiences but manifests genetic associations as well. For example, Ma et al. (2015) found that reflection of one's own unfavorable compared with favorable personality traits induced greater activity in the dorsal anterior cingulate and right anterior insula, and that the anterior insular activity predicted self-report distress feelings. Moreover, it was found that short/short relative to long/long allele carriers of 5-HTTLPR reported stronger distress feelings during reflection of their own unfavorable traits and showed greater activity in the dorsal anterior cingulate and right anterior insula during negative self-reflection. In addition, the 5-HTTLPR effect on the distress feelings was mediated by the anterior insular activity elicited by negative self-reflection. Another study also discovered 5-HTTLPR association with the neural activity underlying reflection on personality traits of one's own ideal self (i.e., attributes an individual wishes to possess) (Shi et al. 2016). By scanning the two variants of 5-HTTLPR while reflecting on the distance between actual and ideal self in personality traits, Shi et al. found that larger actual/ideal self-discrepancy was associated with activations in the ventral/dorsal striatum and dorsal medial and lateral prefrontal cortices. Moreover, these brain activities were stronger in short/short than in long/long allele carriers of 5-HTTLPR. Given that brain activity related to the processing of one's own personality traits manifested both cultural and genetic influences and the frequency of 5-HTTLPR variants was associated with cultural traits (Chiao and Blizinsky 2010), Ma et al. (2014b) predicted that the 5-HTTLPR would interact with interdependent self-construals to shape activity in the social brain network during reflection of oneself.

Owing to the small proportion of l/l allele carrier of the 5-HTTLPR in the Chinese population, Ma et al. (2014b) first collected blood samples from 901 university students aged between 18 and 33 years to genotype 5-HTTLPR and identified seventeen short/short and seventeen long/long allele carriers matched in age, gender, self-construal, and anxiety trait for fMRI scanning. To assess whether 5-HTTLPR polymorphism modulates the association between interdependence of self-construals and neural activity underlying reflection of personal attributes of oneself and close others, short/short and long/long genotype groups were asked to make judgments on personal attributes including personality traits, social roles, and physical features of oneself, one's mother, and a celebrity during fMRI scanning. This design allowed them to test whether 5-HTTLPR effects on the association between a cultural trait, and neural substrates underlying self-reflection were independent of dimensions of personal attributes for judgments. Interdependence of self-construals—a cultural trait that significantly differentiates East Asian and Western culture—was estimated for each participant using the Self-Construal Scale (Singelis, 1994). Ma et al. first conducted whole-brain simple regression analyses to identify brain regions in which activations related to the reflection of oneself (defined in the contrast of self-judgments versus celebrity judgments) or of one's mother (defined in the contrast of mother judgments versus celebrity judgments). These brain regions were then used as masks in further hierarchical regression analyses to examine 5-HTTLPR moderation effects on the association between the activities in these brain regions and self-report of interdependence. There were several interesting findings. First, across all participants, interdependence as a cultural trait was correlated with neural activity during self-reflection in the social brain network including in the medial and lateral prefrontal cortex, temporoparietal junction, superior parietal cortex, insula, hippocampus, and cerebellum. Thus, brain activity involved in reflection of oneself and close others varies significantly across individuals with different levels of interdependence. Second, the association between interdependence and the social brain network activity was moderated by 5-HTTLPR polymorphism because the neural activity in multiple nodes of the social brain network underlying self-reflection on personality traits was associated with interdependence in long/long allele carriers but not in short/short allele carriers (Figure 7.1). Specifically, for long/long carriers,

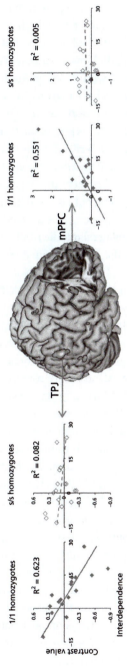

Figure 7.1 Illustration of the interaction between interdependence and 5-HTTLPR on brain activity involved in reflection of one's own personality traits. The middle panel illustrates the TPJ and mPFC in which the neural activity showed significant gene-interdependence interactions in the hierarchical regression analyses. Long/long but not short/short allele carriers showed significant associations between brain activity and interdependence. (See colour plate.)

Adapted from Yina Ma, Dan Bang, Chenbo Wang, Micah Allen, Chris Frith, Andreas Roepstorff, and Shihui Han, Sociocultural patterning of neural activity during self-reflection, *Social Cognitive and Affective Neuroscience*, 9 (1), pp. 73–80, DOI: 10.1093/scan/nss103, Copyright © 2014, Oxford University Press.

those who reported higher interdependence showed stronger activations in the medial prefrontal cortex, left frontal cortex, left hippocampus, and cerebellum, but weaker activation in the bilateral temporoparietal junction. However, the 5-HTTLPR moderation effect was not observed on the neural activity engaged in self-reflection on one's social roles and physical attributes. Third, self-report of interdependence was also correlated with the magnitude of neural activity in response to reflection on one's mother's personality traits, social roles, and physical features in the social brain network including the insula, medial prefrontal cortex, middle/superior frontal cortex, superior temporal cortex, and superior parietal cortex. However, the 5-HTTLPR moderator effects were observed in the neural activity only related to reflection on one's mother's personality traits, with reliable associations between interdependence and neural responses to mother-reflection in long/long but not short/short carriers. Long/long carriers who reported higher interdependence showed stronger activations in the medial prefrontal cortex, bilateral middle frontal cortex, and bilateral insula, but weaker activations in the inferior frontal cortex and inferior/superior parietal cortex.

A general conclusion arising from these findings is that the association between a cultural trait and brain activity involved in social cognition may vary across individuals from the same cultural population owing to their genetic makeup. These findings also have other novel implications. First, the 5-HTTLPR moderator effects covered multiple regions of the social brain network that are involved in self-reflection (e.g., the ventral medial prefrontal cortex; Kelley et al. 2002; Zhu et al. 2007; Ma and Han 2010; Ma et al. 2014a), episodic memory (e.g., hippocampus; Cavanna and Trimble 2006), mental attribution of others (e.g., the dorsal medial prefrontal cortex and temporoparietal junction; Gallagher et al. 2000; Saxe and Kanwisher 2003), causal attribution (e.g., the medial prefrontal cortex and cerebellum; Han et al. 2011). Similarly, the previous research found that life stress also interacts with 5-HTTLPR polymorphism to modulate brain activity in multiple brain regions including the anterior cingulate, middle frontal cortex, and caudate nucleus (Canli et al. 2006). Given that different brain regions in the social brain network contribute to distinct (cognitive and affective) components of social cognition, these finding suggest that a single gene such as the 5-HTTLPR may play a broad role in the moderation of the relationship between cultural/life experiences and brain activity involved in multiple cognitive/affective processes. Second, because the interaction of 5-HTTLPR and brain activity was evident during judgments on personality traits but not social and physical attributes of the self and a close other, one may speculate that the neural substrates engaged in different tasks are differentially vulnerable to gene-culture interaction. Third, although it has been long assumed that genetic polymorphism may influence the probability that a particular cultural trait will be adopted by individuals (Feldman and Laland 1996), it is unknown how this may occur in the brain. Ma et al.'s (2014b) findings suggest that genes may alter individuals' acculturation by moderating the coupling of a cultural trait and brain activity linked to specific cognitive/affective processes. Finally, one may ask why there was a stronger association between a cultural trait and neural activity in the social brain network in long/long than in short/short carriers. This cannot be explained by group differences in traits because the two variants were matched in self-report of interdependence and other traits. One possible account is that long/long carriers, as a minority in the Chinese population, might be more sensitive to a cultural trait such as interdependence than short/short carriers are and thus show a greater association between the brain activity and interdependent self-construals. This is different from the previous finding that depressive symptoms in short allele carriers are more sensitive to life experiences (Caspi et al. 2003). Thus, it may be further speculated that that cultural traits shared by a population and an individual's life experiences may interact with genes in different fashions.

A second example of brain imaging research on gene-culture interaction on the brain examined whether OXTR rs53576 moderates the association between a cultural trait (interdependence) and empathic neural responses to others' suffering (Luo et al. 2015b). In daily life every person pursues his/her own interest and likewise cares about the good of others. The measure of interdependence estimates an individual's view of the relationship between the self and others. Empathic neural responses have been proposed to underlie an individual's behavioral tendency to help others. Luo et al.'s (2015b) work was inspired by the findings of two lines of research. Cross-cultural brain imaging studies revealed effects of cultural experiences on brain activity involved in empathy. On the one hand, Cheon et al. (2011) reported that, compared with white Americans, Koreans showed greater empathy and elicited stronger activity in the left temporoparietal junction (TPJ) in response to in-group versus out-group members' emotional pain. de Greck et al. (2012) also found that, during empathic processing of anger, Chinese adults showed stronger hemodynamic responses in the left dorsolateral prefrontal cortex, whereas Germans manifested stronger activity in the right TPJ, right inferior and superior temporal gyrus, and left middle insula. On the other hand, as aforementioned, Kim and colleagues have shown evidence for the interaction between OXTR rs53576 and cultural (Western/East Asian) experiences in shaping emotion-related trait and behavioral tendencies (Kim et al. 2010, 2011).

Luo et al. (2015b) aimed to address two issues arising from the previous studies, that is, whether a specific dimension of cultural traits—interdependence—interacts with OXTR rs53576 to shape empathy and whether the interaction between interdependence and OXTR rs53576 occurs at both behavioral and neural levels. The G/G allele carriers exhibited increased sympathetic and subjective arousal in response to social interactions (Smith et al. 2014) and stronger empathic neural responses to perceived pain in in-group members (Luo et al. 2015a). The G allele carriers also confer greater susceptibility to influences of cultural environments (Kim et al. 2010, 2011). Based on these findings, Luo et al. hypothesized that there would be a stronger link between empathy and interdependence in G than in A allele carriers of OXTR rs53576. In their first experiment, Luo et al. recruited 1536 undergraduate and graduate Chinese students who were asked to complete the Self-Construal Scale (Singelis 1994) and the Interpersonal Reactivity Index (IRI) (Davis 1994) to estimate interdependence and empathy ability. A hierarchical regression analysis was conducted to examine whether OXTR genotype affected the relationship between interdependence and individuals' empathy. The analyses first confirmed that the interaction of OXTR rs53576 genotype and interdependence reliably predicted the participants' IRI score. This was due to stronger associations between interdependence and empathy in G allele carriers than those with A/A genotype (Figure 7.2). Another way to examine the interaction between OXTR rs53576 and interdependence was to separate individuals into two groups according to high and low interdependence. This analysis revealed that OXTR rs53576 G allele was correlated with higher IRI scores in the high-interdependence group but with lower IRI scores in the low-interdependence group. There was a reliable interaction between OXTR rs53576 and interdependence on both the IRI score and a subscore of perspective taking. Thus, the behavioral measures indicate that the association between interdependence and empathy traits is significantly moderated by OXTR rs53576, with G/G homozygotes showing a stronger link between interdependence and empathy trait compared with A allele carriers.

In a second experiment Luo et al. further investigated whether OXTR rs53576 moderates the association between interdependence and neural responses to others' suffering—an objective measures of empathy—by scanning a small cohort of 30 A/A and 30 G/G homozygous of OXTR rs53576 using fMRI. Empathic neural responses to others' suffering were quantified by contrasting brain activity resulting from viewing video clips of models who received painful (needle penetration) or non-painful (Q-tip touch) stimuli applied to the left or right cheeks (a similar procedure to that employed in the previous research, Xu et al. 2009; Luo et al. 2014). A whole-brain hierarchical regression analysis was applied to the fMRI data, which revealed significant interactions between OXTR rs53576 and interdependence on empathic neural responses (in the contrast of painful vs. non-painful stimuli) in the bilateral insula, amygdala, and superior temporal cortex, indicating that OXTR rs53576 moderated the

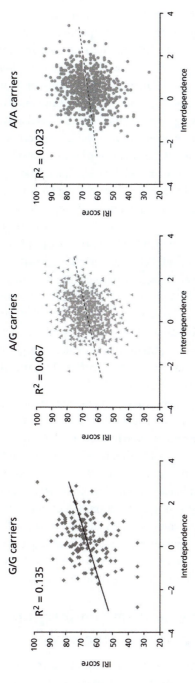

Figure 7.2 Illustration of the interaction between interdependence and OXTR rs53576 on empathy ability in a cohort of Chinese adults. There was stronger coupling between interdependence and empathy ability indexed by the IRI scores in G/G than in A carriers. (See colour plate.) Adapted from Siyang Luo, Yina Ma, Yi Liu, Bingfeng Li, Chenbo Wang, Zhenhao Shi, Xiaoyang Li, Wenxia Zhang, Yi Rao, and Shihui Han, Interaction between oxytocin receptor polymorphism and interdependent culture values on human empathy, *Social Cognitive and Affective Neuroscience*, 10 (9), pp. 1273–1281, Figure 1a, DOI: 10.1093/scan/nsv019, Copyright © 2015, Oxford University Press.

association between interdependence and neural activity in these brain regions in response to others' suffering. Post hoc whole-brain regression analyses confirmed significant associations between interdependence and empathic neural responses in these brain regions in G/G but not A/A carriers (Figure 7.3). G/G carriers with higher interdependence showed stronger activation in the bilateral insula, amygdala, and superior temporal gyrus in response to others' pain. Among G/G carriers, the two subcomponents of empathy ability (i.e., empathic concern and perspective taking) were predicted by the insular activity and the activity in the amygdala and superior temporal cortex, respectively.

These findings demonstrate that the interaction between interdependence and OXTR rs53576 on empathy occurs in both behavioral tendency of empathy and the neural correlates of empathy. The results provide evidence for a stronger coupling between interdependence and empathy (and empathic neural responses) in G allele carriers than in A allele carriers of OXTR rs53576. The findings complement the previous findings that OXTR rs53576 shapes behavioral/dispositional empathy (Rodrigues et al. 2009) and empathic neural responses (Luo et al. 2015a). Interestingly, the interaction between interdependence and OXTR rs53576 was evident mainly in the brain regions related to emotion (such as the insula, amygdala, and STG), contrasting with Ma et al.'s (2014b) findings that 5-HTTLPR moderated the association between interdependence and brain activity underling self-reflection mainly in brain regions related to cognitive processing (e.g., the medial prefrontal and lateral frontal cortex, TPJ, and hippocampus). Thus, it is likely that different genes are specifically associated with emotional or cognitive processes in terms of gene-culture interaction on the underlying brain mechanisms. Interestingly, both Ma et al. (2014b) and Luo et al. (2015b) showed that a minority of the Chinese population in terms of allele frequency (i.e., long allele of 5-HTTLPR and G allele of OXTR rs53576) demonstrated a stronger coupling of brain activity with a cultural trait (i.e., interdependence) compared with the majority of the population. This finding suggests that a minority of the population is more sensitive to dominant cultural values/norms than the majority in the same population. If the dominant cultural beliefs/values/norms are created by the majority of a population in terms of allele frequency, the minority of the population needs to be more sensitive to the cultural beliefs/values/norms and social rules in order to survive and develop in the society.

Neurobiological mechanisms underlying gene-culture interaction on the brain

The findings of the aforementioned brain imaging studies suggest that one variant of a gene showed stronger association between brain activity and a cultural

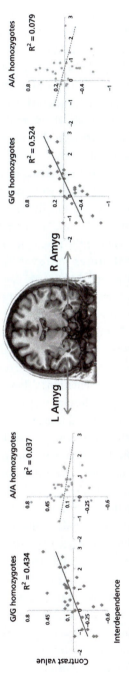

Figure 7.3 Illustration of the interaction between interdependence and OXTR rs53576 on amygdala responses to perceived pain in others in a cohort of Chinese adults. The scatter plots illustrate positive and negative associations between interdependence and amygdala activities in response to perceived pain in others in the two variants of OXTR rs53576. (See colour plate.)

Adapted from Siyang Luo, Yina Ma, Yi Liu, Bingfeng Li, Chenbo Wang, Zhenhao Shi, Xiaoyang Li, Wenxia Zhang, Yi Rao, and Shihui Han, Interaction between oxytocin receptor polymorphism and interdependent culture values on human empathy, *Social Cognitive and Affective Neuroscience*, 10 (9), pp. 1273–1281, Figure 2, DOI: 10.1093/scan/nsv019, Copyright © 2015, Oxford University Press.

trait compared with another variant of the same gene. These findings may be accounted for by assuming that the activity of a large neural population, as indexed by BOLD signals recorded from a brain region, is more sensitive to cultural experiences in one compared with another variant of a gene. Nevertheless, these studies do not tell how cultural experiences interact with the gene to affect neural activity at the microstructure level. We have known little about the neurobiological and molecular mechanisms underlying genetic moderation effects on the coupling of brain activity and cultural traits. However, the findings of recent studies allow us to speculate possible neuromolecular mechanisms underlying the influences of cultural experiences on the brain.

For example, two recent studies reported variations of oxytocin effects on behavioral and brain activity across individuals with different cultural traits. By recording ERPs during judgments of personality traits of oneself and a celebrity, Liu et al. (2013) found that intranasal administration of oxytocin compared with placebo treatment reduced the neural activity associated with self-reflection of personality traits. Moreover, the oxytocin effect on the brain activity underlying self-reflection was positively correlated with a measure of interdependence of self-construals. Participants who self-reported being more interdependent showed stronger oxytocin effects on the brain activity associated with self-reflection. Similarly, Pfundmair et al. (2014) found that intranasal administration of oxytocin versus a placebo attenuated negative affect in responses to ostracism, and the oxytocin effect was more salient in individuals with collectivistic than individualistic orientations. These findings implicate an interaction of a culture trait and a molecular effect on brain activity and behavior and suggest that individuals' cultural traits may moderate the effects of oxytocin, which functions as both neurotransmitter and hormone. If intranasal administration of oxytocin affects behavior and brain activity by changing synaptic transmission, one can then speculate that cultural experiences and traits are likely to modulate oxytocin combination with receptors and thus to influence information processing at the synaptic level in the brain.

Another possible neurobiological mechanisms underlying gene-culture interaction on the brain is that cultural experiences may shape gene expression. Accumulating findings of epigenetic research have demonstrated changes in gene expression that are not based on changes in DNA sequence but can be inherited (Holliday 2006). It is now known that epigenetic changes owing to environmental factors may induce changes of gene expression through DNA methylation and histone modifications (Nikolova and Hariri 2015). Older monozygous twins exhibited remarkable differences in their overall content and genomic distribution of 5-methylcytosine DNA and histone acetylation (Fraga et al. 2005), indicating novel influences of environments and experiences. There has been increasing evidence that increased methylation within or near the promoter of a gene is associated with reduced gene expression and affects downstream neurobiological processes to shape brain structure and function (Nikolova and Hariri 2015). For example, Nikolova et al. (2014) measured the percentage of methylation of the proximal promoter region of the serotonin transporter gene (SLC6A4) in saliva-derived DNA from a discovery cohort of 80 young adults and blood-derived DNA from an independent replication cohort of 96 adolescents. They found that the percentage of methylation of the SLC6A4 proximal promoter was positively correlated with threat-related amygdala reactivity in the left hemisphere, suggesting potential influences of epigenetic changes on the functional organization of emotion-related neural structures. If DNA methylation patterns reflect at least partially the effect of an individual's unique environment, it is then likely that cultural experiences and environments may interact with genes through epigenetic changes of DNA, which, in addition to the transmission of cultural knowledge from one to the next generation, provide a potential way to explain the cultural influences across generations. Future research is needed to measure cultural traits, DNA methylation patterns, and brain activity related to cognition and behavior from two or more cultural groups, to examine the relationship between cultural traits and DNA methylation patterns across individuals, and to test whether the interaction between cultural traits and DNA methylation patterns can predict individuals' behavioral tendencies and related brain activity.

Chapter 8

A culture–behavior–brain-loop model of human development

The brain stands between culture and behavior

As I mentioned in Chapter 1, cross-cultural psychological studies that focus on the comparison of behaviors between East Asians and Westerners have revealed considerable evidence that East Asian cultures encourage individuals to attend to a broad perceptual field and the relationships between objects (Kitayama et al. 2003; Nisbett and Masuda 2003), to categorize objects in terms of their relationships (Chiu 1972), to emphasize contextual effects during causal attribution of physical and social events (Chio et al. 1999; Morris and Peng 1994), to view oneself as being interdependent of significant others and social contexts (Markus and Kitayama 1991), and to inspire low-arousal positive affective states (Tsai 2007). In contrast, Westerners are inclined to attend to a focal object during perception, to categorize objects in terms of their internal attributes, to view the self as being independent of others and social contexts, and to promotes high-arousal positive affective states. The cultural differences in these mental activities have been integrated into a conceptual framework that posits that the collectivistic East Asian cultures foster a holistic style of thinking, whereas the individualistic Western cultures cultivate an analytic style of thinking (Nisbett et al. 2001). The theoretical framework of cultural variations in perceptual, cognitive, and affective processes has been used to interpret the observed cultural differences in behavior.

The findings of cross-cultural psychological research inevitably lead to inquiry about the relationship between the brain and culture because the brain carries the complicated mental processes and culture has played a pivotal role in defining social environments in which the brain develops. Cultural neuroscientists are not the first to ponder the relationship between the brain and social experiences. There have been many debates about the relationship between brain size and complexity of social interactions during evolution, and studies have led to the novel and interesting findings that, in all anthropoid primates, the ratio of neocortex volume to the volume of the rest of the brain is correlated with social group size—an index of social complexity (Dunbar 1992; Dunbar and Shultz 2007)—and with the frequency of social learning (Reader and Laland 2002). Although the findings of this line of research do not elucidate the relationships between the brain size and a particular cognitive skill, one may speculate that the large neocortex in humans may play a key role particularly in the ability to understand others' minds and to imagine how other individuals see the world, because these cognitive skills are critical for dealing with complicated social interactions. Indeed, it has been shown that children of 2.5 years of age have more sophisticated social cognitive skills (e.g., social learning, communication, and understanding others' intentions) than chimpanzees aged between 3 and 21 years do, for dealing with the social world, whereas children and chimpanzees show comparable cognitive skills for dealing with the physical world (e.g., locating a reward, discriminating quantity, and understanding causality; Herrmann et al. 2007). The findings support a cultural intelligence hypothesis that assumes that the human brain is different from that of other primates in size, in order to support our powerful skills of social-cultural cognition developed during the early stage in ontogeny. Because social cognitive skills, such as understanding others' minds, provide a fundamental basis for imitating others' behavior and sharing others' beliefs/values, which lie at the heart of cultural transmission, it is likely that the large size of neocortex in humans (which has developed over the course of evolution) provides neural resources to support cultural transmission among individuals in a social group. This line of research considers the relationship between culture and brain during evolution, but it lacks evidence because research methods for comparing brain functions involved in the same cognitive tasks between humans and other primates and for testing the association between cultural values/beliefs and brain activity in animals have not yet been possible.

Cultural neuroscience is armed with brain imaging techniques such fMRI and EEG/ERP that can be integrated with research paradigms from cross-cultural psychology to explore cultural effects on the brain. The cultural neuroscience findings introduced in the previous chapters indicate reliable cultural influences on the functional organization of the human brain. To reiterate, cross-cultural brain imaging studies have shown evidence for differences in brain activity between East Asians and Westerners related to visual perception, attention, causal attribution, semantic relationship processing, musical processing, mental calculation, self-face recognition, self-reflection, perception of bodily expression, mental state reasoning, empathy, and trait inference, for example. Cultural priming research has also reported evidence that temporary activations of specific cultural beliefs/values modulate the brain activity involved in pain perception, visual perception, self-face recognition, self-reflection, reward, motor processing, and resting state activity. The brain regions in which the activity exhibits cultural influences vary across stimuli and task demands used in the previous studies. Are there specific brain regions that exert cultural modulations of neural activities common to different tasks? This question cannot be answered by examining the results of a single cross-cultural neuroimaging study that employs one cognitive task. Fortunately, the increasing numbers of cultural neuroscience studies allow us to conduct a meta-analysis of the findings to explore whether there are common neural networks that underlie cultural variations in the human brain activity in different tasks.

Han and Ma (2014) summarized the results of 35 fMRI studies that examined Western/East Asian cultural differences in human brain activity published before December 2013, and conducted a whole-brain quantitative meta-analysis to identify cultural differences in brain activities that are activated independently of the stimuli and tasks used in these studies. These fMRI studies compared participants from East Asian (Chinese, Japanese, and Korean) and Western (American and European) societies and were classified into three domains according to the nature of the task (i.e., social cognitive, social affective, and non-social cognitive tasks). Social cognitive tasks engage social cognitive processes related to oneself and others, including self-reflection, theory of mind, face perception, moral judgment, persuasion, and self-recognition. Social affective tasks induce emotional responses during empathy, emotion recognition, emotion, and reward attainment. Non-social tasks examine the neural correlates underlying visual attention, visual spatial or object processing, arithmetic, and physical causal attribution. Among these studies 56 contrasts (28 contrasts of East Asians > Westerners and 28 contrasts of Westerners > East Asians) examined cultural differences in social cognitive processes. The meta-analysis revealed that, relative to Western participants, East Asian participants showed greater activity in the right insula/inferior frontal cortex, dorsal medial prefrontal cortex, left inferior frontal cortex, right inferior parietal cortex, and right temporoparietal junction (Figure 8.1). In contrast, Western compared with East Asian participants showed stronger activity in the anterior cingulate cortex, ventral medial prefrontal cortex, bilateral insula, right superior frontal cortex, left precentral gyrus, and right claustrum. The meta-analysis of the studies of affective processes in social cognition uncovered stronger activity in the right dorsal lateral prefrontal cortex when comparing East Asian with Western participants (based on 8 contrasts) but greater activity in the left insula and right temporal pole in Western versus East Asian participants (based on 11 contrasts). The meta-analysis of fMRI studies on cultural differences in non-social processes included 13 contrasts to compare East Asian versus Western participants and 11 contrasts to compare Western versus East Asian participants.

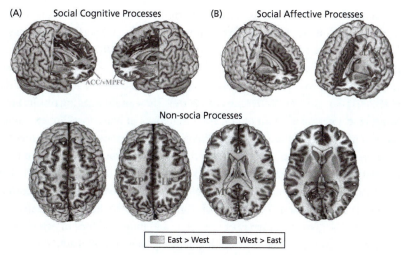

(A) Social Cognitive Processes   (B) Social Affective Processes

Non-socia Processes

East > West   West > East

Figure 8.1 Illustration of East Asian vs. Western cultural differences in brain activity. Yellow-to-orange color shows brain regions that indicate stronger activity in East Asians compared to Westerners. Light-to-dark blue color shows brain regions that indicate stronger activity in the reverse comparison. (A) Cultural differences in brain activity involved in social cognitive processes during self-reflection, mentalizing, and moral judgment; (B) cultural differences in brain activity involved in social affective processes during empathy, emotion recognition, and reward; (C) cultural differences in brain activity involved in non-social processes during visual spatial or object processing, visual attention, arithmetic, and causal judgments on physical events. (See colour plate.)

Adapted from *NeuroImage*, 99 (1), Shihui Han and Yina Ma, Cultural differences in human brain activity: A quantitative meta-analysis, pp. 293–300, DOI:10.1016/j.neuroimage.2014.05.062, Copyright © 2014 Elsevier Inc. Published by Elsevier Inc., with permission from Elsevier.

There was evidence for stronger activity in the left inferior parietal cortex, left middle occipital, and left superior parietal cortex in East Asian compared with Western participants. Western participants, however, showed greater activations in the right lingual gyrus, right inferior parietal cortex, and precuneus relative to East Asian participants.

The meta-analysis of cultural neuroscience findings indicates that cultural influences cover most of the key nodes of the social brain network. Specifically, the social brain network in East Asian cultures is characterized by enhanced activity in brain regions that are activated during inference of others' mental states (dorsal medial prefrontal cortex and temporoparietal junction; Gallagher et al. 2000; Saxe and Kanwisher 2003; Han et al. 2005; Ge and Han 2008), and self-control/emotional regulation (lateral prefrontal cortex; Figner et al. 2010; Ochsner et al. 2012). In contrast, the social brain network in Western cultures is characterized by enhanced activity in brain regions that have been shown to be engaged in self-reflection (ventral medial prefrontal cortex; Kelley et al. 2002; Northoff et al. 2006; Ma and Han 2011; Ma et al. 2014a), socioemotional processing (temporal pole; Olson et al. 2007), and emotional responses (anterior cingulate cortex and insula; Singer et al. 2004; Jackson et al. 2005; Saarela et al. 2007; Gu and Han 2007; Han et al. 2009). These brain imaging results help to provide a neural account of cultural differences in behaviors. For example, the enhanced activity underlying perception and inference of others' mental states in the dorsal medial prefrontal cortex and temporoparietal junction may mediate greater behavioral sensitivity to social contexts in East Asians relative to Westerners. The enhanced activity of the ventral medial prefrontal cortex involved in coding the self-relevance of stimuli provides a neural mechanism in support of the greater tendency of self-focus and independence in behavior in Westerners relative to East Asians. The increased lateral frontal activity underlies self-control and emotional regulation in East Asians, whereas the increased activity in the anterior cingulate cortex and insula mediates Westerners' preference for behaviors that can bring high-arousal emotional states. Thus, these findings indicate that Western/East Asian cultures influence human social behavior by modulating the magnitude of activity in different nodes of the social brain network resulting in culturally specific cognitive/neural strategies, and allowing individuals to accommodate to their sociocultural environments and behave in culturally appropriate ways during social interactions.

The increasing numbers of cultural neuroscience findings have triggered the notion of a new conceptual framework that will elucidate the dynamic interactions between culture, behavior, and the brain. Such a framework should help us to understand how culture shapes the brain by contextualizing behavior and clarifying how the brain modifies culture via behavioral influences. It would also be pivotal in providing a new perspective on how genes and culture shape behavior and the brain during long-term gene-cultural coevolution and during lifespan gene-culture interactions. It has long been believed that human evolution cannot be understood as purely a biological process or a cultural process, and the feedback between biological and cultural processes must be taken into consideration when elucidating the nature of human development (Dobzhansky 1962). There have been attempts to clarify the nature of the interactions between culture and genes and culture-gene coevolution (e.g., Li 2003; Richerson et al. 2010; Ross and Richerson 2014). For example, Li (2003) proposed a cross-level dynamic biocultural co-constructive framework that views lifespan development as occurring simultaneously within different time scales (lifespan ontogeny and human phylogeny) and encompassing multiple levels of mechanisms (neurobiological, cognitive, behavioral, and sociocultural) that underlie human development. However, not much consideration of the role of culture-brain interactions occurs in these early discussions, owing to the lack of cultural neuroscience findings, which have since revealed possible patterns of cultural influences on the brain. Moreover, the early discussions focused on interpretations of the development of human behavior because of gene-culture interaction, rather than taking behavior as a factor that also affects the human brain and culture.

The cultural neuroscience findings summarized in the previous chapters have shown that the brain, as a key node that connects culture and behavior, must be taken into consideration to clarify the relationship between culture and behavior. It is essential to construct a framework that can integrate the interactions between culture and the brain in two opposing directions: one where culture shapes the brain by framing behavior and the other where the brain modifies culture via behavioral influences. This framework should characterize the dynamic nature of the interaction between culture, behavior, and the brain, and improve our understanding of human development in terms of both human phylogeny and lifespan ontogeny. In addition, given gene-culture coevolution (Richerson and Boyd 2005; Richerson et al. 2010) and gene-culture interaction on behavior (Kim and Sasaki 2014), the new framework must consider genes in relation to the interaction between culture, behavior, and the brain at both the population and individual levels. Han and Ma (2015) proposed a *culture–behavior–brain (CBB)-loop model* of human development on the ground of recent cultural neuroscience findings. The CBB-loop model distinguishes culturally contextualized and culturally voluntary behaviors and clarifies behavior-mediated and direct culture-brain interactions. The CBB-loop model also provides a new perspective on the relationship between genes and the interacting CBB loop during human development by highlighting the differential effects of culture and genes on the brain and behavior. This model also provides a conceptual basis for hypotheses relating to possible future changes of brain functional organization.

The CBB-loop model of human development

The CBB-loop model

The CBB-loop model proposed by Han and Ma (2015) is illustrated in Figure 8.2. This model aims to provide a framework for understanding human development regarding both human phylogeny and lifespan ontogeny. This model posits that novel ideas are created by individuals in a society and are diffuse in a population through social learning and interactions in a specific ecological environment to become dominant shared beliefs and behavioral scripts—the

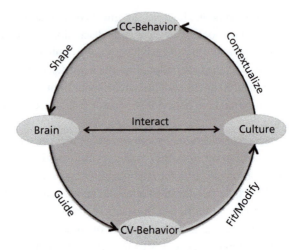

Figure 8.2 Illustration of the CBB-loop model of human development. According to the CBB-loop model, new concepts emerge and diffuse in a population to become shared beliefs and behavioral scripts and to contextualize and influences human behavior. Absorbing new beliefs/traits and practice of new behavioral scripts in turn modifies the functional organization of the brain. The modified brain then guides individual behavior to fit into current cultural contexts and create new cultures. Direct interactions also occur between culture and brain. "Behavior" on the top of the model is culturally contextualized, whereas "Behavior" at the bottom is culturally voluntary.
Adapted from *Trends in Cognitive Sciences*, 19 (11), Shihui Han and Yina Ma, A Culture–Behavior–Brain Loop Model of Human Development, pp. 666–76, DOI:10.1016/j.tics.2015.08.010, Copyright © 2015 Elsevier Ltd., with permission from Elsevier.

two core components of a cultural system—that influence and contextualize human behavior. The functional and/or structural organization of the brain, owing to its inherent plasticity, changes because of absorbing cultural beliefs and performing culturally patterned behaviors. The modified brain then guides an individual's behavior to fit into specific cultural contexts, and the outcome of the behavior can modify concurrent sociocultural environments.

The CBB-loop model proposes two types of behaviors in terms of the driving force behind these behaviors. Culturally contextualized behavior (CC-behavior) refers to overt actions that are mainly governed or constrained by a specific cultural context. In a new cultural environment, an individual's behavior is explicitly guided by new cultural norms and behavioral scripts, and such CC-behavior obtained through social learning plays a key role in acculturation, such as adjustments/adaptations made by immigrants. CC-behaviors may not be performed when individuals depart from the new cultural environment. Culturally voluntary behavior (CV-behavior) refers to overt actions that are guided by internalized cultural beliefs/values and behavioral scripts and culturally patterned brain activity formed through cultural learning and practice. CV-behaviors can occur independently of a specific cultural context if a cultural system has been internalized in the brain and remains stable. Defining these two types of behaviors is pivotal to the understanding of distinct motivations of apparently similar behaviors. For example, a Chinese student, who is accustomed to accepting a professor's opinion in China, when taking a position in a US laboratory, may follow American students' patterns of performance and argue with his supervisor. An American student, who is accustomed to informality in the United States and who calls his American professor by his first name, may imitate other Chinese students to call his Chinese professor "Teacher Han" ("Han" is a family name) when he starts working in a laboratory in China. Such behaviors are driven by a social context rather than internalized cultural belief/value (e.g., independence/interdependence) and thus exemplify CC-behaviors. After the Chinese student has studied in the United States for a long time and has internalized the Western cultural values, such as independence, he may voluntarily argue with his American supervisor rather than conforming to the actions of peers. Similarly, after the American student lives in China for a period and has internalized Chinese cultural values, such as to honor a teacher and respect his teaching, he may voluntarily call his Chinese professor "Teacher Han." These examples exemplify CV-behaviors. In general, a new immigrant, who starts a new life in a different culture, has to pay much attention to the social norms/rules in the new society. His/her behavior at the early stage of immigration is influenced and constrained by the new sociocultural context. However, once he/she lives in the new cultural environment long enough, he/she can behave voluntarily and automatically to fit into the local social norms/rules. Thus, the apparently same behavior can be driven by either sociocultural context or internalized cultural beliefs/values.

The CBB-loop model also distinguishes two types of cultural influences on the brain. *Behavior-mediated culture-brain interaction* refers to the interplay between culture and the brain via overt behavioral practice. For instance, Western cultural values, such as independence in the United States, encourage the Chinese student to argue with his supervisor, and practicing such behaviors may influence his brain. *Direct culture-brain interaction* refers to the interplay between culture and the brain that does not involve overt actions. For example, reminding individuals of specific cultural values such as independence or interdependence in a laboratory setting can directly modulate brain activity. Thus, in the CBB-loop model, behavior is not simply considered a consequence of culture-brain interaction. Instead, behavior is considered part of the interacting CBB loop that constitutes the mechanisms of human development. The three key nodes, culture, behavior, and the brain, dynamically interact through their mutual connections and constitute a loop. Each node and the connection between two nodes of the CBB loop vary continuously across time and influence human ontogeny and phylogeny.

The properties of the CBB loop of human development can be understood on different levels. I call the first level property *mutability*, which applies to each node of the CBB loop. *Mutability* describes how easily the nodes of the CBB loop can change across time. The mutability of a culture is characterized by how fast new cultural beliefs/values/ concepts are created in a population and how easily a contemporary cultural system can be changed or even replaced by a new cultural system. Although cultural knowledge is delivered from one generation to the next, and cultural intergenerational continuity is important for heredity of culture, cultural intergenerational change also occurs frequently and widely among humans. Some cultural changes took place over a long time, such as from hunting/gathering to agriculture-based communities, whereas some cultural changes took place much quicker in two successive generations of the same group of families (Greenfield 1999). Using the data from the three waves of the World Values Surveys that covered 65 societies, Inglehart and Baker (2000) revealed evidence of massive change of cultural traditions in 16 years (1981 to 1997), which was characterized by shifts away from absolute norms/ values toward rational, tolerant, and trusting values, particularly in the developed countries. Both innovation of new ideas/techniques and environmental changes promote changes of both cultural knowledge and the very processes of cultural learning/transmission. The *mutability of behavior* refers to how quickly new behavior scripts are created and how quickly the behaviors of an individual or a population follow the new behavioral scripts, which fit with new cultural values and social norms in a society. Some behaviors have remained invariant for a long time in the human history, such as parenting, whereas new behaviors can emerge quickly in a society, such as online shopping. For an individual, learning new behaviors is critical for survival in a society and for fitting into new sociocultural environments. This is particularly important for individuals in the modern society that is developing and changing more and more rapidly. As proposed earlier, new behaviors can be driven by sociocultural contexts (CC-behavior) and by internalized cultural values/norms and behavioral scripts (CV-behavior). The mutability of the brain reflects neural plasticity that refers to the fact that both the structure and function of the brain, at either the individual or the population level, alters in response to environmental changes and social experiences. Although there has been little evidence for intergenerational changes in the human brain because of social experiences, cultural neuroscience findings have shown substantial evidence for changes of brain functional organization owing to long-term cultural experiences. Brain imaging findings from cultural priming studies indicate that changes of human brain functional organization can occur quickly in response to recent use of different cultural values/norms, and this provides a neurobiological basis of cultural influences on human behavior.

I define the second-level property of the CBB loop as "*interactivity*," which describes the interacting relationships between two nodes of the CBB loop. Cultural impact on human behavior occurs in both the history of humankind and concurrent societies. A survey of the history of humankind (Harari 2014) suggests that the agricultural revolution that occurred about 10,000 years ago and changed human behaviors from gathering/hunting to farming was possibly driven by the belief that farming would provide more food and a more stable life. The scientific revolution during the last 500 years was also driven by the belief that observations and mathematical understanding of the observations are the right source of our knowledge. In current societies, an individualistic culture encourages independence and allows an infant to sleep separately from his/her parents in his/her own room and permits parents to split bills with their adult children at a restaurant. In contrast, in a collectivistic culture that advances interdependence, a child can share a bedroom with his/her parents until early adulthood, and family members never split the restaurant bill. A large number of such behaviors manifest cultural influences on human behavior at both population and individual levels in two directions. On the one hand, culture can change an individual's behavior quickly and in time modify behavior patterns of a population through cultural transmission. On the other hand, human beings never stop modifying the existing culture and creating new cultural beliefs/concepts. Human behaviors during the transition from a collecting/hunting society to a farming society and then to an industrial society created not only new social rules and behavioral scripts but new values and beliefs as well. People of low and high social classes behave differently and create their own cultural values (Snibbe and Markus 2005). New techniques developed during human history always influence our behavior and produce new cultural values. For instance, the widespread use of the Internet brings revolutionary changes to our experience of community (Porter 2013) by providing virtual acquaintances and frequent anonymous encounters with familiar or unfamiliar individuals who are digitally identified. Words delivered via the Internet, which are often striped of context, replace traditional face-to-face communications, which are characterized by inflections, gestures, and embraces. The invention of the smartphone and other portable connected devices has liberated people from nine-to-five working constraints but has created an "always on" culture that blurs the boundary of work and leisure and leads to a new state of the self that is digitally tethered with someone absent (but is separated from physically proximate individuals) (Turkle 2006). These new cultures will change human behaviors and in turn will further modify our brain.

The brain interacts with behavior in two ways. The intrinsic nature of plasticity allows the brain to change both structurally and functionally in response to the environment and experience (Pascual-Leone et al. 2005). For instance, short-term practice of juggling gives rise to transient and selective structural changes of the posterior intraparietal cortex (Draganski et al. 2004). Long-term practice of playing musical instruments causes functional and anatomical changes of the motor cortex in musicians (Münte et al. 2002). Driving a taxi for years induces changes in functional organization of the hippocampus related to spatial memory (Maguire et al. 1997). Chinese who have experienced living in a Western country for years have modification in their empathic neural responses in the anterior cingulate and insula to other-race individuals' pain (Zuo and Han 2013). Life experiences with close others in a collectivistic culture results in overlapped neural coding of oneself and one's mother in the medial prefrontal cortex whereas life experiences in an individualistic culture dissociate the neural coding of the self and mother in the medial prefrontal cortex (Zhu et al. 2007). Taken together, such evidence has demonstrated that the brain is an organ of which the functional and structural organization is highly flexible, although current cultural neuroscience findings mainly reveal modulations of functional (but not anatomical) organization of the brain by sociocultural environments and practices. On the other hand, the brain provides the neurobiological basis of human behavior. The CBB-loop model emphasizes that a culturally shaped brain guides behaviors that conform to specific social norms/rules and fit into specific sociocultural contexts. For example, collectivistic relative to individualistic cultures lead to enhanced activity in the temporoparietal junction during self-reflection on social roles (Ma et al. 2014a), greater activity in the caudate nucleus and medial prefrontal cortex to gestures indicating social dominance (Freeman et al. 2009), and stronger activity in the prefrontal and parietal cortices during tasks requiring context-independent rather than context-dependent judgments (Hedden et al. 2008). These patterned brain activities make individuals in a collectivistic culture coordinate with close others more easily, behave according to social norms that emphasize social relationships, and pay attention to contextual information and others' expectations. A brain that does not attempt to have such culturally specific functional organization may have to work harder to avoid conflict with behavioral scripts and social rules in a collectivistic culture.

There are also mutual interactions between culture and the brain. On the one hand, cultural education shapes the neural substrates of multiple cognitive/

affective processes in the brain as indicated by cultural neuroscience findings. People can be imbued with new cultural values and learn new behavioral scripts by observing others' behavior. This is particularly true for children during education that results in significant modifications of their brains. Even for adults, religious beliefs produce specific patterns of brain activity that differentiate between believers and non-believers. While non-religious individuals employ the ventral medial prefrontal cortex during reflection on one's own personality traits, self-reflection activates the dorsal medial prefrontal cortex in Christians (Han et al. 2008) and the anterior cingulate in Buddhists (Han et al. 2010). The findings of cultural priming studies indicate that that short-time exposure to interdependent or independent cultural values can lead to changes of brain activity involved in multiple cognitive and affective processes, illustrating direct interactions between culture and brain activity. On the other hand, environmental pressure forces humans to create new ideas/concepts that can be transmitted across individuals in a population and finally accepted as cultural norms or values. However, at the current stage of evolution, the human brain may create new cultural concepts and values under no direct environmental pressure. Most of the current techniques are the products of human creativities that were not made for survival but for satisfaction in life. New cultural concepts can be created by a small group of social members who are not satisfied with concurrent sociocultural environments or by just wanting to become unique among peers.

The third-level property of the CBB loop of human development can be called "*spin time*," which characterizes the time required for a circular interaction to occur in the CBB loop. The spin time is a global feature of the CBB loop and is associated with the local properties of the three nodes and their interactivity. At the individual level, the spin time can be used to depict an individual's ability to change his/her behavior and brain activity to fit into new cultural beliefs/norms and to create new ideas to modify contemporary culture. Spin time may vary remarkably across individuals owing to their genetic makeup that influences the coupling between brain activity and cultural values (Ma et al. 2014b; Luo et al. 2015a), and thus it plays a fundamental role in an individual's development. At the population level, spin timing characterizes the ability of a species or a population to create new ideas and accordingly modifies behavior and brain activity during phylogeny. Human beings surpass other primates in rapid creation of novel ideas and new behavioral scripts as evidenced by the changes of living styles from gathering/hunting to agricultural and industrial societies. Though we lack empirical findings comparing changes of functional organization between human and other primates during the past thousands of years, cultural neuroscience findings have shown evidence that the human brain is extremely flexible in the alternation of functional organization in response to new cultural experiences.

To illustrate human development in the CBB-loop framework, let us consider a key cultural trait—interdependence/independence—which differentiates individuals from East Asian and Western societies (Markus and Kitayama 1991, 2010). Previous research has suggested that the idea of interdependence/independence emerged during specific social practice and dynamic changes in ecological environments. Farming and fishing communities emphasize harmonious social interdependence, whereas herding communities emphasize individual decision making and foster social independence (Uskul et al. 2008). By analyzing the relative frequencies of words indexing these values from the years 1800 to 2000 in American English books and books published in the United Kingdom, Greenfield (2013) suggested that adaptation to rural environments prioritizes social obligation/duty and social belonging to promote a strong connection between the self and others, whereas adaptation to urban environments prioritizes choice and personal possessions to foster the unique self. Individuals dominated by interdependence or independence behave differently, such as categorizing objects in terms of their relationships or attributes (Choi et al. 1999). Priming interdependence in laboratories speeds responses to a friend's face, whereas priming independence speeds responses to one's own face (Sui and Han 2007). Interdependence/independence corresponds to distinct patterns of brain activity in different cultures, such as stronger activity in the temporoparietal junction in the East Asians compared with Westerners (Ma et al. 2014a). Priming interdependence/independence also leads to changes of brain activity engaged in multiple cognitive and affective processes, as illustrated by cultural priming findings summarized in Chapter 6. Culturally patterned brain activity, such as the increased activity in the temporoparietal junction in East Asians may be associated with the ability to take others' perspectives voluntarily so that one can easily fit into a collectivistic cultural context (Han and Ma 2014). Therefore, interdependence/independence, behavior, and related brain function constitute a circular interaction that gives rise to dynamic variations of culture, behavior, and the brain in a population.

At an individual level, imagine that a child is born and educated in a culture that advocates interdependence and emphasizes fundamental connections between oneself with close others, such as family members. The child is guided by his/her parents to behavior according to culturally appropriate behavioral scripts such as paying attention to others when sitting around a table during dinner, sharing food and toys with siblings and friends, staying close to family members in a new, unfamiliar environment, making decisions relying on or even by family members, suppressing emotional responses in the public, keeping in mind one's own responsibility for family and searching for social support from family members and others. Long-term practice of these behavioral scripts, guided by culturally specific concepts and values such as interdependence then lead to enhanced functional significance of the brain regions supporting inference of the others' mind (the dorsal medial prefrontal cortex), regulation of emotion (the lateral prefrontal cortex), and shared representations of oneself and close others such as family members (the ventral medial prefrontal cortex). The culturally patterned brain activity, once well developed, then helps to govern the individual's behavior so that he/she can comply with culturally specific norms and scripts without conscious endeavor, and feel comfortable with his/her culturally situated behavior.

Genes and the CBB loop

The CBB-loop model provides a new conceptual framework for the dynamic interactions between culture, behavior, and the brain in terms of both individual ontogeny and group phylogeny. Given the long history of viewing human development as a joint outcome of genetic and environmental factors, it is critical to clarify the relationship between genes and the CBB loop. A simple model has located genes somewhere in the CBB loop because it is believed that genes influence both behavior and the brain (e.g., Li 2003). However, the two tracks of genes and culture reproduce and adapt at quite different rates, with genetic evolution occurring much more slowly (over generations) than cultural evolution (generational). Relative to the time scale that genes moderate the brain at the group level (in thousands or millions of years), cultural and behavioral influences on the brain occur much faster (in days or months or even in a few minutes during manipulations of cultural priming in laboratories). In addition, while there is substantial evidence for novel cultural influences on human behaviors (Triandis 1994; Chapter 1 in this book), the causal pathway from genes to behavioral phenotypes is rarely direct (Flint et al. 2010), and this is particularly true for human behavior. Findings of published studies have shown that the strength of the association between genes and behavioral phenotypes is quite weak. For instance, a genome-wide association study of 101,069 individuals and a replication sample of 25,490 reported that a linear polygenic score from all measured single-nucleotide polymorphisms could account for about 2% of the variance in educational attainment (approximately 1 month of schooling per allele; Rietveld et al. 2013). Given these differences in the pace of genetic and cultural influences on the brain and behavior, Han and Ma (2015) proposed that genes provide a fundamental biological basis for the CBB loop to operate, as shown in the conceptual framework of the relationship between gene and the

CBB loop illustrated in Figure 8.3. The interactions between genes and the CBB loop occur over a long period and are depicted as dashed lines, whereas the interactions within the CBB loop take place over a short-time scale and are indexed using solid lines.

The conceptual model shown in Figure 8.3 suggests several ways in which genes influence the properties of each node of the CBB loop and the interactivity between two nodes. First, genes by and large shape the anatomy of the human brain by influencing brain size (Evans et al. 2004; Boyd et al. 2015) and affecting both cortical and subcortical structures (Thompson et al. 2001; Hibar et al. 2015). Genetic influences make the human brain different from non-human anthropoid primates' brains in some important aspects, such as larger

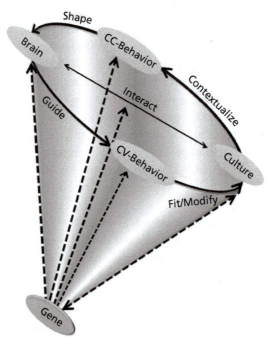

Figure 8.3 Illustration of the relationship between genes and the CBB loop. Genes provide a fundamental basis for the CBB loop in several ways, including genetic influences on the brain and behavior, mutual interactions between genes and culture, and genetic moderations of the association between brain and culture. The solid lines in the CBB loop indicate fast interactions between two nodes, whereas the dashed lines linking the gene and the CBB loop indicate slow interactions between the gene and the CBB loop.

Adapted from *Trends in Cognitive Sciences*, 19 (11), Shihui Han and Yina Ma, A Culture–Behavior–Brain Loop Model of Human Development, pp. 666–76, DOI:10.1016/j.tics.2015.08.010, Copyright © 2015 Elsevier Ltd., with permission from Elsevier.

neocortices and more cortical folding in the prefrontal cortex (Rilling and Insel 1999) but smaller sensory and motor regions than expected (Holloway et al. 1992). Research of resting state brain activity has revealed three neural networks that exist in humans but not in macaque monkeys, including two fronto-parietal networks being related to tool use and one anterior cingulate-insula network being involved in empathy (Mantini et al. 2013). Our genes may bestow high plasticity on our brain so that its structural and functional organization can vary in responses to changes of physical and sociocultural environments. Indeed, the hominid brain has undergone a consistent enlargement over the last two million years with its volume increasing from 500 cc to about 1500 cc (Tattersall 2008). The increased brain size grants its higher degree of mutability, possibly underlain by connections of a large number of neurons, which provides a basis for diversity of behaviors, renders a potential for modifications by cultural experiences, and endows the brain with the ability to create new cultural concepts and values.

Second, although knowledge about the causal pathway from gene to behavioral phenotypes is lacking (Flint et al. 2010), the findings from twin and adoption studies indicate that some behavioral characteristics are to a certain degree heritable (McGue and Bouchard 1998). Candidate gene and genome-wide association studies have linked specific genes to multiple behaviors such as smoking (Kremer et al. 2005) and schooling (Rietveld et al. 2013). The findings of these studies, however, suggest genetic association rather than genetic determination of human behavior. Environments and life experiences produce strong constraints on how a genotype gives rise to a behavioral phenotype (e.g., McGue and Bouchard 1998; Caspi et al. 2003).

Third, the gene-culture coevolution theory suggests that genes and culture are two systems that are important parts of each other's environments so that evolutionary changes in one system induce evolutionary modifications in the other (Boyd and Richerson 1985; also see Chapter 7 of this book). On a historical time scale, cultural beliefs/values may influence the social and physical environments under which genetic selection operates and shapes the human genome, such as that culturally learned mating preferences favor specific biological traits in the opposite sex (Richerson et al. 2010; Laland et al. 2010). On a lifespan scale, genes may affect to what degree an individual is influenced by cultural contexts given that some allele carriers are more easily susceptible to environmental influences relative to other allele carriers (Belsky et al. 2009; Way and Lieberman 2010; Kim et al. 2010a; Kim and Sasaki 2014). The empirical findings of cultural neuroscience studies have suggested a new type of gene-cultural interaction, that is, genes can moderate the degree to which brain activity is associated with cultural traits (e.g., Ma et al. 2014b; Luo et al. 2015a), which suggests a possible mechanism of how the brain learns new cultural values and mediates gene-cultural interactions on behavior.

Finally, genes provide a biological basis for the spin time—the global property of the CBB loop of human development. The change of each single node of the CBB loop is not sufficient to prompt human development. For example, if an individual or a population can change behaviors quickly in response to new cultural environments whereas the behavioral changes cannot rapidly modify the brain and lead to internalized cultural beliefs/values and CV-behavior, it is hard to imagine that the individual or the population can develop quickly to fit into new cultural environments. The fact that human beings have surpassed other species of animals in development during the last hundreds of thousands of years cannot be fully comprehended if we only consider genetic effects on the brain. Only by examining genetic influences on the CBB loop as a whole can researchers fully understand the difference in multiplex cultures, diverse behaviors, and functional brains between human beings and other species of animals and between different cultural populations of human beings. The CBB loop supported by genes exists dynamically in a specific environment during evolution, and the spin time of the CBB loop might be long and constrained by the environment when humans mainly produced adaptive responses to natural environments and were unable to make radical changes to the environment. However, the CBB loop can be accelerated when human influences on the physical environment increase, such as is happening in current human societies where our behaviors have produced huge changes of the global environment by innovation of new cultural beliefs/values and new techniques.

A CBB-loop-based understanding of human nature

Innumerable philosophers, historians, authors, and scientists have pondered the nature of human beings by asking questions such as what kind of animal we—homo sapiens—are, how we came to be this way, in what aspects humans are different from other primates, what allow humans to develop the most divergent cultures on earth, etc. (Spiro et al. 1987; Degler 1991; Hume 1978; Wilson 2012). Researchers from different fields have addressed the issue of "human nature" by proposing a number of unique human features that may differentiate between humans and other primates. The features that have been examined so far and are believed to make us distinct from other primates and made us "human," include cognitive skills, such as language and tool use, and biological properties, such as brain size. However, none of these has been demonstrated to be unique for humans and thus do not constitute a sharp boundary between human nature and that of other primates. For instance, there is evidence for the presence of incipient language abilities in apes, such as the capacity to comprehend and manipulate symbols, to understand syntax, and to communicate various emotions through vocalization (Premack 2004; Schurr 2013). There is also evidence that tool use occurs in most ape species (Mulcahy et al. 2005; Hernandez-Aguilar et al. 2007). Certain chimpanzees are capable of producing stone tools (Mercader et al. 2007), and tool use can be transmitted between individuals (Premack 2004). Other social cognitive and affective abilities such as theory of mind and empathy are observed in both humans (Batson 2011; Baron-Cohen et al. 2013) and other primates such as chimpanzees (De Waal 2009). Unique cultural profiles are also observed in a local community of chimpanzees, such that each chimpanzee community displays a subset of traditions such as distinct ant dipping (Humle and Matsuzawa 2002) and nut cracking (Luncz et al. 2012) techniques. In addition, immigrants into different chimpanzee communities can modify their own nut-cracking techniques learned before they disperse and converge on the way of nut cracking that the local community adopts (Luncz et al. 2012).

The biological approach to the exploration of human nature focuses on the properties of the human brain that may differentiate between human and other animals. The structure of the human brain is characterized by an evolutionary expansion of the cerebral cortex, which is thought to be the most distinctive morphological features of the mammalian brain. The human brain shows a large volume of cortical gray matter as indexed by the percentage of total brain volume, but it is not the largest among primates (Human, 49.2%; Macaca mulatta [one of the best-known species of Old World monkeys], 55.1%; Hofman 1988). The human brain is characterized by the large relative size of the entire cerebral cortex (human, 80%; mice, 40%) and the largest relative white matter volume (about 35%) among primates (Hofman 1988; Herculano-Houzel 2012). The human brain is distinguished by its greater proportion of cortical surface allocated to the higher-order association cortex such as the prefrontal cortex and temporal lobe rather than primary sensory and motor areas (Van Essen and Dierker 2007; Rilling and Seligman 2002; Glasser et al. 2014). The unique properties of human brain anatomy in comparison with other primates may arise from the difference in genetic makeup between these species. It is now known that the difference in a single-copy sequence in DNA, possibly owing to genome accumulated mutations such as single base-pair substitutions, is about 6.5% between humans and rhesus macaques (Gibbs et al. 2007) and about 1.4% between humans and chimpanzees (Scally et al. 2012). Humans also differ from other primates in the number of species-specific insertions in DNA and the levels of intraspecies genetic variation (Rogers and Gibbs 2014). Gene expression also differs between human and other primates because patterns of DNA methylation in the prefrontal cortex are different between humans and chimpanzees, and correlate with differences in gene expression (Zeng et al. 2012). Recent research has discovered specific genes that are linked to human brain structure. Hibar and colleagues (2015) conducted genome-wide association studies of the volumes of seven subcortical regions and the intracranial volume derived from magnetic resonance images of over 30,000 individuals from 50 cohorts. They identified five novel genetic variants that influence the volumes of subcortical structures such as the putamen and caudate nucleus. Boyd and colleagues (2015) took advantage of a novel transgenic technique to introduce a particular regulator of gene activity (dubbed HARE5) from a human or chimpanzee into a mouse embryo. Interestingly, this manipulation led to a 12% bigger brain in the embryos treated with HARE5 sequence from humans compared with those treated with the HARE5 sequence from chimpanzees. This finding suggests that humans compared with other primates are possibly equipped with specific genes that give rise to some distinctive anatomical features of the human brain.

However, these empirical findings still do not allow researchers to explain the remarkable differences in both ontogeny and phylogeny between humans and other primates. Examination of human achievements such as the invention of tools (e.g., boats, needles, and arrows) between 70,000 and 30,000 years ago suggests that Homo sapiens underwent a "cognitive revolution" during which their cognitive abilities, particularly unprecedented ways of thinking and communicating were improved amazingly (Hariri 2014). However, the invention of tools such as boats required very complicated cognitive skills and was difficult to be directly connected with the function of a specific brain structure or a specific gene. To obtain such skills requires creation and transmission of new ideas and concepts and applying them to behavior that in turn gives rise to additional deep thoughts. What is even more surprising is that such circular processes took place in a short period during evolution only in humans.

The CBB-loop model provides a new perspective on the understanding of human development. Cultural neuroscience findings indicate that the structure, or the hardware, of the brain, which is strongly coined by our genes, provides the possibility of what and how the brain finally does. The functional organization of the brain depends upon the interaction between the brain, behavior, and cultural contexts in a way formulated in the CBB-loop model of human development. It is not one of the nodes in the CBB loop but the CBB loop as a whole, which can provide a comprehensive understanding of what makes humans distinct from other primates and bring humans to the top position among the living beings on earth. Based on findings from cultural neuroscience and other fields, it can be proposed that the global properties of the

CBB loop, including the mutability of each node, the interactivity between two nodes, and the spin time of the CBB loop, provide the basis of human development and make humans different from primates in terms of their success during evolution. In particular, our genes may allow humans, relative to other animals, to have a shorter spin time of the CBB loop. The fast dynamic interactions between culture, behavior, and the brain during evolution and lifespan development make humans stand out among other animals.

What happened to human sapiens during the last 10,000 years? According to Hariri (2014), humans started the initial transition from lives that depended on hunting and gathering, to living in settled agriculture communities and relying on the ability to farm crops and domesticate animals. In less than 2,000 years, the agricultural revolution brought more diversity to farming and better food-producing technology that were able to support large populations in limited geographical space. The Industrial Revolution that occurred during the last 250 years changed human lives even more rapidly and radically. The transition from hand production methods to machines, new chemical manufacturing, and iron production processes, and the more recent transition of information exchange from sending relatively slow-moving letters to computer/Internet/smartphone interactions have changed human behavior and thoughts extensively. However, our relatives (e.g., monkeys and chimpanzees) have existed as long as humans have but have been living in a similar way for hundreds of thousands of years (e.g., keeping the way of gathering food). Humans are the only species on earth who consciously organized teaching practices so that their offspring are able to repeat the behaviors that their ancestors performed and the social learning delivers values and norms from one generation to the next. The cultural neuroscience findings introduced in this book have revealed that sociocultural learning also shapes the functional organization of the brain and determines how the brain perceives the world, thinks about the self and others, makes decisions, etc. By contrast, other animals, even our close relatives such as chimpanzees, do not have the capacity to perform consciously large amounts of routine and well-organized social learning. The animals do have the ability to transmit cultural knowledge, but the learning process appears to occur randomly, so it is difficult to shape the functional organization of their brains through the randomly occurring social learning processes. The consciously routine teaching of behaviors and beliefs/values in humans leads to reorganization of the brain so that it is competent for specific tasks and, more importantly, different patterns of the brain activity that can be observed to solve the same task in different sociocultural contexts, such as East Asian and Western societies. We know little about whether animals of other species show group differences in patterns of brain activity underlying the same cognitive or motor tasks.

We would not expect a large differences in the functional brain activity between different groups of monkeys or chimpanzees because these animals, from different groups, demonstrate behaviors such as grooming, mating, and searching for food in quite similar fashions. The special social learning process in humans may play a pivotal role in speeding the CBB loop to accomplish the interacting processes in the CBB loop. Further, the brain bridges the gap between genes and culture during gene-cultural coevolution at the population all levels in a large time scale and during gene-cultural interaction at the individual level in a lifespan.

Brain changes in the future

Cultural neuroscience findings have demonstrated extensive cultural influences on the functional organization of the human brain. Such influences will continue given that humans keep on creating new cultures. New concepts and new techniques are created one after another and transmitted in the contemporary society. The innovative concepts/techniques bring new behavioral scripts and practices and the new behaviors in turn give rise to new patterns of brain activity. According to the CBB-loop model of human development, functional reorganization of the human brain owing to the interactions between culture, behavior, and the brain occurs continuously as adaptive responses to the changing cultural environments. The CBB-loop model provides a framework for understanding how the human brain was shaped in the past and for speculating what will happen to the human brain in the future.

Looking back to the recent history of human development, the Industrial Revolution has changed and is changing human lives in many amazing ways. Among these is the alteration of the basic unit of human social activity. As Harari (2014, 355–356), pointed out,

> As best we can tell, from the earliest times, more than a million years ago, humans lived in small, intimate communities, most of whose members were kin. The Cognitive Revolution and the agricultural revolution did not change that. They glued together families and communities to create tribes, cities, kingdoms and empires, but families and communities remained the basic building blocks of all human societies. The Industrial Revolution, on the other hand, managed within little more than two centuries to break these building blocks into atoms. Most of the traditional functions of families and communities were handed to states and markets.

What Harari describes is also happening now in regions where societies and people are undergoing transition from farming to industry. How is the Industrial Revolution changing the human brain in terms of variation of the basic unit of social activity? Family, as the basic unit of social activity in a farming society, determines whom an individual spends most of his/her time with and can seek social support from. The tight social and affective connections between family members play a significant role in shaping neural representations of people, and lead to shared neural coding of oneself and family members. Once the traditional functions of families such as economic/emotional support are replaced by states and markets, the psychological and neural coupling of oneself and family members can be dampened gradually. This, indeed, has been demonstrated by cultural neuroscience findings that compared functional organization of the brain in those living in the industrialized (or developed and Western) and agricultural (or developing and East Asian) regions in the world. Chinese university students showed overlapping neural activity in the medial prefrontal cortex in response to reflection on oneself and family members, whereas such overlapped neural representations of oneself and close others were degraded in Westerner university students (Zhu et al. 2007; Wang et al. 2012). Such cultural group differences in neural representation of the self and close others were observed during the first few years of twenty-first century. However, as industrialization is developing rapidly in large cities in China, more and more young people from traditional rural areas are moving into cities to pursue good jobs and life styles. These young people are going through the baptism of the Industrial Revolution, which encourages independence and autonomy and downplays the role of family in economic and affective support. Consequently, individuals have to become more and more independent during social interactions. This in turn may dampen the shared neural representations of oneself and family members in the future, even in traditional East Asian cultures.

New techniques that are bringing new ways of social communication in contemporary societies can also bring new behavioral scripts, and change the functional organization of the brain in the future. Conventional face-to-face social interactions allow the development of multiple neurocognitive processes and related neural networks that support our ability to infer others' mental states and other social cognitive abilities (Baron-Cohen et al. 2013). Humans get used to face-to-face communication, which delivers social information about others' mental states and facilitates the development of the neural network consisting of the dorsal medial prefrontal cortex, temporoparietal junction, and temporal pole for inference of others' mental states or theory-of-mind ability (Frith and Frith 2003; Amodio and Frith 2006). Face-to-face communication also helps us to understand and share others' emotional states and develop empathy-related neural networks consisting of the anterior cingulate cortex, anterior insular, and the somatosensory cortex (Singer et al. 2004; Jackson et al. 2005; Gu and Han 2007; Han et al. 2009; Rütgen et al. 2015a, 2015b). These neurocognitive processes are specific to social interactions among real human beings, as suggested by brain imaging studies. For example, Sanfey et al. (2003) found that, in a Ultimatum Game where two players split a sum of money and one player proposes a division and the other can accept or reject this, unfair offers elicited activity in brain areas related to both emotion (anterior insula) and cognition (dorsolateral prefrontal cortex), and the heightened activity was much stronger when playing with a human partner than with a computer partner. Ge and Han (2008) also found that to infer the reasoning processes conducted by human agents but not by computers induced increased activity in the precuneus but decreased activity in the ventral medial prefrontal cortex, and enhanced functional connectivity between the two brain areas. These findings illustrate unique neurocognitive strategies involved in social cognition underlying face-to-face social interactions between humans. However, the traditional face-to-face social interactions in everyday life are changing notably because of the invention of new techniques. Computers, the Internet, and smartphone have been used more and more widely since 1990s, and they alter how people communicate with each other (including family members and friends). Teenagers are becoming accustomed to texting messages rather than talking to the person sitting beside them. The development of Internet social networks has made more and more people in the contemporary societies rely on the Internet for social interaction. A consequence of social interactions in cyberspace is the abatement (or even elimination in some situations) of face-to-face communications that people conventionally depend upon. Lack of experience in interpreting others' intentions and emotional states by perceiving social cues from others' faces/gestures may influence our theory-of-mind ability and the underlying neural strategy.

The Internet and relevant behaviors have created a new "Internet culture" that contextualizes human behavior in the cyberspace (Porter 2013). The wide use of the Internet during learning has significantly altered the way students obtain knowledge. Extensive literature libraries stored on the Internet constitute a large database that can be reached by anyone who can get access to the Internet and has sufficient skills. Internet search engines such as Google Scholar are so powerful that literature or relevant knowledge can be found in a few seconds. As Wegner and Ward (2013) noted, "the Internet is taking the place not just of other people as external sources of memory but also of our own cognitive faculties. The Internet may not only eliminate the need for a partner with whom to share information—it may also undermine the impulse to ensure that some important, just learned facts get inscribed into our biological memory banks." The impact of computer and Internet techniques on our memory processes have been demonstrated by Sparrow and colleagues (2011). They had participants read and type in items of memorable trivia. Among these items, they made participants believe that one-third would be generically saved on a computer, one-third would be saved into a specific folder on a computer, and one-third would be erased. Participants were given the expectation that they would have access to what they saved. In a later recognition task, participants were given all 30 statements they had typed, but half had been altered slightly. Participants had to judge whether the statement they were shown for recognition was exactly what they had read, whether the statement had been saved or erased, and finally, if the statement had been saved to a folder, which folder to which it had been saved. Interestingly, it was found that participants had the best memory of those statements they believed to be erased compared with the statements participants believed they would continue to have access to. However, when answering the question "Was this statement saved or erased?" participants accurately remembered what they had saved more than they accurately remembered what they had erased. These findings illustrate the general experience of remembering something you have read online that you would like to see again but no longer remembering where you saw it, or even knowing when and where they had been saved onto your hard drive but having to use the search feature to find it. The Internet has gradually become a primary form of external memory where information is stored collectively outside our brain but can be easily accessed. For students who study through the Internet, it is much more important to learn and practice how to find information using search engines relative to remembering as much knowledge as possible. Thus, the Internet tends to replace the function of brain structures such as the inferior frontal cortex, inferior parietal lobe, and temporal lobe that have been used to store and retrieve semantic knowledge (Thompson-Schill et al. 1997; Binder and Desai 2011). The increasing reliance on the Internet for "memorizing" knowledge may endow the original neural system of memory with other functions such as reasoning and inference.

The Internet and smartphones keep people continuously digitally connected with others and generate an "always-on" culture (Turkle 2006; Park 2013). Many people switch on their smartphones 24 hours a day. The first and last thing they do in a day is to check e-mails or text messages. More and more people get used to frequently checking e-mails or text messages and responding to others' messages once being signaled on the arrival of a message. Such an "always-on" culture leads to a high level of discontinuity in the execution of our activities (González and Mark 2004) owing to multiple tasks that may bring various changes of the brain functions (Levitin 2015). Last, the Internet and smartphones are becoming more and more time consuming and result in directing our mind toward others during most of the waking time, leaving much less time for self-reflection. It is well known that self-reflection is mediated by the mid-line brain structure consisting of the brain regions such as the medial prefrontal cortex and posterior cingulate cortex (Kelley et al. 2002; Northoff et al. 2006). Sustained mental activity such as focusing on others or external environments implicates changes in the mid-line brain structure or the default mode brain system that is engaged in self-reflection. Thus, Internet culture may lead to reorganization of human brain function to fit decreased face-to-face communication but increase digital connections among people. The potential changes of the functional organization of the brain may help the next generation to adopt more easily the Internet culture and, meanwhile, the brain shaped by the Internet culture may produce new cultural concepts and new behavioral scripts in the future.

Chapter 9

Implications of the sociocultural brain

To date, cultural-neuroscience research has shown an increasing amount of evidence for cultural-group differences in brain activity underlying a variety of human cognitive and affective processes. The studies that have integrated brain imaging and cultural priming have provided further evidence for the causal relationships between cultural beliefs/values and changes in the functional organization of the human brain. The findings of gene–culture interaction on the brain activity underlying social cognition cast new light on the biological and sociocultural drive of the development of cognitive and affective neural processes. These findings improve our understanding of the nature of the brain and culture, and have numerous scientific and social implications. I discuss a few of them below.

The biosocial nature of the brain

Human beings have the capacity for creating new beliefs/concepts and transmitting them quickly through social media, both within a population and across populations. New beliefs/concepts, once spreading in a population and accepted by the public, have a powerful effect on our behaviors, encouraging the creation of the rich and colorful sociocultural environment on earth. In contemporary societies, children are fostered in unique, artificial environments. People speak a mother language, behave in accordance with specific social rules, act as members of social institutions, and interact with people who share specific cultural beliefs and values. As a result, the human brain develops in a specific sociocultural environment during interactions with others and this allows individuals to fit into a specific sociocultural context and to cooperate efficiently with others.

Traditional neurophysiology and neuroscience research investigates animals that are usually raised in the same, well-controlled environment in order to exclude many influences resulting from a complicated social environment and experience. This approach, taking the brain as a biological organ, aims to clarify the biological (e.g., genetic) drive of the development of multiple-level brain functional organization. The approach helps explain how animals' sensory experiences affect the functional organization of their brains, and it has been very successful in revealing the fundamental principles of brain development. The development of the human brain, however, is different from the development of animals' brains in that the human brain develops within a complex, dynamic sociocultural environment where each person has unique personal experiences. In addition, the human brain has evolved a novel capacity of social learning via communication and education that allows people to create, transmit, and learn new beliefs, concepts, and behavioral scripts. Cultural-neuroscience findings have indicated that culture-specific neurocognitive processes that arise during human development can help individuals to adapt to specific sociocultural environments. Most of the social functions of the human brain (e.g., mental-state inference and self-reflection) would be impossible without the individual's sociocultural experiences of interacting with others, and this reflects the sociocultural-context-dependent nature of the functional organization of the human brain.

Cultural-neuroscience research has opened a new pathway between traditional "biological" and "social" approaches to understanding the nature of the human brain. On the one hand, by comparing the brain activity related to cognition and behavior in different cultural groups, cultural neuroscientists have shown that individuals from different cultures can recruit common neural circuits for multiple cognitive processes (e.g., individuals from both Western and East Asian cultures recruit the lateral occipital cortex in object-processing tasks [Goh et al. 2007] and the ventral medial prefrontal cortex in self-reflection [Zhu et al. 2007; Ma et al. 2014a]). These findings have revealed culturally universal brain mechanisms of cognition and emotion that, largely, may be determined by our biological (e.g., genetic) factors and common social experiences across cultures. On the other hand, cultural-neuroscience findings have also shown that the brain activity underlying other cognitive and affective processes strongly depends on a person's cultural experience, which will vary across different cultural groups (e.g., the premotor activity during mental calculation [Tang et al. 2006] and the activity in the temporoparietal junction and its functional connectivity with the medial prefrontal cortex during self-reflection [Ma et al. 2014a]).

The differing patterns of brain activity underlying cognition and behavior across cultures may reflect either the use of culturally different task-solving strategies or changes in the functional/structural aspects of the neural basis of human cognition. In the former condition, the culturally different stimuli or culturally preferred tasks in daily life merely modulate already preexisting neural activity that can remain independent of any contextual effects. For example, individuals from both East Asian and Western cultures have been shown to recruit the frontoparietal network during visuospatial tasks; however, the magnitude of the activity in the network can vary as a function of task demands for absolute and relative judgments (Hedden et al. 2008). This type of cultural difference in brain activity amounts to what has been called modulatory-context dependence (Han and Northoff 2008; Northoff 2014), with the suggestion that neuronal and social activities interact with each other while remaining independent from each other in their respective constitutions. If being modulatory-context dependent, the function of a brain region or a neural network is mainly determined by biological factors such as genes, whereas sociocultural experiences can only change the degree to which the brain region or the neural network is engaged in a specific cognitive task. In the latter condition, however, the functional organization of a specific brain region and connections between different brain regions are dependent upon the sociocultural context. In other words, the function of a brain region or a neural network is mainly determined by personal experience in a particular sociocultural environment. Whereas, biological factors such as genes only drive the formation of anatomical structure of the brain region or the neural network (e.g., the overlapping ventral medial prefrontal activity during reflection of personality traits of oneself and one's mother was observed in Chinese but not Western participants [Zhu et al. 2007]). This amounts to what can be described as constitutive-context dependence (Han and Northoff 2008; Northoff 2014). If the constitution of brain activity underlying specific cognitive/affective processes depends on the respective sociocultural context, a clear-cut distinction between the biological domain of the brain and the social domain of culture would not make sense. In these circumstances, the brain and its neuronal activity must be considered a hybrid of both biological and social influences. In this sense, the human brain is essentially a biosocial organ functioning to bridge the gap between the biological world of the organism and the social world of the environment and its culture (Northoff 2014; Han et al. 2013). Cultural-neuroscience findings have suggested that some neural activities in response to cognition and emotion may mainly be modulated by cultural differences, whereas other neural activities might depend constitutionally on individuals' sociocultural experiences.

The emerging body of studies on cultural influences on human brain function and structure is challenging the dichotomy between neuroscience (describing biologically determined variations between people) and social sciences (interpreting sociocultural differences in human minds and behaviors). The findings of gene–culture interactions on human behavior (Kim and Sasaki 2014) and human brain activity (Ma et al. 2014b; Luo et al. 2015b) further extend the current gene–behavior–brain approach to the understanding of human behavior by providing new perspectives on the relationship between genes and behavior. In particular, as illustrated by the CBB loop model of human development (Han and Ma 2015), cultural-neuroscience findings open a new avenue toward the understanding of human behavior in a specific sociocultural environment by considering how genes modulate the associations between cultural beliefs/values and the brain activity that guides our social behavior. Genetic modulations of the relationship between culture and the brain provide a new mechanism that mediates gene–culture interaction and gene–culture coevolution.

The sociobiological nature of culture

As I mentioned in Chapter 1, from the perspective of cultural psychology, culture consists of both material components (e.g., social environments and culturally patterned behaviors) and subjective components (e.g., shared beliefs, values, and behavioral scripts in our minds). The material components of culture are essentially the outcome of shared beliefs, values, and norms, for example. Although social environments have a significant impact on human behavior, the subjective components of culture are more fundamental and stable in guiding behavior and can be passed on from one generation to the next through social learning. The findings of cultural-neuroscience research indicate that the brain is a key node that connects and integrates the material and subjective components of culture and mediates the dynamic interaction between culture and behavior. Cultural-neuroscience findings also drive us to rethink the exact nature of culture.

Given that the functional organization of the brain is highly sensitive to sociocultural environments and experiences (in particular, if the brain shows constitutive-context dependence) and that the brain must be regarded as a biosocial (rather than a purely biological) organ, it is then reasonable to propose that culture is not as purely social and subjective as has been often assumed. Culture is neither absolutely external and in the material-social environment nor absolutely subjective and a pure mental process. In terms of the psychological mechanisms of culture, cultural effects on behavior reflect the influence of the shared beliefs/values in a population. In terms of neural mechanisms of culture, cultural effects on the brain reflect the influence of shared beliefs/values on the neural processes underlying cognition and emotion in a social group. These claims make even more sense when embedding culture in the —CBB-loop of human development (Han and Ma 2015). Cultural beliefs/values are represented in the neuronal structures and functional organization of the brain activity and guide behaviors via brain activity. Therefore, rather than being completely and exclusively social and subjective, culture should be considered sociobiological. Cultural-neuroscience findings break down the old dichotomy between biology as *nature* and culture as *nurture* and indicate that the human brain is significant in creating new cultural concepts and beliefs. Moreover, culture must be considered a part of human-sociobiological nature.

The current cultural-neuroscience findings also raise important issues about culture from a neuroscience perspective. For example, while there has been increasing evidence that cultural beliefs/values shape the functional organization of the brain, little is known about the nature of neural representations of cultural beliefs/values. One possibility is that no brain region or neural network is specific for representing and coding abstract cultural knowledge. Instead, cultural beliefs/values/norms are essentially embedded in patterned brain activities underlying multiple cognitive and affective processes engaged in tasks and behavior, and cultural learning simply modifies these patterned brain activities rather than coding and storing cultural knowledge in specific brain regions or neural networks. Alternatively, cultural beliefs/values/norms may be represented and stored in a specific brain region, and this brain region may function as a central hub to influence the activity in other brain regions engaged in cognitive and affective tasks. A neural model of culture such as this may not be practical because any damage to the brain region encoding culture would result in loss of all cultural knowledge, and yet there has been no neuropsychological finding showing impaired cultural knowledge resulting from a lesion to a specific brain region. The third model of neural representations of cultural knowledge is that cultural beliefs/values/norms are encoded in a distributed neural circuit, similar to the neural representation of semantic knowledge. Current brain imaging studies have suggested two theoretical positions regarding the neuroanatomical distribution of a cortical semantic network that is organized to conform to the neuroanatomy of sensory, motor, and linguistic systems (Patterson et al. 2007). The distributed-only model suggests that there are widely distributed regions, along with the diverse connections between them, that constitute the complete semantic network, and that the different dimensions of semantic knowledge (e.g., name, color, and action) are distributed in different nodes of that semantic network. The distributed-plus-hub model assumes that the modality-specific distributed regions connect to and communicate through a shared, anodal "hub" in the anterior temporal lobes, where the associations between different dimensions of semantic knowledge are processed by a common set of neurons. Similar to the neural representation of semantic knowledge, different cultural beliefs/values/norms such as individualism/collectivism (Triandis 2001), independence/interdependence (Markus and Kitayama 1991; 2010), loose/tightness (Gelfand et al. 2011), may be encoded in multiple nodes of a neural circuit. In addition, this neural circuit may have connections with and exert modulatory influences on other neural networks underlying perception, cognition, emotion, and decision making, for example. Evidence supporting this model comes from Wang et al. (2013) who found that, relative to a calculation task, priming both interdependent and independent self-construals (by asking participants to read essays containing single or plural pronouns) activated the ventral medial prefrontal cortex and posterior cingulate cortex. Moreover, priming interdependent compared with independent self-construals induced greater activity in the dorsal medial prefrontal cortex and left middle frontal cortex. One may expect, based on these findings, that cultural knowledge such as interdependence and independence will be coded in the ventral medial prefrontal cortex and posterior cingulate cortex and that encoding of interdependence will further engage the dorsal medial prefrontal cortex and left middle frontal cortex. However, this should be tested using different types of stimuli and paradigms if neural representations of independence/interdependence are independent of stimuli and tasks. A big challenge for future cultural-neuroscience research is to create new paradigms that can be integrated with brain imaging to clarify the nature of neural coding of cultural knowledge in the human brain.

Another important question arising from cultural-neuroscience research is how culture is inherited across generations and transmitted among individuals in a population. It is commonly acknowledged that biological information is encoded and delivered from one generation to the next by genes, whereas cultural information is transmitted through social learning (e.g., Richerson and Boyd 2005). This view separates heredity and transmission of genes, which is purely biological, and heredity and transmission of cultural information, which is purely social. However, given the sociobiological nature of culture mentioned above, and in particular, if the culturally patterned brain activity underlying cognitive and affective processes is a prominent component of culture, cultural heredity and transmission then should also be sociobiological (rather than purely social). Social learning from parents and teachers and among peers not only delivers cultural beliefs/values and behavioral scripts across individuals but also transmits culturally patterned brain activity in accordance with these cultural beliefs/values and behavioral scripts. Similarly, selection of new cultural beliefs/values not only results in learning of culturally specific beliefs/values and behavioral scripts but also gives rise to new patterned brain activity in a cultural population as well. Therefore, cultural heredity should be considered as both heredity of cultural knowledge and heredity of culturally induced biology (i.e., culturally patterned brain activity or culturally specific functional organization of the brain) from one generation to the next via sociocultural learning. In this sense, cultural transmission and selection must be considered as sociobiological processes.

Education

In 2014, the BBC recorded an interesting "sociocultural experiment"—five Chinese teachers from middle schools in China were invited by the Bohunt School in a Hampshire town in the UK, to take over the education of 50 British teenage students. The idea of the project, according to the headmaster of the Bohunt School, was that teenagers in the UK face a competitive world, and British teachers should know what is happening outside of the UK regarding education. For example, mathematics education policies in schools vary greatly across cultures, and the international studies of mathematics achievement have revealed higher average scale scores among Chinese students, as compared with student scores from the UK and other countries (Leung 2014). Thus of particular interest was whether anything from the Chinese education system could be transferred to schools in the UK to improve the students' school achievements. This was tested by having the Chinese teachers introduce the education program of a typical Chinese middle school to the British students at the Bohunt School. In the early morning at school, the Chinese teachers lead the students in body building exercise. Chinese teachers believe that such exercise is good for health and that working together on the exercises may help students to learn to coordinate with each other, which may then benefit the teaching of other topics. All 50 students were organized to take lectures in science, mathematics, English, and other subjects, taught by the five Chinese teachers in one classroom. All of the students in this "Chinese" class were to be tested in exams, and their performance would be compared with that of the students taught by the British teachers.

The final exam results were similar among all students, whether taught by Chinese or British teachers. Therefore, students seemed to learn knowledge and skills equally well from the Chinese and British teachers. However, there were very interesting incidents in the Chinese class that manifested overt inconsistency in cultural beliefs, values, and norms between the Chinese teachers and their British students. For example, the Chinese teachers emphasized discipline in the classroom, asking the students to remain silent and pay attention to the lectures given by the teachers. The purpose of the discipline was to emphasize the authority of the teachers, who deliver knowledge and should be respected according to the Chinese culture, and to make students work in coordination with each other, because "the class is a unit," according to one of the Chinese teachers. However, the British students, who were used to speaking their minds in class, giving their opinions, and working in small groups to advance their skills and improve their knowledge, found it difficult to sit in a classroom full of 50 students and simply take notes and practice repetition. They soon became disengaged with the lessons, chatting to each other and not listening to their teachers. As a punishment, when a student could not help talking to others during a lecture, the student was punished by the Chinese teacher, who asked her to sit in front of the classroom in order to separate her from the other students. However, the desired effect was not obtained. The student, rather than feeling embarrassed, seemed to feel excited about being singled out from the others. Obviously, in this *sociocultural experiment*, Chinese teachers' cultural beliefs/values were on a collision course with those of British students, who had expected their views to be considered during school teaching. Further, the differences in cultural beliefs/values between the Chinese teachers and the British students led to unexpected educational outcomes. For instance, in Chinese culture, it is a punishment to isolate an individual from a collective group, whereas, in Western cultures, being independent and different from others can be a reward. Thus, what is perceived as punishment in the Chinese culture can be taken as a chance to show one's uniqueness in the English culture.

The *sociocultural experiment* recorded by the BBC illustrates well that schoolteachers are significant in establishing strong cultural imprints, either explicit or implicit. They not only pass on their skilled knowledge but also deliver cultural beliefs, values, and norms to their students because of the way they teach (e.g., relaxed vs. disciplining). Moreover, because education can be taken as a process that guides learning to ensure proper brain development and functionality (Koizumi 2004), the cultural-neuroscience findings introduced in this book suggest that teaching in schools can strongly shape the functional organization of a student's brain with indelible cultural imprints in several aspects. First, although the scientific knowledge of physics and chemistry, for example, delivered to students can be similar at schools in different cultural environments, some knowledge about, for instance, music, gestures, and brands are obviously culturally specific. Cultural-neuroscience research has shown that cultural familiarity with music, brands, and gestures can modulate brain activity so that the motor cortex responds automatically to support perception-production integration by internal tapping or swinging when listening to culturally familiar music (Nan et al. 2008). The theory-of-mind network (the posterior cingulate cortex, dorsal medial prefrontal cortex, and bilateral temporal-parietal junctions) engages in detecting the mental states of others, based on culturally familiar gestures (Liew et al. 2011), and the reward system (the ventral striatum, orbitofrontal cortex, and anterior cingulate) responds to culturally familiar brands to generate good feelings (Erk et al. 2002). Thus, education assigns culturally familiar stimuli with specific meanings and values that are represented and stored in the brain.

Moreover, education in schools modulates the functional organization of the brain to support culturally specific cognitive styles and strategies that are utilized during multiple tasks. During simple mathematical operations, such as comparison and addition, students from different cultures engage either language-related brain regions (i.e., the Broca and Wernicke areas) in English-speaking Westerners or the premotor association area in Chinese students (Tang et al. 2006). Students learn how to make causal attributions of physical and social events and can focus on either external contextual factors or internal dispositions in different cultures, and the culturally preferred styles of causal attribution are mediated by distinct patterns of the frontal and parietal activity (Han et al. 2011). Thus, students during their school life learn cognitive styles and strategies employed during problem solving, and these are not culturally universal. The neural underpinnings also vary across cultures accordingly. When solving the same problem, students with different cultural experiences may adopt different neurocognitive strategies even if they may finally give the same answer to the same problem.

Further, involvement in school life can influence students' brain activity in realms of affective responses and emotion regulation. Western cultures (such as American) actively encourage high-arousal positive affect such as excitement, whereas the Chinese culture favors low-arousal positive affect such as calm (Tsai et al. 2006). The different cultural affects were also apparent in the BBC documentary. British students were accustomed to interactive talking and raising questions during lectures, whereas the Chinese teachers demanded calm and quiet while their students watched and listened in the class, with the aim of indoctrinating them with the concepts of discipline and coordination, rather than criticizing and challenging. The different rules and atmospheres in British and Chinese classes can lead to increased brain activity mediating affective responses in the anterior cingulate and insula in Westerners and increased brain activity in the lateral prefrontal cortex that supports emotional regulation in East Asians (Han and Ma 2014). It is therefore the case that education in schools can be significant in shaping the neural substrates of emotional responses and emotion regulation.

Finally, school education can also foster the fundamental cultural beliefs/ values such as interdependence/independence, together with the underlying neural substrates. Now, lectures at schools have not been designed explicitly to teach students about local cultural beliefs/values. However, the way in which education is organized in different cultures may have novel effects on the learning of cultural beliefs/values and may shape students' neural roots. In Chinese elementary schools, a number (usually 20 to 50) of students are organized into a "class" to study together for a few years. A Head Teacher, who plays roles of both a teacher and a parental guardian for the students in his or her class, is assigned to and stays with the class through these years. Students from the same class will study the same topic at the same time, and which lectures and when they are taken are scheduled by the school rather than by students themselves. This organizational system continues from elementary schools to universities in China. A Head Teacher will be remembered by the students from the same class for the rest of their lives, and classmates from the same class meet for parties or dinners even after they have retired. The organization of a "class" is a social unit that gives Chinese students a strong collective identity with which to be affiliated. In contrast, starting from middle or high schools, students in the USA and UK (and other Western countries) are not affiliated with a specific "class." Instead, a student attends a lecture in a classroom with other students who share the same interest for a short period and then moves to another classroom for a different lecture with a different group of students. The educational systems in Western societies encourage personal interests and downplay the role of a class group for social affiliation. Thus, school teaching can provide students with very different cultural experiences that will promote distinct cultural beliefs/values, such as individualism/collectivism and interdependence/independence, through the manner in which education is organized. Because teenagers are probably the most sensitive population to new cultural beliefs/values during acculturation (Cheung et al. 2010), and because the frontal lobe of their brains, which possibly engages in neural representation of cultural beliefs/values, is experiencing rapid changes of gray matter density at this time of their lives (Gogtay et al. 2004), it is highly possible that teaching at middle schools can produce remarkable influences on the functional organization of the brain related to fundamental cultural beliefs/values.

Education can be significant in inducing culture-related brain changes in adults as well. Currently, there are millions of immigrants around the world, and globalization has inevitably brought intercultural contacts to people from very different cultural backgrounds. It is important for immigrants to attempt to integrate smoothly in order to be accepted. They need to do this so they can improve the quality of their lives in a new cultural environment. New immigrants have to adjust to culturally unfamiliar information, learn the cognitive styles of local residents, and understand their emotions. Critically, immigrants have to learn local cultural beliefs/values/norms and internalize them in the brain through their social interaction and education. How might it be possible for adult immigrants to change the brain activity underlying the fundamental cultural beliefs through cultural learning? Given that cultural priming studies in laboratories have shown that short-term exposures to cultural symbols can modulate brain activity when an individual is involved in multiple cognitive/affective tasks (Han et al. 2013), it is highly likely that immigrants can undergo changes of brain functional organization during cultural learning that will help them to integrate into a new society quickly. Without the appropriate cultural education (and relevant changes of brain activity), it would be harder for immigrants to develop in and fit into a new cultural environment.

There has been much consideration of the relationship between neuroscience findings and education (Bruer 1997, 2016; Hinton et al. 2012). Researchers have used the results from neuroscience research (e.g., neurogenesis and continuous reorganization of the brain during development) for reconsidering school teaching methods and other educational practices (Sousa 2011). Cultural-neuroscience findings are clearly of significance here in the demonstration that teaching at schools can significantly modify students' brains with strong cultural imprints, which, without a doubt, will influence students' development and lives in the future. Attention to such results should inspire changes in educational practices. To date, it is unknown if there are critical and sensitive periods of cultural learning when the brain may more easily adjust to culturally unfamiliar information and internalize new cultural beliefs/values. Answers to questions like this have important implications for the timing and content of education in specific cultural contexts and for making policies related to the cultural integration of immigrants.

Cross-cultural communication and conflict

Communication between people with distinct cultural beliefs and cultural experiences is ubiquitous in the contemporary society, given the increasing global migration and the international nature of commerce, cooperation, and personal relationships. For instance, the ease of international travel has remarkably increased the number of tourists who are confronted with different cultures during travel. International business inevitably has engaged employees from different nations with different cultural backgrounds. Millions of immigrants have to communicate with people from local cultures during job training and working. Education at universities consists of frequent interactions between international students and their professors, who may have very different cultural experiences and cultural beliefs/values. Even at home, people may have to deal with others with different cultural beliefs/values such as those in cross-cultural marriages and the first and second generations in immigration families. During cross-cultural communication, people have to be careful about when to talk and what to say so as not to break social norms in a local culture. It is obvious that efficient and pleasant cross-cultural communication is pivotal to the success of various intercultural interactions, such as when making political policies and decisions regarding international relationships, pursuing the business goals of cross-national corporations, or improving family well-being in cross-cultural marriages.

Failures of cross-cultural communications may produce intercultural misunderstandings and even cross-cultural conflict between cultural groups (e.g., during international cooperation between companies from different counties) or two individuals (e.g., couples in a cross-cultural marriage). Although social conflict often occurs because of competition for resources or economic interests, this is not always the reason. Cross-cultural conflict can occur between two cultural groups who pursue the same goal during international business and academic cooperation or between two individuals who share the same interests but have different cultural backgrounds (e.g., a student and his/her supervisor or a married couple). What is in common in the failure of cross-cultural communication is the difference in cultural beliefs/values/norms between parties, which may lead to incongruent or opposite opinions about the same issue. The problem in such cross-cultural conflict is that the incongruent or opposite opinions do not simply arise from language differences. Often, such differences can be misunderstood as reflecting intentions to approach different (rather than the same) goals, even when the two parties are pursuing the same goal, and this causes difficulties for further communication.

However, cultural differences in beliefs/values/norms do not necessarily produce conflict between groups or individuals. Understanding the cause of apparently different opinions is important for cross-cultural communication and for reducing cross-cultural conflict. From a cultural-neuroscience perspective, each individual obtains a culturally default neurocognitive style through cultural learning and experience during development; however, this does not exclude that individuals can obtain knowledge from multiple cultures and learn more than one neurocognitive strategy. For example, as I mentioned in the previous chapters, individuals educated in Western cultures develop specific patterns of neural activity in the parietal/temporal/occipital cortices. Those patterns allow them to focus attention on salient objects or local properties of visual input and specific patterns of neural activity in the frontal and parietal cortices, which support their culturally preferred causal attribution of physical and social events in terms of objects' internal attributes or individuals' personality traits. By contrast, individuals educated in East Asian cultures acquire unique patterns of the parietal/temporal/occipital activity that facilitate distributed attention to contextual information, and global properties of visual input and patterns of the frontal/parietal activity that mediate their culturally preferred causal attribution of physical and social events in terms of contextual reasons. Although these culturally preferred neurocognitive strategies employed during cognition can be shifted temporarily (such as when individuals are primed with interdependence or independence), they guide perception, cognition, and decision making in daily life as a default. In addition, brain responses to culturally familiar and unfamiliar products can be different and can be associated with different reward values and different affects. Neural representations of the fundamental beliefs about the relationships between people and between objects can vary greatly across different cultural groups. Given these cultural-neuroscience findings, it may not be surprising that when perceiving and discussing the same issue, two parties engaged in cross-cultural communication (e.g., between Westerners and East Asians, or between any individuals with different cultural backgrounds) adopt their default neurocognitive strategies and cultural values, which may lead to differing opinions or conclusions. Consequently, during cross-cultural cooperation with a target of common interests of the two parties, culturally default neurocognitive strategies may give rise to discrepant views and result in unpleasant outcomes or even conflict.

I believe that, during cross-cultural communication, knowing other people's culturally preferred neurocognitive strategies is helpful for understanding their perspectives and for predicting their opinions and decisions. On the other hand, one also has to be aware of one's own culturally default neurocognitive strategies for perception, attention, causal judgment, and decision making. Understanding both cultural distinctiveness and cultural universality in the neural mechanisms underlying human cognition and behavior is important for mutual understanding, resolving cross-cultural conflict, and reaching agreement during cross-cultural communication and intercultural cooperation. However, the cultural-neuroscience findings of cultural differences in neurocognitive strategies do not necessarily indicate the validity of cultural stereotypes that prevent us from understanding people with different cultural experiences. Rather, cultural-neuroscience research has shown evidence that both long- and short-term cultural experiences can shape neurocognitive strategies. These findings imply that cross-cultural communication can bring changes in the neurocognitive strategies of the parties involved and as a result, may provide opportunities for coordination of the different parties.

People usually intend to assert and maintain their own cultural beliefs/values during cross-cultural communication. An optimistic or positive view of cultural differences in neurocognitive strategies is that, through cross-cultural communication, one can learn new perspectives and new thinking styles from other people with different cultural backgrounds. This can be particularly important for international students who study and work with supervisors in a new culture because learning new neurocognitive strategies for thinking can help students to think about research questions and work toward solutions from multiple perspectives. Encouraging different cognitive strategies for problem solving in international cooperative projects or business can promote critical examination of an issue from multiple points of view and lead to unexpected innovations. In this sense, inconsistency of different culturally default neurocognitive strategies does not necessarily produce negative outcomes during cross-cultural communication: it can benefit human societies.

Psychiatry

Mental disorders such as depression, anxiety, and schizophrenia are problematic for large populations of human beings. Clinical treatments of these mental disorders have become increasingly expensive to both government and civilians. Current biomedical research has focused on finding multiple-level biomarkers (e.g., neuronal, molecular, and genetic) for these neuropsychiatric disorders in order to reveal the underlying mechanisms and highlight possible targets for biomedical treatments. There is a long history of clinical psychiatry documenting cultural variations in the onset, course, and outcome of major psychiatric disorders (Kirmayer and Minas 2000). For example, early research reported that Europeans and Euro-Americans tended to report lower symptom levels of depression as compared with Asians and Asian-Americans (Shong 1977; Marsella et al. 1975; Cheung 1982). Moreover, migrants, especially refugees, reported elevated symptom levels, especially depressive symptoms (Westermeyer et al. 1983). Black immigrants to the UK and other countries have demonstrated elevated rates of schizophrenia, and this effect has persisted and even become worse in the second generation (Cantor-Graae 2007; Cantor-Graae and Selton 2005; Coid et al. 2008). It has been assumed that culture may generate multiple influences on the sources of mental disorders, the form of illness experience, the interpretation of symptoms, social responses to the mental disorders, and models of coping with the neuropsychiatric disorders (Kirmayer 2001). For instance, the conceptual models of depression differ greatly across cultures. Karasz (2005) presented South Asians and European Americans with a vignette describing depressive symptoms and then asked them to participant in semistructured interview designed to elicit representation models of the symptoms in terms of the identity of the illness, antecedents, or causes of the illness, consequences, timeline, and treatment strategies. Karasz found that European Americans tended to interpret the symptoms described in the vignette as a disease disorder, whereas South Asians were prone to interpret them in terms of social situations, such as emotional reactions to various pathogenic situations. The findings on cultural differences in the interpretation of depression are consistent with the cultural differences shown in the conceptual models of depression, with a dominant disease model in Western societies (emphasizing the roots of the disorder in anatomy, heredity, and disease process; Keyes 1985), and a dominant "situational" model (emphasizing social context and structured perceptions of cause, consequence, timeline, and treatment) in East Asian societies and minority communities in Western societies (Patel 1995). The culturally unique models of mental disorders are also in agreement with the proposition of cultural differences in strategies for causal attribution that emphasize internal dispositions in Westerners but contextual constraints in East Asians (Choi et al. 1999; Morris and Peng 1994; Peng and Knowles 2003).

Cultural-neuroscience research raises new and important issues concerning cross-cultural differences in the prevalence (and neural correlates) of psychiatric disorders. For example, an interesting question is whether symptomatic expressions of mental disorders are influenced by cultural predispositions, such that the symptoms of psychiatric patients educated in cultures that encourage collectivism are different from those from cultures that encourage individualism. Another issue that is particularly related to cultural-neuroscience findings is whether the symptomatology of neuropsychiatric disorders is mediated by similar patterns of abnormal neural activity across cultures. Taking depression as an example, a study that examined the relationship between anger suppression and depressive symptoms found that a cultural trait (i.e., interdependent self-construal) moderated the suppression–depression link such that Asian (as compared with European) American status and a stronger interdependent self-construal attenuated the relation between anger suppression and depressive symptoms (Cheung and Park 2010). A study of Asian American college students also found that interdependence moderated the relationship between maladaptive perfectionism and depressive symptoms, such that highly interdependent Asian American students appeared more vulnerable to depression when demonstrating perfectionistic tendencies (Yoon and Lau 2008). Such findings suggest a potential function of cultural traits (e.g., interdependence) in the expression and moderation of depressive symptoms.

A typical cognitive model of depression emphasized an enhanced self-focus and a negative view about oneself or a distorted negative schema of the self (Beck 1976; Beck et al. 1979). In line with this cognitive model of depression, recent brain imaging research has led to the development of a neural model of depression related to self-referential processing that is characterized by greater activity in the medial prefrontal cortex during self-referential processing in depressed patients, as compared with healthy controls (Lemogne et al. 2009).

Unlike healthy controls, depressed patients showed a failure to reduce activity in the medial prefrontal cortex during cognitive tasks such as examining negative pictures passively or reappraising these pictures actively (Sheline et al. 2009). Lemogne and colleagues (2012) further suggested, based on brain imaging studies of individuals with major depression, using different paradigms, that an elevated tonic ventral medial prefrontal activation in response to transient self-reflective thought may embody automatic aspects of depressive self-focus, such as attracting attention to self-relevant incoming information. An elevated phasic dorsal medial prefrontal activation in response to sustained self-reflection may embody strategic aspects of depressive self-focus, such as comparing the self with inner standards. Most of the previous brain imaging studies of depression tested patients from Western societies, and the results of the studies suggest that the abnormal pattern of the increased medial prefrontal activity provides a neural basis for enhanced self-focus in depressed patients relative to nondepressed individuals. However, considering the cultural-neuroscience findings that healthy individuals from an East Asian (e.g., Chinese) culture, compared with those from a Western (e.g., Danish) culture, showed decreased medial prefrontal activity during self-reflection (Ma et al. 2014a), one may ask whether depressed patients in East Asian cultures would show a similar magnitude of the abnormal enhanced medial prefrontal activity (compared with healthy controls) as that observed in depressed patients in Western cultures. In addition, the healthy individuals from the East Asian (e.g., Chinese) culture, as compared with the Western (e.g., Danish) culture, showed greater activations during self-reflection in the temporoparietal junction, which is mediated by the cultural trait of interdependence and is associated with taking others' perspectives on oneself (Ma et al. 2014a). Thus, one may ask whether depressed patients from both cultures would exhibit abnormal activity in the temporoparietal junction during self-reflection and whether the abnormal activity in the temporoparietal junction is associated with similar depressive symptoms in depressed patients in both East Asian and Western cultures.

Another issue related to the neural underpinnings of depression arising from cultural-neuroscience findings is how cultural traits interact with an individual's genetic makeups to shape the biomarker of depression in the brain. Because one compared with another variant of the same gene (e.g., the short vs. long alleles of 5-HTTLPR) is more vulnerable to aversive life experiences, and thus, is more likely to exhibit more depressive symptoms (Caspi et al. 2003); is more prone to negative self-reflection and to show greater responses in the emotion-related neural circuit (Ma et al. 2014c); and shows stronger coupling of cultural values and brain activity underlying self-reflection (Ma et al. 2014b), it is likely that genetic influences on mental disorders and the underlying neural substrates are moderated by individuals' cultural trait and experiences. Future research could test this by comparing neuromarkers of mental disorders, such as depression, in genotyped patients from different cultures, to examine how genetic effects on neuromarkers of mental disorders vary across cultures, and how they are moderated by cultural context and/or specific cultural traits.

Understanding both universal and culture-specific aspects of neuromarkers of neuropsychiatric disorders has important clinical implications in determining whether the same treatments are appropriate for mental disorders in different cultures and for finding effective prevention and intervention efforts across diverse cultures. There has been evidence for distinct responses to antidepressant treatment in individuals from different cultures. Wade et al. (2010) recruited adult patients from Sweden and Turkey who had been diagnosed with a depressive or anxiety disorder by a primary care physician and prescribed an antidepressant in the class of selective serotonin reuptake inhibitors. Both physicians and patients recorded presenting symptoms based on questionnaire measures just before and 8 weeks after starting treatment with an antidepressant. The measures suggested that the degree of improvement was greater in Turkish patients than in Swedish patients for three prominent symptoms, including depression, stress, and pain. Researchers have realized that several factors influence ethnic differences in the utilization of mental health care for neuropsychiatric disorders, including socioeconomic context, cultural beliefs/attitudes, and patient–physician communications (Stewart et al. 2012). Future cultural-neuroscience research could help to clarify potential neural underpinnings of cultural-group differences in response to antidepressant treatment during mental health care by comparing the effects of antidepressants on the neuromarkers of depression in patients from different cultures.

References

Adams Jr, R.B., Rule, N.O., and Franklin Jr, R.G. et al. (2010). Cross-cultural reading the mind in the eyes: an fMRI investigation. *Journal of Cognitive Neuroscience* 22, 97–108.

Adolphs, R., Tranel, D., Damasio, H., and Damasio, A. (1994). Impaired recognition of emotion in facial expressions following bilateral damage to the human amygdala. *Nature* 372, 669–72.

Aharon, I., Etcoff, N., Ariely, D., Chabris, C.F., O'Connor, E., and Breiter, H.C. (2001). Beautiful faces have variable reward value: fMRI and behavioral evidence. *Neuron* 32, 537–51.

Albahari, M. (2006). *Analytical Buddhism: the two-tiered illusion of self.* New York: Palgrave Macmillan.

Allman, J.M., Watson, K.K., Tetreault, N.A., and Hakeem, A.Y. (2005). Intuition and autism: a possible role for Von Economo neurons. *Trends in Cognitive Sciences* 9, 367–73.

Amato, P.R., and Gilbreth, J.G. (1999). Nonresident fathers and children's well-being: a meta- analysis. *Journal of Marriage and Family* 61, 557–73.

Ambady, N., and Bharucha, J. (2009). Culture and the brain. *Current Directions in Psychological Science* 18, 342–5.

Ames, D.L., and Fiske, S.T. (2010). Cultural neuroscience. *Asian Journal of Social Psychology* 13, 72–82.

Amodio, D.M., and Frith, C.D. (2006). Meeting of minds: the medial frontal cortex and social cognition. *Nature Reviews Neuroscience* 7, 268–77.

Amsterdam, B. (1972). Mirror self-image reactions before age two. *Developmental Psychobiology* 5, 297–305.

Archer, D. (1997). Unspoken diversity: cultural differences in gestures. *Qualitative Sociology* 20, 79–105.

Asendorpf, J.B., Warkentin, V., and Baudonniere, P.M. (1996). Self-awareness and other-awareness II: mirror self-recognition, social contingency awareness, and synchronic imitation. *Development Psychology* 32, 313–21.

Azari, N.P., Nickel, J., and Wunderlich, G. et al. (2001). Neural correlates of religious experience. *European Journal of Neuroscience* 13, 1649–52.

Baars, B.J. (1997). *In the theater of consciousness.* New York Oxford: Oxford University Press.

Bakermans-Kranenburg, M.J., and van IJzendoorn, M.H. (2014). A sociability gene? Meta-analysis of oxytocin receptor genotype effects in humans. *Psychiatric Genetics* 24, 45–51.

Baron-Cohen, S., Lombardo, M., Tager-Flusberg, H., and Cohen, D. (eds.) (2013). *Understanding Other Minds: Perspectives from Developmental Social Neuroscience.* New York: Oxford University Press.

Baron-Cohen, S., Ring, H., and Wheelwright, S. et al. (1999). Social intelligence in the normal and autistic brain: an fMRI study. *European Journal of Neuroscience* 11, 1891–8.

Baron-Cohen, S., Wheelwright, S., Hill, J., Raste, Y., and Plumb, I. (2001). The "Reading the Mind in the Eyes" test revised version: a study with normal adults, and adults with Asperger syndrome or high-functioning autism. *Journal of Child Psychology and Psychiatry* 42, 241–51.

Batson, C.D. [2009] (2011). These things called empathy: eight related but distinct phenomena. In: J. Decety and W. Ickes (eds.), *The social neuroscience of empathy*. Cambridge, MA: MIT Press, pp. 3–15.

Batson, C.D. (2011). *Altruism in humans*. New York: Oxford University Press.

Beck, A.T. (1976). *Cognitive therapy and emotional disorders*. New York: International University Press.

Beck, A.T., Rush, A.J., Shaw, B.F., and Emery, G. (1979). *Cognitive therapy of depression*. New York: Guilford Press.

Belsky, J., Jonassaint, C., Pluess, M., Stanton, M., Brummett, B., and Williams, R. (2009). Vulnerability genes or plasticity genes & quest. *Molecular Psychiatry* 14, 746–54.

Belsky, J., and Pluess, M. (2009). Beyond diathesis stress: differential susceptibility to environmental influences. *Psychological Bulletin* 135, 885–908.

Benet-Martínez, V., Leu, J., Lee, F., and Morris, M.W. (2002). Negotiating biculturalism cultural frame switching in biculturals with oppositional versus compatible cultural identities. *Journal of Cross-Cultural Psychology* 33, 492–516.

Bentin, S., Allison, T., Puce, A., Perez, E., and McCarthy, G. (1996). Electrophysiological studies of face perception in humans. *Journal of Cognitive Neuroscience* 8, 551–65.

Binder, J.R., and Desai, R.H. (2011). The neurobiology of semantic memory. *Trends in Cognitive Sciences* 15, 527–36.

Blais, C., Jack, R.E., Scheepers, C., Fiset, D., and Caldara, R. (2008). Culture shapes how we look at faces. *PLoS One* 3, e3022.

Blakemore, S.J. (2008). The social brain in adolescence. *Nature Reviews Neuroscience* 9, 267–77.

Blokland, G.A., McMahon, K.L., Thompson, P.M., Martin, N.G., de Zubicaray, G.I., and Wright, M.J. (2011). Heritability of working memory brain activation. *Journal of Neuroscience* 31, 10882–90.

Bochud, M. (2012). Estimating heritability from nuclear family and pedigree data. In: R.C. Elston, J.M. Satagopan, and S. Sun (eds.), *Statistical human genetics*. Totowa, NJ: Humana Press, pp.171–86.

Bohlken, M.M., Mandl, R.C., and Brouwer, R.M. et al. (2014). Heritability of structural brain network topology: a DTI study of 156 twins. *Human Brain Mapping* 35, 5295–305.

Bookheimer, S. (2002). Functional MRI of language: new approaches to understanding the cortical organization of semantic processing. *Annual Review of Neuroscience* 25, 151–88.

Botvinick, M.M., Cohen, J.D., and Carter, C.S. (2004). Conflict monitoring and anterior cingulate cortex: an update. *Trends in Cognitive Sciences* 8, 539–46.

Boyd, J.L., Skove, S. L., and Rouanet, J. P. et al. (2015). Human-chimpanzee differences in a FZD8 enhancer alter cell-cycle dynamics in the developing neocortex. *Current Biology* 25, 772–9.

Boyd, R., and Richerson, P.J. (1985). *Culture and the evolutionary Process*. Chicago: Chicago University Press.

Brewer, M.B., and Gardner, W.L. (1996). Who is this 'we'? Levels of collective identity and self representations. *Journal of Personality and Social Psychology* 71, 83–93.

Bromm, B., and Chen, A.C. (1995). Brain electrical source analysis of laser evoked potentials in response to painful trigeminal nerve stimulation. *Electroencephalogry of Clinical Neurophysiology* **95**, 14–26.

Bruce, A.S., Bruce, J.M., and Black, W.R. et al. (2014). Branding and a child's brain: an fMRI study of neural responses to logos. *Social Cognitive and Affective Neuroscience* **9**, 118–22.

Bruce, A.S., Martin, L.E., and Savage, C.R. (2011). Neural correlates of pediatric obesity. *Preventive Medicine* **52**, S29–35.

Bruer, J.T. (1997). Education and the brain: a bridge too far. *Educational Researcher* **26**, 4–16.

Bruer, J.T. (2016). Where is educational neuroscience? *Educational Neuroscience* **1**, 1–12.

Burns, C. (2003). "Soul-less" Christianity and the Buddhist empirical self: Buddhist Christian convergence? *Buddhist Christian Studies* **23**, 87–100.

Burton, H., Snyder, A.Z., Diamond, J.B., and Raichle, M.E. (2002). Adaptive changes in early and late blind: a fMRI study of verb generation to heard nouns. *Journal of Neurophysiology* **88**, 3359–71.

Calvo-Merino, B., Glaser, D., Grezes, J., Passingham, R., and Haggard, P. (2005). Action observation and acquired motor skills: an fMRI study with expert dancers. *Ceberal Cortex* **15**, 1243–9.

Campbell, J.I., and Xue, Q. (2001). Cognitive arithmetic across cultures. *Journal of Experimental Psychology General* **130**, 299–315.

Campbell, P.S. (1997). Music, the universal language: fact or fallacy? *International Journal of Music Education* **1**, 32–9.

Canli, T., and Lesch, K.P. (2007). Long story short: the serotonin transporter in emotion regulation and social cognition. *Nature Neuroscience* **10**, 1103–9.

Canli, T., Qiu, M., and Omura, K. et al. (2006). Neural correlates of epigenesis. *Proceedings of the National Academy of Sciences* **103**, 16033–8.

Cantor-Graae, E. (2007). The contribution of social factors to the development of schizophrenia: a review of recent findings. *Canadian Journal of Psychiatry* **52**, 277–86.

Cantor-Graae, E., and Selten, J.P. (2005). Schizophrenia and migration: a meta-analysis and review. *American Journal of Psychiatry* **162**, 12–24.

Carter, C.S., Braver, T.S., Barch, D.M., Botvinick, M.M., Noll, D., and Cohen, J.D. (1998). Anterior cingulate cortex, error detection, and the online monitoring of performance. *Science* **280**, 747–9.

Caspi, A., and Moffitt, T.E. (2006). Gene–environment interactions in psychiatry: joining forces with neuroscience. *Nature Reviews Neuroscience* **7**, 583–90.

Caspi, A., Sugden, K., and Moffitt, T. E. et al. (2003). Influence of life stress on depression: moderation by a polymorphism in the 5-HTT gene. *Science* **301**, 386–9.

Cavalli-Sforza, L.L., and Feldman, M.W. (1981). *Culture and the evolutionary process.* Chicago: University of Chicago Press.

Cavanna, A.E., and Trimble, M.R. (2006). The precuneus: a review of its functional anatomy and behavioral correlates. *Brain* **129**, 564–83.

Cesarini, D., Dawes, C.T., Fowler, J.H., Johannesson, M., Lichtenstein, P., and Wallace, B. (2008). Heritability of cooperative behavior in the trust game. *Proceedings of the National Academy of Sciences* **105**, 3721–6.

Chang, L., Fang, Q., Zhang, S., Poo, M.M., and Gong, N. (2015). Mirror-induced self-directed behaviors in rhesus monkeys after visual-somatosensory training. *Current Biology* **25**, 212–17.

Chen, C.H., Gutierrez, E.D., and Thompson, W. et al. (2012). Hierarchical genetic organization of human cortical surface area. *Science* 335, 1634–6.

Chen, P.H.A., Heatherton, T.F., and Freeman, J.B. (2015). Brain-as-predictor approach: an alternative way to explore acculturation processes. In: E. Warnick and D. Landis (eds.), *Neuroscience in intercultural contexts*. New York: Springer, pp.143–70.

Chen, P.H.A., Wagner, D.D., Kelley, W.M., and Heatherton, T.F. (2015). Activity in cortical midline structures is modulated by self-construal changes during acculturation. *Culture and Brain* 3, 39–52.

Chen, P.H.A., Wagner, D.D., Kelley, W.M., Powers, K.E., and Heatherton, T.F. (2013). Medial prefrontal cortex differentiates self from mother in Chinese: evidence from self-motivated immigrants. *Culture and Brain* 1, 3–15.

Chen, X., Hastings, P.D., Rubin, K.H., Chen, H., Cen, G., and Stewart, S.L. (1998). Child-rearing attitudes and behavioral inhibition in Chinese and Canadian toddlers: a cross-cultural study. *Developmental Psychology* 34, 677–86.

Cheon, B.K., Im, D.M., and Harada, T. et al. (2011). Cultural influences on neural basis of intergroup empathy. *NeuroImage* 57, 642–50

Cheon, B.K., Im, D.M., and Harada, T. et al. (2013). Cultural modulation of the neural correlates of emotional pain perception: the role of other-focusedness. *Neuropsychologia* 51, 1177–86.

Cheung, B.Y., Chudek, M., and Heine, S.J. (2011). Evidence for a sensitive period for acculturation younger immigrants report acculturating at a faster rate. *Psychological Science* 22, 147–52.

Cheung, F.M. (1982). Psychological symptoms among Chinese in urban Hong Kong. *Social Science and Medicine* 16, 1339–44.

Cheung, R.Y., and Park, I.J. (2010). Anger suppression, interdependent self-construal, and depression among Asian American and European American college students. *Cultural Diversity and Ethnic Minority Psychology* 16, 517–25.

Chiao, J.Y. (2010). At the frontier of cultural neuroscience: introduction to the special issue. *Social Cognitive and Affective Neuroscience* 5, 109–10.

Chiao, J.Y., and Ambady, N. [2007] (2010). Cultural neuroscience: parsing universality and diversity across levels of analysis. In: S. Kitayama and D. Cohen (eds.), *Handbook of cultural psychology*. New York: Guilford, pp.237–54.

Chiao, J.Y., and Bebko, G.M. (2011). Cultural neuroscience of social cognition. In: S. Han and E. Poppel (eds.), *Culture and neural frames of cognition and communication*. Berlin: Springer, pp.19–40.

Chiao, J.Y., and Blizinsky, K.D. (2010). Culture-gene coevolution of individualism-collectivism and the serotonin transporter gene. *Proceedings of the Royal Society of London B: Biological Sciences* 277, 529–37.

Chiao, J.Y., Cheon, B.K., Pornpattananangkul, N., Mrazek, A.J., and Blizinsky, K.D. (2013). Cultural neuroscience: progress and promise. *Psychological Inquiry* 24, 1–19.

Chiao, J.Y., Harada, T., and Komeda, H. et al. (2010). Dynamic cultural influences on neural representations of the self. *Journal of Cognitive Neuroscience* 22, 1–11.

Chiao, J.Y., Iidaka, T., and Gordon, H.L. et al. (2008). Cultural specificity in amygdala response to fear faces. *Journal of Cognitive Neuroscience* 20, 2167–74.

Chiao, J.Y., Li, S.C., Seligman, R., and Turner, R. (eds.) (2016). *The Oxford handbook of cultural neuroscience*. New York: Oxford University Press.

Ching, J. (1984). Paradigms of the self in Buddhism and Christianity. *Buddhist-Christian Studies* 4, 31–50.

Chiu, C.Y., and Hong, Y.Y. (2013). *Social psychology of culture*. New York: Psychology Press.

Chiu, L.H. (1972). A cross-cultural comparison of cognitive styles in Chinese and American children. *International Journal of Psychology* 7, 235–42.

Choi, I., Nisbett, R.E., and Norenzayan, A. (1999). Causal attribution across cultures: variation and universality. *Psychological Bulletin* 125, 47–63.

Christmann, C., Koeppe, C., Braus, D., Ruf, M., and Flora, H. (2007). A simultaneous EEG–fMRI study of painful electrical stimulation. *NeuroImage* 34, 1428–37.

Chung, T., and Mallery, P. (1999). Social comparison, individualism-collectivism, and self-esteem in China and the United States. *Current Psychology* 18, 340–52.

Coid, J.W., Kirkbride, J.B., and Barker, D. et al. (2008). Raised incidence rates of all psychoses among migrant groups: findings from the East London first episode psychosis study. *Archives of General Psychiatry* 65, 1250–8.

Coley, R.L. (1998). Children's socialization experiences and functioning in single-mother households: the importance of fathers and other men. *Child Development* 69, 219–30.

Colzato, L.S., de Bruijn, E.R., and Hommel, B. (2012). Up to "me" or up to "us"? The impact of self-construal priming on cognitive self-other integration. *Frontiers in Psychology* 3, 341.

Constantine, M.G., and Sue, D.W. (2006). Factors contributing to optimal human functioning in people of color in the United States. *Counseling Psychologist* 34, 228–44.

Coon, K.A., and Tucker, K.L. (2002). Television and children's consumption patterns. A review of the literature. *Minerva Pediatrica* 54, 423–36.

Cross, E., Hamilton, A., and Grafton, S. (2006). Building a motor simulation de novo: observation of dance by dancers. *Neuroimage* 31, 1257–67.

Cunningham, W.A., Johnson, M.K., Gatenby, J.C., Gore, J.C., and Banaji, M.R. (2003). Neural components of social evaluation. *Journal of Personality and Social Psychology* 85, 639–49.

Cuthbert, B.N., Schupp, H.T., Bradley, M.M., Birbaumer, N., and Lang, P.J. (2000). Brain potentials in affective picture processing: covariation with autonomic arousal and affective report. *Biological Psychology* 52, 95–111.

Dannlowski, U., Kugel, H., and Grotegerd, D. et al. (2015). Disadvantage of social sensitivity: interaction of oxytocin receptor genotype and child maltreatment on brain structure. *Biological Psychiatry* 15, 1053–7.

D'Argembeau, A., Ruby, P., and Collette, F. et al. (2007). Distinct regions of the medial prefrontal cortex are associated with self-referential processing and perspective taking. *Journal of Cognitive Neuroscience* 19, 935–44.

Davidson, R.J., and Irwin, W. (1999). The functional neuroanatomy of emotion and affective style. *Trends in Cognitive Sciences* 3, 11–21.

Davis, M.H. (1994). *Empathy: a social psychological approach*. Boulder, CO: Westview Press.

De Greck, M., Shi, Z., and Wang, G. et al. (2012). Culture modulates brain activity during empathy with anger. *NeuroImage* 59, 2871–82.

De Waal, F.B.M. (2008). Putting the altruism back into altruism: the evolution of empathy. *Annual Review of Psychology* **59**, 279–300.

De Waal, F.B.M. (2009). *The age of empathy.* New York: Harmony.

Debener, S., Makeig, S., Delorme, A., and Engel, A.K. (2005). What is novel in the novelty P3 event-related potential as revealed by independent component analysis. *Cognitive Brain Research* **22**, 309–21.

Decety, J., and Lamm, C. (2007). The role of the right temporoparietal junction in social interaction: how low-level computational processes contribute to meta-cognition. *Neuroscientist* **13**, 580–93.

Deco, G., Jirsa, V.K., and McIntosh, A.R. (2011). Emerging concepts for the dynamical organization of resting-state activity in the brain. *Nature Reviews Neuroscience* **12**, 43–56.

Degler, C.N. (1991). *In search of human nature: the decline and revival of Darwinism in American social thought.* New York: Oxford University Press.

Demorest, S.M., Morrison, S.J., Stambaugh, L.A., Beken, M., Richards, T.L., and Johnson, C. (2010). An fMRI investigation of the cultural specificity of music memory. *Social Cognitive and Affective Neuroscience* **5**, 282–91.

Demorest, S.M., and Osterhout, L. (2012). ERP responses to cross-cultural melodic expectancy violations. *Annals of the New York Academy of Sciences* **1252**, 152–7.

Descartes, R. (1912). Meditations on the First Philosophy, meditation 2 (in English). In: *everyman's library, 570, philosophy.* London: J. M. Dent and Sons LTD.

Dobzhansky, T. (1962). *Mankind evolving: the evolution of the human species.* New Haven: Yale University Press.

Donchin, E., and Coles, M.G.H. (1988). Precommentary: is the P300 component a manifestation of context updating? *Behavioral and Brain Sciences* **11**, 357–74.

Draganski, B., Gaser, C., Busch, V., Schuierer, G., Bogdahn, U., and May, A. (2004). Neuroplasticity: changes in grey matter induced by training. *Nature* **427**, 311–12.

Drwecki, B.B., Moore, C.F., Ward, S.E., and Prkachin, K.M. (2011). Reducing racial disparities in pain treatment: the role of empathy and perspective-taking. *Pain* **152**, 1001–6.

Dunbar, R.I. (1992). Neocortex size as a constraint on group size in primates. *Journal of Human Evolution* **22**, 469–93.

Dunbar, R.I., and Shultz, S. (2007). Evolution in the social brain. *Science* **317**, 1344–7.

Durham, W.H. (1991). *Coevolution: genes, culture, and human diversity.* Stanford: Stanford University Press.

Eichenbaum, H. (2000). A cortical-hippocampal system for declarative memory. *Nature Reviews Neuroscience* **1**, 41–50.

Eimer, M. (2000). The face-specific N170 component reflects late stages in the structural encoding of faces. *Neuroreport* **11**, 2319–24.

Ekman, P., Friesen, W.V., and O'Sullivan, M. et al. (1987). Universals and cultural differences in the judgments of facial expressions of emotion. *Journal of Personality & Social Psychology* **53**, 712–17.

Epstein, R., and Kanwisher, N. (1998). A cortical representation of the local visual environment. *Nature* **392**, 598–601.

Erk, S., Spitzer, M., Wunderlich, A.P., Galley, L., and Walter, H. (2002). Cultural objects modulate reward circuitry. *Neuroreport* **13**, 2499–503.

Etkin, A., Büchel, C., and Gross, J.J. (2015). The neural bases of emotion regulation. *Nature Reviews Neuroscience* **16**, 693–700.

Evangelou, E., and **Ioannidis, J.P.** (2013). Meta-analysis methods for genome-wide association studies and beyond. *Nature Reviews Genetics* **14**, 379–89.

Evans, P.D., Anderson, J.R., Vallender, E.J., Choi, S.S., and Lahn, B.T. (2004). Reconstructing the evolutionary history of microcephalin, a gene controlling human brain size. *Human Molecular Genetics* **13**, 1139–45.

Falkenstein, M., Hohnsbein, J., Hoorman, J., and Blanke, L. (1991). Effects of crossmodal divided attention on late ERP components: II. Error processing in choice reaction tasks. *Electroencephalography and Clinical Neurophysiology* **78**, 447–55.

Fan, Y., Duncan, N.W., de Greck, M., and Northoff, G. (2011). Is there a core neural network in empathy? An fMRI based quantitative meta-analysis. *Neuroscience & Biobehavioral Reviews* **35**, 903–11.

Feldman, M.W., and Laland, K.N. (1996). Gene–culture coevolutionary theory. *Trends in Ecology & Evolution* **11**, 453–7.

Ferguson, G.A. (1956). On transfer and the abilities of man. *Canadian Journal of Psychology/Revue Canadienne de Psychologie* **10**, 121–31.

Festinger, L. (1954). A theory of social comparison processes. *Human Relations* **7**, 117–40.

Figner, B., Knoch, D., and Johnson, E.J. et al. (2010). Lateral prefrontal cortex and self-control in intertemporal choice. *Nature Neuroscience* **13**, 538–9.

Flint, J., Greenspan, R.J., and Kendler, K.S. (2010). *How genes influence behavior.* New York: Oxford University Press.

Fogassi, L., Ferrari, P.F., Gesierich, B., Rozzi, S., Chersi, F., and Rizzolatti, G. (2005). Parietal lobe: from action organization to intention understanding. *Science* **308**, 662–7.

Folstein, J.R., and Van Petten, C. (2008). Influence of cognitive control and mismatch on the N2 component of the ERP: a review. *Psychophysiology* **45**, 152–70.

Fong, M.C., Goto, S.G., Moore, C., Zhao, T., Schudson, Z., and Lewis, R.S. (2014). Switching between Mii and Wii: the effects of cultural priming on the social affective N400. *Culture and Brain* **2**, 52–71.

Ford, J.A. (1949). Cultural dating of prehistoric sites in Virú Valley, Peru. *Anthropological Papers of the American Museum of Natural History* **43**, 31–78.

Fortun, K., and Fortun, M. (2009). *Cultural anthropology.* London: SAGE.

Fox, P. T., Raichle, M. E., Mintun, M. A., and Dence, C. (1988). Nonoxidative glucose consumption during focal physiologic neural activity. *Science* **241**, 462–4.

Fraga, M.F., Ballestar, E., and Paz, M.F. et al. (2005). Epigenetic differences arise during the lifetime of monozygotic twins. *Proceedings of the National Academy of Sciences of the United States of America* **102**, 10604–9.

Freeman, J.B., Rule, N.O., Adams Jr, R.B., and Ambady, N. (2009). Culture shapes a mesolimbic response to signals of dominance and subordination that associates with behavior. *Neuroimage* **47**, 353–9.

Friederici, A.D. (2002). Towards a neural basis of auditory sentence processing. *Trends in Cognitive Sciences* **6**, 78–84.

Friederici, A.D. (2012). Thecortical language circuit: from auditory perception to sentence comprehension. *Trends in Cognitive Sciences* **16**, 262–8.

Frith, U., and Frith, C.D. (2003). Development and neurophysiology and mentalizing. *Philosophical Transactions of the Royal Society of London* **358**, 459–73.

Fung, Y. (1948/2007). *A short history of Chinese philosophy.* Tian Jin: Tian Jin Social Science Academy Press.

Furukawa, E., Tangney, J., and Higashibara, F. (2012). Cross-cultural continuities and discontinuities in shame, guilt, and pride: a study of children residing in Japan, Korea and the USA. *Self and Identity* 11, 90–113.

Gallagher, H.L., Happé, F., Brunswick, N., Fletcher, P.C., Frith, U., and Frith, C.D. (2000). Reading the mind in cartoons and stories: an fMRI study of "theory of mind" in verbal and nonverbal tasks. *Neuropsychologia* 38, 11–21.

Gallese, V., Fadiga, L., Fogassi, L., and Rizzolatti, G. (1996). Action recognition in the premotor cortex. *Brain* 119, 593–610.

Gallup, G.G. (1970). Chimpanzees: self-recognition. *Science* 167, 86–7.

Gardner, W.L., Gabriel, S., and Lee, A.Y. (1999). "I" value freedom, but "we" value relationships: self-construal priming mirrors cultural differences in judgment. *Psychological Science* 10, 321–6.

Gazzaniga, M.S. (ed.). (2004). *The cognitive neurosciences*. Cambridge, MA: MIT Press.

Ge, J., Gu, X., Ji, M., and Han, S. (2009). Neurocognitive processes of the religious leader in Christians. *Human Brain Mapping* 30, 4012–24.

Ge. J., and Han, S. (2008). Distinct neurocognitive strategies for comprehensions of human and artificial intelligence. *PLoS ONE* 3, e2797.

Geary, D.C. (2000). Evolution and proximate expression of human paternal investment. *Psychological Bulletin* 126, 55–77.

Gehring, W.J., Coles, M.G.H., Meyer, D.E., and Donchin, E. (1990). The error-related negativity: an event-related brain potential accompanying errors. *Psychophysiology* 27, S34.

Gehring, W.J., Himle, J., and Nisenson, L.G. (2000). Action-monitoring dysfunction in obsessive–compulsive disorder. *Psychological Science* 11, 1–6.

Gelfand, M.J., Raver, J.L., and Nishii, L. et al. (2011). Differences between tight and loose cultures: a 33-nation study. *Science* 332, 1100–4.

Geng, H., Zhang, S., Li, Q., Tao, R., and Xu, S. (2012). Dissociations of subliminal and supraliminal self-face from other-face processing: behavioral and ERP evidence. *Neuropsychologia* 50, 2933–42.

Gibbs, R.A., Rogers, J., and Katze, M.G. et al. (2007). Evolutionary and biomedical insights from the rhesus macaque genome. *Science* 316, 222–34.

Gimpl, G., and Fahrenholz, F. (2001). The oxytocin receptor system: structure, function, and regulation. *Physiological Reviews* 81, 629–83.

Glasser, M.F., Goyal, M.S., Preuss, T.M., Raichle, M.E., and Van Essen, D.C. (2014). Trends and properties of human cerebral cortex: correlations with cortical myelin content. *Neuroimage* 93, 165–75.

Gogtay, N., Giedd, J.N., and Lusk, L. et al. (2004). Dynamic mapping of human cortical development during childhood through early adulthood. *Proceedings of the National Academy of Sciences of the United States of America* 101, 8174–9.

Goh, J. O., Chee, M. W., and Tan, J. C. et al. (2007). Age and culture modulate object processing and object-scene binding in the ventral visual area. *Cognitive, Affective, & Behavioral Neuroscience* 7, 44–52.

Goh, J.O., Hebrank, A.C., Sutton, B.P., Chee, M.W., Sim, S.K., and Park, D. C. (2013). Culture-related differences in default network activity during visuo-spatial judgments. *Social Cognitive and Affective Neuroscience* 8, 134–42.

Goh, J.O., Siong, S.C., Park, D., Gutchess, A., Hebrank, A., and Chee, M.W. (2004). Cortical areas involved in object, background, and object-background processing revealed with functional magnetic resonance adaptation. *Journal of Neuroscience* 24, 10223–8.

Gold, N., Colman, A.M., and Pulford, B.D. (2014). Cultural differences in responses to real-life and hypothetical trolley problems. *Judgment & Decision Making* 9, 65–76.

González, V.M., and Mark, G. (2004). Constant, constant, multi-tasking craziness: managing multiple working spheres. *Proceedings of the SIGCHI Conference on Human Factors in Computing Systems* pp.113–20.

Gornotempini, M.L., Pradelli, S., and Serafini, M. et al. (2001). Explicit and incidental facial expression processing: an fMRI study. *Neuroimage* 14, 465–73.

Goto, S.G., Ando, Y., Huang, C., Yee, A., and Lewis, R.S. (2010). Cultural differences in the visual processing of meaning: detecting incongruities between background and foreground objects using the N400. *Social Cognitive and Affective Neuroscience* 5, 242–53.

Goto, S.G., Yee, A., Lowenberg, K., and Lewis, R.S. (2013). Cultural differences in sensitivity to social context: detecting affective incongruity using the N400. *Social Neuroscience* 8, 63–74.

Gougoux, F., Belinb, P., Vossa, P., Leporea, F., Lassondea, M., and Zatorre, R.J. (2009). Voice perception in blind persons: a functional magnetic resonance imaging study. *Neuropsychologia* 47, 2967–74.

Greene, J., and Haidt, J. (2002). How (and where) does moral judgment work? *Trends in Cognitive Sciences* 6, 517–23.

Greenfield, P.M. (1999). Cultural change and human development. *New Directions for Child and Adolescent Development* 83, 37–59.

Greenfield, P.M. (2013). The changing psychology of culture from 1800 through 2000. *Psychological Science* 24, 1722–31.

Greenwald, A.G. (1980). The totalitarian ego: fabrication and revision of personal history. *American Psychologist* 35, 603–18.

Greenwald, A.G., McGhee, D.E., and Schwartz, J.L.K. (1998). Measuring individual differences in implicit cognition: the implicit association test. *Journal of Personality and Social Psychology* 74, 1464–80.

Grill-Spector, K., Henson, R., and Martin, A. (2006). Repetition and the brain: neural models of stimulus-specific effects. *Trends in Cognitive Sciences* 10, 14–23.

Grill-Spector, K., Kourtzi, Z., and Kanwisher, N. (2001). The lateral occipital complex and its role in object recognition. *Vision Research* 41, 1409–22.

Grön, G., Schul, D., Bretschneider, V., Wunderlich, A.P., and Riepe, M.W. (2003). Alike performance during nonverbal episodic learning from diversely imprinted neural networks. *European Journal of Neuroscience* 18, 3112–20.

Groner, R., Walder, F., and Groner, M. (1984). Looking at faces: local and global aspects of scanpaths. In: A.G. Gale and F. Johnson (eds.), *Theoretical and Applied Aspects of Eye Movements Research*. Amsterdam: Elsevier, pp.523–33.

Gu, X., and Han, S. (2007). Attention and reality constraints on the neural processes of empathy for pain. *NeuroImage* 36, 256–67.

Guan, L., Qi, M., Zhang, Q., and Yang, J. (2014). The neural basis of self-face recognition after self-concept threat and comparison with important others. *Social Neuroscience* 9, 424–35.

Gutchess, A.H., Hedden, T., Ketay, S., Aron, A., and Gabrieli, J.D. (2010). Neural differences in the processing of semantic relationships across cultures. *Social Cognitive and Affective Neuroscience* **5**, 254–63.

Gutchess, A.H., Welsh, R.C., Boduroğlu, A., and Park, D.C. (2006). Cultural differences in neural function associated with object processing. *Cognitive, Affective, & Behavioral Neuroscience* **6**, 102–9.

Haber, S. N., and Knutson, B. (2010). The reward circuit: linking primate anatomy and human imaging. *Neuropsychopharmacology* **35**, 4–26.

Haidt, J. (2001). The emotional dog and its rational tail: a social intuitionist approach to moral judgment. *Psychological Review* **108**, 814–34.

Hajcak, G., and Nieuwenhuis, S. (2006). Reappraisal modulates the electrocortical response to unpleasant pictures. *Cognitive, Affective and Behavioral Neuroscience* **6**, 291–7.

Han, H., Glover, G.H., and Jeong, C. (2014). Cultural influences on the neural correlate of moral decision making processes. *Behavioural Brain Research* **259**, 215–28.

Han, S. (2013). Culture and brain: a new journal. *Culture and Brain* **1**, 1–2.

Han, S. (2015). Cultural neuroscience. In: A.W. Toga (ed.), *Brain mapping: an encyclopedic reference*. Oxford: Elsevier, pp.217–20.

Han, S., Fan, S., Chen, L., and Zhuo, Y. (1997). On the different processing of wholes and parts: a psychophysiological analysis. *Journal of Cognitive Neuroscience* **9**, 687–98.

Han, S., Fan, S., Chen, L., and Zhuo, Y. (1999). Modulation of brain activities by hierarchical processing: a high-density ERP study. *Brain Topography* **11**, 171–83.

Han, S., and Fan, Y. (2009). Empathic neural responses to others' pain are modulated by emotional contexts. *Human Brain Mapping* **30**, 3227–37.

Han, S., Gu, X., Mao, L., Ge, J., Wang, G., and Ma, Y. (2010). Neural substrates of self-referential processing in Chinese Buddhists. *Social Cognitive and Affective Neuroscience* **5**, 332–9.

Han, S., and Humphreys, G.W. (2016). Self-construal: a cultural framework for brain function. *Current Opinion in Psychology* **8**, 10–14.

Han, S., Jiang, Y., and Gu, H. et al. (2004). The role of human parietal cortex in attention networks. *Brain* **127**, 650–9.

Han, S., Jiang, Y., Humphreys, G.W., Zhou, T., and Cai, P. (2005). Distinct neural substrates for the perception of real and virtual visual worlds. *NeuroImage* **24**, 928–35.

Han, S., and Ma, Y. (2014). Cultural differences in human brain activity: a quantitative meta-analysis. *NeuroImage* **99**, 293–300.

Han, S., and Ma, Y. (2015). A culture-behavior-brain loop model of human development. *Trends in Cognitive Sciences* **19**, 666–76.

Han, S., Ma, Y., and Wang, G. (2016). Shared neural representations of self and conjugal family members in Chinese brain. *Culture and Brain* **2**, 72–86.

Han, S., Mao, L., Gu, X., Zhu, Y., Ge, J., and Ma, Y. (2008). Neural consequences of religious belief on self-referential processing. *Social Neuroscience* **3**, 1–15.

Han, S., Mao, L., Qin, J., Friederici, A.D., and Ge, J. (2011). Functional roles and cultural modulations of the medial prefrontal and parietal activity associated with causal attribution. *Neuropsychologia* **49**, 83–91.

Han, S., Mao, L., Qin, J., Friederici, A.D., and Ge, J. (2015). Neural substrates underlying contextual and dispositional causal judgments of physical events in Germany. unpublished manuscript.

Han, S., and **Northoff, G.** (2008). Culture-sensitive neural substrates of human cognition: a transcultural neuroimaging approach. *Nature Reviews Neuroscience* 9, 646–54.

Han, S., and **Northoff, G.** (2009). Understanding the self: a cultural neuroscience approach. *Progress in Brain Research* 178, 203–12.

Han, S., **Northoff, G., Vogeley, K., Wexler, B.E., Kitayama, S.,** and **Varnum, M.E.W.** (2013). A cultural neuroscience approach to the biosocial nature of the human brain. *Annual Review of Psychology* 64, 335–59.

Han, S., and Poppel, E., (eds.), (2011). *Culture and neural frames of cognition and communication.* Berlin: Springer.

Han, S., **Yund, E.W.,** and **Woods, D.L.** (2003). An ERP study of the global precedence effect: the role of spatial frequency. *Clinical Neurophysiology* 114, 1850–65.

Harada, T., **Li, Z.,** and **Chiao, J.Y.** (2010). Differential dorsal and ventral medial prefrontal representations of the implicit self modulated by individualism and collectivism: an fMRI study. *Social Neuroscience* 5, 257–71.

Harari, Y.N. (2014). *Sapiens: a brief history of humankind.* London: Harvill Secker.

Hariri, A.R., **Mattay, V.S.,** and **Tessitore, A.** et al. (2002). Serotonin transporter genetic variation and the response of the human amygdala. *Science* 297, 400–3.

Harris, J.R. (2000). Context-specific learning, personality, and birth order. *Current Directions in Psychological Science* 9, 174–7.

Harris, M. (1999). *Theories of culture in postmodern times.* Walnut Creek, CA: AltaMira.

Hatemi, P.K., **Smith, K., Alford, J.R., Martin, N.G.,** and **Hibbing, J.R.** (2015). The genetic and environmental foundations of political, psychological, social, and economic behaviors: a panel study of twins and families. *Twin Research and Human Genetics* 18, 243–55.

Haviland, W.A., **Prins, H.E.L., Walrath, D.,** and **McBride, B.** (2008). *Cultural anthropology.* Belmont, CA: Thomson Wadsworth.

Haxby, J.V., and **Gobbini, M.I.** (2011). Distributed neural systems for face perception. In: A.J. Calder, G. Rhodes, M.H. Johnson, and J.V. Haxby (eds.), *The Oxford handbook of face perception.* Oxford University Press, pp. 93–110.

Haxby, J.V., **Hoffman, E.A.,** and **Gobbini, M.I.** (2000). The distributed human neural system for face perception. *Trends in Cognitive Sciences* 4, 223–33.

Hedden, T., **Ketay, S., Aron, A., Markus, H.R.,** and **Gabrieli, J.D.** (2008). Cultural influences on neural substrates of attentional control. *Psychological Science* 19, 12–17.

Heisz, J.J., **Watter, S.,** and **Shedden, J.M.** (2006). Automatic face identity encoding at the N170. *Vision Research* 46, 4604–14.

Henderson, J.M., **Williams, C.C.,** and **Falk, R.J.** (2005). Eye movements are functional during face learning. *Memory & Cognition* 33, 98–106.

Henrich, J., **Heine, S.J.,** and **Norenzayan, A.** (2010). Most people are not WEIRD. *Nature* 466, 29.

Henson, R.N., **Rylands, A., Ross, E., Vuilleumeir. P.,** and **Rugg, M.D.** (2004). The effect of repetition lag on electrophysiological and hemodynamic correlates of visual object priming. *NeuroImage* 21, 1674–89.

Herculano-Houzel, S. (2012). Neuronal scaling rules for primate brains: the primate advantage. *Progress in Brain Research* 195, 325–40.

Hernandez-Aguilar, R.A., **Moore, J.,** and **Pickering, T.R.** (2007). Savanna chimpanzees use tools to harvest the underground storage organs of plants. *Proceedings of the National Academy of Sciences* 104, 19210–13.

Herrmann, C.S., and **Knight, R.T.** (2001). Mechanisms of human attention: Event-related potentials and oscillations. *Neuroscience and Biobehavioral Reviews* 25, 465–76.

Herrmann, E., **Call, J.**, Hernández-Lloreda, M.V., Hare, B., and **Tomasello, M.** (2007). Humans have evolved specialized skills of social cognition: the cultural intelligence hypothesis. *Science* 317, 1360–6.

Hibar, D.P., **Stein, J.L.**, and **Renteria, M.E.** et al. (2015). Common genetic variants influence human subcortical brain structures. *Nature* 520, 224–9.

Hickok, G., and **Poeppel, D.** (2007). The cortical organization of speech processing. *Nature Reviews Neuroscience* 8, 393–402.

Higgins, E.T. (1987). Self-discrepancy: a theory relating self and affect. *Psychological Review* 94, 319–40.

Hinton, C., **Fischer, K.W.**, and **Glennon, C.** (2010). Mind, brain, and education. *Mind* 6, 49–50.

Hodges, E.V.E., **Finnegan, R.A.**, and **Perry, D.G.** (1999). Skewed autonomy–relatedness in preadolescents' conceptions of their relationships with mother, father, and best friend. *Developmental Psychology* 35, 737–48.

Hofman, M.A. (1988). Size and shape of the cerebral cortex in mammals. *Brain, Behavior and Evolution* 32, 17–26.

Hofstede, G. (1980). *Culture's consequences: international differences in work-related values.* Beverly Hills, CA: Sage.

Hofstede, G. (2001). *Culture's consequences: comparing values, behaviors, institutions, and organizations across nations.* Thousand Oaks, CA: Sage.

Holland, R.W., **Roeder, U.R.**, Brandt, A.C., and **Hannover, B.** (2004). Don't stand so close to me the effects of self-construal on interpersonal closeness. *Psychological Science* 15, 237–42.

Holliday, R. (2006). Epigenetics: a historical overview. *Epigenetics* 1, 76–80.

Holloway, R.L. (1992). The failure of the gyrification index (GI) to account for volumetric reorganization in the evolution of the human brain. *Journal of Human Evolution* 22, 163–70.

Hong, Y. (2009). A dynamic constructivist approach to culture: moving from describing culture to explaining culture. In: R.S. Wyer, C.Y. Chiu, and Y.Y. Hong (eds.), *Problems and Solutions in Cross-cultural Theory, Research and Application.* New York: Psychology Press, pp. 3–24.

Hong, Y., **Ip, G.**, Chiu, C., **Morris, M.W.**, and **Menon, T.** (2001). Cultural identity and dynamic construction of the self: collective duties and individual rights in Chinese and American cultures. *Social Cognition* 19, 251–68.

Hong, Y., **Morris, M.**, Chiu, C., and **Benet-Martinez, V.** (2000). Multicultural minds: a dynamic constructivist approach to culture and cognition. *American Psychologist* 55, 709–20.

Hong, Y., **Wan, C.**, No, S., and **Chiu, C.** [2007] (2010). Multicultural identities. In: S. Kitayama and D. Cohen. (eds.), *Handbook of cultural psychology.* New York: Guilford Press, pp. 323–46.

Hopfinger, J.B., **Buonocore, M.H.**, and **Mangun, G.R.** (2000). The neural mechanisms of topdown attentional control. *Nature Neuroscience* 3, 284–91.

Hu, S. (1929/2006). *An outline of the history of Chinese philosophy (in Chinese).* Beijing: Uniting Press.

Huff, S., **Yoon, C.**, Lee, F., **Mandadi, A.**, and **Gutchess, A.H.** (2013). Self-referential processing and encoding in bicultural individuals. *Culture and Brain* 1, 16–33.

Hughes, H.C., Nozawa, G., and Kitterle, F. (1996). Global precedence, spatial frequency channels, and the statistics of natural images. *Journal of Cognitive Neuroscience* 8, 197–230.

Hume, D. (1978). *A treatise of human nature*. Oxford: Oxford University Press

Humle, T., and Matsuzawa, T. (2002). Ant-dipping among chimpanzees of Bossou, Guinea, and some comparisons with other sites. *American Journal of Primatology* 58, 133–48.

Huntington, E. (1945). *Mainsprings of civilization*. New York: Wiley.

Iacoboni, M., Woods, R.P., Brass, M., Bekkering, H., Mazziotta, J.C., and Rizzolatti, G. (1999). Cortical mechanisms of human imitation. *Science* 286, 2526–8.

Iidaka, T., Matsumoto, A., Nogawa, J., Yamamoto, Y., and Sadato, N. (2006). Frontoparietal network involved in successful retrieval from episodic memory. Spatial and temporal analyses using fMRI and ERP. *Cerebral Cortex* 16, 1349–60.

Imbo, I., and LeFevre, J.A. (2009). Cultural differences in complex addition: Efficient Chinese versus adaptive Belgians and Canadians. *Journal of Experimental Psychology, Learning, Memory, and Cognition* 35, 1465–76.

Inglehart, R., and Baker, W.E. (2000). Modernization, cultural change, and the persistence of traditional values. *American Sociological Review* 61, 19–51.

Ishigami-Iagolnitzer, M. (1997). The self and the person as treated in some Buddhist texts. *Asian Philosophy* 7, 37–45.

Ishii, K., Kim, H.S., Sasaki, J.Y., Shinada, M., and Kusumi, I. (2014). Culture modulates sensitivity to the disappearance of facial expressions associated with serotonin transporter polymorphism (5-HTTLPR). *Culture and Brain* 2, 72–88.

Ishii, K., Miyamoto, Y., Mayama, K., and Niedenthal, P.M. (2011). When your smile fades away: cultural differences in sensitivity to the disappearance of smiles. *Social Psychological and Personality Science* 2, 516–22.

Jack, R.E., Blais, C., Scheepers, C., Schyns, P. G., and Caldara, R. (2009). Cultural confusions show that facial expressions are not universal. *Current Biology* 19, 1543–8.

Jack, R.E., Garrod, O.G., Yu, H., Caldara, R., and Schyns, P.G. (2012). Facial expressions of emotion are not culturally universal. *Proceedings of the National Academy of Sciences* 109, 7241–4.

Jackson, P.L., Meltzoff, A.N., and Decety, J. (2005). How do we perceive the pain of others? A window into the neural processes involved in empathy. *NeuroImage* 24, 771–9.

James, W. [1890] (1950). *The principles of psychology. Vols. 1 and 2*. New York: Dover.

Jenkins, A.C., and Mitchell, J.P. (2011). Medial prefrontal cortex subserves diverse forms of self-reflection. *Social Neuroscience* 6, 211–18.

Jenkins, L.J., Yang, Y.J., Goh, J., Hong, Y.Y., and Park, D.C. (2010). Cultural differences in the lateral occipital complex while viewing incongruent scenes. *Social Cognitive and Affective Neuroscience* 5, 236–41.

Ji, L.J., Peng, K., and Nisbett, R.E. (2000). Culture, control, and perception of relationship in the environment. *Journal of Personality and Social Psychology* 78, 943–55.

Ji, L.J., Zhang, Z., and Nisbett, R.E. (2004). Is it culture or is it language? Examination of language effects in cross-cultural research on categorization. *Journal of Personality and Social Psychology* 87, 57–65.

Jiang, C., Varnum, M.E., Hou, Y., and Han, S. (2014). Distinct effects of self-construal priming on empathic neural responses in Chinese and Westerners. *Social Neuroscience,* 9, 130–38.

Jiang, Y., and Han, S. (2005). Neural mechanisms of global/local processing of bilateral visual inputs: an ERP study. *Clinical Neurophysiology* 116, 1444–54.

Johnson, J.D., Simmons, C.H., Jordan, A., MacLean, L., Taddei, J., and Thomas, D. (2002). Rodney King and O.J. revisited: the impact of race and defendant empathy induction on judicial decisions. *Journal of Applied Social Psychology* 32, 1208–23.

Johnson, R.Jr. (1988). The amplitude of the P300 component of the event-related potential. Review and synthesis. *Advances in Psychophysiology*, 3, 69–137.

Johnson, S.C., Baxter, L.C., Wilder, L.S., Pipe, J.G., Heiserman, J.E., and Prigatano, G.P. (2002). Neural correlates of self-reflection. *Brain* 125, 1808–14.

Kan, K.J., Wicherts, J.M., Dolan, C.V., and van der Maas, H.L. (2013). On the nature and nurture of intelligence and specific cognitive abilities the more heritable, the more culture dependent. *Psychological Science* 24, 2420–8.

Kang, P., Lee, Y., Choi, I., and Kim, H. (2013). Neural evidence for individual and cultural variability in the social comparison effect. *Journal of Neuroscience* 33, 16200–8.

Kanwisher, N., McDermott, J., and Chun, M.M. (1997). The fusiform face area: a module in human extrastriate cortex specialized for face perception. *Journal of Neuroscience* 17, 4302–11.

Karasz, A. (2005). Cultural differences in conceptual models of depression. *Social Science and Medicine* 60, 1625–35.

Keenan, J.P., McCutcheon, B., Sanders, G., Freund, S., Gallup, G.G., and Pascual-Leone, A. (1999). Left hand advantage in a self-face recognition task. *Neuropsychologia* 37, 1421–5.

Keenan, J.P., Wheeler, M.A., Gallup, G.G., and Pascual-Leone, A. (2000). Self-recognition and the right prefrontal cortex. *Trends in Cognitive Science* 4, 338–44.

Kelley, W.M., Macrae, C.N., Wyland, C.L., Caglar, S., Inati, S., and Heatherton, T.F. (2002). Finding the self? An event-related fMRI study. *Journal of Cognitive Neuroscience*, 14, 785–94.

Kelly, D.J., Liu, S., Rodger, H., Miellet, S., Ge, L., and Caldara, R. (2011). Developing cultural differences in face processing. *Developmental Science* 14, 1176–84.

Kelly, W., Macrae, C.N., Wyland, C.L., Caglar, S., Inati, S., and Heatherton, T.F. (2002). Finding the self? An event-related fMRI study. *Journal of Cognitive Neuroscience* 14, 785–94.

Kemmelmeier, M., and Cheng, B.Y.M. (2004). Language and self-construal priming a replication and extension in a Hong Kong sample. *Journal of Cross-Cultural Psychology* 35, 705–12.

Kendon, A. (1997). Gesture. *Annual Review of Anthropology* 26, 109–28.

Keyes, C.F. (1985). The interpretive basis of depression. In: A. Kleinman and B. Goodeds (eds.), *Culture and depression: studies in the anthropology and cross-cultural psychiatry of affect and disorder.* Berkeley: University of California Press, pp. 153–75.

Keyes, H., Brady, N., Reilly, R.B., and Fox, J.J. (2010). My face or yours? Event-related potential correlates of self-face processing. *Brain and Cognition* 72, 244–54.

Kim, B., Sung, Y.S., and McClure, S.M. (2012). The neural basis of cultural differences in delay discounting. *Philosophical Transactions of the Royal Society B: Biological Sciences* 367, 650–6.

Kim, H.S., and Sasaki, J.Y. (2014). Cultural neuroscience: biology of the mind in cultural contexts. *Annual Review of Psychology* 65, 487–514.

Kim, H.S., Sherman, D.K., and Mojaverian, T. et al. (2011). Gene–culture interaction oxytocin receptor polymorphism (OXTR) and emotion regulation. *Social Psychological and Personality Science* **2**, 665–72.

Kim, H.S., Sherman, D.K., and Sasaki, J.Y. et al. (2010). Culture, distress, and oxytocin receptor polymorphism (OXTR) interact to influence emotional support seeking. *Proceedings of the National Academy of Sciences* **107**, 15717–21.

Kim, Y., Sohn, D., and Choi, S.M. (2011). Cultural difference in motivations for using social network sites: a comparative study of American and Korean college students. *Computers in Human Behavior* **27**, 365–72.

Kirmayer, L.J. (2001). Cultural variations in the clinical presentation of depression and anxiety: implications for diagnosis and treatment. *Journal of Clinical Psychiatry* **62**, 22–30.

Kirmayer, L.J., and Minas, H. (2000). The future of cultural psychiatry: an international perspective. *Canadian Journal of Psychiatry* **45**, 438–46.

Kita, S. (2009). Cross-cultural variation of speech-accompanying gesture: a review. *Language and Cognitive Processes* **24**, 145–67.

Kitayama, S., and Cohen, D. (eds.) (2010). *Handbook of cultural psychology.* New York: Guilford.

Kitayama, S., and Park, J. (2014). Error-related brain activity reveals self-centric motivation: culture matters. *Journal of Experimental Psychology: General* **143**, 62–70.

Kitayama, S., and Uskul, A.K. (2011). Culture, mind, and the brain: current evidence and future directions. *Annual Review of Psychology* **62**, 419–49.

Kitayama, S., Duffy, S., Kawamura, T., and Larsen, J.T. (2003). Perceiving an object and its context in different cultures: a cultural look at new look. *Psychological Science* **14**, 201–6.

Kitayama, S., Ishii, K., Imada, T., Takemura, K., and Ramaswamy, J. (2006). Voluntary settlement and the spirit of independence: evidence from Japan's "northern frontier." *Journal of Personality and Social Psychology* **91**, 369–84.

Kitayama, S., King, A., Hsu, M., Liberzon, I., and Yoon, C. (2016). Dopamine-system genes and cultural acquisition: the norm sensitivity hypothesis. *Current Opinion in Psychology* **8**, 167–74.

Kitayama, S., King, A., Yoon, C., Tompson, S., Huff, S., and Liberzon, I. (2014). The dopamine D4 receptor gene (DRD4) moderates cultural difference in independent versus interdependent social orientation. *Psychological Science* **25**, 1169–77.

Kitayama, S., Park, H., Sevincer, A.T., Karasawa, M., and Uskul, A.K. (2009). A cultural task analysis of implicit independence: comparing North America, Western Europe, and East Asia. *Journal of Personality and Social Psychology* **97**, 236–55.

Klein, S.B. (2012). The self and its brain. *Social Cognition* **30**, 474–518.

Klein, S.B., Cosmides, L., Tooby, J., and Chance, S. (2002). Decisions and the evolution memory: multiple systems, multiple functions. *Psychological Review* **109**, 306–29.

Klein, S.B., and Loftus, J. (1993). Behavioral experience and trait judgments about the self. *Personality & Social Psychology* **19**, 740–6.

Klein, S.B., Loftus, J., and Burton, H.A. (1989). Two self-reference effects: the importance of distinguishing between self-descriptiveness judgments and autobiographical retrieval in self-referent encoding. *Journal of Personality and Social Psychology* **56**, 853–65.

Klein, S.B., Loftus, J., Trafton, J.G., and Fuhrman, R.W. (1992). Use of exemplars and abstractions in trait judgments: a model of trait knowledge about the self and others. *Journal of Personality & Social Psychology* 63, 739–53.

Klein, S.B., Robertson, T.E., Gangi, C.E., and Loftus, J. (2007). The functional independence of trait self-knowledge: commentary on Sakaki. *Memory* 16, 556–65.

Kluckhohn, C., and Kelly, W.H. (1945). The concept of culture. In: R. Linton (ed.), *The Science of man in the world crisis*. New York: Columbia University Press, pp. 78–105.

Kobayashi, C., Glover, G.H., and Temple, E. (2006). Cultural and linguistic influence on neural bases of 'theory of mind': an fMRI study with Japanese bilinguals. *Brain & Language* 98, 210–20.

Kobayashi, C., Glover, G.H., and Temple, E. (2007). Cultural and linguistic effects on neural bases of 'theory of mind' in American and Japanese children. *Brain Research* 1164, 95–107.

Kogan, A., Saslow, L.R., Impett, E.A., Oveis, C., Keltner, D., and Saturn, S.R. (2011). Thin-slicing study of the oxytocin receptor (OXTR) gene and the evaluation and expression of the prosocial disposition. *Proceedings of the National Academy of Sciences of the United States of America* 108, 19189–92.

Kogan, N. (1961). Attitudes toward old people: the development of a scale and an examination of correlates. *Journal of Abnormal and Social Psychology* 62, 44–54.

Kohlberg, L. [1969] (1971). Stage and sequence: the cognitive-developmental approach to socialization. In: D.A. Goslin (ed.), *Handbook of socialization theory and research*. Chicago: Rand McNally, pp. 347–480.

Koizumi, H. (2004). The concept of "developing the brain": a new natural science for learning and education. *Brain and Development* 26, 434–41.

Korn, C.W., Fan, Y., Zhang, K., Wang, C., Han, S., and Heekeren, H.R. (2014). Cultural influences on social feedback processing of character traits. *Frontiers in Human Neuroscience* 8, 192.

Koten, J.W., Wood, G., Hagoort, P., Goebel, R., Propping, P., Willmes, K., and Boomsma, D.I. (2009). Genetic contribution to variation in cognitive function: an FMRI study in twins. *Science* 323, 1737–40.

Kotlewska, I., and Nowicka, A. (2015). Present self, past self and close-other: event-related potential study of face and name detection. *Biological Psychology* 110, 201–11.

Kotz, S.A., Cappa, S.F., von Cramon, D.Y., and Friederici, A.D. (2002). Modulation of the lexical-semantic network by auditory semantic priming: an event-related functional MRI study. *Neuroimage* 17, 1761–72.

Krämer, K., Bente, G., and Kuzmanovic, B. et al. (2014). Neural correlates of emotion perception depending on culture and gaze direction. *Culture and Brain* 2, 27–51.

Kremer, I., Bachner-Melman, R., and Reshef, A. et al. (2005). Association of the serotonin transporter gene with smoking behavior. *American Journal of Psychiatry* 162, 924–30.

Krendl, A.C. (2016). An fMRI investigation of the effects of culture on evaluations of stigmatized individuals. *NeuroImage* 124, 336–49.

Kringelbach, M. L. (2005). The human orbitofrontal cortex: linking reward to hedonic experience. *Nature Reviews Neuroscience* 6, 691–702.

Krishna, A., Zhou, R., and Zhang, S. (2008). The effect of self-construal on spatial judgments. *Journal of Consumer Research* 35, 337–48.

Kroeber, A.L., and Kluckhohn, C. (1952). *Culture: a critical review of concepts and definitions. Papers of the Peabody Museum*. Cambridge, MA: Harvard University.

Kubota, J.T., and Ito, T.A. (2007). Multiple cues in social perception: the time course of processing race and facial expression. *Journal of Experimental Social Psychology* **43**, 738–52.

Kuhn, M.H., and Mcpartland, T.S. (1954). An empirical investigation of self-attitudes. *American Sociological Review* **19**, 68–76.

Kühnen, U., and Oyserman, D. (2002). Thinking about the self influences thinking in general: cognitive consequences of salient self-concept. *Journal of Experimental Social Psychology* **38**, 492–9.

Kuper, A. (1999). *Culture: the anthropologists' account*. Cambridge, MA: Harvard University Press.

Kutas, M., and Hillyard, S.A. (1980). Reading senseless sentences: Brain potentials reflect semantic incongruity. *Science* **207**, 203–5.

Laland, K.N., Odling-Smee, J., and Myles, S. (2010). How culture shaped the human genome: bringing genetics and the human sciences together. *Nature Reviews Genetics* **11**, 137–48.

Lampl, Y., Eshel, Y., Gilad, R., and Sarova-Pinhas, I. (1994). Selective acalculia with sparing of the subtraction process in a patient with left parietotemporal hemorrhage. *Neurology* **44**, 1759–61.

Lao, J., Vizioli, L., and Caldara, R. (2013). Culture modulates the temporal dynamics of global/local processing. *Culture and Brain* **1**, 158–74.

Lau, E.F., Phillips, C., and Poeppel, D. (2008). A cortical network for semantics: (de) constructing the N400. *Nature Reviews Neuroscience* **9**, 920–33.

LeClair, J., Janusonis, S., and Kim, H.S. (2014). Gene–culture interactions: a multi-gene approach. *Culture and Brain* **2**, 122–40.

Lee, K.M. (2000). Cortical areas differentially involved in multiplication and subtraction: A functional magnetic resonance imaging study and correlation with a case of selective acalculia. *Annals of Neurology* **48**, 657–61.

Lefevre, J.A., Bisanz, J., Daley, K.E., Buffone, L., Greenham, S.L., and Sadesky, G.S. (1996). Multiple routes to solution of single-digit multiplication problems. *Journal of Experimental Psychology* **125**, 284–306.

Lemogne, C., Delaveau, P., Freton, M., Guionnet, S., and Fossati, P. (2012). Medial prefrontal cortex and the self in major depression. *Journal of Affective Disorders* **136**, e1–e11.

Lemogne, C., le Bastard, G., and Mayberg, H. et al. (2009). In search of the depressive self: extended medial prefrontal network during self-referential processing in major depression. *Social Cognitive and Affective Neuroscience* **4**, 305–12.

Lemonde, S., Turecki, G., and Bakish, D. et al. (2003). Impaired repression at a 5-hydroxytryptamine 1A receptor gene polymorphism associated with major depression and suicide. *Journal of Neuroscience* **2**, 8788–99.

Lesch, K.P., Bengel, D., and Heils, A. et al. (1996). Association of anxiety-related traits with a polymorphism in the serotonin transporter gene regulatory region. *Science* **274**, 1527–31.

Leung, K., Koch, P., and Lu L. (2002). A dualistic model of harmony and its implications for conflict management in Asia. *Asia Pacific Journal of Management* **19**, 201–20.

Leung, F. K. (2014). What can and should we learn from international studies of mathematics achievement? *Mathematics Education Research Journal* **26**, 579–605.

Levanen, S., Jousmaki, V., and Hari, R. (1998). Vibration-induced auditory-cortex activation in a congenitally deaf adult. *Current Biology* **8**, 869–72.

Levitin, D.J. (2015). *Why the modern world is bad for your brain* [Online] (Updated 18 Jan 2015) Available at: http://www.theguardian.com/science/2015/jan/18/modern-world-bad-for-brain-daniel-j-levitinorganized-mind-information-overload.

Lewis, M. (2011). The origins and uses of self-awareness or the mental representation of me. *Consciousness & Cognition* 20, 120–9.

Lewis, R.S., Goto, S.G., and Kong, L.L. (2008). Culture and context: East Asian American and European American differences in P3 event-related potentials and self-construal. *Personality and Social Psychology Bulletin* 34, 623–34.

Li, H.Z., Zhang, Z., Bhatt, G., and Yum, Y. (2006). Rethinking culture and self-construal: China as a middle land. *Journal of Social Psychology* 146, 591–610.

Li, S.C. (2003). Biocultural orchestration of developmental plasticity across levels: the interplay of biology and culture in shaping the mind and behavior across the life span. *Psychological Bulletin* 129, 171–94.

Lieberman, M.D. (2007). Social cognitive neuroscience: a review of core processes. *Annual Review of Psychology* 58, pp.259–89.

Liew, S.L., Han, S., and Aziz-Zadeh, L. (2011). Familiarity modulates mirror neuron and mentalizing regions during intention understanding. *Human Brain Mapping* 32, 1986–97.

Liew, S.L., Ma, Y., Han, S., and Aziz-Zadeh, L. (2011). Who's afraid of the boss: cultural differences in social hierarchies modulate self-face recognition in Chinese and Americans. *PLoS ONE* 6, e16901.

Lin, H. (2005). Religious wisdom of no-self. In: Y. Wu, P. Lai, and W. Wang (eds.), *Dialogue between Buddhism and Christianity*. Beijing, China: Zhong Hua Book Company, pp. 317–38.

Lin, Z., and Han, S. (2009). Self-construal priming modulates the scope of visual attention. *Quarterly Journal of Experimental Psychology* 62, 802–13.

Lin, Z., Lin, Y., and Han, S. (2008). Self-construal priming modulates visual activity underlying global/local perception. *Biological Psychology* 77, 93–7.

Liu, D.Z. (1984). *History of ancient Chinese architecture*. 2nd ed. Beijing: China Architecture and Building Press.

Liu, Y., Sheng, F., Woodcock, K.A., and Han, S. (2013). Oxytocin effects on neural correlates of self-referential processing. *Biological Psychology* 94, 380–7.

Locke, J. [1690] (1731). *An essay concerning human understanding*. London: Edmund Parker.

Logothetis, N.K. (2008). What we can do and what we cannot do with fMRI. *Nature* 453, 869–78.

Lou, H.C., Luber, B., and Crupain, M. et al. (2004). Parietal cortex and representation of the mental self. *Proceedings of the National Academy of Sciences of the United States of America* 101, 6827–32.

Luck, S.J. (2014). *An introduction to the event-related potential technique*. Cambridge, MA: MIT press.

Luncz, L.V., Mundry, R., and Boesch, C. (2012). Evidence for cultural differences between neighboring chimpanzee (Pan troglodytes) communities. *Current Biology* 22, 922–6.

Luo, S., and Han, S. (2014). The association between an oxytocin receptor gene polymorphism and cultural orientations. *Culture and Brain* 2, 89–107.

Luo, S., Li, B., Ma, Y., Zhang, W., Rao, Y., and Han, S. (2015a). Oxytocin receptor gene and racial ingroup bias in empathy-related brain activity. *NeuroImage* **110**, 22–31.

Luo, S., Ma, Y., and Liu, Y. et al. (2015b). Interaction between oxytocin receptor polymorphism and interdependent culture on human empathy. *Social Cognitive and Affective Neuroscience* **10**, 1273–81.

Luo, S., Shi, Z., Yang, X., Wang, X., and Han, S. (2014). Reminders of mortality decrease midcingulate activity in response to others' suffering. *Social Cognitive and Affective Neuroscience* **9**, 477–86.

Lupien, S.J., McEwen, B.S., Gunnar, M.R., and Heim, C. (2009). Effects of stress throughout the lifespan on the brain, behaviour and cognition. *Nature Reviews Neuroscience* **10**. 434–45.

Lynch, M.P., and Eilers, R.E. (1992). A study of perceptual development for musical tuning. *Perception & Psychophysics* **52**, 599–608.

Ma, Y., and Han, S. (2009). Self-face advantage is modulated by social threat—boss effect on self-face recognition. *Journal of Experimental Social Psychology* **45**, 1048–51.

Ma, Y., and Han, S. (2010). Why respond faster to the self than others? An implicit positive association theory of self advantage during implicit face recognition. *Journal of Experimental Psychology: Human Perception and Performance* **36**, 619–33.

Ma, Y., and Han, S. (2011). Neural representation of self-concept in sighted and congenitally blind adults. *Brain* **134**, 235–46.

Ma, Y., and Han, S. (2012). Functional dissociation of the left and right fusiform gyrus in self-face recognition. *Human Brain Mapping* **33**, 2255–67.

Ma, Y., Bang, D., and Wang, C. et al. (2014a). Sociocultural patterning of neural activity during self-reflection. *Social Cognitive and Affective Neuroscience* **9**, 73–80.

Ma, Y., Bang, D., Wang, C. et al. (2014b). Sociocultural patterning of neural activity during self-reflection. *Social Cognitive and Affective Neuroscience* **9**, 73–80.

Ma, Y., Li, B., and Wang, C. et al. (2014c). 5-HTTLPR polymorphism modulates neural mechanisms of negative self-reflection. *Cerebral Cortex* **24**, 2421–9.

Ma, Y., Li, B., Wang, C., Zhang, W., Rao., Y., and Han, S. (2015). Genetic difference in acute citalopram effects on human emotional network. *British Journal of Psychiatry* **206**, 385–92.

Ma, Y., Wang, C., Li, B., Zhang, W., Rao, Y., and Han, S. (2014). Does self-construal predict activity in the social brain network? A genetic moderation effect. *Social Cognitive and Affective Neuroscience* **9**, 1360–7.

Macrae, C.N., Moran, J.M., Heatherton, T.F., Banfield, J.F., and Kelley, W.M. (2004). Medial prefrontal activity predicts memory for self. *Cerebral Cortex* **14**, 647–54.

Maess, B., Koelsch, S., Gunter, T.C., and Friederici, A.D. (2001). Musical syntax is processed in Broca's area: an MEG study. *Nature Neuroscience* **4**, 540–5.

Maguire, E.A., Frackowiak, R.S., and Frith, C.D. (1997). Recalling routes around London: activation of the right hippocampus in taxi drivers. *Journal of Neuroscience,* **17**, 7103–10.

Ma-Kellams, C., Blascovich, J., and McCall, C. (2012). Culture and the body: East–West differences in visceral perception. *Journal of Personality and Social Psychology* **102**, 718–28.

Malpass, R.S., and Kravitz, J. (1969). Recognition for faces of own and other race. *Journal of Personality & Social Psychology* **13**, 330–4.

Mantini, D., Corbetta, M., Romani, G.L., Orban, G.A., and Vanduffel, W. (2013). Evolutionarily novel functional networks in the human brain? *Journal of Neuroscience* **33**, 3259–75.

Markowitsch, H.J., Vandekerckhovel, M.M., Lanfermann, H., and Russ, M.O. (2003). Engagement of lateral and medial prefrontal areas in the ecphory of sad and happy autobiographical memories. *Cortex* **39**, 643–65.

Markus, H.R., and Hamedani, M.G. [2007] (2010). Sociocultural psychology: the dynamic interdependence among self systems and social systems. In: S. Kitayama and D. Cohen (eds.), *Handbook of cultural psychology*. New York: Guilford, pp. 3–39.

Markus, H.R., and Kitayama, S. (1991). Culture and the self: implications for cognition, emotion, and motivation. *Psychological Review* **98**, 224–53.

Markus, H.R., and Kitayama, S. (2010). Cultures and selves: a cycle of mutual constitution. *Perspectives on Psychological Science* **5**, 420–30.

Mars, R.B., Jbabdi, S., and Sallet, J. et al. (2011). Diffusion-weighted imaging tractography-based parcellation of the human parietal cortex and comparison with human and macaque resting-state functional connectivity. *Journal of Neuroscience* **31**, 4087–100.

Marsella, A.J., Sanborn, K.O., Kameoka, V., Shizuru, L., and Brennan, J. (1975). Cross-validation of self-report measures of depression among normal populations of Japanese, Chinese, and Caucasian ancestry. *Journal of Clinical Psychology* **31**, 281–7.

Martin, A., Wiggs, C.L., Ungerleider, L.G., and Haxby, J.V. (1996). Neural correlates of category-specific knowledge. *Nature* **379**, 649–52.

Martinez, A., Anllo-Vento, L., and Sereno, M.I. et al. (1999). Involvement of striate and extrastriate visual cortical areas in spatial attention. *Nature Neuroscience* **2**, 364–9.

Masuda, T., and Nisbett, R.E. (2001). Attending holistically vs. analytically: comparing the context sensitivity of Japanese and Americans. *Journal of Personality & Social Psychology* **81**, 922–34.

Mathur, V.A., Harada, T., Lipke, T., and Chiao, J.Y. (2010). Neural basis of extraordinary empathy and altruistic motivation. *NeuroImage* **51**, 1468–75.

Matsunaga, R., Yokosawa, K., and Abe, J.I. (2012). Magnetoencephalography evidence for different brain subregions serving two musical cultures. *Neuropsychologia* **50**, 3218–27.

McClure, S.M., Li, J., Tomlin, D., Cypert, K.S., Montague, L.M., and Montague, P.R. (2004). Neural correlates of behavioral preference for culturally familiar drinks. *Neuron* **44**, 379–87.

McGue, M. (1993). From proteins to cognitions: the behavioral genetics of alcoholism. In: R. Plomin, and G.E. McClearn (eds.), *Nature, nurture and psychology*. Washington, DC: American Psychological Association, pp. 245–68.

McGue, M., and Bouchard Jr, T.J. (1998). Genetic and environmental influences on human behavioral differences. *Annual Review of Neuroscience*, **21**, 1–24.

Mead, M. (1937). Public opinion mechanisms among primitive peoples. *Public Opinion Quarterly* **1**, 5–16.

Menon, V., Levitin, D.J., and Smith, B.K. et al. (2002). Neural correlates of timbre change in harmonic sounds. *Neuroimage* **17**, 1742–54.

Mercader, J., Barton, H., Gillespie, J. et al. (2007). 4,300-year-old chimpanzee sites and the origins of percussive stone technology. *Proceedings of the National Academy of Sciences USA* **104**, 3043–8.

Michalska, K.J., Decety, J., and Liu, C. et al. (2014). Genetic imaging of the association of oxytocin receptor gene (OXTR) polymorphisms with positive maternal parenting. *Frontiers in Behavioral Neuroscience* **8**, 21.

Miellet, S., Vizioli, L., He, L., Zhou, X., and Caldara, R. (2013). Mapping face recognition information use across cultures. *Frontiers in Psychology* **4**, 1–12.

Minami, M., and McCabe, A. (1995). Rice balls and bear hunts: Japanese and North American family narrative patterns. *Journal of Child Language* **22**, 423–45.

Mitchell, J.P., Banaji, M.R., and MacRae, C.N. (2005). The link between social cognition and self-referential thought in the medial prefrontal cortex. *Journal of Cognitive Neuroscience* **17**, 1306–15.

Mitchell, J.P., Heatherton, T.F., and Macrae, C.N. (2002). Distinct neural systems subserve person and object knowledge. *Proceedings of National Academy of Sciences* **99**, 15238–43.

Miyamoto, Y., Nisbett, R.E., and Masuda, T. (2006). Culture and the physical environment holistic versus analytic perceptual affordances. *Psychological Science* **17**, 113–19.

Moffitt, T.E. (2005). Genetic and environmental influences on antisocial behaviors: evidence from behavioral–genetic research. *Advances in Genetics* **55**, 41–104.

Moll, J., de Oliveira-Souza, R., Bramati, I.E., and Grafman, J. (2002). Functional networks in emotional moral and nonmoral social judgments. *Neuroimage* **16**, 696–703.

Molnar-Szakacs, I., Wu, A.D., Robles, F.J., and Iacoboni, M. (2007). Do you see what I mean? Corticospinal excitability during observation of culture-specific gestures. *PLoS ONE*, **2**, e626.

Montepare, J.M., and Zebrowitz, L.A. (1993). A cross-cultural comparison of impressions created by age-related variations in gait. *Journal of Nonverbal Behavior* **17**, 55–68.

Moran, M.A., Musfson, E.J., and Mesulam, M.M. (1987). Neural inputs into the temporopolar cortex of the rhesus monkey. *Journal of Comparative Neurology* **256**, 88–103.

Morelli, G.A., Rogoff, B., Oppenheim, D., and Goldsmith, D. (1992). Cultural variation in infants' sleeping arrangements: questions of independence. *Developmental Psychology* **28**, 604–13.

Morikawa, H., Shand, N., and Kosawa, Y. (1998). Maternal speech to prelingual infants in Japan and the United States: relationships among functions, forms, and referents. *Journal of Child Language* **15**, 237–56.

Morris, D., Collett, P., Marsh, P., and O'Shaughnessy, M. (1979). *Gestures, their origins and distribution.* New York: Stein and Day.

Morris, M., and Peng, K. (1994). Culture and cause: American and Chinese attributions for social and physical events. *Journal of Personality and Social Psychology* **67**, 949–71.

Morris, M., and Peng, K. (1994). Culture and cause: American and Chinese attributions for social and physical events. *Journal of Personality and Social Psychology* **67**, 949–71.

Moya, P., and Markus, H.R. (2011). Doing race: a conceptual overview. In: H.R. Markus, and P. Moya (eds.), *Doing race: 21 essays for the 21st century*. New York: Norton, pp. 1–102.

Mrazek, A.J., Chiao, J.Y., Blizinsky, K.D., Lun, J., and Gelfand, M.J. (2013). The role of culture–gene coevolution in morality judgment: examining the interplay between tightness–looseness and allelic variation of the serotonin transporter gene. *Culture and Brain* **1**, 100–17.

Mu, Y., and Han, S. (2010). Neural oscillations involved in self-referential processing. *NeuroImage* **53**, 757–68.

Mu, Y., and Han, S. (2013). Neural oscillations dissociate between self-related attentional orienting versus evaluation. *NeuroImage* **67**, 247–56.

Mu, Y., Kitayama, S., Han, S., and Gelfand, M. (2015). How culture gets embrained: cultural differences in event-related potentials of social norm violations. *Proceedings of the National Academy of Sciences* **112**, 15348–53.

Mulcahy, N.J., Call, J., and Dunbar, R.I. (2005). Gorillas (Gorilla gorilla) and orangutans (Pongo pygmaeus) encode relevant problem features in a tool-using task. *Journal of Comparative Psychology* **119**, 23–32.

Munafò, M.R., Brown, S.M., and Hariri, A.R. (2008). Serotonin transporter (5-HTTLPR) genotype and amygdala activation: a meta-analysis. *Biological Psychiatry* **63**, 852–7.

Münte, T.F., Altenmüller, E., and Jäncke, L. (2002). The musician's brain as a model of neuroplasticity. *Nature Reviews Neuroscience* **3**, 473–8.

Murata, A., Moser, J.S., and Kitayama, S. (2013). Culture shapes electrocortical responses during emotion suppression. *Social Cognitive and Affective Neuroscience* **8**, 595–601.

Mutti, D.O., Zadnik, K., and Adams, A.J. (1996). The nature versus nurture debate goes on. *Investigative Ophthalmology & Visual Science* **37**, 952–7.

Nan, Y., Knösche, T. R., and Friederici, A. D. (2006). The perception of musical phrase structure: a cross-cultural ERP study. *Brain Research* **1094**, 179–91.

Nan, Y., Knösche, T.R., Zysset, S., and Friederici, A.D. (2008). Cross-cultural music phrase processing: an fMRI study. *Human Brain Mapping* **29**, 312–28.

Navon, D. (1977). Forest before trees: The precedence of global features in visual perception. *Cognitive Psychology* **9**, 353–83.

Nelson, N.L., and Russell, J.A. (2013). Universality revisited. *Emotion Review* **5**, 8–15.

Neumann, R., Steinhäuser, N., and Roeder, U.R. (2009). How self-construal shapes emotion: cultural differences in the feeling of pride. *Social Cognition* **27**, 327–37.

Ng, S.H. (2009). Effects of culture priming on the social connectedness of the bicultural self. *Journal of Cross-Cultural Psychology* **40**, 170–86.

Ng, S.H., Han, S., Mao, L., and Lai, J.C. (2010). Dynamic bicultural brains: fMRI study of their flexible neural representation of self and significant others in response to culture primes. *Asian Journal of Social Psychology* **13**, 83–91.

Nikolova, Y.S., and Hariri, A.R. (2015). Can we observe epigenetic effects on human brain function? *Trends in Cognitive Sciences* **19**, 366–73.

Nikolova, Y.S., Koenen, K.C., and Galea, S. et al. (2014). Beyond genotype: serotonin transporter epigenetic modification predicts human brain function. *Nature Neuroscience* **17**, 1153–5.

Nisbett, R.E. (2003). *The geography of thought: how Asians and Westerners think differently, and why*. New York: Free Press.

Nisbett, R.E., and Cohen, D. (1996). *Culture of honor: the psychology of violence in the South*. Boulder: Westview Press.

Nisbett, R.E., and Masuda, T. (2003). Culture and point of view. *Proceedings of the National Academy of Sciences* **100**, 11163–70.

Nisbett, R.E., Peng, K., Choi, I., and Norenzayan, A. (2001). Culture and systems of thought: holistic versus analytic cognition. *Psychological Review* **108**, 291–310.

Nishimura, H., Hashikawa, K., Doi, K., Iwaki, T., Watanabe, Y., and Kusuoka, H. (1999). Sign language "heard" in the auditory cortex. *Nature* **397**, 116.

Nobre, A.C., Sebestyen, G.N., Gitelman, D.R., Mesulam, M.M., Frackowiak, R.S., and Frith, C.D. (1997). Functional localization of the system for visuospatial attention using positron emission tomography. *Brain* **120**, 515–33.

Norenzayan, A., Smith, E.E., Kim, B.J., and Nisbett, R.E. (2002). Cultural preferences for formal versus intuitive reasoning. *Cognitive Science* **26**, 653–84.

Northoff, G. (2014). *Unlocking the brain*. Oxford, UK/New York: Oxford University Press.

Northoff, G., Heinze, A., de Greck, M., Bermpoh, F., Dobrowolny, H., and Panksepp, J. (2006). Self-referential processing in our brain--a meta-analysis of imaging studies on the self. *NeuroImage* **31**, 440–57.

O'Doherty, J.P. (2004). Reward representations and reward-related learning in the human brain: insights from neuroimaging. *Current Opinion in Neurobiology* **14**, 769–76.

Obhi, S.S., Hogeveen, J., and Pascual-Leone, A. (2011). Resonating with others: the effects of self-construal type on motor cortical output. *Journal of Neuroscience* **31**, 14531–5.

Ochsner, K.N., and Gross, J.J. (2005). The cognitive control of emotion. *Trends in Cognitive Sciences* **9**, 242–9.

Ochsner, K.N., and Lieberman, M.D. (2001). The emergence of social cognitive neuroscience. *American Psychologist* **56**, 717–34.

Ochsner, K.N., Silvers, J.A., and Buhle, J.T. (2012). Functional imaging studies of emotion regulation: a synthetic review and evolving model of the cognitive control of emotion. *Annals of the New York Academy of Sciences* **1251**, E1–E24.

O'Doherty, J., Kringelbach, M.L., Rolls, E.T., Hornak, J., and Andrews, C. (2001). Abstract reward and punishment representations in the human orbitofrontal cortex. *Nature Neuroscience* **41**, 95–102.

Olson, I.R., Plotzker, A., and Ezzyat, Y. (2007). The enigmatic temporal pole: a review of findings on social and emotional processing. *Brain* **130**, 1718–31.

Or, C.C.F., Peterson, M.F., and Eckstein, M.P. (2015). Initial eye movements during face identification are optimal and similar across cultures. *Journal of Vision* **15**, 1–25.

Oyserman, D. (2011). Culture as situated cognition: cultural mindsets, cultural fluency, and meaning making. *European Review of Social Psychology* **22**, 164–214.

Oyserman, D., Coon, H.M., and Kemmelmeier, M. (2002). Rethinking individualism and collectivism: evaluation of theoretical assumptions and meta-analyses. *Psychological Bulletin* **128**, 3–72.

Oyserman, D., and Lee, S.W.S. [2007] (2010). Priming "culture." In: S. Kitayama, and D. Cohen. (eds.), *Handbook of cultural psychology*. New York: Guilford, pp. 255–79.

Oyserman, D., Novin, S., Flinkenflögel, N., and Krabbendam, L. (2014). Integrating culture-as-situated-cognition and neuroscience prediction models. *Culture and Brain* **2**, 1–26.

Oyserman, D., Sorensen, N., Reber, R., and Chen, S.X. (2009). Connecting and separating mind-sets: culture as situated cognition. *Journal of Personality and Social Psychology* **97**, 217–35.

Paladino, P. M., Leyens, J. P., Rodriguez, R. T., Rodriguez, A. P., Gaunt, R., and Demoulin, S. (2002). Differential association of uniquely and nonuniquely human emotions to the ingroup and the outgroups. *Group Processes and Intergroup Relations* **5**, 105–17.

Paquette, D., Coyl-Shepherd, D.D., and Newland, L.A. (2013). Fathers and development: new areas for exploration. *Early Child Development and Care* **183**, 735–45.

Park, B.K., Tsai, J.L., Chim, L., Blevins, E., and Knutson, B. (2015). Neural evidence for cultural differences in the valuation of positive facial expressions. *Social Cognitive & Affective Neuroscience* 11, 243–52.

Park, D.C., and Huang, C.M. (2010). Culture wires the brain: a cognitive neuroscience perspective. *Perspectives on Psychological Science* 5, 391–400.

Park, S. (2013). Always on and always with mobile tablet devices: a qualitative study on how young adults negotiate with continuous connected presence. *Bulletin of Science Technology & Society* 33, 182–90.

Parke, R.D. (1996). *Fatherhood*. Cambridge, MA: Harvard University Press.

Paschou, P., Lewis, J., Javed, A., and Drineis, P. (2001). Ancestry informative markers for fine-scale individual assignment to worldwide populations. *Journal of Medical Genetics* 47, 835–47.

Pascual-Leone, A., Amedi, A., Fregni, F., and Merabet, L.B. (2005). The plastic human brain cortex. *Annual Review of Neuroscience* 28, 377–401.

Pascual-Marqui, R.D., Esslen, M., Kochi, K., and Lehmann, D. (2002). Functional imaging with low-resolution brain electromagnetic tomography (LORETA): a review. *Methods and Findings in Experimental and Clinical Pharmacology* 24, 91–5.

Patel, V. (1995). Explanatory models of mental illness in Sub-Saharan Africa. *Social Science and Medicine* 40, 1291–8.

Patterson, K., Nestor, P.J., and Rogers, T.T. (2007). Where do you know what you know? The representation of semantic knowledge in the human brain. Nature Reviews Neuroscience, 8, 976–87.

Peng, K., and Knowles, E.D. (2003). Culture, education, and the attribution of physical causality. *Personality and Social Psychology Bulletin* 29, 1272–84.

Penn, D.C., and Povinelli, D.J. (2007). Causal cognition in human and nonhuman animals: a comparative, critical review. *Annual Review of Psychology* 58, 97–118.

Peper, J.S., Brouwer, R.M., Boomsma, D.I., Kahn, R.S., and Hulshoff, P.H.E. (2007). Genetic influences on human brain structure: a review of brain imaging studies in twins. *Human Brain Mappin*, 28, 464–73.

Perry, S.E. (2006). What cultural primatology can tell anthropologists about the evolution of culture. *Annual Review of Anthropology* 35, 171–90.

Peyron, R., Laurent, B., and García-Larrea, L. (2000). Functional imaging of brain responses to pain. A review and meta-analysis. *Neurophysiologie Clinique* 30, 263–88.

Pezawas, L., Meyer-Lindenberg, A., and Drabant, E.M. et al. (2005). 5-HTTLPR polymorphism impacts human cingulate-amygdala interactions: a genetic susceptibility mechanism for depression. *Nature Neuroscience* 8, 828–34.

Pfundmair, M., Aydin, N., Frey, D., and Echterhoff, G. (2014). The interplay of oxytocin and collectivistic orientation shields against negative effects of ostracism. *Journal of Experimental Social Psychology* 55, 246–51.

Platek, S.M., Keenan, J.P., Gallup, G.G., and Mohamed, F.B. (2004). Where am I? The neurological correlates of self and other. *Brain Research Cognitive Brain Research* 19, 114–22.

Platek, S.M., Loughead, J.W., and Gur, R.C. et al. (2006). Neural substrates for functionally discriminating selfface from personally familiar faces. *Human Brain Mapping* 27, 91–8.

Platel, H., Baron, J.C., Desgranges, B., Bernard, F., and **Eustache, F.** (2003). Semantic and episodic memory of music are subserved by distinct neural networks. *Neuroimage* **20**, 244–56.

Plomin, R., and **Daniels, D.** (1987). Why are children in the same family so different from one another? *Behavioral and Brain Sciences,* **10**, 1–16.

Plotnik, J.M., De Waal, F.B., and **Reiss, D.** (2006). Self-recognition in an Asian elephant. *Proceedings of the National Academy of Sciences* **103**, 17053–7.

Pluess, M., Belsky, J., Way, B.M., and **Taylor, S.E.** (2010). 5-HTTLPR moderates effects of current life events on neuroticism: differential susceptibility to environmental influences. *Progress in Neuro-Psychopharmacology and Biological Psychiatry* **34**, 1070–4.

Porter, D. (ed.) (2013). *Internet culture.* New York: Routledge.

Prado, J., Lu, J., Liu, L., Dong, Q., Zhou, X., Booth, J.R. (2013). The neural bases of the multiplication problem-size effect across countries. *Frontiers in Human Neuroscience* **7**, 189.

Prado, J., Mutreja, R., and **Zhang, H.** et al. (2011). Distinct representations of subtraction and multiplication in the neural systems for numerosity and language. *Human Brain Mapping* **32**, 1932–47.

Premack, D. (2004). Is language the key to human intelligence? *Science* **303**, 318–20.

Premack, D., and **Woodruff, G.** (1978). Does the chimpanzee have a theory of mind? *Behavioral and Brain Sciences* **1**, 515–26.

Ptito, M., Moesgaard, S.M., Gjedde, A., and **Kupers, R.** (2005). Cross-modal plasticity revealed by electrotactile stimulation of the tongue in the congenitally blind. *Brain* **128**, 606–14.

Ranganath, C., and **Rainer, G.** (2003). Neural mechanisms for detecting and remembering novel events. *Nature Reviews Neuroscience* **4**, 193–202.

Reader, S.M., and **Laland, K.N.** (2002). Social intelligence, innovation, and enhanced brain size in primates. *Proceedings of the National Academy of Sciences* **99**, 4436–41.

Reiss, D. and **Marino, L.** (2001). Mirror self-recognition in the bottlenose dolphin: a case of cognitive convergence. *Proceedings of the National Academy of Sciences of the United States of America* **98**, 5937–42.

Reist, C., Ozdemir, V., Wang, E., Hashemzadeh, M., Mee, S., and **Moyzis, R.** (2007). Novelty seeking and the dopamine D4 receptor gene (DRD4) revisited in Asians: haplotype characterization and relevance of the 2-repeat allele. *American Journal of Medical Genetics Part B: Neuropsychiatric Genetics* **144**, 453–7.

Renninger, L.B., Wilson, M.P., and **Donchin, E.** (2006). The processing of pitch and scale: an ERP study of musicians trained outside of the western musical system. *Empirical Musicology Review* **1**, 185–97.

Richerson, P.J., and **Boyd, R.** (2005). *Not by genes alone.* Chicago: University of Chicago Press.

Richerson, P.J., Boyd, R., and **Henrich, J.** (2010). Gene-culture coevolution in the age of genomics. *Proceedings of the National Academy of Sciences* **107**, 8985–92.

Richiardi, J., Altmann, A., and **Milazzo, A.C.** et al. (2015). Correlated gene expression supports synchronous activity in brain networks. *Science* **348**, 1241–4.

Richman, A.L., Miller, P.M., and **Solomon, J.J.** (1988). The socialization of infants in suburban Boston. In: R.A. LeVine, P.M. Miller, and M.M. West (eds.), *Parental behavior in diver societies.* San Francisco: Jossey-Bass, pp. 65–74.

Rietveld, C.A., Medland, S.E., and Derringer, J. et al. (2013). GWAS of 126,559 individuals identifies genetic variants associated with educational attainment. *Science* 340, 1467–71.

Rilling, J.K., and Insel, T.R. (1999). The primate neocortex in comparative perspective using magnetic resonance imaging. *Journal of Human Evolution* 37, 191–223.

Rilling, J.K., and Seligman, R.A. (2002). A quantitative morphometric comparative analysis of the primate temporal lobe. *Journal of Human Evolution* 42, 505–33.

Rizzolatti, G., and Craighero, L. (2004). The mirror-neuron system. *Annual Review of Neuroscience* 27, 169–92.

Robinson, T.N., Borzekowski, D.L., Matheson, D.M., and Kraemer, H.C. (2007). Effects of fast food branding on young children's taste preferences. *Archives of Pediatric and Adolescent Medicine* 161, 792–7.

Rodrigues, S.M., Saslow, L.R., Garcia, N., John, O.P., and Keltner, D. (2009). Oxytocin receptor genetic variation relates to empathy and stress reactivity in humans. *Proceedings of the National Academy of Sciences of the United States of America* 106, 21437–41.

Rogers, C. (1961). On becoming a person: a therapist's view of psychotherapy. Boston: Houghton Mifflin Harcourt.

Rogers, J., and Gibbs, R.A. (2014). Comparative primate genomics: emerging patterns of genome content and dynamics. *Nature Reviews Genetics* 15, 347–59.

Rogers, T.B., Kuiper, N.A., and Kirker, W.S. (1977). Self-reference and the encoding of personal information. *Journal of Personality and Social Psychology* 35, 677–88.

Rogoff, B. (2003). *The cultural nature of human development.* New York: Oxford University Press.

Ross, C.T., and Richerson, P.J. (2014). New frontiers in the study of human cultural and genetic evolution. *Current Opinion in Genetics & Development* 29, 103–9.

Rossion, B., Schiltz, C., Robaye, L., Pirenne, D., and Crommelinck, M. (2001). How does the brain discriminate familiar and unfamiliar faces?: a PET study of face categorical perception. *Journal of Cognitive Neuroscience* 13, 1019–34.

Rowe, D.C. (1994). *The limits of family influence: genes, experience, and behavior.* New York: Guilford Press.

Rubens, M., Ramamoorthy, V., and Attonito, J. et al. (2016). A review of 5-HT transporter linked promoter region (5-HTTLPR) polymorphism and associations with alcohol use problems and sexual risk behaviors. *Journal of Community Genetics* 7, 1–10.

Rule, N.O., Freeman, J.B., and Ambady, N. (2013). Culture in social neuroscience: a review. *Social Neuroscience* 8, 3–10.

Russell, M.J., Masuda, T., Hioki, K., and Singhal, A. (2015). Culture and social judgments: the importance of culture in Japanese and European Canadians' N400 and LPC processing of face lineup emotion judgments. *Culture and Brain* 3, 131–47.

Rütgen, M., Seidel, E.M., and Riecansky, I. et al. (2015). Reduction of empathy for pain by placebo analgesia suggests functional equivalence of empathy and first-hand emotion experience. *Journal of Neuroscience* 35, 8938–47.

Rütgen, M., Seidel, E.M., and Silani, G. et al. (2015). Placebo analgesia and its opioidergic regulation suggest that empathy for pain is grounded in self pain. *Proceedings of the National Academy of Sciences of the United States of America* 112, E5638–E5646.

Saarela, M. V., Hlushchuk, Y., Williams, A. C. D. C. et al. (2007). The compassionate brain: humans detect intensity of pain from another's face. Cerebral Cortex 17, 230–7.

Sadato, N., Pascual-Leone, A., and Grafman, J. et al. (1996). Activation of the primary visual cortex by Braille reading in blind subjects. *Nature* **380**, 526–8.

Samson, S., and Zatorre, R.J. (1992). Learning and retention of melodic and verbal information after unilateral temporal lobectomy. *Neuropsychologia* **30**, 815–26.

Sanfey, A.G., Rilling, J.K., Aronson, J.A., Nystrom, L.E., and Cohen, J.D. (2003). The neural basis of economic decision-making in the ultimatum game. *Science* **300**, 1755–8.

Santos, J.P., Moutinho, L., Seixas, D., and Brandão, S. (2012). Neural correlates of the emotional and symbolic content of brands: a neuroimaging study. *Journal of Customer Behaviour* **11**, 69–93.

Sasaki, J.Y. (2013). Promise and challenges surrounding culture–gene coevolution and gene–culture interactions. *Psychological Inquiry* **24**, 64–70.

Sasaki, J.Y., Kim, H.S., Mojaverian, T., Kelley, L.D., Park, I.Y., and Janušonis, S. (2013). Religion priming differentially increases prosocial behavior among variants of the dopamine D4 receptor (DRD4) gene. *Social Cognitive and Affective Neuroscience* **8**, 209–15.

Sasaki, J.Y., Kim, H.S., and Xu, J. (2011). Religion and well-being: the moderating role of culture and the oxytocin receptor (OXTR) gene. *Journal of Cross-Cultural Psychology* **42**, 1394–405.

Saw, S.M., Chua, W.H., Wu, H.M., Yap, E., Chia, K.S., and Stone, R.A. (2000). Myopia: gene-environment interaction. *Annals of the Academy of Medicine of Singapore* **29**, 290–7.

Saxe, R., and Kanwisher, N. (2003). People thinking about thinking people. The role of the temporo-parietal junction in "theory of mind." *Neuroimage* **19**, 1835–42.

Scally, A., Dutheil, J.Y., and Hillier, L.W. et al. (2012). Insights into hominid evolution from the gorilla genome sequence. *Nature* **483**, 169–75.

Schaefer, M., Berens, H., Heinze, H.J., and Rotte, M. (2006). Neural correlates of culturally familiar brands of car manufacturers. *Neuroimage* **31**, 861–5.

Schaefer, M., and Rotte, M. (2007). Thinking on luxury or pragmatic brand products: brain responses to different categories of culturally based brands. *Brain Research* **1165**, 98–104.

Scheepers, D., Derks, B., and Nieuwenhuis, S. et al. (2013). The neural correlates of in-group and self-face perception: is there overlap for high identifiers? *Frontiers in Human Neuroscience* **7**, 528.

Schubotz, R.I., and von Cramon, D.Y. (2001). Functional organization of the lateral premotor cortex: fMRI reveals different regions activated by the anticipation of object properties, location and speed. *Cognitive Brain Research* **11**, 97–112.

Schurr, T.G. (2013). When did we become human? Evolutionary perspectives on the emergence of the emergence of the modern human mind, brain, and culture. In: G. Hatfield, and H. Pittman (eds.), *Evolution of mind, brain, and culture.* Philadelphia: University of Pennsylvania Press, pp. 45–90.

Searle, J.R. (2004). *Mind: a brief introduction.* New York: Oxford University Press.

Sedikides, C. and Spencer, S.J. (eds.). (2007). *The self.* New York: Psychology Press.

Seeger, G., Schloss, P., and Schmidt, M.H. (2001). Marker gene polymorphisms in hyperkinetic disorder—predictors of clinical response to treatment with methylphenidate? *Neuroscience Letters* **313**, 45–8.

Segall, M.H., Campbell, D.T., and Herskovits, M.J. (1966). *The influence of culture on visual perception.* Indianapolis: Bobbs-Merrill.

Seigel, J. (2005). *The idea of the self: thought and experience in Western Europe since the seventeenth century.* Cambridge: Cambridge University Press.

Seitz, R.J., and Angel, H.F. (2012). Processes of believing—a review and conceptual account. *Reviews in the Neurosciences* 23, 303–9.

Sergent, J., Ohta, S., and MacDonald, B. (1992). Functional neuroanatomy of face and object processing. A positron emission tomography study. *Brain* 115, 15–36.

Shackman, A.J., Salomons, T.V., Slagter, H.A., Fox, A.S., Winter, J.J., and Davidson, R.J. (2011). The integration of negative affect, pain and cognitive control in the cingulate cortex. *Nature Reviews Neuroscience* 12, 154–67.

Shah, N.J., Marshall, N.C., Zafiris, O., Schwab, A., Zilles, K., and Markowitsch, H.J. et al. (2001). The neural correlates of person familiarity—a functional magnetic resonance imaging study with clinical implications. *Brain* 124, 804–15.

Shariff, A.F., and Norenzayan, A. (2007). God is watching you: priming god concepts increases prosocial behavior in an anonymous economic game. *Psychological Science* 18, 803–9.

Shaw, C., and McEachern, J. (eds.) (2001). *Toward a theory of neuroplasticity*. London: Psychology Press.

Sheline, Y.I., Barch, D.M., and Price, J.L. et al. (2009). The default mode network and self-referential processes in depression. *Proceedings of the National Academy of Sciences* 106, 1942–7.

Sheng, F., and Han, S. (2012). Manipulations of cognitive strategies and intergroup relationships reduce the racial bias in empathic neural responses. *NeuroImage* 61, 786–97.

Sheng, F., Han, X., and Han, S. (2016). Dissociated neural representations of pain expressions of different races. *Cerebral Cortex* 26, 1221–33.

Sheng, F., Liu, Q., Li, H., Fang, F., and Han, S. (2014). Task modulations of racial bias in neural responses to others' suffering. *NeuroImage* 88, 263–70.

Shi, Z., Ma, Y., Wu, B., Wu, X., Wang, Y., and Han, S. (2016). Neural correlates of reflection on actual versus ideal self-discrepancy. *NeuroImage* 124, 573–80.

Shong, O.K.M. (1977). A study of the self-rating depression scale (SDS) in a psychiatric out-patient clinic. *Journal of the Korean Neuropsychiatric Association* 16, 84–94.

Shulman, G.L., Sullivan, M.A., Gish, K., and Sakoda, W.J. (1986). The role of spatial-frequency channels in the perception of local and global structure. *Perception* 15, 259–73.

Shweder, R. (1991). *Thinking through cultures*. Cambridge, MA: Harvard University Press.

Simon, J.R. (1969). Reactions toward the source of stimulation. *Journal of Experimental Psychology* 81, 174–6.

Singelis, T.M. (1994). The measurement of independent and interdependent self-construals. *Personality and Social Psychology Bulletin* 20, 580–91.

Singer, T., Seymour, B., O'Doherty, J., Kaube, H., Dolan, R.J., and Frith, C.D. (2004). Empathy for pain involves the affective but not sensory components of pain. *Science* 303, 1157–62.

Smith, K.E., Porges, E.C., Norman, G.J., Connelly, J.J., and Decety, J. (2014). Oxytocin receptor gene variation predicts empathic concern and autonomic arousal while perceiving harm to others. *Social Neuroscience* 9, 1–9.

Snibbe, A.C., and Markus, H.R. (2005). You can't always get what you want: educational attainment, agency, and choice. *Journal of Personality and Social Psychology* 88, 703–20.

Solomon, R.C. (1990). *The big questions: a short introduction to philosophy* (3rd ed.). San Diego, CA: Harcourt Brace Jovanovich, Publishers.

Sousa, D. (2011). Mind, brain and education: the impact of educational neuroscience on the science of teaching. *Learning Landscapes* 5, 37–43.

Sparrow, B., Liu, J., and **Wegner, D.M.** (2011). Google effects on memory: cognitive consequences of having information at our fingertips. *Science* 333, 776–8.

Spiro, M.E., Killborne, B., and Langness, L.L.L. (eds.). (1987). *Culture and human nature.* New Brunswick: Transaction Publishers.

Stanley, J.T., Zhang, X., Fung, H.H., and Isaacowitz, D.M. (2013). Cultural differences in gaze and emotion recognition: Americans contrast more than Chinese. *Emotion* 13, 36–46.

Stein, J.L., Medland, S.E., and Vasquez, A.A. (2012). Identification of common variants associated with human hippocampal and intracranial volumes. *Nature Genetics* 44, 552–61.

Stenberg, G., Wiking, S., and Dahl, M. (1998). Judging words at face value: interference in word processing reveals automatic processing of affective facial expressions. *Cognition and Emotion* 12, 755–82.

Stewart, S.M., Simmons, A., and Habibpour, E. (2012). Treatment of culturally diverse children and adolescents with depression. *Journal of Child and Adolescent Psychopharmacology* 22, 72–9.

Strike, L.T., Couvy-Duchesne, B., Hansell, N.K., Cuellar-Partida, G., Medland, S.E., and Wright, M.J. (2015). Genetics and brain morphology. *Neuropsychology Review* 25, 63–96.

Suddendorf, T., and Butler, D.L. (2013). The nature of visual self-recognition. *Trends in Cognitive Sciences* 17, 121–7.

Sugiura, M., Watanabe, J., Maeda, Y., Matsue, Y., Fukuda, H., and Kawashima, R. (2005). Cortical mechanisms of visual self-recognition. *NeuroImage* 24, 143–9.

Sui, J., and Han, S. (2007). Self-construal priming modulates neural substrates of self-awareness. *Psychological Science* 18, 861–6.

Sui, J., Hong, Y., Liu, C.H., Humphreys, G.W., and Han, S. (2013). Dynamic cultural modulation of neural responses to one's own and friend's faces. *Social Cognitive and Affective Neuroscience* 8, 326–32.

Sui, J., and Humphreys, G. W. (2015). The integrative self: How self-reference integrates perception and memory. *Trends in Cognitive Sciences* 19, 719–28.

Sui, J., Liu, C.H., and Han, S. (2009). Cultural difference in neural mechanisms of self-recognition. *Social Neuroscience* 4, 402–11.

Sui, J., Zhu, Y., and Chiu, C.Y. (2007). Bicultural mind, self-construal, and self-and mother-reference effects: consequences of cultural priming on recognition memory. *Journal of Experimental Social Psychology* 43, 818–24.

Sui, J., Zhu, Y., and Han, S. (2006). Self-face recognition in attended and unattended conditions: an ERP study. *NeuroReport* 17, 423–7.

Sullivan, E.V., Pfefferbaum, A., Swan, G.E., and Carmelli, D. (2001). Heritability of hippocampal size in elderly twin men: equivalent influence from genes and environment. *Hippocampu* 11, 754–62.

Sutherland, R.L., and Woodward, J.L. (1940). *An introduction to sociology.* Chicago: University of Chicago Press.

Tang, Y., Zhang, W., and Chen, K. et al. (2006). Arithmetic processing in the brain shaped by cultures. *Proceedings of the National Academy of Sciences* 103, 10775–80.

Tangney, J.P., Wagner, P.E., Burggraf, S.A., Gramzow, R., and Fletcher, C. (1990). *The test of self-conscious affect for children.* Fairfax, VA: George Mason University.

Tarkka, I.M., and **Treede, R.D.** (1993). Equivalent electrical source analysis of pain-related somatosensory evoked potentials elicited by a CO2 laser. *Journal of Clinical Neurophysiology* **10**, 513–19.

Tattersall, I. (2008). An evolutionary framework for the acquisition of symbolic cognition by Homo sapiens. *Comparative Cognition & Behavior Reviews* **3**, 99–114.

Taylor, S.E., **Way, B.M., Welch, W.T.,** Hilmert, C.J., Lehman, B.J., and **Eisenberger, N.I.** (2006). Early family environment, current adversity, the serotonin transporter promoter polymorphism, and depressive symptomatology. *Biological Psychiatry* **60**, 671–6.

The concise Oxford dictionary. (1990). 8th ed. New York.

Thompson, P.M., **Cannon, T.D.,** and **Narr, K.L.** et al. (2001). Genetic influences on brain structure. *Nature Neuroscience* **4**, 1253–8.

Thompson-Schill, S.L., **D'Esposito, M., Aguirre, G.K.,** and **Farah, M.J.** (1997). Role of left inferior prefrontal cortex in retrieval of semantic knowledge: a reevaluation. *Proceedings of the National Academy of Sciences* **94**, 14792–7.

Thomsen, L., **Sidanius, J.,** and **Fiske, A.P.** (2007). Interpersonal leveling, independence, and self-enhancement: a comparison between Denmark and the US, and a relational practice framework for cultural psychology. *European Journal of Social Psychology* **37**, 445–69.

Toga, A.W., and **Thompson, P.M.** (2005). Genetics of brain structure and intelligence. *Annual Review of Neuroscience* **28**, 1–23.

Tomasello, M., **Kruger, A.C.,** and **Ratner, H.H.** (1993). Cultural learning. *Behavioral and Brain Sciences* **16**, 495–511.

Tong, F., and **Nakayama, K.** (1999). Robust representations for faces: evidence from visual search. *Journal of Experiment Psychology: Human Perception and Performance* **25**, 1016–35.

Tost, H., **Kolachana, B.,** and **Hakimi, S.** et al. (2010). A common allele in the oxytocin receptor gene (OXTR) impacts prosocial temperament and human hypothalamic-limbic structure and function. *Proceedings of the National Academy of Sciences* **107**, 13936–41.

Trafimow, D., **Silverman, E.S.,** Fan, R.M.T., and **Law, J.S.F.** (1997). The effects of language and priming on the relative accessibility of the private self and the collective self. *Journal of Cross-Cultural Psychology* **28**, 107–23.

Trafimow, D., **Triandis, H.C.,** and **Goto, S.G.** (1991). Some tests of the distinction between the private self and the collective self. *Journal of Personality and Social Psychology* **60**, 649–55.

Triandis, H.C. (1989). The self and social behavior in differing cultural contexts. *Psychological Review* **96**, 506–20.

Triandis, H.C. (1994). *Culture and social behavior.* New York: McGraw-Hill Book Company.

Triandis, H.C. (1995). *Individualism and collectivism.* Boulder, CO: Westview.

Triandis, H.C. (2001). Individualism-collectivism and personality. *Journal of Personality* **69**, 907–24.

Triandis, H.C., **Bontempo, R., Villareal, M.J.,** Asai, M., and **Lucca, N.** (1988). Individualism and collectivism: cross-cultural perspectives on self-ingroup relationships. *Journal of Personality and Social Psychology* **54**, 323–38.

Triandis, H.C., and **Gelfand, M.J.** (1998). Converging measurement of horizontal and vertical individualism and collectivism. *Journal of Personality and Social Psychology* **74**, 118–28.

Tsai, J.L. (2007). Ideal affect: cultural causes and behavioral consequences. *Perspectives on Psychological Science* **2**, 242–59.

Tsai, J.L., Knutson, B., and Fung, H.H. (2006). Cultural variation in affect valuation. *Journal of Personality and Social Psychology* 90, 288–307.

Turkheimer, E. (2000). Three laws of behavior genetics and what they mean. *Current Directions in Psychological Science* 9, 160–4.

Turkle, S. [2006] (2008). Always-on/always-on-you: the tethered self. In: J.E. Katz. *Handbook of mobile communication and social change.* Cambridge, MA: MIT Press.

Uddin, L.Q., Kaplan, J.T., Molnar-Szakaca, I., Zaidel, E., and Iacoboni, M. (2005). Self-face recognition activates a frontoparietal "mirror" network in the right hemisphere: an event-related fMRI study. *NeuroImage* 25, 926–35.

Ungerleider, L.G., and Haxby, J.V. (1994). "What" and "where" in the human brain. *Current Opinion in Neurobiology* 4, 157–65.

Ungerleider, S.K.A.L.G. (2000). Mechanisms of visual attention in the human cortex. *Annual Review of Neuroscience* 23, 315–41.

Uskul, A.K., Kitayama, S., and Nisbett, R.E. (2008). Ecocultural basis of cognition: farmers and fishermen are more holistic than herders. *Proceedings of the National Academy of Sciences* 105, 8552–6.

Utz, S. (2004). Self-construal and cooperation: is the interdependent self more cooperative than the independent self? *Self and Identity* 3, 177–90.

Van Beijsterveldt, C.E., Molenaar, P.C., De Geus, E.J., and Boomsma, D.I. (1996). Heritability of human brain functioning as assessed by electroencephalography. *American Journal of Human Genetics* 58, 562–73.

Van Beijsterveldt, C.E.M., and Van Baal, G.C.M. (2002). Twin and family studies of the human electroencephalogram: a review and a meta-analysis. *Biological Psychology* 61, 111–38.

Van der Elst, W., Van Boxtel, M.P., Van Breukelen, G.J., and Jolles, J. (2008). Is left-handedness associated with a more pronounced age-related cognitive decline? *Laterality* 13, 234–54.

Van Essen, D.C., and Dierker, D.L. (2007). Surface-based and probabilistic atlases of primate cerebral cortex. *Neuron* 56, 209–25.

Van Pelt, S., Boomsma, D.I., and Fries, P. (2012). Magnetoencephalography in twins reveals a strong genetic determination of the peak frequency of visually induced gamma-band synchronization. *Journal of Neuroscience* 32, 3388–92.

Varnum, M.E., Shi, Z., Chen, A., Qiu, J., and Han, S. (2014). When "Your" reward is the same as "My" reward: self-construal priming shifts neural responses to own vs. friends' rewards. *NeuroImage* 87, 164–9.

Volkow, N.D., Wang, G.J., and Fowler, J.S. et al. (2002). "Nonhedonic" food motivation in humans involves dopamine in the dorsal striatum and methylphenidate amplifies this effect. *Synapse* 44, 175–80.

Wade, A.G., Johnson, P.C., and Mcconnachie, A. (2010). Antidepressant treatment and cultural differences—a survey of the attitudes of physicians and patients in Sweden and Turkey. *Bmc Family Practice* 11, 93.

Wagner, A.D., Shannon, B.J., Kahn, I., and Buckner, R.L. (2005). Parietal lobe contributions to episodic memory retrieval. *Trends in Cognitive Sciences* 9, 445–53.

Walther, D.B., Caddigan, E., Fei-Fei, L., and Beck, D.M. (2009). Natural scene categories revealed in distributed patterns of activity in the human brain. *Journal of Neuroscience* 29, 10573–81.

Wan, X.H., Nakatani, H., Ueno, K., Asamizuya, T., Cheng, K., and Tanaka, K. (2011). The neural basis of intuitive best next-move generation in board game experts. *Science* 331, 341–6.

Wang, C., Ma, Y., and Han, S. (2014). Self-construal priming modulates pain perception: event-related potential evidence. *Cognitive Neuroscience* 5, 3–9.

Wang, C., Oyserman, D., Li, H., Liu, Q., and Han, S. (2013). Accessible cultural mindset modulates default mode activity: evidence for the culturally situated brain. *Social Neuroscience* 8, 203–16.

Wang, C., Wu, B., Liu, Y., Wu, X., and Han, S. (2015). Challenging emotional prejudice by changing self-concept: priming independent self-construal reduces racial in-group bias in neural responses to other's pain. *Social Cognitive & Affective Neuroscience* 10, 1195.

Wang, E., Ding, Y.C., and Flodman, P. et al. (2004). The genetic architecture of selection at the human dopamine receptor D4 (DRD4) gene locus. *American Journal of Human Genetics* 74, 931–44.

Wang, G., Mao, L., and Ma, Y. et al. (2012). Neural representations of close others in collectivistic brains. *Social Cognitive and Affective Neuroscience* 7, 222–9.

Wang, J., Qin, W., and Liu, B. et al. (2014). Neural mechanisms of oxytocin receptor gene mediating anxiety-related temperament. *Brain Structure and Function* 219, 1543–54.

Wang, Q. (2001). Culture effects on adults' earliest childhood recollection and self-description: implications for the relation between memory and the self. *Journal of Personality and Social Psychology* 81, 220–33.

Wang, Q. (2004). The emergence of cultural self-constructs: autobiographical memory and self-description in European American and Chinese children. *Developmental Psychology* 40, 3–15.

Watanabe, M. (1996). Reward expectancy in primate prefrontal neurons. *Nature* 382, 629–32.

Way, B.M., and Lieberman, M.D. (2010). Is there a genetic contribution to cultural differences? Collectivism, individualism and genetic markers of social sensitivity. *Social Cognitive and Affective Neuroscience* 5, 203–11.

Wegner, D., and Ward, A. (2013). The internet has become the external hard drive for our memories. *Scientific American* 309, 6.

Westermeyer, J., Vang, T.F., and Neider, J. (1983). A comparison of refugees using and not using a psychiatric service: an analysis of DSM-III criteria and self-rating scales in cross-cultural context. *Journal of Operational Psychiatry* 14, 36–41.

Wexler, B.E. (2006). *Brain and culture: neurobiology, ideology and social Change.* Cambridge, MA: MIT Press.

Whalen, P.J., Rauch, S.L., Etcoff, N.L., McInerney, S.C., Lee, M.B., and Jenike, M.A. (1998). Masked presentations of emotional facial expressions modulate amygdala activity without explicit knowledge. *Journal of Neuroscience* 18, 411–18.

White, K., and Lehman, D.R. (2005). Culture and social comparison seeking: the role of self-motives. *Personality and Social Psychology Bulletin* 31, 232–42.

Whiting, J.W.M. (1964). The effects of climate on certain cultural practices. In: W.H. Goodenough (ed.), *Explorations in cultural anthropology: essays in honor of Gerrge Peter Murdock.* New York: McGraw-Hill, pp. 511–44.

Wilkins, D. (2003). Why pointing with the index finger is not a universal (in sociocultural and semiotic terms). In: S. Kita (ed.), *Pointing: where language, culture, and cognition meet.* Mahwah, NJ: Lawrence Erlbaum, pp. 171–215.

Wilkinson, P.O., Trzaskowski, M., Haworth, C., and Eley, T.C. (2013). The role of gene–environment correlations and interactions in middle childhood depressive symptoms. *Development and Psychopathology* 25, 93–104.

Wilson, E.O. (2012). *On human nature*. Cambridge, MA: Harvard University Press.

Wong, R.Y.M., and Hong, Y.Y. (2005). Dynamic influences of culture on cooperation in the prisoner's dilemma. *Psychological Science* 16, 429–34.

Wright, I.C., Sham, P., Murray, R.M., Weinberger, D.R., and Bullmore, E.T. (2002). Genetic contributions to regional variability in human brain structure: methods and preliminary results. *Neuroimage* 17, 256–71.

Wright, M.J., Hansell, N.K., Geffen, G.M., Geffen, L.B., Smith, G.A., and Martin, N.G. (2001). Genetic influence on the variance in P3 amplitude and latency. *Behavior Genetics* 31, 555–65.

Wu, S., and Keysar, B. (2007). The effect of culture on perspective taking. *Psychological Science* 18, 600–6.

Xu, X., Zuo, X., Wang, X., and Han, S. (2009). Do you feel my pain? Racial group membership modulates empathic neural responses. *Journal of Neuroscience* 29, 8525–9.

Yang, J., Benyamin, B., and McEvoy, B.P. et al. (2010). Common SNPs explain a large proportion of the heritability for human height. *Nature Genetics* 42, 565–9.

Yilmaz, O., and Bahçekapili, H. G. (2015). Without God, everything is permitted? The reciprocal influence of religious and meta-ethical beliefs. *Journal of Experimental Social Psychology* 58, 95–100.

Yoon, J., and Lau, A.S. (2008). Maladaptive perfectionism and depressive symptoms among Asian American college students: contributions of interdependence and parental relations. *Cultural Diversity and Ethnic Minority Psychology* 14, 92–101.

Zang, Y., Jiang, T., Lu, Y., He, Y., and Tian, L. (2004). Regional homogeneity approach to fMRI data analysis. *NeuroImage* 22, 394–400.

Zaslansky, R., Sprecher, E., Tenke, C., Hemli, J., and Yarnitsky, D. (1996). The P300 in pain evoked potentials. *Pain* 66, 39–49.

Zeng, J., Konopka, G., Hunt, B.G., Preuss, T.M., Geschwind, D., and Soojin, V.Y. (2012). Divergent whole-genome methylation maps of human and chimpanzee brains reveal epigenetic basis of human regulatory evolution. *American Journal of Human Genetics* 91, 455–65.

Zhang, H., and Zhou, Y. (2003). The teaching of mathematics in Chinese elementary schools. *International Journal of Psychology* 38, 286–98.

Zhang, S.Y. (2005). *An introduction to philosophy*. Beijing: Peking University Press.

Zhou, X., Chen, C., and Zang, Y. et al. (2007). Dissociated brain organization for single-digit addition and multiplication. *Neuroimage* 35, 871–80.

Zhu, Y., and Han, S. (2008). Cultural differences in the self: from philosophy to psychology and neuroscience. *Social and Personality Psychology Compass* 2, 1799–811.

Zhu, Y., and Zhang, L. (2002). An experimental study on the self-reference effect. *Sciences in China, Series C* 45, 120–8.

Zhu, Y., Zhang, L., Fan, J., and Han, S. (2007). Neural basis of cultural influence on self-representation. *Neuroimage* 34, 1310–16.

Zuo, X., and Han, S. (2013). Cultural experiences reduce racial bias in neural responses to others' suffering. *Culture and Brain* 1, 34–46.

Index